Peer Heinlein • Peer Hartleben

The Book of IMAP

Building a Mail Server with Courier and Cyrus

Munich

San Francisco

The Book of IMAP: Building a Mail Server with Courier and Cyrus. Copyright © 2008 Open Source Press GmbH

All rights reserved. No part of this work may be reproduced or transmitted in any form or by any means, electronic or mechanical, including photocopying, recording, or by any information storage or retrieval system, without the prior written permission of the copyright owner and the publisher.

Printed on recycled paper in the United States of America.

1 2 3 4 5 6 7 8 9 10 — 08 07 06 05

No Starch Press and the No Starch Press logo are registered trademarks of No Starch Press, Inc. Other product and company names mentioned herein may be the trademarks of their respective owners. Rather than use a trademark symbol with every occurrence of a trademarked name, we are using the names only in an editorial fashion and to the benefit of the trademark owner, with no intention of infringement of the trademark.

Publisher: William Pollock
Cover Design: Octopod Studios
U.S. edition published by No Starch Press, Inc.
555 De Haro Street, Suite 250, San Francisco, CA 94107
phone: 415.863.9900; fax: 415.863.9950; info@nostarch.com; http://www.nostarch.com

Original edition © 2007 Open Source Press GmbH
Published by Open Source Press GmbH, Munich, Germany
Publisher: Dr. Markus Wirtz
Original ISBN 978-3-937514-11-6
For information on translations, please contact
Open Source Press GmbH, Amalienstr. 45 Rg, 80799 München, Germany
phone +49.89.28755562; fax +49.89.28755563; info@opensourcepress.de; http://www.opensourcepress.de

The information in this book is distributed on an "As Is" basis, without warranty. While every precaution has been taken in the preparation of this work, neither the author nor Open Source Press GmbH nor No Starch Press, Inc. shall have any liability to any person or entity with respect to any loss or damage caused or alleged to be caused directly or indirectly by the information contained in it.

Library of Congress Cataloging-in-Publication Data

```
Heinlein, Peer
   [POP3 und IMAP. English]
   The book of IMAP: building a mail server with Courier and Cyrus / Peer Heinlein
and Peer Hartleben.--
       p. cm.
   Includes index.
   ISBN-13: 978-1-59327-177-0
   ISBN-10: 1-59327-177-8
1. Electronic mail systems-Computer programs.  2. Electronic mail
systems-Standards.  3. Computer network protocols.  4. Web servers.  I.
Hartleben, Peer.  II. Title.
   TK5105.73.H45 2008
   004.692-dc22
                                              2008012396
```

Contents

Introduction 13

I How To Set Up and Maintain IMAP Servers 15

1 Protocols and Terms 17
  1.1 Why Is IMAP So Complex? 19
  1.2 Comparing Courier and Cyrus 20

2 POP3 and IMAP at the Protocol Level 23
  2.1 POP3 23
    2.1.1 Test Session 24
    2.1.2 Authentication via APOP and KPOP 27
  2.2 IMAP 28
    2.2.1 The Design of the IMAP Protocol 29
    2.2.2 Transcript of an IMAP Session 31
    2.2.3 A Practical View of IMAP 33
    2.2.4 Subscribing to IMAP Folders 41

3 Load Distribution and Reliability 43
  3.1 Load Balancer 45
    3.1.1 DNS Round Robin 46
    3.1.2 Round Robin via `iptables` 46
    3.1.3 Linux Virtual Server 47
  3.2 IMAP Proxies 50

4 Selecting a Filesystem   53

- 4.1 A Performance Test 55
- 4.2 Tuning the Performance of the Filesystem 57
  - 4.2.1 The `atime` 57
  - 4.2.2 Access Control Lists 58
  - 4.2.3 The Ext2/Ext3 Option `dir_index` 58
  - 4.2.4 Journal Mode 60
  - 4.2.5 Optimized `fstab` Entries 62
- 4.3 RAID 62
- 4.4 NFS 63
  - 4.4.1 Disabling `atime` and Optimizing Block Size 64
  - 4.4.2 NFS Version 3 64
  - 4.4.3 Fast I/O 65

5 Complementary Webmail Clients   67

- 5.1 Squirrelmail 68
- 5.2 Horde/IMP 70
- 5.3 Fast Access via the IMAP Cache Proxy 73

6 Migrating IMAP servers   75

- 6.1 Migration Using `imapsync` 76
- 6.2 Converting mbox to maildir 78
- 6.3 Modifying Folder Names 79
- 6.4 Determining Cleartext Passwords 81

II Courier-IMAP   83

7 Structure and Basic Configuration   85

- 7.1 Installing the Software 86
- 7.2 What Is Where? 87
- 7.3 Initial Start-Up 89
- 7.4 Courier and MTAs 90
  - 7.4.1 Courier and Postfix 92
  - 7.4.2 Courier and QMail 94
  - 7.4.3 Courier and Exim 94

7.5 Optimizing the Configuration 95
    7.5.1 Real and "False" Configuration Parameters 96
    7.5.2 POP3 Configuration in `/etc/courier/pop3d` 96
    7.5.3 Configuring the IMAP Daemon in `/etc/courier/imapd` 99
7.6 The Configuration Files for SSL 102

8 Maildir as Email Storage Format   107
8.1 The IMAP Namespace 110
8.2 Filenames of Emails 111
    8.2.1 Keywords: Custom IMAP Flags 115

9 User Data   119
9.1 `authtest` and `DEBUG_LOGIN` for Debugging Assistance 121
9.2 The `authdaemond` 122
9.3 Authentication via PAM 123
9.4 The `authuserdb` Module 124
    9.4.1 Converting `passwd` into a `userdb` 125
    9.4.2 Maintaining Account Data with `userdb` 127
    9.4.3 Creating a Binary Version of the User Database 128
    9.4.4 Separating the `userdb` into Multiple Files 129
    9.4.5 The `atime` 130
9.5 Using QMail's `vchkpw` Library for Authentication 130
9.6 Implementing Custom Authentication Methods 130
9.7 Integrating External Authentication Programs 131
9.8 Authentication via MySQL 133
9.9 Authentication via PostgreSQL 139
9.10 Authentication via LDAP 140
9.11 Obsolete Authentication Modules 143
    9.11.1 The `authpwd` Module 143
    9.11.2 The `authshadow` Module 143
    9.11.3 The `authcram` Module 144
9.12 User Options 144
    9.12.1 Saving User Options in the `userdb` 146
    9.12.2 Individual User Options in an LDAP Directory 146

Contents

   9.12.3 Storing User Options in Dedicated Fields in an SQL Table 147
 9.13 Saving Passwords: Cleartext or Hash? 147
 9.14 Username Selection When Maintaining Multiple Domains . . . 150

10 The Work of a Courier Administrator   153

 10.1 Shared Folders 153
   10.1.1 Setting Up Virtual Shared Folders 154
   10.1.2 Creating Filesystem-Based Shared Folders 163
 10.2 Quotas 166
   10.2.1 Quotas for Courier 167
   10.2.2 Quotas and the MDA 172
 10.3 Building an IMAP Proxy with Courier 175
 10.4 Push Instead of Pull: The IDLE Command 176
 10.5 Sending Emails via the IMAP Server 178

III   Cyrus-IMAP   181

11 Structure and Basic Configuration   183

 11.1 Installing Cyrus 184
   11.1.1 OpenSuSE/SuSE Linux Enterprise Server (SLES) 185
   11.1.2 Fedora Core/Red Hat 186
   11.1.3 Debian 186
 11.2 The Cyrus Hierarchy and Permissions System 187
 11.3 Features and Functions 188
 11.4 Quick Start 190
   11.4.1 Authentication and Mailboxes 194
   11.4.2 Tests 195

12 A Closer Look at the Configuration Files   199

 12.1 /etc/cyrus.conf 199
   12.1.1 The START{} Section 200
   12.1.2 The SERVICES{} Section 200
   12.1.3 The EVENTS{} Section 201
 12.2 /etc/imapd.conf 203

13 Authentication and Safeguards 207

13.1 Encrypting with SSL/TLS 208

    13.1.1 SSL Transmission Types 208

    13.1.2 Real and Fake Certificates 208

    13.1.3 Creating and Integrating SSL Certificates 209

13.2 Cyrus SASL 211

    13.2.1 Cyrus SASL Modules 212

    13.2.2 The `auxprop` Module 213

    13.2.3 The Authentication Process 214

13.3 Calling Different Data Sources 215

    13.3.1 Standard Authentication Methods for Unix 215

    13.3.2 `sasldb2` 216

    13.3.3 Cyrus and MySQL 216

    13.3.4 Cyrus and LDAP 220

    13.3.5 Cyrus and Kerberos 223

14 Advanced Cyrus Configuration 225

14.1 Mailbox Quotas 225

    14.1.1 Automatic Quotas 226

    14.1.2 Manual Quotas 228

14.2 Shared Folders and ACLs 230

14.3 Virtual Domains 232

    14.3.1 The Underlying Concept 232

    14.3.2 Effects on ACLs 236

    14.3.3 Domain Administrators 237

14.4 Sorting Emails into Subdirectories 237

14.5 Email Partitions 239

14.6 The Sieve Email Filter 240

    14.6.1 The Email Filter Daemon `timsieved` 240

    14.6.2 Configuring and Testing 240

    14.6.3 The `sieveshell` Administration Tool 242

    14.6.4 The Sieve Script Language 246

    14.6.5 Setting Up Sieve Scripts Automatically for New Accounts 251

    14.6.6 Adapting Sieve Scripts 252

Contents

    14.7 The `notifyd` Daemon 252

        14.7.1 Drums or Smoke Signals? 253

    14.8 Cyrus and Other MTAs 254

    14.9 Backing Up and Restoring Data 255

        14.9.1 Using `reconstruct` to Repair Mailboxes 255

        14.9.2 Restoring Quotas 257

    14.10 Performance Tuning 257

        14.10.1 Parameters in `/etc/imapd.conf` that influence performance 258

15 Internal Structure and Modules   261

    15.1 The Cyrus Daemons 262

    15.2 Tools for Analysis, Maintenance, and Repairs 263

        15.2.1 Statistics and Analysis 263

        15.2.2 Maintenance and Repair 266

        15.2.3 Internal Tools 268

    15.3 Other In-House Tools 269

    15.4 The `cyradm` Administration Tool 271

16 Cyrus at the Filesystem Level   275

    16.1 The Email Directory 275

    16.2 The Administration Directory 277

17 Cyrus in a Cluster   281

    17.1 The Cyrus Aggregator 281

        17.1.1 The Aggregator Concept 282

        17.1.2 The Cluster Setup 283

    17.2 Cyrus Replication 291

        17.2.1 Replicating the Authentication Data 291

Appendixes 293

A IMAP Command Reference 295
    A.1 Commands Always Available to Clients 296
    A.2 Commands Available in the Not-Authenticated Status 297
    A.3 Commands Available in the Authenticated Status 298
    A.4 Commands Available in the Selected Status 303
    A.5 IMAP Extensions 314
    A.6 Experimental Commands 316

B POP3 Command Reference 317
    B.1 An Overview of All Commands 318

C Installing from the Source Code 321
    C.1 Courier 321
    C.2 Cyrus 325
        C.2.1 Cyrus Sources 325
        C.2.2 Creating a System User 325
        C.2.3 Installing Cyrus SASL 326
        C.2.4 Installing the Cyrus IMAP Server 329
        C.2.5 Convenient Starting and Stopping 330

Introduction

There is very little specialist literature available on IMAP servers, and no current documentation deals with the subject in sufficient depth.

There is a real need for a guide to IMAP. A quick look at relevant mailing lists shows that they are full of questions and problems, indicating that the software solutions now in use raise many issues. IMAP may seem to be a simple affair and to require little in the way of configuration, but there are plenty of pitfalls when an IMAP server is designed for a large number of users or when elaborate additional features are added to a basic installation.

We have specialized in Courier and Cyrus during the last few years. Both offer distinct advantages and disadvantages, so the appropriate choice of software depends on the project. Peer Heinlein mainly works with Courier IMAP, and he uses it to implement mail servers for large ISPs that are designed to accommodate tens or hundreds of thousands of users. Peer Hartleben uses Cyrus IMAP for mail servers in small and large companies, which require Cyrus user administration—sometimes via a console—and server-based filtering of mail using Sieve. Peer Heinlein has therefore written the introduction and the Courier section of this book, and Peer Hartleben has written the section on Cyrus.

Neither Courier nor Cyrus have had suitable documentation (until now). We have to admit: This book was hard work. There were many behaviors and call parameters that we had to debug and test by trial and error, or understand by analyzing the source code, because their significance was not documented *anywhere*. The project mailing lists often were not helpful, frequently containing more questions than answers.

The detailed work on this book took far longer than we had originally suspected it would, and there were repeated delays in publication. But, finally, we have an exhaustive and up-to-date reference on the subjects of IMAP, Courier, and Cyrus. Considering the importance of email communication, we hope that this book will help many administrators and postmasters in their work.

This book is in its first edition and is still not *truly* complete. We had to postpone discussion of some small details until the second edition. Also, when interpreting behavior that had no or insufficient documentation, we ran as many tests as possible to try to gain an accurate picture; nevertheless, we cannot rule out errors and omissions.

We will therefore provide corrections and additions at `http://www.imap-buch.com/`. You are very welcome to leave helpful suggestions, references, or corrections for us there. This kind of help is very important to us. Please tell us which subjects you found interesting, which topics remained unclear after you read our explanations, and where you suspect we made a mistake. The website contains a link to the mailing list `imap-buch`, which, we hope, will soon develop into a lively and competent discussion.

Once this book has been sent to the printers, many people will heave a large sigh of relief. We are very grateful to these people. First, we have to thank our editor, Patricia Jung, for her perseverance in adding the finishing touches and questioning every detail. We authors often despaired of relief from her scrutiny, but she is the reason for the high quality of this book. Thanks to her specialist knowledge, she also was able to provide many suggestions and explanations.

The rest of the Open Source Press team, Markus Wirtz and Ulrich Wolf, also played an important part in making this book a reality—and gained not a few grey hairs during the process. (Sorry!)

Arnt Gulbrandsen and his detailed knowledge of IMAP were also a great help, and we would like to thank him for his commitment. We would also like to thank Frank Richter from TU Chemnitz for helping us in our battle with the Cyrus cluster.

We also had behind-the-scenes help from members of the Heinlein Support team, who did the preliminary work, made measurements (to be honest, they did the heavy lifting), researched details, and did some of our own tasks as well, so that we were able to concentrate on the book itself: Thank you, Stefan, Holger, Chrizz, Henri, Christian, Matthias, and Christiane.

As customary when writing a book, we want to thank our loved ones, and tell them that "it will all get better now." So we would like to tell our *four* ladies: *Now we can spend more time with you again!* Thanks to our grown-up ladies, Anja and Ivonne, who have gone through the whole process with us, and who have had to live with *the book* hanging over every moment of spare time like the sword of Damocles. And to our tiny women: Lara Hartleben, who does not yet sleep through the night, and Heinlein Junior, who does not yet have a name but has already entered the first contest of her life: Who will be born first—her or *The Book of IMAP*? It seems as if the book will win...

Peer Heinlein and Peer Hartleben   Berlin, September 2007

Part I

How To Set Up and Maintain IMAP Servers

Chapter 1

Protocols and Terms

What is a mail server? This term could describe the particular machine in a computer center that is responsible for sending and receiving users' emails. However, such a mail server actually consists of a variety of components and programs, which use various protocols to communicate among themselves. The same is true of commercial software applications that combine the many necessary functions into one product. In most cases, the different mail server tasks can be distributed to more than one computer, which means that "the mail server" may in fact consist of several machines that together fulfill the different functions.

Mail servers use the *Simple Mail Transport Protocol (SMTP)* to communicate and to deliver emails. Clients such as Outlook, KMail, Thunderbird, and Evolution usually deliver emails to the *relay server* via SMTP. However, SMTP is suitable only for *sending* emails, not for *receiving* them. This means that SMTP cannot be used to query a mailbox or create email directories in it. Likewise, a *Mail Transfer Agent (MTA)* transports emails received from clients or other servers to their destination, but has nothing to do with mail-receiving protocols such as POP3 or IMAP. This book will not deal with SMTP servers such as Postfix, QMail, Exim, or Sendmail, except marginally. We simply assume that they work correctly.[1]

Post Office Protocol Version 3 (POP3) is a comparatively simple protocol with few configuration options, so pure POP3 servers require very little administration. Once they have been started or entered in the configuration of the X(Inet) Daemon, emails can be retrieved on port 110 using POP3.

Internet Message Access Protocol (IMAP), the "grown-up" version of POP3, is far more complex. This book will focus on the numerous ways that email retrieval can be configured and on the administration of emails. Once you have read it, you will be able to implement even demanding mail-handling scenarios. Common IMAP servers also contain a small POP3 daemon, so programmers who deal with the complexity of managing the IMAP protocol will have no difficulty in providing a POP3 protocol "on the side."

This book deals with the two most common open source IMAP protocols: Courier IMAP and Cyrus IMAP. Both contain a POP3 server. When we refer to "IMAP servers," we mean both services, unless we are specifically discussing the features of one of them.

The *Local Message Transfer Protocol (LMTP)* is closely related to SMTP, but it is only used locally; for example, to transfer an email from a Mail Transfer Agent (such as Postfix) to another component of the mail system, specifically to a *Mail Delivery Agent (MDA)*. In this case, LMTP has an advantage over SMTP: With LMTP, it is possible to determine the email addresses for which a local transfer succeeds. Unlike SMTP, LMTP returns a status message for each recipient *after* the DATA command. The status message specifies the mailbox in which the email was actually saved. SMTP only indicates whether the server was able to place an email for the recipient in a queue for delivery at a later point in time. LMTP is also better in high-performance environments.

You should only use LMTP locally within your own network; for example, to transfer emails from the front relay (which receives via SMTP) to the actual mail backend that does the saving. The protocol can be used, for example, to connect Cyrus to the MTA (see section 11.4 on page 191).

Groupware is software that manages tasks, calendars, email contacts, and address books on behalf of multiple users. Depending on the version, it can also manage resources, rooms, files, or other kinds of objects. Email is thus only a part of the functionality offered by groupware, but groupware usually contains an email service. The IMAP servers introduced here are *not* groupware servers, but some free groupware solutions such as Kolab, OpenGroupware, and eGroupWare are based on IMAP, so this book may be helpful when adapting such software to your needs as well.

---

[1] See *The Book of Postfix* (No Starch Press, 2005) by Ralf Hildebrandt and Patrick Koetter for more information on this subject.

1.1 Why Is IMAP So Complex?

The POP3 server waits until a user has logged on and then transfers the unread messages that are saved in that user's mailbox to the user's mail client. Depending on the client requirements, the messages are deleted after transfer to save space, or flagged as read and retained. This is not particularly demanding, so there is not much that can go wrong with the software here.

An IMAP server operates differently: Not only does it deliver emails to users, it also organizes the entire end-user email administration. The user's email client now functions as a kind of "remote control" for manipulating the mailbox stored on the server.

An IMAP server provides storage space and stores all emails. For this reason, it makes sense to use quotas, which force users to clean up occasionally and free up valuable space. When a user creates folders for his or her emails, the IMAP server has to represent this folder structure and sort the emails correspondingly. IMAP also enables users to search messages for specified senders or text and to flag emails, for example, as read, unread, or answered. Users can also access shared folders in parallel.

An IMAP server enables a user to manage a mailbox from different computers; the contents of the mailbox always consist of the same data records no matter where it is accessed from, and the mailbox does not need to be synchronized among the machines.

All these features make great demands on the IMAP protocol and the programmer. The configuration of an IMAP server does not require much attention from the administrator once the server has been connected to a user database. However, the operation of IMAP servers does contain a few traps and technical difficulties, which we will examine in this book:

Performance
    As the number of users increases, the load on the IMAP server becomes noticeable. In a large organization, the server has to manage millions of emails, operate hundreds or thousands of IMAP connections in parallel, and deal with email searches and extensive copying actions. Depending on the scenario, IMAP servers can consume considerable RAM or create high I/O loads on the data carriers.

Availability
    Nowadays, email needs to be available around the clock, as any extended outage can endanger business. Once a certain number of users has been reached, the infrastructure should be secured by using multiple servers, even if a robust IMAP server has been selected.

Storage
    Email storage can increase to sizeable proportions, which necessi-

tates the use of an NAS or SAN. Also, when an IMAP server is part of a server cluster, it is no longer sufficient to use a directly attached hard disk for storage.

Quotas
Implementing storage restrictions as quotas is not always easy and requires precise planning.

Legal Situation
Emails are subject to the laws on privacy of communications. Not many people are aware that administrators can be prosecuted for negligence. However, this is a general problem with all email management, and this book will not deal with the topic further.

1.2 Comparing Courier and Cyrus

The requirements and size of the installation play an important part in the selection of an IMAP server. Both Courier and Cyrus make low demands on the CPU; fast I/O is required in both cases if there are more than approximately 20,000 users.

Both Courier and Cyrus enable users to share IMAP folders and administrators to limit the number of simultaneous logins. The user data can be transferred from Unix accounts, read out via PAM, and stored in a LDAP directory or in a MySQL or a PostgreSQL database.

In terms of user management, the real difference between the two lies in secure authentication via *Simple Authentication and Security Layer (SASL)*, which is specified as an Internet standard in RFC 2222 (and used by Postfix and other MTAs). In Cyrus, it is simple to implement, but in Courier, it requires numerous kludges and dodges that are too much even for good administrators. Instead, Courier uses a specially developed authentication library, *Authlib*, whose central program is the `authdaemond` daemon. Cyrus also supports the authentication library as an SASL module (see page 213).

Both servers allow POP3 and IMAP via SSL/TLS, either via the dedicated ports 995 (POP3 via SSL) and 993 (IMAP via SSL) or via the commands STLS (POP3, see page 319) and STARTTLS (IMAP, see page 297), and both support virtual domains.

The most noticeable difference between Courier and Cyrus is the way they manage email accounts and metadata. Courier uses only the filesystem and ASCII files. The benefit is that nothing can break down; as long as the filesystem is okay, Courier works. Courier uses the maildir format, which is suitable for use via NFS, as no file locking is required.

On a Courier IMAP server, accounts automatically exist as long as, and as soon as, they are listed in the user database. On the other hand, once

Cyrus knows the login data of a new user, it creates the account structure automatically when the user first logs in. It is also possible to initialize new mailboxes using the administration tool `cyradm`.

Courier administrators can use shell scripts to intervene in the system, but Cyrus administrators always use `cyradm` to administer their servers.

Cyrus stores emails and administration information in small filesystem-based databases. This is intended to speed up access when there are a large number of emails, but the disadvantage is that accessing mail messages via an index is more prone to errors. Simple manipulations to the email store, such as the deletion or addition of messages, are complex to carry out. As NFS accesses internal databases, and index files are destroyed if multiple Cyrus nodes access them in parallel, a functioning file locking system is essential. The suitability of NFS therefore mainly depends on the NFS version and the maturity of the locking mechanisms it provides; however, most administrators prefer not to use this solution.

Cyrus has the advantage of being able to use the mail filter language Sieve. It also provides a system of permissions for shared IMAP folders that is easier to use to implement access control policies.

POP3 and IMAP at the Protocol Level

You should take the intended environment into account when choosing whether to support POP3 or IMAP as the protocol for mail retrieval. One is simple and robust, the other is powerful and flexible. Courier and Cyrus speak both protocols, and by using them you can provide IMAP and POP3 to your users without any additional work.

2.1 POP3

Version 3 of the *Post Office Protocol (POP3)* is comparatively simple, and only allows the user to download emails from the server to the client. The user can log in to an account, view the contents of the mailbox, transfer and delete emails, and log out, all via server port 110. This requires few resources, and there is little to configure, which means few sources of error.

Emails are stored locally on the user's PC, which saves precious storage space on the server and reduces backup times. The user usually has to download all emails before deciding which ones are worth reading, based on the subject and/or the sender, although by now most clients support filters for screening incoming mail messages.

Because email messages are stored locally, the user can process them offline using the client application. This reduces the time spent online, and is especially suitable for laptops. However, POP3 does not provide any mechanisms for ensuring that mail clients on different machines will all see the same data if the user accesses a mailbox from several computers (from a laptop and from a desktop PC, for example).

POP3 client software only allows the user to decide whether or not to delete emails from the server after they are retrieved. A simple way to guarantee that multiple clients are always in synch with each other is to never delete any messages. If all the emails remain on the server, every mail client can download them at all times. Good clients will recognize newly arrived messages by storing message IDs and avoid transferring old emails a second time.

This method has some disadvantages: Because the emails are never deleted, the mailbox on the server continually grows. In addition, each client receives all messages, including ones that have already been read and (locally) deleted by another client. There is also no automatically maintained, common record of sent emails, since each client manages its outbox independently.

2.1.1 Test Session

The POP3 protocol is simple enough to use directly, in an interactive session:

```
user@linux:$ telnet mail.example.com 110
Trying 192.168.50.50...
Connected to mail.example.com.
Escape character is '^]'.
+OK Hello there.
USER tux
+OK Password required.
PASS secret
+OK logged in.
```

We are now in the POP3 INBOX. (It is not possible to access other types of mail stores, such as IMAP folders, using a POP3 client.) The LIST command summarizes all the messages it contains (nine in the following example) and their lengths:

2.1 POP3

```
LIST
+OK POP3 clients that break here, they violate STD53.
1 9586
2 1125022
3 53125
4 2451
5 5931
6 4943
7 4206
8 5231
9 9481
.
```

The message from Courier in the +OK answer refers to POP3 clients that erroneously expect the server to return the number of messages in answer to the LIST command:

```
LIST
+OK 2 messages (320 octets)
1 120
2 200
.
```

The given example is listed in RFCs 1081, 1225, 1460, 1725, and 1939, but the RFCs add that this example does not define how the server's answer should look, i. e. the number and size of messages shown in the example are not a mandatory part of the answer. The authors of Courier could have made the server reply more helpful (and less arrogant); an example could have been POP3 clients that expect a specific string here violate RFC 1939..

RETR is used to retrieve a message from the server:

```
RETR 2
Return-Path: <p.heinlein@heinlein-support.de>
X-Original-To: p.heinlein@heinlein-support.de
Delivered-To: tux@example.com
Received: from [10.0.42.2] (unknown [10.0.42.2])
        (using TLSv1 with cipher DHE-RSA-AES256-SHA (256/256 bits))
        (Client did not present a certificate)
        by plasma.heinlein-support.de (Postfix) with ESMTP id BEA0581A4B
        for <tux@example.com>; Sat,  7 Apr 2007 01:02:01 +0200 (CEST)
From: Peer Heinlein <p.heinlein@heinlein-support.de>
To: Tux <tux@example.com>
Subject: Test message 2
Date: Sat, 7 Apr 2007 01:02:01 +0200
User-Agent: KMail/1.9.5
MIME-Version: 1.0
Content-Type: text/plain; charset="iso-8859-1"
Content-Transfer-Encoding: quoted-printable
```

```
Content-Disposition: inline
Message-Id: <200704070102.01895.p.heinlein@heinlein-support.de>
X-Length: 1519
Status: R
X-Status: NC
X-UID: 0

Hello!
I am a test message.

=2D-=20
Heinlein Professional Linux Support GmbH
Linux: Academy - Support - Hosting

http://www.heinlein-support.de

Legally required information according to =A735a HGB (German Commercial
Code)
HRB 93818 B / Amtsgericht Berlin-Charlottenburg,=20
Manager: Peer Heinlein =A0-- Seat: Berlin
```

Flagging message 2 for deletion after it has been read is just as simple:

```
DELE 2
DELE 2
+OK Deleted.
```

However, it will not actually be deleted until the user logs out. This allows us to undo the setting of the deletion flag:

```
RSET
+OK Resurrected.
```

If we do not wish to transfer an entire message to the client, we can use the TOP command to retrieve only the message headers and a specified number of lines of the mail body, given in a second argument to the command (seven in this case):

```
TOP 2 7
Return-Path: <p.heinlein@heinlein-support.de>
X-Original-To: p.heinlein@heinlein-support.de
Delivered-To: tux@example.com
Received: from [10.0.42.2] (unknown [10.0.42.2])
        (using TLSv1 with cipher DHE-RSA-AES256-SHA (256/256 bits))
        (Client did not present a certificate)
        by plasma.heinlein-support.de (Postfix) with ESMTP id BEA0581A4B
        for <tux@example.com>; Sat,  7 Apr 2007 01:02:01 +0200 (CEST)
From: Peer Heinlein <p.heinlein@heinlein-support.de>
To: Tux <tux@example.com>
```

```
Subject: Test message 2
Date: Sat, 7 Apr 2007 01:02:01 +0200
User-Agent: KMail/1.9.5
MIME-Version: 1.0
Content-Type: text/plain; charset="iso-8859-1"
Content-Transfer-Encoding: quoted-printable
Content-Disposition: inline
Message-Id: <200704070102.01895.p.heinlein@heinlein-support.de>
X-Length: 1519
Status: R
X-Status: NC
X-UID: 0

Hello!
I am a test message.

=2D-=20
Heinlein Professional Linux Support GmbH
Linux: Academy - Support - Hosting
.
```

There is also an "idle" command that enables the client to keep the connection open:

NOOP
+OK Yup.

The QUIT command is used to terminate the connection:

QUIT
+OK Bye-bye.
Connection closed by foreign host.

2.1.2 Authentication via APOP and KPOP

Unlike the "standard" login to the POP server described on page 24, the *Authenticated Post Office Protocol (APOP)* authentication procedure protects the password by encrypting it. This is tricky to accomplish, because if the client/server communication is vulnerable to unauthorized eavesdropping at all, then the eavesdropper can listen in on the entire connection, including the initial exchange between the client and server that establishes the encryption parameters as defined by the protocol.

When APOP is used, the POP3 server provides a *timestamp* at the beginning of each connection, which differs for every POP session. In the sample session below, the timestamp is highlighted in bold:

```
user@linux:$ telnet localhost 110
Trying 127.0.0.1...
```

```
Connected to localhost.
Escape character is '^]'.
+OK ready <13226.1017708644@mail.example.com>
APOP tux c4c9334bac560ecc979e580001b3e22fb
+OK maildrop has 42 messages 43231 octets
[...]
```

The email client can now use a standard cryptographic hash procedure to calculate an encrypted login password from the cleartext password it already knows and the server-provided timestamp. Because this encrypted password depends on the timestamp, it is valid only for the current connection.

The server also knows the user's unencrypted password and performs the same calculation. If the encrypted password it receives from the client agrees with the result it computes, the server can conclude that the client genuinely represents the user and accept the login.

This is because it is (theoretically) not possible to calculate the original password from the encrypted login data transferred by the client, even when the hash procedure is known. Likewise, recording the APOP login dialog for a legitimate connection and replaying it to the server later will not allow an eavesdropper to impersonate the real user, because the timestamp for the eavesdropper's session with the server will be different.

Kerberos Post Office Protocol (KPOP) is a Kerberos enhancement for POP3, but it is rarely used. Like APOP, it does not transmit the password in cleartext. However, it is not easy to implement a Kerberos system. A free implementation of Kerberos is available from the Massachusetts Institute of Technology (MIT).[1]

2.2 IMAP

The *Internet Mail Access Protocol Version 4 (IMAP)*, provided by a server on port 143, functions in an entirely different manner from POP3. It is far more complex than POP3, supports mail subfolders on the server (including those shared by multiple users) and complex search queries, and permits emails to be uploaded onto the server. All emails always remain on the server; clients simply keep local copies of the mail store and synchronize them with the server.

Emails are only transferred to the client when they are accessed, and only stored temporarily by the client (this is similar to the way websites are accessed by web browsers). This means that multiple email clients can access the same mailbox in parallel—they all find the same set of data syn-

---

[1] See http://web.mit.edu/kerberos/www.

chronized by the server. Users can also use the contents directory of the mailbox to decide which emails are transferred to the client.

Storing the data on the server requires valuable storage space. However, this is offset by the fact that a simple backup of the server[2] will suffice to preserve the emails for all users. If the hard disk of a client computer breaks, the messages for that user's email account are not affected, apart from those that are only saved locally.

IMAP is designed to be used online and in real time. With dial-up connections, email retrieval may be slow. Good mail clients are capable of an *offline IMAP* mode of operation, which combines the behavior of POP3 (local email storage) and IMAP (synchronizing emails with the server). This means that an IMAP mailbox can be transferred to a laptop and then manipulated offline.

2.2.1 The Design of the IMAP Protocol

Unlike the SMTP and POP3 protocols, which have simple commands that can be issued interactively in a terminal session if necessary, IMAP is very complicated. To make up for this, it has far more functions than the other mail protocols.

IMAP has almost no restrictions on the status information (read, unread, important, new) that can be assigned to an email message. The system flags specified by the IMAP standard are listed in Table 8.1 on page 113. The server and client can agree their own additional *permanent flags*. In addition to permanent flags, there are also *session-based flags* (see also section 8.2.1 on page 115). Both types can be defined for each mail folder. The server and the client have to agree on the flags that can be used, and on their type.

IMAP provides the client with functions that perform search and selection against the data stored on the server. These enable searches such as "All emails with the unread flag AND from sender geeko@example.com AND with message number larger than 300."

IMAP also provides functions that enable the client to store many details locally and to use them repeatedly in different logins—a locally saved directory of mail folder contents, for example. This is not trivial to implement, as changes could result to the underlying folder contents after the local summary is created. For this reason, IMAP numbers email messages sequentially using both an *arithmetically increasing sequence number* without punctuation (1–399, for example) and *unique IDs* that are unambiguous and should not change. *Should* does not mean *must*, and so the server and client must communicate if any unique ID does change.

---

[2] Using `rsync` in an ingenious manner for example.

This is made easier by the *unique ID value*, which the client and the server both memorize. As long as this value does not change, the server's assignment of unique IDs to emails has not changed. When a change occurs in the email folders on the server, the server changes the unique ID value as well, so that it now differs from the value the client has. The client thus knows it must import the complete list of emails, with their unique IDs, anew.

Thanks to this complex design, IMAP is future-proof and flexible, as it is possible to introduce new options and flags without changing the protocol.

Disconnected IMAP, also known as *offline IMAP*, is a good example of how this can be used. The email client saves the entire contents of the mailbox locally. The user can then create folders and move, flag, or delete emails while working offline. The next time the client connects to the IMAP server, the client and server synchronize all changes. In spite of some early teething problems in its deployment, this method now works surprisingly well and combines the advantages of POP3 and IMAP.

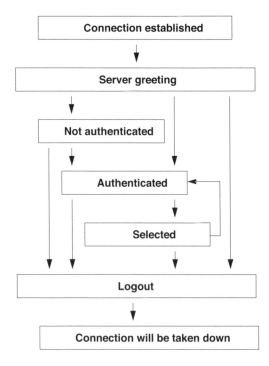

Figure 2.1: IMAP connections can be in different states.

What makes IMAP sessions even more complex and exciting is that the client can send multiple commands to the server without having to wait for the server to answer—the server can send the answers in a different sequence. This means it is possible to send a complex search query to the server and still upload emails or create folders while the search is being processed. For this reason, all client requests are *tagged*, or provided with a unique ID selected by the client. The server replies are marked with this unique ID, which enables the client to identify the answer.

These tags must be used during login, too:

```
a1 login username password
a1 OK LOGIN OK
```

The choice of a1 as the tag was purely arbitrary; we could have used 001 or abc instead.

Unfortunately, some server replies occupy more than one line. Therefore we have to differentiate between tagged and untagged server replies. *Untagged* server replies begin with a star, while *tagged* replies start with the identifier selected by the user and mark the end of a complete reply to a client request.

The NOOP command is a case in point; the server can send a multiline reply, giving rise to untagged reply lines. NOOP is actually used to carry out *no* operation. A client can send it to prevent a timeout and keep the connection open. However, some servers react to it by returning the status information of the mailbox, such as (in this example) the number of messages received since login (3), the number of read messages (14), or the number of emails flagged for deletion (22):

```
a2 NOOP
* 22 EXPUNGE
* 23 EXISTS
* 3 RECENT
* 14 FETCH (FLAGS (\Seen \Deleted))
a2 OK NOOP completed
```

The server reply consists of multiple untagged replies (beginning with *) and ends with a tagged reply OK NOOP.

2.2.2 Transcript of an IMAP Session

A successful IMAP session begins when the server has greeted the client, and consists of four states as shown in Figure 2.1:

Not Authenticated
    The status between connection and successful authentication of username and password. Only a few commands, such as STARTLS, LOGIN, LOGOUT, and NOOP are available (see sections A.1 and A.2 on page 296).

Authenticated
: The client has been authenticated but has not selected a folder. It can get information on available folders, subscribe or unsubscribe to them, create new folders, or delete existing ones (see section A.3 on page 298).

    It can *not* read or save emails here, as it is not clear which emails or directories are being referred to.

Selected
: The client has shown its colors and selected a directory using SELECT, EXAMINE, or STATUS. It may now issue commands that apply to the messages in this directory. If the client uses CLOSE or EXPUNGE to deselect a directory, the connection state switches back to the Authenticated status. For an overview of all commands available here, see section A.4 on page 303.

Logout
: The client has used LOGOUT to announce that it wishes to log out . Only then does the server delete messages marked as \Deleted —if the connection is terminated unintentionally, these messages should not be deleted. The server then ends and terminates the connection.

A standard IMAP connection switches back and forth between "Authenticated" and "Selected." As a consequence, not all commands are available all the time.

This means that IMAP is a *session-based protocol*, like FTP or SMTP, as opposed to a *stateless protocol* such as HTTP, in which each client request is independent of previous events. IMAP connections between the server and the client are usually kept open indefinitely, and can remain so for hours.

Usually, clients check for new emails every few minutes; however, the server can also inform the client when new messages are received. PR and web terminology refers to the first option as the *pull* procedure, and to the second as the *push* procedure. From the server perspective, the push procedure is more efficient and desirable. If the server monitors some directories for change and then informs the client, this requires far fewer resources than if the client roots through three dozen IMAP folders every few minutes, only to discover that nothing has changed. Unfortunately, few clients have the ability at present to support this mode of operation; we will examine Courier's functionality in section 10.4 on page 176. Cyrus implements this in a daemon, `idled` (see page 200 and page 262).

There are some disadvantages when clients keep connections open permanently: Assuming that a Courier IMAP server uses between 1.5 and 2MB RAM for each session, it quickly becomes obvious that a mail server with 4GB RAM cannot serve 2,500 IMAP users simultaneously . In case of POP3, these resources would suffice for 25,000 active email accounts, as each client logs out immediately and thereby frees up resources. There is more information on this subject in Chapter 3, page 43.

2.2.3 A Practical View of IMAP

RFC 3501 defines the IMAP standard. This document is more than 100 pages long, but it only provides a limited explanation of the protocol. Its author, Marc Crispin, admits: "Beyond the protocol overview in section 2, it [the RFC] is not optimized for someone trying to understand the operation of the protocol."[3]

In order to operate a mail server, you do not need to have read the RFCs or even to know all the details of the protocol as described in Appendix A on page 295; you certainly do not need to know it by heart. You should, however, understand its basic workings and know the technical options the server offers the client.

It is easier to remember procedures that you have carried out at least once, so it is worth testing the IMAP commands discussed below on an IMAP server. This experience will be useful when an error occurs, and it is always pleasant to understand the server you are responsible for.

You do not require `root` permissions for the server; indeed, you can use your own email account on the mail server of an Internet service provider or other email provider, as long as you can access it through IMAP. Begin by connecting to the IMAP port on the server (port 143):

```
user@linux:~$ telnet imap.example.com 143
Trying 192.0.2.12...
Connected to imap.example.com.
Escape character is '^]'.
* OK [CAPABILITY IMAP4rev1 UIDPLUS CHILDREN NAMESPACE THREAD=ORDEREDSUB
JECT THREAD=REFERENCES SORT IDLE AUTH=CRAM-MD5 AUTH=CRAM-SHA1 ACL] Cour
ier-IMAP ready. Copyright 1998-2005 Double Precision, Inc.  See COPYING
 for distribution information.
```

In reply, the server will present its *capabilities*. Not every server supports all IMAP features. *IMAP extensions* provide features that are not part of the core protocol, and are therefore optional. In our example, the server displays the version of the IMAP protocol (`IMAP4rev1`) and the extensions that it supports. Often, but not always, the extensions offer IMAP commands with the same name to the client.

---

[3] See http://www.faqs.org/rfcs/rfc3501.html.

Some extensions, including sorting functions such as THREAD[4] or SORT[5] shift tasks from the client to the server, whereas others simplify the querying of email and directory structures, which saves time and traffic (these include UIDPLUS, described in RFC 2359, CHILDREN, described in RFC 3348, and NAMESPACE, defined in RFC 2342).

IMAP prescribes only the login methods LOGIN and PLAIN, in which the password is transmitted in plaintext. The server can offer alternative, better authentication methods, such as CRAM-MD5 or CRAM-SHA1, as shown in the example.

In the example, the server also states that it supports the extensions IDLE (RFC 2177, see pages 176 and 200) and ACL (RFC 4314). The latter extension enables multiple users to access a single IMAP folder (see section 10.1 on page 153 and section 14.2 on page 230).

Next, log on with your username and (plaintext) password:

```
a1 LOGIN "tux" "hidden"
a1 OK LOGIN completed
```

The server returns the reply OK, which lets us know that we have authenticated ourselves successfully and now have the "Authenticated" status. Now we can call up a list of all available directories:

```
a2 LIST "" "*"
* LIST (\HasNoChildren)   "." "INBOX.Private.Holiday"
* LIST (\HasNoChildren)   "." "INBOX.Private.Orchestra"
* LIST (\HasChildren)     "." "INBOX.Private"
* LIST (\HasNoChildren)   "." "INBOX.ToDo"
* LIST (\HasNoChildren)   "." "INBOX.Test"
* LIST (\HasChildren)     "." "INBOX.Book stuff"
* LIST (\HasNoChildren)   "." "INBOX.Book stuff.LPIC-1"
* LIST (\HasNoChildren)   "." "INBOX.Book stuff.Postfix 3"
* LIST (\HasNoChildren)   "." "INBOX.Book stuff.Snort"
* LIST (\HasNoChildren)   "." "INBOX.Book stuff.IMAP"
* LIST (\Unmarked \HasChildren) "." "INBOX"
a2 OK LIST completed
```

The flags in the third column show whether the corresponding directory contains subfolders (\HasChildren—yes, \HasNoChildren—no) and messages. If a folder is flagged as \Unmarked, no new messages have been received since it was last accessed.

---

[4] In the example shown here, the server states that it supports the threading algorithm ORDEREDSUBJECT. This algorithm is very simple and assumes that all emails with identical subjects belong to a single shared thread. The THREAD extension itself is specified in http://tools.ietf.org/rfcmarkup?doc=draft-ietf-imapext-thread. This document also describes the threading algorithm REFERENCES.

[5] See http://www3.tools.ietf.org/rfcmarkup?doc=draft-ietf-imapext-sort.

The fourth column specifies the hierarchy separator used in the next folder: In our example, the full stop symbol (.) separates the hierarchies; if a backslash were used instead, the first directory specification would be `INBOX/Private/Holiday`.

If you have many folders, you can also specify a restrictive pattern for folder names:

```
a3 LIST "" "INBOX.Priv*"
* LIST (\HasNoChildren) "." "INBOX.Private.Holiday"
* LIST (\HasNoChildren) "." "INBOX.Private.Orchestra"
* LIST (\HasChildren)   "." "INBOX.Private"
a3 OK LIST completed
```

You can now use the `SELECT` command to select a folder. Here we select the `Test` folder, which is a subfolder of the `INBOX`:

```
a4 SELECT INBOX.Test
* FLAGS (\Draft \Answered \Flagged \Deleted \Seen \Recent)
* OK [PERMANENTFLAGS (\Draft \Answered \Flagged \Deleted \Seen)] Limited
* 3 EXISTS
* 1 RECENT
* OK [UIDVALIDITY 1175900586] Ok
* OK [MYRIGHTS "acdilrsw"] ACL
a4 OK [READ-WRITE] Ok
```

The server uses the `FLAGS` keyword to tell us which flags are permitted for emails in this folder, as these may include ones not specified by the IMAP standard. The following flags are usually available:

- `\Answered` shows that the email has been marked as answered.
- `\Deleted` means that the email has been marked for deletion.
- `\Draft` shows that an email is a draft message that has not yet been sent.
- `\Flagged` shows that the email is important.
- `\Seen` shows that an email has been marked as read.
- `\Recent` shows that a message has been received since the last login and no other client has seen it yet.[6] Unlike the other five system flags that have been mentioned, the `\Recent` flag cannot be set using the `STORE` command (see page 39).
- If the server announces the `\*` flag (this flag does not appear in our example), it is permissible to use custom flags (see section 8.2.1 on page 115).

[6] If more than one client accesses a single mailbox, all of them see the same messages, but only one of them will ever see a given email flagged as `\Recent`.

n EXISTS shows how many emails this folder contains in all—in this case, three. n RECENT tells us how many new messages have been received since the last login (here, only one).

OK [PERMANENTFLAGS (flag1 flag2 ...)] lists all those flags that the client can change permanently. If the server does not return this keyword, the client can assume that all flags can be modified and stored.

OK [UIDVALIDITY n] shows the unique ID value that is currently valid.

OK [MYRIGHTS n] tells the client what read, write, or delete permissions it has for emails in this directory (see Table 2.1).

Table 2.1: Permissions that can be assigned for IMAP folders

Permission	Explanation
r	The user is permitted to view the contents of a mailbox.
l	The user may view the name of a mailbox. Users that know the name of a folder can access it even if they possess only the r flag and not the l flag. This condition does *not* apply to shared folders in Cyrus; here, users that do not own the folder require both the r and the l permission to access it.
s	The user may flag a message as read or unread. The effects of this permission depend on whether the server sets flags by file or by email and user. Under Courier, users who allow other users to access directories can use this permission to determine whether third parties can change the \Seen flag. If that is the case, the owner of the directory sees the message as read if other users have already accessed it. In contrast, Cyrus saves flags based on users. If a user changes the \Seen flag on a message, this will not affect the message status for other users of the same folder.
w	The user has write permissions and may set flags and so on. w does *not* permit the user to delete emails.
i	The user may add and delete messages.
p	This permission must be set on Cyrus for users to be able to sort emails into directories and subdirectories (the abbreviation stands for *post*); for example, if they are addressed directly to a subfolder (see section 14.4 on page 237) or if the messages are moved automatically using filter scripts (see page 240). Without this permission, messages are placed in the INBOX. This permission is not available in Courier, as the corresponding function is not available.

continued:

Permission	Explanation
c	The user may create a new mailbox or a mailbox subdirectory. In Cyrus, the user may also rename or delete a mailbox or mailbox subdirectory.
d	This permission is only assigned in Cyrus and allows the user to request the deletion of a message or mailbox. In Courier, the combination tex is used for the same permission.
t	This permission is unique to Courier and allows users to flag messages as \Deleted.
e	This permission is unique to Courier and allows the user to have messages deleted from the server if they have already been flagged as \Deleted.
x	This permission is unique to Courier and allows users to delete or rename the directory.
a	The user is permitted to set ACLs.

Finally, the answer OK [READ-WRITE] Ok together with the tag of the query shows that the reply to the SELECT command is now complete. If the client has write permissions for the folder, the server *should* add the information [READ-WRITE] to the OK keyword. If the client only has read permissions, the server *must* return [READ-ONLY].

Viewing, Copying, and Deleting Emails

The client can now view messages or parts of messages. For example, only the email headers are required to create a table of contents. You can use the FETCH command to specify exactly which emails (the following example specifies messages with sequence numbers from 1 to 3)[7] and which parts of these emails should be transmitted. If you use the ALL keyword, the server returns the flags, the time of arrival, the message size in bytes, and the header fields From, To, Cc, Reply-to, Message-ID, Date, and Subject:

```
a5 FETCH 1:3 ALL
* 1 FETCH (FLAGS (\Seen) INTERNALDATE "07-Apr-2007 01:03:06 +0200" RFC822
.SIZE 1647 ENVELOPE ("Sat, 7 Apr 2007 01:01:51 +0200" "Test message 1" (
("Peer Heinlein" NIL "p.heinlein" "heinlein-support.de")) (("Peer Heinlei
n" NIL "p.heinlein" "heinlein-support.de")) (("Peer Heinlein" NIL "p.hein
lein" "heinlein-support.de")) (("Tux" NIL "tux" "example.com")) NIL NIL N
IL "<200704070101.52187.p.heinlein@heinlein-support.de>"))
```

[7] If you wish to specify unique IDs instead of sequence numbers, you would use the UID FETCH command (see page 313).

```
* 2 FETCH (FLAGS () INTERNALDATE "07-Apr-2007 01:03:06 +0200" RFC822.SIZE
 1646 ENVELOPE ("Sat, 7 Apr 2007 01:02:01 +0200" "Test message 2" (("Pee
r Heinlein" NIL "p.heinlein" "heinlein-support.de")) (("Peer Heinlein" NI
L "p.heinlein" "heinlein-support.de")) (("Peer Heinlein" NIL "p.heinlein"
"heinlein-support.de")) (("Tux" NIL "tux" "example.com")) NIL NIL NIL "<2
00704070102.01895.p.heinlein@heinlein-support.de>"))
* 3 FETCH (FLAGS () INTERNALDATE "07-Apr-2007 01:03:06 +0200" RFC822.SIZE
 1651 ENVELOPE ("Sat, 7 Apr 2007 01:02:10 +0200" "And test message 3" (("
Peer Heinlein" NIL "p.heinlein" "heinlein-support.de")) (("Peer Heinlein"
 NIL "p.heinlein" "heinlein-support.de")) (("Peer Heinlein" NIL "p.heinle
in" "heinlein-support.de")) (("Tux" NIL "tux" "example.com")) NIL NIL NIL
 "<200704070102.11133.p.heinlein@heinlein-support.de>"))
a5 OK FETCH completed.
```

Let's look at the complete message for message number 2, using the FETCH subcommand BODY[]:

```
a6 FETCH 2 BODY[]
* 2 FETCH (BODY[] 1646
Return-Path: <p.heinlein@heinlein-support.de>
X-Original-To: p.heinlein@heinlein-support.de
Delivered-To: p.heinlein@heinlein-support.de
Received: from [10.0.42.2] (unknown [10.0.42.2])
        (using TLSv1 with cipher DHE-RSA-AES256-SHA (256/256 bits))
        (Client did not present a certificate)
        by plasma.heinlein-support.de (Postfix) with ESMTP id BEA0581A4B
        for <tux@example.com>; Sat,  7 Apr 2007 01:02:01 +0200 (CEST)
From: Peer Heinlein <p.heinlein@heinlein-support.de>
To: Tux <tux@example.com>
Subject: Test message 2
Date: Sat, 7 Apr 2007 01:02:01 +0200
User-Agent: KMail/1.9.5
MIME-Version: 1.0
Content-Type: text/plain;
  charset="iso-8859-1"
Content-Transfer-Encoding: quoted-printable
Content-Disposition: inline
Message-Id: <200704070102.01895.p.heinlein@heinlein-support.de>
X-Length: 1519
Status: R
X-Status: NC
X-UID: 0

Hello!
I am a test message.

=2D-=20
Heinlein Professional Linux Support GmbH
Linux: Academy - Support - Hosting
```

```
http://www.heinlein-support.de

Obligatory information according to =A735a HGB (German Commercial Code)
HRB 93818 B / Berlin Charlottenburg Local Court,=20
Managing Director: Peer Heinlein =A0-- Registered Office: Berlin
)
a6 OK FETCH completed.
```

It is also possible to download individual header lines:

```
a7 FETCH 2 BODY[HEADER.FIELDS Message-ID]
* 2 FETCH (BODY[HEADER.FIELDS ("Message-ID")] 59
Message-Id: <200704070102.01895.p.heinlein@heinlein-support.de>

)
a7 OK FETCH completed.
```

We can also copy messages, either to another folder or (just to make life easier) back to INBOX.Test.

```
a8 COPY 2:3 INBOX.Test
a8 OK [COPYUID 1175900586 2:3 4:5] COPY completed.
```

Messages 2 and 3 are now duplicated as messages 4 and 5. It does not make sense to keep duplicates in a folder, so we assign the \Deleted flag to them. This means that they will be deleted the next time an EXPUNGE, SELECT, or CLOSE command is executed (see pages 304, 298, and 303):[8]

```
a9 STORE 2,3 +FLAGS \Deleted
* 2 FETCH (FLAGS (\Deleted))
* 3 FETCH (FLAGS (\Deleted))
a9 OK STORE completed
```

The IMAP server now provides updated status information for this folder. It does not mention any new messages, even though our copying has increased the number of messages significantly:

```
a10 NOOP
* 5 EXISTS
* 0 RECENT
a10 OK NOOP completed
```

It is still possible to use the messages that have been flagged for deletion. The message only disappears from the server when we leave the folder, e. g. by selecting a new directory.

[8] ...but not when we leave the folder using UNSELECT, according to the IMAP extension from RFC 3691.

Searching for Email Contents

There are many complex and powerful query methods available for searching email on the server. You can search by age and size of the message, as well as by sender, header line, IMAP flag, and actual content of the email. The following query asks the server to return the sequence numbers of all unread messages:

```
a11 SEARCH UNSEEN
* SEARCH 3 5
a11 OK SEARCH done
```

Email 1 is not returned, as it was flagged as \Seen when the session began (as shown by the FETCH command on page 37).

If you wish to find all messages that are marked for deletion among first four messages, you should use the command:

```
a12 SEARCH 1:4 DELETED
* SEARCH 2 3
a12 OK SEARCH done
```

You can also search message contents. The SEARCH command is *not* case sensitive:

```
a13 SEARCH ALL TEXT Heinlein
* SEARCH 1 2 3 4 5
a13 OK SEARCH done
```

Warning: Because the TEXT option searches through the raw data, this search query may overlook certain emails that contain the search term. This example will not return any hits for messages in which the only occurrence of the word "heinlein" contains a soft line break in the quoted-printable-coded email text and therefore looks like this: hein=(crlf)lein. It usually makes more sense to use the SEARCH subcommand BODY[] instead of TEXT (see page 305).

These simple examples show that the IMAP protocol offers the client multiple options that can transfer complex tasks efficiently to the server and thereby reduce the volume of data transmitted. Unfortunately, implementations of the IMAP protocol in mail clients are of varying degrees of quality.

Even web mailers, who should be grateful for the variety of options, hardly take advantage of them. Instead of pulling only those emails off the server that are to be displayed and then preparing them for display, many access all emails, and then make their selection in a manner that is cumbersome and requires a lot of storage space.

2.2.4 Subscribing to IMAP Folders

A client can use the `SUBSCRIBE` command to select a folder from the list of all folders in an IMAP mailbox and subscribe to it, and use the `UNSUBSCRIBE` command to unsubscribe from that folder again. The list of subscribed folders is stored directly on the IMAP server, which must support this feature. Courier and Cyrus are both able to do this without any additional configuration.

Whether a subscription exists for a directory only makes a difference for the `LIST` and `LSUB` IMAP commands: `LIST` lists all IMAP folders, whether they have been subscribed to or not. It returns all IMAP folders even if the server contains a list of subscriptions. If the `LSUB` command (the name is an abbreviation of *list subscribed*) is sent, the server returns only the subscribed directories.

Apart from this difference, `LIST` and `LSUB` behave identically. Clients can use these commands each time they retrieve emails to specify whether only the subscribed directories or all directories are returned.

The second option is advantageous for clients on laptops that use UMTS dial-up, or at locations that have expensive traffic or slow connections. When the mailbox is retrieved, only the subscribed IMAP folders are synchronized, if the IMAP client is configured correspondingly. This option saves time and money when emails are retrieved on the go. On the other hand, the IMAP client at a stationary machine can be configured not to support subscribed folders for the same mailbox. It will continue to send the `LIST` command and thereby synchronize itself with the entire set of data.

Your IMAP client will determine how and where you can subscribe to IMAP directories. You will usually find a function enabling you to select individual directories for subscription from all folders listed; you should also be able to configure whether subscriptions should be observed or not.

Load Distribution and Reliability

A web server can deal with many thousands of hits per hour, but IMAP servers encounter new and far-reaching problems when dealing with that many users. The Courier and Cyrus IMAP processes consume between 1.5 and 2MB RAM for each online session, even if the connection is idle and the client is hardly active. A server with 4GB RAM can therefore run out of memory when serving approximately 2,500 simultaneous connections.

Unlike POP3, where the client logs on separately for each query and the memory used to process a query is freed up for other connections once the server is finished with it (this is similar to HTTP and SMTP, where RAM is only consumed when work is being processed), IMAP is unfortunately far more greedy because clients often attempt to remain permanently connected to the server when users wish to maintain a dedicated connection.

This is not a problem if there are only 20, 50, or even as many as 100 users, as a server usually has 250MB RAM available. However, if there are a thousand or more users and a corresponding number of parallel IMAP connections, the main memory can quickly become a bottleneck. Besides the amount of available RAM, the number of connections that can be served efficiently is also limited by the physical (disk) storage. Processor performance is rarely a problem for large IMAP servers. If, for example, clients in 2,500 parallel connections retrieve emails every three minutes, this still only amounts to 10 or 20 parallel requests per second. This is manageable for a fast enough computer with a single processor. Disk I/O is likely to become a more noticeable limiting factor for overall system performance, since hard drive performance has not changed significantly in recent years, compared to CPU speed. At present, disk caching is used to attempt to alleviate this problem as far as possible.

RAM and memory I/O are the weak points when the number of users reaches four or five digits; these weak points are balanced out by using shared IMAP clusters or fast hard disks.

If your IMAP server can barely deal with the number of simultaneous logins and/or the size of the mailboxes, there are two strategies available: You can either use *load balancers* or *proxies*.

Under load balancing, multiple IMAP servers use a central filesystem (SAN/NAS) to access all email data, so that every node can service every user account. A central load balancer distributes the load to an arbitrary number of identically configured IMAP servers. To prevent filenames from being duplicated in the shared mail space, you should provide each node with a different hostname. The advantages of this solution include the following:

- Load balancing can be done very simply, even using Round Robin DNS (but without guarantee of system stability), although a load balancer is better.

- Individual user accounts do not need to be assigned permanently to individual nodes.

- The load is balanced optimally between all the servers.

There are also disadvantages, though: A load balancer (an appliance or a homegrown solution) is required, and the central filesystem bears the entire I/O load of the IMAP cluster. Furthermore, they both become single points of failure unless they are designed to be redundant.

An IMAP proxy receives connection requests from all clients and transfers each to the responsible IMAP server. Each of the IMAP servers therefore manages only a certain part of the account base, for which it saves the relevant mail data locally. There is an additional list of all accounts and passwords that is maintained separately (for example, in a MySQL database or in an LDAP directory). This has the following advantages:

- No problems with a single I/O bottleneck, as multiple local hard disks are used

- No (expensive) central mail storage

- No load balancer

However, a central proxy IMAP server can become overloaded if there is a very large number of users; individual IMAP servers can become overloaded even though other nodes still have capacity available; and each individual IMAP server is a single point of failure for the accounts that reside on it, although accounts on other servers are not affected by such a failure.

3.1 Load Balancer

If all mail hosts access a shared storage solution, as shown in Figure 3.1 (whether this is an NFS, a SAN, or an iSCSI with a cluster filesystem), it is unimportant which host is used to connect the client. In this case, there is no reason not to use a load balancer. Even on a simple Linux router, it only takes a few steps to configure a load balancer; the Linux kernel offers different options for distributing IP connections.

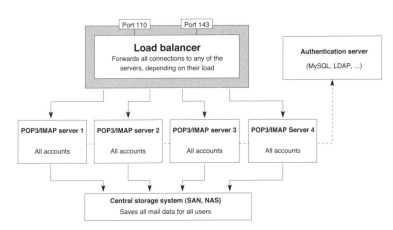

Figure 3.1:
If all mail servers access the same email database, every incoming connection can be assigned to a server individually.

If the central storage system becomes a performance bottleneck due to numerous simultaneous accesses to numerous files, the only option is to use a large number of very fast hard disks, which can make this system organization very expensive.

During configuration, you should ensure that *persistence* is maximized. This means that the balancer attempts to assign a new client connection to the same server that was last used for that client whenever possible, in order to take advantage of any user and account information still present in that server's local disk cache.

3.1.1 DNS Round Robin

DNS enables a (very) simple load distribution technique. If you specify several DNS entries for the name of your host, the clients are assigned an IP number, and thus an actual host server, at random for each query.

The following entries in a DNS zone file ensure that all queries are (randomly) assigned one of the three servers with the IP numbers mentioned:

```
mail.example.com.        IN A    192.168.10.11
mail.example.com.        IN A    192.168.10.12
mail.example.com.        IN A    192.168.10.13
```

However, this makes you reliant on DNS data, which is often cached for a long time, and which is correspondingly difficult to influence. This means that DNS Round Robin is only a first attempt at load balancing rather than a proper strategy. If necessary, you can adapt the `iptables` rule described on the following pages and switch IPs on or off. This raises the question: Why not do it like this from the start?

3.1.2 Round Robin via `iptables`

`iptables` can use the `DNAT` target to distribute connections to a number of *consecutive* IP numbers. This does not achieve real load distribution, as the connections are distributed via the round-robin method. Cache times are of no importance here (unlike DNS Round Robin), which means the solution can be adapted and changed as required.

If you use a Linux router as a central gateway anyway, little effort is required to forward all POP3/IMAP connections to multiple servers with different IP addresses in order to balance the load.

The following example illustrates how to externally provide a single POP3-IMAP server under IP 192.168.10.10 while the requests are distributed internally to the three servers 192.168.10.11, 192.168.10.12, and 192.168.10.13 via DNAT:[1]

```
linux: # iptables -A PREROUTING -t nat -p tcp --dport 110 -d 192.168.10.
10   -j DNAT --to-destination 192.168.10.11-192.168.10.13
linux: # iptables -A PREROUTING -t nat -p tcp --dport 143 -d 192.168.10.
10   -j DNAT --to-destination 192.168.10.11-192.168.10.13
```

[1] Line breaks have been inserted in the single-line commands to make them easier to read.

```
linux: # iptables -A PREROUTING -t nat -p tcp --dport 993 -d 192.168.10.
10   -j DNAT --to-destination 192.168.10.11-192.168.10.13
linux: # iptables -A PREROUTING -t nat -p tcp --dport 995 -d 192.168.10.
10   -j DNAT --to-destination 192.168.10.11-192.168.10.13
```

You can also use the `iptables` targets `BALANCE` and `CLUSTERIP` to implement complex setups that exceed the scope of this book. For more information, see `man (5) iptables`.

However, `iptables` is not able to divert queries that a failed host or service receives in this manner; in the worst case, the client will receive a timeout or "Connection Refused" message. Even if this option is unsuitable for high availability requirements, it can be recommended as a simple, robust, and functioning initial solution.

3.1.3 Linux Virtual Server

The Linux Virtual Server (LVS) project[2] has nothing to do with *virtual root servers (VServers)* as provided by some ISPs. Rather, it provides the kernel function and control commands that can be used to set up a *real* load balancer on any Linux system with very little effort. Unlike the simple `iptables DNAT` method, LVS enables the connections to be distributed to individual hosts according to available criteria; For example, it could favor individual (higher-performance) servers or take existing connections into account.

The LVS project connects to the target hosts in three different ways. In most cases, *Direct Routing* will be the first choice.[3]

Direct Routing is based on the principle of supplying the servers with an external production IP, which is identical for all nodes (in this case, `192.168.10.10`), in addition to their actual maintenance IPs (in this case, `192.19.10.11`, `192.168.10.12`, and `192.168.10.13`). This IP is attached to the loopback interface as a virtual IP on every server, so as to prevent IP conflicts and interference between the servers. The subnetwork must be set to `255.255.255.255` to prevent the server from attempting to contact other nodes in the network via the loopback interface.

```
linux: # ifconfig lo:1 192.168.10.10 netmask 255.255.255.255 broadcast \
192.168.10.255
```

At the same time, the Linux kernel must be taught not to return the MAC address of `eth0` to ARP queries for this IP. The Linux kernel usually returns the IP of the receiving interface to ARP requests even if the requested IP

---

[2] See http://www.linuxvirtualserver.org/.
[3] It is described in detail at http://www.linuxvirtualserver.org/VS-DRouting.html.

address is on *any* of its interfaces. At the same time, it arbitrarily selects one of its own IP addresses for outgoing requests.

In order to prevent this, you should enter the following entries into the file `/etc/sysctl.conf`:

```
net.ipv4.conf.all.arp_ignore = 1
net.ipv4.conf.lo.arp_ignore = 1
```

This ensures that the kernel only replies to ARP requests if they are received on the intended interface. It ignores ARP requests for the IP address hidden behind `lo:1`, as they are received on `eth0`. Instead, the kernel should only use the actual IP address of the outgoing interface `eth0`. Add two more entries to `/etc/sysctl.conf`:

```
net.ipv4.conf.all.arp_announce = 2
net.ipv4.conf.lo.arp_announce = 2
```

During setup you load these parameters manually; later on, they are activated automatically during booting. This is the call for SuSE:

```
linux: # /etc/init.d/boot.sysctl start
Setting current sysctl status from /etc/sysctl.conf
net.ipv4.icmp_echo_ignore_broadcasts = 1
net.ipv4.conf.all.rp_filter = 1
net.ipv4.conf.all.arp_ignore = 1
net.ipv4.conf.lo.arp_ignore = 1
net.ipv4.conf.all.arp_announce = 2
net.ipv4.conf.lo.arp_announce = 2
```

Debian users use the command `/etc/init.d/procps.sh start` instead.

Now, multiple servers have the same IP, but none of them reply to ARP requests. This means that this IP is not available—at least until we introduce the LVS load balancer.

Now enter the production IP in your load balancer; this time, enter it on `eth0` or as an additional IP on `eth0:1`. The settings in `/etc/sysctl.conf` are no longer required on the balancer, as you want it to be available.

While you are here, you should also set up the IP forwarding. You can either do this in the command line, as shown in this example, or enter the required parameters in the corresponding configuration files of your distributor (or use setup programs such as SuSE's YaST):

```
linux: # ifconfig eth0:0 192.168.10.10 netmask 255.255.255.0 broadcast \
  192.168.10.255 up
linux: # echo 1 > /proc/sys/net/ipv4/ip_forward
```

The LVS server now replies to this IP. If you wish to forward the POP/IMAP requests to the host that currently has the fewest open connections, you have to instruct LVS to distribute the connections according to the *Least Connection* (`lc`) procedure. To do this, enter the *actual* IP address of eth0 as the target on the individual hosts. For POP3 and IMAP, you will require two sets of rules: one rule for TCP port 110 (POP3) and one rule for TCP port 143 (IMAP):[4]

```
linux: # ipvsadm -A -t 192.168.10.10:110 -s lc
linux: # ipvsadm -a -t 192.168.10.10:110 -r 192.168.10.11 -g
linux: # ipvsadm -a -t 192.168.10.10:110 -r 192.168.10.12 -g
linux: # ipvsadm -a -t 192.168.10.10:110 -r 192.168.10.13 -g
linux: # ipvsadm -A -t 192.168.10.10:143 -s lc
linux: # ipvsadm -a -t 192.168.10.10:143 -r 192.168.10.11 -g
linux: # ipvsadm -a -t 192.168.10.10:143 -r 192.168.10.12 -g
linux: # ipvsadm -a -t 192.168.10.10:143 -r 192.168.10.13 -g
```

When a new connection is made, LVS determines the most suitable target host. Then LVS replaces the MAC address in the TCP/IP package. The package is still addressed to the same production IP address (`192.168.10.10`), but on the Ethernet level (layer 2 in the OSI layer model) it is addressed to the eth0 interface of a specific target host in the server pool. This host receives the package without detecting the short detour. The package is addressed to its IP address, which is linked to `lo:1`, but it is received via the external interface eth0 because the MAC address has been replaced. As it owns the target IP, it is immaterial which interface is used to transfer the package.

Unlike the `DNAT` procedure, this procedure sends the reply packages directly to the default gateway instead of rerouting them to the LVS balancer. This entire setup scales well, because the LVS balancer channels very little data from the client to the server, and because the large amount of data transferred from the server to the client does not place any load on the network interface of the LVS.

As the LVS balancer maintains a table of existing connections, packages that belong to a connection in that table are always transferred to the same production server.

For more in-depth information on the subject of load balancing, please refer to the comprehensive online documentation.[5] This also describes in detail how to monitor the availability of an individual host automatically, and how to dynamically adapt the load balancing to handle failed hosts.

---

[4] Enter the settings for ports 993 (POP3 via SSL) and 995 (IMAP via SSL) in the same manner if you use SSL/TLS.

[5] See http://www.linuxvirtualserver.org/.

3.2 IMAP Proxies

If you set up multiple IMAP servers with local hard disk systems, rather than a single shared filesystem, these no longer need to know about all users or have access to all email accounts; instead, each of them can manage a portion of all the user mailboxes. A central IMAP proxy then no longer needs to cache entire (IMAP) sessions (like the Squid HTTP proxy, for example); instead, it assigns incoming connection requests to the responsible IMAP server (see Figure 3.2).

Every user data set must contain a separate field specifying the IMAP server the user's account is stored on. The IMAP proxy queries this data during login and then transfers the IMAP request transparently to the required IMAP server. As every user is directed to his or her "own" server, no shared file area is required. This means that no load distribution among different servers is needed if this solution is used.

In very large environments, it may make sense to combine IMAP proxies *and* the load balancing technique: The proxy assigns connections to balancers on the basis of the user ID, and each balancer distributes its share of the connections to multiple IMAP servers. It is then possible to construct separate mail stores if an individual storage system is overloaded.

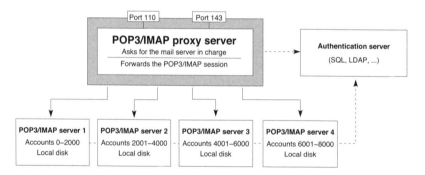

Figure 3.2: Autarkic mail servers with a local filesystem are fast, but they are also single points of failure. The AuthServer knows where each account is located.

However, most IMAP proxies consume as much RAM as the IMAP client, as the entire authentication routine and the IMAP protocol have to be implemented on them. As a result, the IMAP proxy itself can become overloaded and run out of RAM. This type of solution is therefore effective at distributing the I/O load rather than the RAM load. The following software is suitable:

Courier IMAP Proxy
> Courier IMAP contains the proxy function starting from version 4.0. For a Courier server, the simplest choice is the internal proxy. The implementation is described in section 10.3 on page 175.

Cyrus Murder Cluster
: The new versions of Cyrus also contain a native IMAP proxy, the *Cyrus-Aggregator* used in Cyrus Murder Clusters (see section 17.1 on page 281). At present (February 2008), it is still deployed "at your own risk."[6]

Perdition
: Perdition[7] is designed to work with any IMAP server as a fully-featured IMAP proxy. It can request the IMAP target host from a number of different database sources: ODBC, MySQL, PostgreSQL, GDBM, and NIS. It is also possible to assign usernames to IMAP hosts using regular expressions. Unfortunately, LDAP is not supported.

  As Courier and Cyrus each contain their own proxy, it does not really make sense to use Perdition with these servers; after all, you can only use user databases that are suitable for your IMAP backend. The project also seems to be either "'perfect"' (in the eyes of its developers) or hibernating, as there has been no new release since June 2005.

The following is *not* suitable for operating an IMAP cluster:

IMAP Proxy
: Unlike the previously mentioned proxies, IMAP proxy[8] attempts to cache the connections permanently instead of transferring them to other IMAP servers. For this reason it is mainly used to speed up web mailers, which have to log on to the IMAP server constantly because of the individual PHP calls. The program `in.imapproxyd` keeps this connection to the IMAP server open, which reduces the load on the IMAP server and speeds up the PHP application. It is described in section 5.3 on page 73.

---

[6] See http://cyrusimap.web.cmu.edu/imapd/install-murder.html.
[7] See http://www.vergenet.net/linux/perdition/.
[8] See http://www.imapproxy.org/.

Selecting a Filesystem

On small mail servers for 20 users or so, performance is hardly affected by the way the operating system organizes the data on the hard disk. When it comes to Internet or mail service providers with hundreds or thousands of users, it is a different story. Here, even if the emails are stored on fast hard disks, it can be tricky to find a filesystem capable of efficiently handling large numbers of small files, which is typical of the contents of an email database.

There is a lot of disagreement on this subject, and it is unlikely that consensus will be reached. Unfortunately, there is a wide variety of opinions and evaluation criteria regarding the speed and advantages of different filesystems; not only are they confusing, they are also often contradictory, as the different kernel versions and distributions can differ widely. If one version of a filesystem is slow, the very next kernel release may improve its speed considerably.

4 Selecting a Filesystem

Focusing on common, tested, and stable free systems that include journaling considerably reduces the number of available filesystems to consider.

Under Linux, the classic Ext2/Ext3 filesystems are not to be underestimated: Processing speed has increased so much in recent years that it may no longer be noticeably slower than ReiserFS, which has been praised for its performance with tens of thousands of files. Without question, there used to be a difference between them; however, this chapter contains test results showing that Ext2/Ext3 has overtaken ReiserFS where speed is concerned.

Admittedly, ReiserFS utilizes disk space more efficiently than Ext2 and Ext3 when dealing with large numbers of small files, but it also continues to encounter problems with data security. Whenever we have worked with ReiserFS in recent years, we encountered corrupt Reiser filesystems and inexplicable data loss. The final straw is that even `fsck.reiserfs`, when it ostensibly runs without errors, cannot guarantee that the filesystem is in a consistent state. In many cases, the only recovery solution was to use `fsck.reiserfs --rebuild-btree`, and this is a tricky procedure that can take several hours, causes an unacceptably long downtime on the server, and pumps a year's worth of adrenaline into the administrator's bloodstream.

Where loss of data is not too tragic—for example, on /tmp or in the cache directory of a proxy server—and defective partitions can be reformatted, there is no reason not to use ReiserFS. For older kernel versions, ReiserFS is still the faster solution.

However, the authors refuse to entrust email directories that need to be saved permanently to ReiserFS, and many concur in this view.

There are quite a few people who swear by XFS. It appears that people begin to appreciate it once they have worked with it for some time. It is stable and robust, but it does not, at present, contain features for reducing an existing filesystem (unlike Ext2/Ext3 or ReiserFS)—but enlarging is possible. In addition, tests and benchmark results[1] returned diverging conclusions on the performance of XFS when accessing small files.

The authors do not have much experience with using XFS, but it does not appear to be suitable for use on high-performance servers with *small* files due to insufficient speed.

OpenSolaris uses ZFS, which has only just been ported to Linux and *BSD. In addition to the benefits of the journaling filesystems mentioned above, it also contains a Logical Volume Manager (LVM). The system has one important advantage: It is aware of the physical structure of the underlying hard disk, which enables it to fully exploit the I/O speeds when writing to the hard disk. It is easy to manage, supports software RAID and snapshots, uses checksum processes, and does not require a filesystem check after a

---

[1] See http://www.debian-administration.org/articles/388.

power failure. It is also regarded as very stable; however, software RAID and checksum methods may reduce the speed and thereby diminish its advantages in that respect.

If there is no need to save money on the SAN, administrators often choose the NetApp filers from Network Appliance. WAFL, Network Appliance's own filesystem, is very capable of dealing with accesses to numerous small email files, an access pattern typical for email stores.

4.1 A Performance Test

The standard test tools `iozone` and `bonnie` or `bonnie++` are only of limited use when testing the performance of filesystems on mail servers, as these tools perform very little switching between read and write accesses to the data medium. NetApp's tool `postmark`[2] simulates the work carried out by mail and news servers. During the test, numerous small files are read, written, and deleted in turn, in order to stress the index structure of the filesystem.

The following test results are purely illustrative, as the observed results depend strongly on the kernel in use: Different versions can give rise to very different performance results for an identical filesystem. This explains why there are so many different opinions on the quality of particular filesystems.

The tests confirm our subjective opinion, which is that ReiserFS has lost its advantage in speed over Ext2/Ext3—it has landed firmly in second place. The planned ReiserFS version 4, however, seems to have caught up again and to now be ahead of Ext4 (which is also in the planning stages). A lot may have changed since this book went to press, so you should not base decisions solely on the results presented here.

15,000 RPM SCSI	Ext3	ReiserFS 3	XFS
Transactions per second	162	123	81
Files created per second	1,225	411	457
Files deleted per second	816	924	175
Read accesses per second	81	61	40

Table 4.1: Test results of the SCSI system

---

[2] This was previously at `http://www.netapp.com/tech_library/postmark.html`, but the official website no longer seems to exist.

4 Selecting a Filesystem

continued:

15,000 RPM SCSI	Ext3	ReiserFS 3	XFS
Write accesses per second	80	61	40
Average Read throughput	769.75 KB/s	578.73 KB/s	370.87 KB/s
Average Write throughput	969.20 KB/s	728.69 KB/s	466.96 KB/s

The tests with `postmark` 1.51 were done in the following conditions:

- The default kernel of OpenSuSE 10.2 in version 2.6.18.8 was used as the operating system.

- The 15,000-RPM SCSI hard disk was (see Table 4.1) a Seagate Cheetah ST336753LC FN with an 8 MB disk cache in a computer equipped with a XEON 2.8 GHz dual core (512KB CPU Cache).

- During tests on an IDE hard disk with 7,200 RPM (see Table 4.2), we used a (fairly slow) IBM Deskstar IC35L060AVVA07-0 with 2 MB disk cache on a Pentium-IV 3 GHz HT (512KB CPU Cache).

- There was a maximum number of 125,000 files, distributed among 10,000 subdirectories, and the files contained between 1,500 and 15,000 bytes.

- The test observed one million transactions in journaling mode `ordered` while the kernel and disk caches were switched on.

Some initial test results for Ext4 and ReiserFS version 4 are available on http://www.linuxinsight.com/first_benchmarks_of_the_ext4_file_system.html.

Table 4.2: Performance results of the IDE systems

7,200 RPM IDE	Ext3	ReiserFS 3	XFS
Transactions per second	47	41	26
Files created per second	29	24	15
Files deleted per second	29	24	15
Read accesses per second	23	20	13

continued:

7,200 RPM IDE	Ext3	ReiserFS 3	XFS
Write accesses per second	23	20	12
Average read throughput:	229.33 KB/s	196.48 KB/s	120.86 KB/s
Average write throughput:	288.75 KB/s	247.39 KB/s	152.17 KB/s

4.2 Tuning the Performance of the Filesystem

Speed is affected not only by the choice of filesystem, but also by the way it is used. There are some welcome configuration changes that improve speed slightly and have no disadvantages.

4.2.1 The `atime`

By default, every read access to a file automatically involves a write access, as Linux saves *three* timestamps for every file:

- *Modification time* (`mtime`) is the time displayed in the detailed (`ls -l`) file listing and describes the point in time when the *contents* of the file were last changed.

- *Change time* (`ctime`) saves the time of the most recent change to the file *permissions*, that is to say the read, write, and execute flags and the file owner. A `chmod` command ensures that a new `ctime` is set while the `mtime` remains unchanged.

- *Access time* (`atime`) shows the most recent time a *read* access occurred. Every read access, even a simple `cat`, causes a new `atime` to be saved.

This is a little performance killer. Even if the `atime` is usually only written to the write cache at first, and even if the client only retrieves a few emails, it still involves unnecessary file administration and disk I/O.

As the `atime` is not usually relevant for servers, it can be switched off. To do this, mount the data partition with the option `noatime`, and/or enter this option in the `/etc/fstab`. The Linux kernel will no longer change the atime when read accesses occur. This will not have any negative consequences.[3]

4.2.2 Access Control Lists

For access to an individual file, the Unix filesystem differentiates users into fixed classes: the *owner* of the file, users belonging to the same *group* as the file owner, and all other users (*other/world*). *Access control lists (ACLs)* have been added to improve flexibility. They are used to enable or block file access by individual users according to specific criteria.

Naturally, it takes time to evaluate ACLs. Often it is practically no time, but it does take some time, which can add up quickly on high-performance mail servers. "Practically nothing" can become "10 million times practically nothing" and turn into a relevant performance factor.

Unless you operate filesystem-based shared folders under Courier (see section 10.1.2 on page 163), (filesystem-based) ACLs are not really useful in the mail directories of an IMAP server. In this case, it makes sense to deactivate them for the mail data partition.

In addition to the `noatime` option mentioned above, there is also a `noacl` mount option that prevents the ACLs from being evaluated.[4] You can enter it in the option column in `/etc/fstab` in the usual way.

4.2.3 The Ext2/Ext3 Option `dir_index`

Ext3 used to perform badly when accessing directories containing many thousands of files. If a directory contained 100,000 files, there was literally enough time to fetch a cup of coffee before a `ls -la` returned the output.

ReiserFS clearly had the edge here, but Ext2/Ext3 have caught up and introduced the `dir_index` option, which sorts the files in a folder by a hash index and therefore enables much faster access to individual filenames. However, there is a caveat: This works *in theory*. The test results in Table 4.3 only display a minor increase in speed if `dir_index` is active; the performance actually deteriorates noticeably when it comes to deleting files.

Theodore "Ted" Tso, the central developer of the Ext2/Ext3 filesystem, provided the following explanation: `dir_index` is actually a high-performance solution, but it prevents files that were created in sequence from being stored on the hard disk in order of ascending inode. Instead, they are sorted by hash values. As a consequence, creating and deleting numerous files

---

[3] You can usually mount all your system partitions with the `noatime` option, even the root partition. However, as servers usually cause little activity on the root partition, this latter option does not improve performance noticeably.

[4] It is also valid for ReiserFS, even though `man mount` only lists it for Ext2.

causes more disk head movements than would result if the files could be written in chronological order.

`dir_index` may speed up the access to individual files, but it results in haphazard accesses to the hard disk when many files are accessed. The positioning time required by the disk head (*seek time*) then causes delays.

This does not pose a problem in our case: Good mail server programs import the file directory and then sort the files by their inode numbers in ascending order before executing accesses or deletions; this prevents the disk head from backtracking. Sam Varshavchik, the Courier author, has implemented this sorting function in Courier, but the benchmark tool we used does not contain it. This means that Courier IMAP is optimized for use with `dir_index`, and the test results can not be applied in full to Courier. Unfortunately, the authors did not have the chance to adapt the behavior of the benchmark tool.

Current distributions such as OpenSuSE 10.2 now set the option `dir_index` automatically for Ext3 partitions. Depending on the distribution and version you use, you may be able to skip the following instructions on activating `dir_index`.

For indexed directories, enter the option `dir_index` directly during formatting with `mkfs.ext3`:

```
linux: # mkfs.ext3 -O dir_index /dev/sda5
```

If you wish to activate this feature on a partition that is already being used, use `tune2fs`. In order to activate `dir_index` for directories that already exist, run `fsck` once on the disk (which may not yet be mounted). The `-fD` parameter enforces the optimization of the directory structure; as a result, an index is also created for existing directories.

```
linux: # umount /dev/sda5
linux: # tune2fs -O dir_index /dev/sda5
linux: # fsck.ext3 -fD /dev/sda5
linux: # mount /dev/sda5
```

15,000 RPM SCSI	Ext3 without `dir_index`	Ext3 with `dir_index`
Transactions per second	91	95
Files created per second	4,424	4,065
Files deleted per second	1,360	1,283

Table 4.3: Influence of the `dir_index` option

continued:

15,000 RPM SCSI	Ext3 without `dir_index`	Ext3 with `dir_index`
Read accesses per second	45	47
Write accesses per second	45	47
Average read throughput	426.34 KB/s	445.63 KB/s
Average Write throughput	651.37 KB/s	680.86 KB/s

4.2.4 Journal Mode

The Ext3 and ReiserFS journaling filesystems currently know three different methods of journaling:

`journal`
    This mode guarantees the highest possible data safety, as data is first written to the journal and then to its final destination.

`ordered` (Default)
    The kernel writes the data straight to its destination and then enters information on this transaction in the journal.

`writeback`
    In this method, the data can be written to the journal and the user data area in any order.

    In principle, this method provides as much data safety as `journal`; however, it is possible that deleted data reappears in the filesystem after a crash. You could say that this is an anomaly that is the opposite of data loss. However, this should not be a problem on a maildir system with Courier; the worst-case scenario is that some old emails reappear.

The method is specified by the corresponding `data` option when the partition is mounted or the entry is made in the `/etc/fstab`.

Table 4.4 shows the differences in speed. The results indicate that `ordered` provides the best performance for maildir-based mail servers. We have to admit that we did not expect this result. We sent a query to Ted Tso, but had received no reply when this book went to press. If you have a spare moment, please take a look at `http://www.imap-buch.com/`!

4.2 Tuning the Performance of the Filesystem

Most of us expected `writeback` to come out on top; after all, tests keep on stating that `writeback` improves performance by approximately 10 percent (Ext3) or 30 percent (ReiserFS) in comparison to `journal`. Our tests have put this statement in perspective in regard to the Ext3 system we tested: We could not detect a performance increase of 10 percent, but most operations were slightly faster. However, the main performance killer is the creation of files, and this is where `writeback` lost out. Unlike a web server that mainly delivers, a mail server constantly creates new files on a large scale. `writeback` does not therefore seem suitable for mail servers based on Ext3, in spite of popular opinion.

15,000 RPM SCSI	ordered	journal	writeback
Transactions per second	91	90	91
Files created per second	4,424	1,160	846
Files deleted per second	1,360	1,244	1,320
Read accesses per second	45	45	45
Write accesses per second	45	45	45
Average read throughput	426.34 KB/s	416.95 KB/s	419.01 KB/s
Average Write throughput	651.37 KB/s	637.03 KB/s	640.18 KB/s

Table 4.4: The `writeback` mode does not make Ext3 faster.

Ted Tso confirmed the differences between the `journal` and `writeback` modes, and provided the following explanation: `writeback` is slightly faster during normal operation; this does not apply if the running software often calls `fsync()`, forcing the system to write the data definitively from the cache to the hard disk.

Frequent sync actions can have very different effects depending on the journaling mode: In `writeback` mode, the user data has to be written to the hard disk. This requires numerous single accesses and disk head movements because the data blocks are scattered. In `journal` mode, it suffices if the data is written to the journal when `fsync()` is executed. The filesystem can do this in one access, and without much movement of the disk head, which makes this method a lot faster.

In practice, mail servers constantly call `fsync()` to ensure that the cache is emptied and the emails are safely saved. As such, in the case of a crash or reset, they lose next to no data. This means that `writeback` is now slower rather than faster. In regard to this aspect, a mail server differs substantially from a desktop PC running KDE/Gnome, OpenOffice.org, & Co.

4.2.5 Optimized `fstab` Entries

If you wish to combine all the options suggested here, you should make the following entry in the `/etc/fstab` for Ext3:

```
/dev/sda5 /mail ext3 defaults,noatime,noacl,data=ordered 1 2
```

For a corresponding ReiserFS entry, you only need to change the information on the filesystem: `reiserfs` instead of `ext3`.

4.3 RAID

Sensitive email data should be stored on a RAID system as standard practice. RAID 1 (data is mirrored on two hard disks) performs noticeably better than RAID 5 (data is stored with single parity) and RAID 6 (data is stored with double parity) in regard to computing and processing. This applies especially to write accesses, where RAID 5 and RAID 6 systems provide far less throughput than RAID 1.

In general, RAID 5/RAID 6 performs better for read access to large data blocks and achieves significantly higher throughput rates than RAID 1. The distribution of read accesses improves as the number of hard disks used in RAID 5 increases. RAID 5/RAID 6 is, however, unsuitable for mail servers, as mail servers (unlike web servers) are subject to constant write accesses. RAID 5/RAID 6 cannot utilize its high read throughput, as a mail directory consists of too many tiny files. Quite the opposite: The large number of hard disks and the consequently increased positioning times required by the disk heads slow down the access to many small files significantly when compared to RAID 1. Our experience has shown that RAID 1 is therefore more suitable for mail servers because its write throughput is better.

RAID 5 is no safer than RAID 1. RAID 1 and RAID 5 can both handle the failure of only one disk. Only RAID 6 is able to cope if two disks fail at the same time.

For this reason, it is safer (!) and more sensible to use three hard disks to build a RAID 1 (two data disks, one spare disk) rather than a RAID 5 (two data disks, one parity disk).

The RAID performs better when writing, and a spare disk is always available. However, a RAID 1 has 50 percent less storage space for user data than a corresponding RAID 5, so you may have to invest in larger hard disks if you require the same entire storage capacity.

Instead of spending money on a RAID 5 controller, you should instead invest in a fourth hard disk and construct the cheaper (but faster) RAID 10, which is a combination of RAID 1 (mirroring) and RAID 0 (striping). Even if you have a spare disk for RAID 5 (two disks for data, one disk for the parity, and one disk as a backup), it makes more sense to use the additional disk for RAID 1 or RAID 10 from a performance point of view. You can combine two disks to one RAID 1 and then combine the two RAIDs to a large filesystem under LVM. You could also combine all four disks into a RAID 10. RAID 10 is currently the highest-performing RAID available.

Even if fast RAID 5 controllers are released in the near future and can smooth out the write drawbacks, you should not underestimate the I/O load caused by large mail directories. Bottlenecks in mail systems are often caused by the shared I/O load of the disk combination when thousands of POP3 and IMAP users access the stored emails in parallel, and not by lack of storage space.

Every hard disk has a limited capacity for I/O operations, resulting from the positioning speed of the disk head and the revolution speed of the disk, which are indirectly related. Disks with 10,000 RPM or 15,000 RPM have the advantage here, but even they will be pushed to the limit if there are more than a few thousand users. The only solution in this case is to parallelize on a large scale; this means that you should use additional Autarkic read heads in RAID 10. If you have a lot of space and many IMAP users, it may be advisable to buy many small hard disks rather than a few large ones.

4.4 NFS

If you store emails on a central system, you can distribute the load onto multiple physical IMAP servers without too much effort. As every server then contains an identical file tree, it no longer matters which computer the user is assigned to. You can use a load balancer or a simple DNS Round Robin method to distribute the load, as described in section 3.1 on page 45.

Courier uses a maildir storage format for emails that was designed specifically for use with NFS. It does not need file locking, which can be tricky for NFS, so multiple servers acting independently can use it in parallel. Courier IMAP can use it to deliver emails, while Postfix and other such servers can use it to store emails.

This is unfortunately not the case for Cyrus. Cyrus index files require file locking. Current implementations of NFS contain a file locking daemon that is intended to solve this problem, but even the developers of Cyrus are cagey about this. The most concrete statement in the Cyrus Wiki is that "NFS4 seems to support the file-locking."[5] However, various discussion forums frequently mention locking errors in conjunction with NFS4. We therefore do not recommend the production use of NFS as a storage location for Cyrus. Because Cyrus (unlike Courier) is not able to write to an identical data set using multiple instances, NFS looks less attractive anyway.

It is fairly simple to mount the (Courier) mail repository via NFS, but there are a few tuning hints that will speed up access considerably.

4.4.1 Disabling `atime` and Optimizing Block Size

NFS offers the option of mounting the entire storage partition using `noatime` (see section 4.2.1 on page 57) on the NFS server and on the NFS client.

You should also specify the options `rsize=8192,wsize=8192` on the NFS client; it will then increase the block size for read and write accesses.

If the client wishes to read or save a large email, it has to distribute it according to the block size. A 16KB email normally is transferred in 16 blocks of 1,024 bytes. The problem is that the parallel processing of NFS requests is limited. The NFS client has to wait for confirmation by the server after every block before it can send the next one. This takes up valuable time. If the block size is increased to 8,192 bytes, a 16KB email can be processed in two requests.

Small block sizes were introduced to limit the amount of data that has to be retransmitted if blocks are lost or errors occur during transmission. However, transmission errors should occur only rarely within a LAN,[6] so there is no reason to keep the blocks small.

Many kernel versions and distributions now use block sizes of 4,096 or 8,192 bytes instead of the original default value of 1,024 bytes.

4.4.2 NFS Version 3

Specify `nfsvers=3` as the mount option on the NFS client, so that it will use protocol version 3 to communicate with the server. Version 3 is currently contained in the common distributions, but the clients of older distributions may use version 2 by default.

Protocol version 3 knows some additional NFS commands that can save time and reduce the load on the client in some circumstances. This option

---

[5] See http://cyrusimap.web.cmu.edu/twiki/bin/view/Cyrus/CyrusCluster.
[6] If they occur more frequently, you should troubleshoot this error!

will not have any negative side effects. If your Linux/Unix does not support this version, your mount attempt will fail. You will then not be able to use this trick, but there are no negative consequences.

4.4.3 Fast I/O

Do not underestimate the I/O load on the server. Simple SATA or IDE disks with 7,200 RPM already perform well on a normal server; normal RAID controllers also return good results, as the speed of the entire system also depends on the CPU and local data processing. Mediocre I/O performance does not have serious effects in this case.

The NFS server, however, delivers the data rather than processing it. All requests from all other hosts are bunched. The local I/O can be a problem here. Mediocre RAID controllers or hard disks reach their limits very quickly, and thereby slow down all other processes unnecessarily.

If you are using an NFS server, pay special attention to the tuning hints for hard disks, mount options, journaling variants, and filesystems that are listed in this chapter. A good disk cache is, as always, beneficial, and the advantage provided by hard disks with 10,000 or 15,000 RPM becomes apparent very quickly.

Complementary Webmail Clients

IMAP lets users access their email anywhere they can run an IMAP client, so a web-based mail client is simply a logical extension of the basic idea. There are two approaches: direct filesystem access to the email repository or access via IMAP.

Large, monolithic email services sometimes contain a native webmail client, which is often designed specifically for the particular system's database format and accesses the email repository directly. Such webmail clients can only be combined with Cyrus if the mail system explicitly supports Cyrus databases. They can be used with Courier if the webmail client is able to work directly with a maildir structure.

Most free webmailers simply use the IMAP protocol to access the email server, so it is not relevant where and how the IMAP server stores emails. This means that these webmailers can theoretically be combined with any IMAP server, because they run in the web browser but communicate with the mail server like standard mail clients that run on the desktop.

5 Complementary Webmail Clients

This chapter will introduce the two best-known free webmailers that are able to work with any IMAP server: Squirrelmail and Horde/IMP. Both are written in PHP and run in a standard web space. They use the IMAP protocol to connect to the mail server, so they do not require access to the email filesystem, and do not need to connect to the user database on the mail server. They transfer the login name and password to the mail server via the IMAP connection.

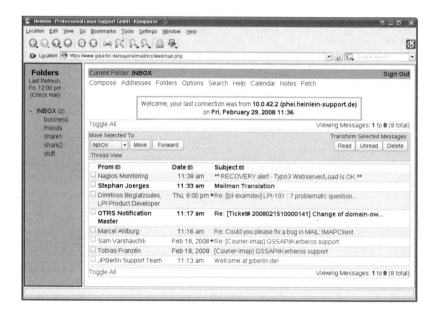

Figure 5.1:
A look at the
Squirrelmail inbox

5.1 Squirrelmail

Squirrelmail[1] (see Figure 5.1) is fast and easy to install. It also provides a number of interesting features by means of numerous plugins, including the following:

- A virtual keyboard during login, to prevent keylogging

- Shared calendars and address books

- A current weather report for the region

- Spam protection and filters

[1] See http://www.squirrelmail.org/.

5.1 Squirrelmail

- A fetchmail plugin for importing POP3 accounts to the IMAP server
- Safety functions for locking users or IP addresses, or for logging the source of the most recent access
- Automatic signatures and headers

This package is recommended for basic distributions, as Debian and SuSE, among others, contain Squirrelmail. The installation of the source code is also simple, as Squirrelmail is only a collection of PHP scripts.

Place the archive into the document directory on your web server:[2]

```
linux: # tar -xvzf squirrelmail-1.4.9a.tar.gz
[...]
linux: # mv squirrelmail-1.4.9a /srv/www/htdocs/squirrelmail
linux: # cd /srv/www/htdocs/squirrelmail
```

Once Squirrelmail is installed, you can configure it via a menu-based interface by invoking a short Perl script:

```
linux:/srv/www/htdocs/squirrelmail # ./configure
SquirrelMail Configuration : Read: config.php (1.4.0)
---------------------------------------------------------
Main Menu --
1.  Organization Preferences
2.  Server Settings
3.  Folder Defaults
4.  General Options
5.  Themes
6.  Address Books
7.  Message of the Day (MOTD)
8.  Plugins
9.  Database
10. Languages

D.  Set pre-defined settings for specific IMAP servers

C   Turn color on
S   Save data
Q   Quit

Command >>
```

Make sure you set up the SMTP and IMAP servers under menu item **2. Server Settings**. Specify the language and character encoding under **10. Languages**:

[2] We recommend that you give the directory an unusual name, rather than `squirrelmail` or `webmail`, as this is a simple way to keep wannabe script hackers at bay.

```
Command >> 10

SquirrelMail Configuration : Read: config.php (1.4.0)
---------------------------------------------------------
Language preferences
1.  Default Language       : en_US
2.  Default Charset        : iso-8859-1
3.  Enable lossy encoding  : false

R   Return to Main Menu
C   Turn color on
S   Save data
Q   Quit

Command >> S

Data saved in config.php
Press enter to continue...
```

Call up the URL for Squirrelmail; for example, `http://www.example.com/squirrelmail`. You should now be able to log on to your email account. Because Squirrelmail uses your login data to log on to the IMAP server, Squirrelmail does not need to be connected to the user database.

For more information on enhancing Squirrelmail, go to the project web page, which contains a number of (more or less useful) plugins, including the ones we mentioned previously (*Virtual Keyboard*, *Calendar*, and *Shared Calendar*). The *Show SSL Link* plugin is also worth mentioning, as it encourages users to log on via SSL—though this only works if the webmailer is run on an HTTPS secure web page.

During operation, you should keep an eye on the `data` subdirectory. This is where the program stores personal user settings, filter settings, address books, and calendar entries. Do not forget this folder during backups or migrations. When you switch to IMAP server software with a different name space, the filter settings may no longer be suitable. Users will no longer be able to log in if the filter rules are faulty (see section 6.3 on page 79).

5.2 Horde/IMP

The IMP webmailer is part of the Horde project.[3] This is a powerful but complex framework for web and groupware applications, but the configuration is not intuitive. The project has existed for nearly ten years and has yielded "standard" webmailers, specialized Ajax and cell phone webmailers, and projects such as (group) calendars, task management tools, file managers, and address books or bookmark tools. Horde has also made its

---

[3] See `http://www.horde.org/`.

5.2 Horde/IMP

way into the standard Linux distributions (the `horde` and `imp` packages in SuSE, and the `horde3` and `imp4` packages in Debian).

In the following section, we will set up IMP so that it (like Squirrelmail) can be used as a pure webmailer for an IMAP server. We will thereby leave out the other impressive Horde functions, as well as Horde's own user management.

After installation, you should have a look at `http://localhost/horde`; you will be logged in automatically. The menu item **Administration/Configuration** contains the settings for Horde and IMP. Strangely enough, you have to make your settings in both sections, even if you only wish to use the webmailer.

You should first determine whether and how users need to be authenticated in the Horde framework. If they use the entire Horde project suite, they will access a MySQL database or LDAP directly at some stage. If they will only use the webmailer, we recommend that you simply transfer the user data to the IMAP server.

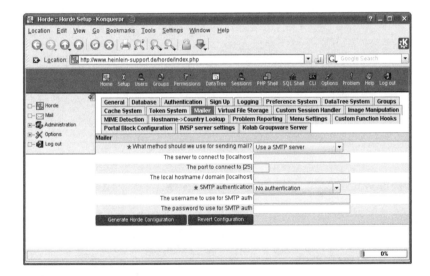

Figure 5.2: Confusing: Horde configuration

First, we require the **Authentication** tab in the Horde configuration. Go to menu item **What backend should we use for authenticating users to Horde?** and select the **IMAP server** menu item. Enter the hostname and port and configure whether contact should be via an SSL/TLS encrypted connection. This informs Horde that the webmailer may only be accessed after authentication through an IMAP username and password.

Caution: Do not lock yourself out of your own web front end. Save your own IMAP username under **Which users should be treated as administrators** before saving your settings if you want to have administrator rights.

5 Complementary Webmail Clients

Go to the **Mailer** tab to configure how the framework should send emails: Do you want them to be forwarded to `/usr/lib/sendmail` via a pipe or transferred to a mail server via SMTP? In Figure 5.2, we chose SMTP. Click **Create Horde configuration** to save the settings.

To choose a display option, specify email sizes, or determine other display details, go to the **IMP** item in **Administration/Configuration**. Don't forget to save the settings by clicking **Create webmail configuration**.

Strangely enough, the most important setting is not available here: Which IMAP mail server should the webmailer connect to? The IMAP server you specified in the first step only served to verify the login to the Horde framework and has nothing to do with email retrieval.

Now, you have to edit the configuration files: Go to the directory containing the Horde PHP files (`/srv/www/htdocs/horde`) and then choose the `imp/config/servers.php` file. Now go to the IMAP server section and complete the setup as described in the example below:

```
$servers['imap'] = array(
        'name' => 'Web and Mail',
        'server' => 'mail.example.com',
        'hordeauth' => false,
        'protocol' => 'imap/notls',
        'port' => 143,
        'maildomain' => 'example.com',
        'smtphost' => 'smtp.example.com',
        'smtpport' => 25,
        'realm' => '',
        'preferred' => 'true',
);
```

Figure 5.3:
A pleasant
webmailer: IMP

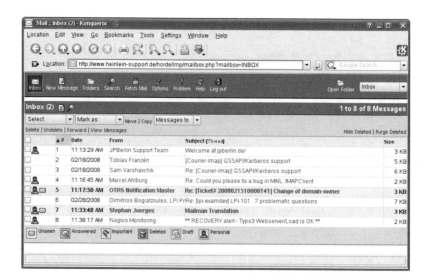

IMP is able to work with multiple IMAP servers in parallel. The user can select the IMAP server during login. In single-server mode (the standard mode), the `preferred => true` setting ensures that the specified server is always used. In multiserver mode, you can suggest a server for preselection by the user.

If possible, we also recommend that you set the `protocol` to `'imap/tls'` so that the connection to the IMAP server is tunneled via SSL/TLS. Now you can log on to the webmailer under `http://localhost/horde/imp` (see Figure 5.3).

5.3 Fast Access via the IMAP Cache Proxy

Webmailers generally have a problem: They are unable to keep a connection to the IMAP server open. Every time a user accesses the webmailer, clicks on an email, or selects a directory, the webmailer's PHP code has to reconnect to the IMAP server. This takes time and puts strain on the server.

The IMAP proxy project has developed a not very well-known program, `in.imapproxyd`, which keeps a connection to an IMAP server open even after the webmailer ends its current session. When the webmailer next accesses the IMAP server, the server recognizes that it is part of the same user-level session by the cached login data, and forwards the request to the IMAP server via the preserved IMAP session. The webmailer still has to identify itself to `in.imapproxyd`, but this uses far less resources than logging on from scratch to the IMAP server.

You will find the source code on `http://www.imapproxy.org/`; there is also a mailing list.[4] The IMAP proxy software is stable and problem free after installation, but it is not yet part of the distributions. There are only a few Red Hat packages from third parties; one of us (Peer Heinlein) has created a package for the current SuSE version, which you will find on the website for this book.[5] This package does the compiling (described below) for you, and also contains an init script more suitable for SuSE than the original script.

The instructions below refer to version 1.2.5 under OpenSuSE 10.2, but the procedure should be similar for other versions or distributions. You require the source code package,[6] `gcc`, the OpenSSL and NCurses libraries with header files (from packages `openssl-devel` and `ncurses-devel`) and Wietse Venema's `tcpd` log utility for networks,[7] as well as the appropriate development package (such as `tcpd-devel`).

---

[4] See `http://lists.andrew.cmu.edu/mailman/listinfo/imapproxy-info`.
[5] See `http://www.imap-buch.com/`.
[6] See `http://www.imapproxy.org/downloads/up-imapproxy-1.2.5.tar.gz`.
[7] See `ftp://ftp.porcupine.org/pub/security/index.html`.

Use the commands `configure`, `make`, and `make install` from the unpacked source directory to compile and install the IMAP cache proxy. The original code also contains an init script, which links the supplied `Makefile` underneath `/etc/rc2.d`. This is correct for Debian, but will result in an error message under SuSE.

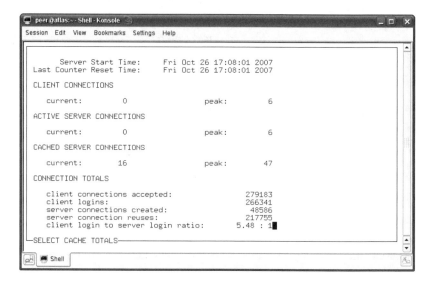

Figure 5.4:
pimpstat shows the potential savings that IMAP proxy can make

The `/etc/init.d/imapproxy` start script does run under OpenSuSE, but is expected in `/etc/init.d/rc3.d` and `rc5.d`:

```
linux:~/up-imapproxy-1.2.5 # cd /etc/init.d
linux:/etc/init.d # ln -s ../imapproxy rc3.d/S99imapproxy
linux:/etc/init.d # ln -s ../imapproxy rc5.d/S99imapproxy
```

The `pimpstat` tool is installed along with the `in.imapproxyd`. Like `top`, it provides an overview, constantly updated, of the number of connections, the number of connections not made because of caching, and other information (see Figure 5.4).

Chapter 6

Migrating IMAP servers

When you change to new IMAP server software or migrate from POP3 to IMAP, you will rarely find a suitable conversion program or import function that will transfer the existing data records perfectly. Unless both programs use identical storage methods for emails (mbox or maildir format), you will not be able to migrate from the old system to the new one by simply copying the files.

However, there is a simple solution: Use the IMAP (or POP3) protocol itself. After all, the software provides a corresponding interface. IMAP can be used to upload all emails of an account to the target IMAP server while retaining all defined IMAP flags (read, deleted, answered) and any custom flags, as long as the target server supports them.

You can use the SELECT command to determine whether this is the case. If the server returns a * when listing the flags, this means that any flag is permitted. Cyrus supports a maximum of 128 flags per folder, while Courier theoretically has no upper limit. This means that there could be problems when migrating from Courier to Cyrus if there are a very large number of custom flags.

There are a number of tools that can carry out the migration. These include:

`imapsync`[1]
: We recommend this flexible and mature migration tool by Gilles Lamiral.

`pop2imap`[2]
: This is `imapsync`'s little brother. It synchronizes the data set of a POP3 server with that of an IMAP server.

`imap_migrate`[3]
: This PHP script expects an empty target mailbox, so it is not suitable for continuous data synchronization. When you try to update an already populated mailbox, it creates duplicates of existing messages. However, it can serve as a basis for any in-house developments.

`imapcopy`[4]
: This tool is still under development, but it may be worth looking at if `imapsync` or `imap_migrate` are not suitable.

`imap_tools`[5]
: This is a collection of Perl scripts, which perform tasks such as copying IMAP server files to mbox files or uploading emails from mbox files to an IMAP server. There is also a tool for migrating from POP3 to IMAP.

6.1 Migration Using `imapsync`

We have had very good experiences with `imapsync`. It is stable and under active development, and allows continuous synchronization of IMAP folders. Thus you can migrate a mailbox from the old system to the new system incrementally without creating duplicates of existing emails in the target system.

This is important because migrating a large system via IMAP takes quite a long time. `imapsync` permits you to begin the migration while the source mail system is still operating. In this way the largest possible number of emails from each account is copied to the target system at the beginning.

[1] See http://www.linux-france.org/prj/imapsync/.
[2] See http://www.linux-france.org/prj/pop2imap/.
[3] See http://freshmeat.net/projects/imapmigration/.
[4] See http://home.arcor.de/armin.diehl/imapcopy/imapcopy.html.
[5] See http://www.athensfbc.com/imap_tools.

For thousands of accounts and many gigabytes of email content, the first transfer cycle can take a number of days. However, as long as the old mail system can continue to operate during this process, it does not really matter.

After the main bulk of data has been copied to the target system, the succeeding `imapsync` cycles take far less time. The time required for synchronization decreases with each cycle. During the final migration period, however, you have to bar user access to the old system and schedule downtime so that all remaining emails and data can be completely transferred to the new system without any new mail arrivals or user updates happening in the meantime. If you have carried out the preparations just described, the downtime for this final synchronization cycle is very short and can take place during a night of the weekend, for example. `imapsync` now only needs to copy all new emails, remove newly deleted emails from the target system, and adapt any newly modified email flags.

The following example copies the `INBOX` and all other IMAP folders of the user `tux`:

```
linux: # imapsync --host1 oldmail.example.com --user1 tux \
  --password1 "secret"  --host2 newmail.example.com --user2 t.tux \
  --password2 "secret"
```

You can automate the processing of many hundreds or thousands of accounts by creating a list of all usernames and passwords and a shell script that feeds them to `imapsync`. However, there are some security concerns when you transfer passwords as call parameters, because they are then entered in the shell's command history. Moreover, unprivileged (!) users can view the invocation of `imapsync` with all entered passwords by displaying the process list. `imapsync` therefore explicitly provides the option of reading the passwords from separate files. These files should be stored in a secure directory and only be readable by `root`:

```
linux: # cat /root/pw1
secretpassword1
linux: # cat /root/pw2
secretpassword2
linux: # imapsync --host1 oldmail.example.com --user1 tux \
  --passfile1 /root/pw1  --host2 newmail.example.com --user2 t.tux \
  --passfile2 /root/pw2
```

The following call parameters are also useful:

- If you add the `--dry` flag, `imapsync` runs the readonly synchronization cycle and does not modify any data. This is perfect for a test run.

- `--delete` deletes the emails on the source host specified in `--host1` after the migration has been completed successfully.

- `--delete2` deletes the emails on the target host specified in `--host2` if they (no longer) exist on the source host.

- `--ssl1` and `--ssl2` activate the SSL encryption on the source and target computers, respectively. These two parameters demonstrate how the script works: It acts as a link *between* the two servers and opens separate connections to each of them.

- `--help` provides a list of the numerous available call parameters. It is possible to specify complex criteria (size, age, folder name) for selecting the emails that are to be migrated, and to adapt the names of the IMAP folders.

When testing the migration, you should pay attention to the following stumbling blocks:

- Were all IMAP folder names converted correctly? Do IMAP folders on the old system contain special characters that the new system cannot interpret properly? In some cases, the old and new systems disagree on whether IMAP folders may be parallel to the `INBOX` (see section 6.3 on page 79).

    `imapsync` also allows you to modify or transform folder names between the old and new systems by using the parameter `--regextrans2` to specify a regular expression corresponding to the desired replacement: for example, `--regextrans2 s/INBOX/INBOX.old-inbox/`.

- Do users need to subscribe to folders on the target system (see section 2.2.4 on page 41)?

    If your users used subscribed folders on the old system, you have to transfer the subscription list to the new server. `imapsync` accepts a suitable call parameter in the `--subscribe` option.

    If mail clients update all IMAP folders as a matter of course, you can ignore this item. However, if a user's client is configured to only synchronize subscribed folders with the server, the user will see *no* emails if the subscription list is empty.

- For a number of email servers and clients, POP3 users will see all migrated emails as new emails and therefore have to download them all completely. The only solution here is to explain this to users in advance.

6.2 Converting mbox to maildir

Even though an mbox contains all emails in one single file, whereas maildir creates a separate file for each email, individual emails are identically formatted in both cases. For this reason, it is fairly easy to convert mbox files to the maildir format.

Juri Haberland currently maintains a tool named mb2md.pl,[6] which performs the required steps more or less automatically and is suitable for converting large data sets. If your target system uses the maildir format, migration on the file level using it will probably be a lot faster than if you use the IMAP tools we just described.

The following example shows how to convert an individual user's mbox file. Use -s to enter the path for the source file and -d to enter the path for the target directory:

```
username@linux:$ mb2md.pl -s /var/mail/username \
  -d /var/maildir/username/Maildir/
Converting /var/mail/username to maildir: /var/maildir/username/Maildir
Source Mbox is /var/mail/username
Target Maildir is /var/maildir/username/Maildir
666 messages.
```

You should execute this command under the user ID of the user rather than as root. Otherwise, mb2md.pl will create the target maildir with incorrect permissions, and the user will (probably) no longer have the necessary read and write permissions to the converted files. When executing a loop to convert the files of many users, you can use an su call to switch to the corresponding user IDs; in this case, the command to invoke mb2md.pl is specified via -c:

```
linux: # su username -c "mb2md.pl -s source_file -d target_directory"
```

6.3 Modifying Folder Names

You might need to modify the names of the IMAP folders during migration, because the target system only permits folders beneath the INBOX. In this case folder names such as Friends are no longer permitted; instead, you have to convert them into INBOX.Friends. Two types of complications can occur at this stage.

First, what happens if a user has Friends *and* INBOX.Friends on the old system? This scenario could easily occur. After all, mail clients cannot agree among themselves on whether the Trash, Sent, and Drafts folders should be created parallel to or beneath the INBOX. If you are unlucky, a user's desktop email client creates the directories in parallel, while the

---

[6] See http://batleth.sapienti-sat.org/projects/mb2md/.

webmailer creates them underneath `INBOX`; this scenario results in two directories being used for the same purpose. They can be copied together during migration, but this has to be done manually.

Second, if you simply move the user's folders without also modifying his filter settings, some user settings can become invalid and have to be reset after the migration. In this case, you have to inform your users in advance and apologize for the inconvenience.

Squirrelmail, the popular webmailer, is particularly sensitive to this problem: Normally, Squirrelmail imports any modified folder structures from the server after IMAP login. However, if filter settings refer to IMAP folders that no longer exist (because the folder names have changed), Squirrelmail freezes and the user can no longer log in. In this case, you should modify the user-specific profile files in the `data` folder under the Squirrelmail folder. If users have defined their own rules, you will find entries of the following form in their profiles:

```
filter0=From,tux@example.com,INBOX.Friends.tux
filter1=From,support@heinlein-support.de,INBOX.Work.heinlein-support
```

The `grep` command enables you to find these lines, so you can detect potential problems at an early stage. If necessary, you can use a `sed` script to modify the folder names appearing in a profile file appropriately:[7]

```
for FILE in * ; do
        sed s/oldname/newname/ $FILE > $FILE.WORK
        cp $FILE $FILE.ORIG
        mv $FILE.WORK $FILE
done
```

If nothing works, you have to delete the filter settings from the profile files and explain this to your users. The following script removes *all* filter settings:

```
for FILE in * ; do
        grep -v ^filter $FILE > $FILE.WORK
        cp $FILE $FILE.ORIG
        mv $FILE.WORK $FILE
done
```

In any case, check the results carefully before overwriting the original profile files with new versions.

[7] The following shell scripts are only examples and should be modified to suit the specific situation.

6.4 Determining Cleartext Passwords

Even though cleartext passwords usually *increase* security (see section 9.13 on page 147), many setups save only hashed user passwords in the user data.

In principle there should be no problem with this, but in practice different programs compute hash values differently. If you have to switch authentication sources during migration, this can lead to disaster. Even if the new authentication database also does not save passwords in cleartext, it may still require the cleartext passwords to calculate the new hashed passwords that it will use. The existing password hashes cannot be used.

Even `imapsync` and other IMAP migration tools assume that you have access to the user data and can log on as if you were the normal user. If you do not have this data, you can not use these extremely convenient data migration tools. At this point, you will wish you had stored the cleartext passwords. But there is a solution.

Check whether the existing product contains a debug mode that logs the passwords. This means you can collect the cleartext passwords of active users as you go along. Pay special attention to ensure that restrictive file permissions are set for the mail log file.

On a Courier-based server, you can use the option `DEBUG_LOGIN=2` in the configuration file `authdaemonrc` (previously `pop3d` and `imapd`). If Courier is in operation, you can use this method to determine the passwords and then enter them into the authentication database.

Systems that do not use cleartext passwords often restrict users to the authentication methods `PLAIN` and `LOGIN`. These methods are not secure, as it is easy to listen in on the network traffic while the password is transferred in cleartext from the client to the server. On the other hand, this safety risk enables you to sniff out login data continuously without much effort. You can then evaluate it and update the authentication database. Standard sniffing tools carry out these tasks automatically and then present a clear list of the sniffed-out user data.[8]

Alternatively, if you need the cleartext passwords, you can also create a web front end that users have to log into in order to trigger the migration of their mailbox to the new server. The called script has to create the user account on the new server and can then start tools such as `imapsync`. This method is usually faster and more reliable than logging or sniffing out passwords.

This is also suitable for migration from MS Exchange servers to other pro-

---

[8] In Germany, it is a criminal offense to use these tools, even if you are using them to prevent user accounts from being hacked, and even if this is the only way you can improve the safety of the system. We do not advise German administrators to use these tools at home or abroad. Administrators of other nationalities may not use these tools within Germany.

grams and authentication services, as this software prohibits the logging of passwords and the exporting of password data (in any form) from the active directory. Even hashed password data remains hidden.[9] We have used this method successfully in a variety of projects.

Ultimately, this is just password phishing by another name. The only difference is that it is being done by the good guys for a legitimate system administration purpose. Do inform your users in advance (by letter if possible). Explain that this is an exceptional request, and that login data will never be requested without such prior notification.

---

[9] The authors would appreciate any information on how to access this *data*.

Part II

Courier IMAP

Chapter 7

Structure and Basic Configuration

Courier IMAP is part of a larger project that provides a full-fledged mail server containing a mail transport agent (Courier-MTA), a webmailer dubbed SqWebMail, a mail delivery agent with a filter engine (Maildrop), a compact command-line mail client (Cone), a generic authentication library (Courier Authlib) to replace the Simple Authentication and Security Layer (SASL) described in RFC 4422, and the aforementioned IMAP and POP3 server with proxy capability.

All of these components can be used independently, which means that Courier IMAP often functions as an IMAP server with, for example, Postfix or Exim as MTA, or with Squirrelmail or Horde/IMP as webmailer. These are more modern, well-developed, and efficient than the corresponding Courier components; of the Courier modules, only Courier IMAP and Maildrop are commonly used.

Work on the Courier project began in 1998, and the software has long since found its way into all standard distributions. Nobody can claim that

7 Structure and Basic Configuration

new, ambitious developments will appear soon. The Courier IMAP CVS on Sourceforge[1] shows some activity, and there are usually half a dozen new emails on the corresponding mailing lists at any given time. However, we probably cannot expect any major hype over a big release with numerous new functions.

This is not really a problem, as the software is capable of all necessary functions, is very robust, and performs very well overall. You can more or less forget about the server once it has been installed properly; it works in the background, requires almost no attention, and has not caused any major security problems.

To simplify matters, we will refer to the IMAP server as *Courier* from now on, even though this name actually refers to the entire software project.

7.1 Installing the Software

The installation process causes some binary programs and simple configuration files to be placed on the system. No additional database systems or configuration decisions are required, and the configuration itself is not arduous. The only difficult part is integrating authentication mechanisms into Courier so that you can use authentication data stored in MySQL, LDAP, and the like.

You should first use shell accounts to get to know Courier and its basic features. This reduces the possible sources of error and resulting annoyance. After you understand how Courier works, you can then move on to including LDAP and MySQL support and be better able to fill in the required configuration fields.

In most cases you can simply install the Courier IMAP packages from the Linux distributon. Debian and Ubuntu contain current .deb packages, enabling `apt-get install courier-imap` to do its work. If you require a package with SSL support, you can additionally call `apt-get install courier-imap-ssl`.

If you prefer to compile Courier IMAP yourself, you will find detailed instructions in section C.1 on page 321. When we went to press, there were no RPM packages for Red Hat Enterprise or Fedora systems, so you will have to do the compiling for these systems.

SuSE delivers Courier IMAP in two separate packages. `yast -i courier-imap` installs the IMAP server. Support for LDAP is contained in a separate RPM package. Use `yast -i courier-imap-ldap` if you need to integrate LDAP.

SuSE packages only contain support for MySQL starting from OpenSuSE

---

[1] See http://www.courier-mta.org/cvs.html.

version 10.2. If you use an earlier version and require support for MySQL, you will have to compile it yourself as described in section C.1 on page 321.

In OpenSuSE 10.0 (and only in this version), the SSL start scripts are bungled in such a way that it is impossible to start Courier so that it offers IMAP and POP3 via SSL/TLS on port 993 or 995. The SSL start scripts use call parameters from the non-SSL start scripts: Instead of `SSL_PORTS`, it contains `PORTS`. When Courier attempts to start `imap-ssl` on the already occupied non-SSL port 143, this can only lead to chaos.[2] Instead of trying to correct the scripts, you can run an online update immediately after installation. This update corrects these errors automatically.

7.2   What Is Where?

In nearly all distributions, the configuration files (see section 7.5 on page 95) are located in `/etc/courier`. The Courier binaries can be found under `/usr/bin/` or `/usr/sbin/`. These also contain the IMAP daemon `/usr/sbin/imapd`, the POP3 module `/usr/sbin/pop3d`, and the following programs:

`/usr/sbin/imaplogin` and `/usr/sbin/pop3login`
These two auxiliary login modules are called automatically by Courier.

`/usr/sbin/couriertls`
This program manages SSL/TLS connections. It is not really designed for manual use.

`/usr/bin/deliverquota`
Every MTA can store emails in the maildir format. MTAs usually contain a little program that functions as a mail delivery agent (MDA). However, not all MDAs observe quotas. `deliverquota` does observe quotas and is available for use by other MTAs; Postfix, for example, can use it if a corresponding entry is made in the `master.cf` (see section 10.2.2 on page 173).

`/usr/bin/maildiracl`
This permits maintenance of the IMAP folder *Access Control Lists*. Clients usually import the required ACLs directly via the IMAP protocol. Administrators can use this tool to carry out this process manually.

`/usr/bin/maildirkw`
This enables the administrator to edit custom IMAP flags (*keywords*,

---

[2] Clearly the maintainer could not have tried starting the `courier-imap` package even once; certainly there were no tests...

see section 8.2.1 on page 115) for individual emails. Clients usually use the STORE IMAP command to do this (see section A.4 on page 312).

/usr/bin/maildirmake
This little script creates the maildir directories for users. It invokes several mkdir commands to create the directories Maildir, cur, new, and tmp and to assign the correct permissions to them (see section 10.1.2 on page 164).

/usr/sbin/mkimapdcert and /usr/sbin/mkpop3dcert
These two bash scripts automatically generate SSL/TLS keys. They are started automatically when Courier first launches, if SSL is used. The configuration is situated in files /etc/courier/pop3d.cnf and imapd.cnf.

/usr/sbin/sharedindexinstall
This script helps you to put in place the index file for email folders shared by multiple users without a restart (see section 10.1.1 on page 156).

/usr/sbin/sharedindexsplit
This partitions a large index file for shared folders into multiple small subfiles according to a number of criteria.

/usr/lib/courier-imap/couriertcpd
This is a type of inet daemon for the Courier project. It monitors the TCP/IP ports and activates the submodules responsible for the corresponding protocol when new connections are made.

As usual, the Courier init scripts are located under /etc/init.d/. This is where the distributions provide an individual start script for every Courier IMAP module:

```
linux: # ls -la /etc/init.d/courier-*
-rwxr-xr-x  1 root root 2307 Nov 18  2004 /etc/init.d/courier-authdaemon
-rwxr-xr-x  1 root root 2288 Nov 18  2004 /etc/init.d/courier-imap
-rwxr-xr-x  1 root root 2677 Nov 18  2004 /etc/init.d/courier-imap-ssl
-rwxr-xr-x  1 root root 2234 Nov 18  2004 /etc/init.d/courier-pop3
-rwxr-xr-x  1 root root 2657 Nov 18  2004 /etc/init.d/courier-pop3-ssl
```

In SuSE, the init scripts can be called directly as rccourier-authdaemon, rccourier-imap, and so on, without entering a path; this is a pleasant luxury not available to users of Debian or Red Hat. These rc scripts are symbolic links to the actual start-stop scripts:

```
linux: # ls -la /usr/sbin/rccourier*
lrwxrwxrwx 1 root root 30 Mar 30 18:41 /usr/sbin/rccourier-authdaemon ->
```

```
/etc/init.d/courier-authdaemon
lrwxrwxrwx 1 root root 24 Mar 30 18:41 /usr/sbin/rccourier-imap -> /etc/
init.d/courier-imap
lrwxrwxrwx 1 root root 28 Mar 30 18:41 /usr/sbin/rccourier-imap-ssl -> /
etc/init.d/courier-imap-ssl
lrwxrwxrwx 1 root root 24 Mar 30 18:41 /usr/sbin/rccourier-pop3 -> /etc/
init.d/courier-pop3
lrwxrwxrwx 1 root root 28 Mar 30 18:41 /usr/sbin/rccourier-pop3-ssl -> /
etc/init.d/courier-pop3-ssl
```

Unfortunately, there is no shared script that starts and stops *all* services at once. This is particularly helpful at the beginning, when you are still experimenting with the configuration files.

The following script provides this convenient option. You can install it as `/usr/local/bin/rccourier`, for example, and make it executable through `chmod u+x`:

```
linux: # cat /usr/sbin/rccourier
/etc/init.d/courier-authdaemon $1
/etc/init.d/courier-pop3 $1
/etc/init.d/courier-pop3-ssl $1
/etc/init.d/courier-imap $1
/etc/init.d/courier-imap-ssl $1
linux: # chmod u+x /usr/sbin/rccourier
```

It uses `$1` to transfer the first call parameter to the start scripts. Thus, the command `rccourier start` or `rccourier stop` starts or stops all services at once, and their status can be queried as follows:

```
linux: # rccourier status
Checking for Courier Authentication Daemon            running
Checking for Courier-POP3                             running
Checking for Courier-POP3 (ssl)                       running
Checking for Courier-IMAP                             running
Checking for Courier-IMAP (ssl)                       running
```

7.3 Initial Start-Up

Regardless of the distribution, Courier should start directly after installation without requiring any further configuration and should then be available on ports 110 (POP3) and 143 (IMAP):

```
linux: # lsof -i :110
COMMAND    PID USER   FD   TYPE DEVICE SIZE NODE NAME
couriertc 4539 root    5u  IPv6  10832      TCP *:pop3 (LISTEN)
```

```
linux: # lsof -i :143
COMMAND     PID USER    FD    TYPE DEVICE SIZE NODE NAME
couriertc 4606 root     5u    IPv6 10931        TCP *:imap (LISTEN)
linux: # telnet localhost 110
Trying 127.0.0.1...
Connected to localhost.
Escape character is '^]'.
+OK Hello there.
QUIT
+OK Better luck next time.
Connection closed by foreign host.
linux: # telnet localhost 143
Trying 127.0.0.1...
Connected to localhost.
Escape character is '^]'.
* OK [CAPABILITY IMAP4rev1 UIDPLUS CHILDREN NAMESPACE THREAD=ORDEREDSUBJ
ECT THREAD=REFERENCES SORT QUOTA IDLE ACL ACL2=UNION] Courier-IMAP ready
. Copyright 1998-2004 Double Precision, Inc.  See COPYING for distributi
on information.
a1 logout
* BYE Courier-IMAP server shutting down
a1 OK LOGOUT completed
Connection closed by foreign host.
```

If you cannot contact the server at this stage, you should check your installation carefully and see whether the components start properly. /var/log/messages or /var/log/mail often contains valuable error messages.

7.4 Courier and MTAs

Unlike Cyrus, Courier IMAP does not provide an interface that mail transport agents might use to transfer emails to it (via LMTP, SMTP, or a similar protocol). It expects that the MTA will store emails in a suitable location within the appropriate maildir directory while observing the file permissions. Courier and the MTA interact through these common directories, as illustrated in Figure 7.1. This means that the MTA and the IMAP server *must* run on the same computer or use a shared filesystem, for example, NFS.

On the other hand, there are no potentially problematic interfaces between the SMTP mail server and Courier. We do not need to worry about the socket or the transport protocol. If Courier and the mail relay are located on different computers, they have to share a filesystem, for example, via NFS. Alternatively, if the mail relay for some reason must use SMTP, it is possible to operate an additional local MTA, such as Postfix, on the Courier server, and have the mail relay forward the emails via SMTP to the local MTA for storage.

Each service can function even when the other is inoperational or faulty. Postfix can continue to receive emails and sort them into the maildir directories even if Courier is not running. Conversely, users can access the emails stored on the IMAP server even when the SMTP mail relay is not running.

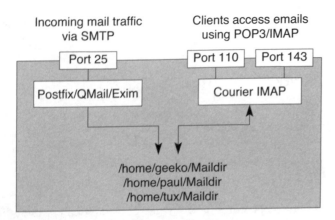

Figure 7.1:
MTA and Courier both access the stored emails.

Postfix, Exim, and sendmail usually store emails in the *mbox* format: All of a user's emails are in one single file. This file is often stored in /var/mail or /var/spool/mail.

The mbox format is not particularly suitable for IMAP servers, as IMAP folder structures, flags, and other types of information such as quotas cannot be mapped into this monolithic file. The mbox format also has some disadvantages due to the way it is implemented:

- Deleting an individual email from a large 25MB mailbox requires extensive file copying actions.

- If software crashes during write access to the mbox file, this can leave incomplete emails that corrupt the internal structure of the mailbox.

- If a file write error occurs, it is difficult to determine afterward whether or not an email was delivered successfully. This means that emails can be lost without being detected.

- Many processes have simultaneous write access to the mbox, so you have to set up file locking to prevent competing writes from destroying the file. The NFS network filesystem is well known for its file-locking problems, which can lead to email corruption when it is used.

Courier therefore relies on its own maildir process, which stores a user's emails in individual files in a filesystem directory (the *maildir*). This makes it easy to determine whether an email was delivered successfully. Individual faulty email files no longer destroy the entire mailbox. Because of the use of temporary directories, file locking is no longer necessary, which means that NFS can be used. Chapter 8 illustrates how maildir actually works.

Standard MTAs usually support the maildir format. Postfix, Exim, and sendmail can be converted to use it in a few short steps, and QMail uses maildir as standard. This makes Courier easy to integrate into any system with little effort.

7.4.1 Courier and Postfix

The `home_mailbox` variable tells Postfix where to store emails. This variable is empty in standard installations:

```
linux: # postconf home_mailbox
home_mailbox =
```

In this case, the MTA stores all messages as an mbox file in the directory specified in `mail_spool_directory`:

```
linux: # postconf mail_spool_directory
mail_spool_directory = /var/spool/mail
linux: # ls -la /var/spool/mail/
total 36
drwxrwxrwt   2 root   root        72 Dec  9 10:36 .
drwxr-xr-x  15 root   root       392 Mar  3 10:31 ..
-rw-------   1 root   root     34356 Dec  9 10:36 root
-rw-------   1 tux    users   237932 Dec 10 12:27 tux
-rw-------   1 geeko  users    92883 Dec  7 21:22 geeko
```

If you enter a path in `home_mailbox`, Postfix will create the path to the location for storing a user's emails by taking the home directory ($HOME) of the user and suffixing it with the specified path. If you set the following parameter in `main.cf`, Postfix will store all emails for `tux` under /home/tux/Maildir/ in the maildir format:

```
home_mailbox = Maildir/
```

It selects the maildir format only because the path in `home_mailbox` ends with /. The trailing slash tells Postfix that it is dealing with a directory, and Postfix then understands that maildir is required. If you forget to enter the / here, Postfix will instead store all emails in the /home/tux/Maildir *file*, which will be in the mbox format. Then it will not be able to collaborate with Courier.

If the maildir directory does not exist, Postfix will create it.[3] The parent directory (/home/tux in this example) does have to exist.

As Postfix adopts the user's permissions to store the emails, the parent directory must be writable for the MTA to be able to create the new maildir structure.

Once you have set `home_mailbox` correctly and remembered to reload Postfix, you can attempt the first test:

```
linux: # echo "Hello" | mail tux@localhost
linux: # tail /var/log/mail
[...]
Apr 2 18:13:12 linux postfix/pickup[7915]: 7094F27FD9: uid=0 from=<root>
Apr 2 18:13:12 linux postfix/cleanup[7930]: 7094F27FD9: message-id=<442F
F7FA.mail5ZO117IBS@linux.site>
Apr 2 18:13:12 linux postfix/qmgr[7916]: 7094F27FD9: from=<root@peer.pos
t.fix>, size=394, nrcpt=1 (queue active)
Apr 2 18:13:12 linux postfix/local[7932]: 7094F27FD9: to=<tux@localhost.
post.fix>, orig_to=<tux@localhost>, relay=local, delay=30, status=sent (
delivered to maildir)
Apr 2 18:13:12 linux postfix/qmgr[7916]: 7094F27FD9: removed
linux: # ls -la /home/tux/Maildir
total 1
drwx------  5 tux users 120 Apr  2 18:13 .
drwxr-xr-x  9 tux users 616 Apr  2 18:13 ..
drwx------  2 tux users  48 Apr  2 18:13 cur
drwx------  2 tux users 104 Apr  2 18:13 new
drwx------  2 tux users  48 Apr  2 18:13 tmp
linux: # ls -la /home/tux/Maildir/new
total 4
drwx------  2 tux users 104 Apr  2 18:13 .
drwx------  5 tux users 120 Apr  2 18:13 ..
-rw-------  1 tux users 482 Apr  2 18:13 1143994392.V305I27fdeM695281.li
nux
linux: # cat /home/tux/Maildir/new/1143994392.V305I27fdeM695281.linux
Return-Path: <root@peer.example.com>
X-Original-To: tux@localhost
Delivered-To: tux@localhost.example.com
Received: by peer.example.com (Postfix, from userid 0)
        id 7094F27FD9; Sun,  2 Apr 2006 18:12:42 +0200 (CEST)
Date: Sun, 02 Apr 2006 18:12:42 +0200
To: tux@localhost.post.fix
Message-ID: <442FF7FA.mail5ZO117IBS@example.com>
User-Agent: nail 11.4 8/29/04
MIME-Version: 1.0
Content-Type: text/plain; charset=us-ascii
```

---

[3] This is pretty nice of Postfix—Courier simply crashes in this case, which is not particularly helpful. This problem is well known, but the Courier programmers believe that Courier need not concern itself with the existence of the maildir and is therefore entitled to terminate the connection in such cases. We therefore cannot expect a solution, even though, as much as we like Courier, this state of affairs is unacceptable.

```
Content-Transfer-Encoding: 7bit
From: root@peer.example.com (root)

Hello
```

Because this newly delivered email has not yet been accessed via POP3 or IMAP, it is stored in the new subdirectory.

If every POP3/IMAP user in your scenario has a shell account as a matter of course, Postfix and Courier will work together after this small adjustment has been made. If you wish to use *virtual users*, that is, email accounts that do not correspond to existing Linux system users, you should define home directories for them in the Postfix configuration somewhere outside of the /home directory tree, for example, under /var/spool/mail.

7.4.2 Courier and QMail

As QMail is already set up for the maildir format, only a few simple steps are required to use it with Courier. You have to set up the correct storage path. If necessary, create the `defaultdelivery` file in the /var/qmail/control directory. It contains the path to the storage location for the emails. As in Postfix, a path ending in / indicates a directory and therefore that the maildir format will be used.

Courier expects the maildir in the home directory of every user by default, but QMail stores it under /var/spool/mail. Enter the following configuration in `defaultdelivery` for QMail:

```
./Maildir/
```

Now you have to restart QMail:

```
linux:/var/qmail/control # qmailctl restart
Restarting qmail:
* Stopping qmail-smtpd.
* Sending qmail-send SIGTERM and restarting.
* Restarting qmail-smtpd.
```

Proceed for the first test email as you would for Postfix (see section 7.4.1 on page 93).

7.4.3 Courier and Exim

Like Postfix, Exim requires only a few steps to switch from using the mbox to the maildir format. You will find the required configuration files in /etc/exim.

Open `exim.conf`, search for the `local_delivery` section, and insert the lines displayed in bold. These lines ensure that a maildir is created in the home directory of every user:

```
local_delivery:
driver = appendfile
group = mail
mode = 0660
mode_fail_narrower = false
envelope_to_add = true
return_path_add = true

directory=${home}/Maildir
maildir_format = true
prefix = ""
```

If you have a more complex setup with virtual users and would like to store all maildirs centrally, you should specify a fixed path instead of ${home}. Don't forget to send a test email after changing the configuration (see section 7.4.1 on page 93).

7.5 Optimizing the Configuration

Now that you are on your feet, you should have a look at the configuration files in `/etc/courier`. Courier has a very modular structure, and each component uses different files. The configuration files include the settings for POP3 and POP3 via SSL/TLS (in pop3d and pop3d-ssl) and for IMAP (imapd) and IMAP via SSL/TLS (imapd-ssl); often, one also finds the central configuration file of the authorization daemon (authdaemonrc) and, depending on the setup, the configuration files for the authorization modules (authldaprc in this example). The authorization configuration may also be located in `/etc/authlib`.

```
linux: # ls -la /etc/courier
-rw-------   1 root root   2688 Jul 20 06:02 authdaemonrc
-rw-------   1 root root   2697 Nov 18 2004 authdaemonrc.dist
-rw-------   1 root root   7318 Jul 15 06:49 authldaprc
-rw-------   1 root root  12625 Mar 30 18:38 imapd
-rw-------   1 root root   6093 Mar 30 18:38 imapd-ssl
-rw-------   1 root root   6093 Nov 18 2004 imapd-ssl.dist
-rw-------   1 root root    343 Nov 18 2004 imapd.cnf
-rw-------   1 root root  12625 Nov 18 2004 imapd.dist
-rw-------   1 root root   3809 Mar 30 18:38 pop3d
-rw-------   1 root root   5704 Mar 30 18:38 pop3d-ssl
-rw-------   1 root root   5704 Nov 18 2004 pop3d-ssl.dist
-rw-------   1 root root    343 Nov 18 2004 pop3d.cnf
-rw-------   1 root root   3809 Nov 18 2004 pop3d.dist
```

```
-r--r--r--   1 root root    516 Nov 18  2004 quotawarnmsg.example
drwxr-xr-x   2 root root   4096 Jul 12 11:30 shared
```

Files `pop3d.cnf` and `imapd.cnf` are only required once, by `mkpop3dcert` or `mkimapdcert` (see section 7.2 on page 88). If Courier has been configured for SSL/TLS support (see section 7.6 on page 102) but does not find any prepared SSL/TLS certificates, it uses `mkpop3dcert`, `mkimapdcert`, and `openssl` to create them. It uses the information on the hostname, certificate owner, and server location from `pop3d.cnf` and `imapd.cnf` to do this (see section 7.6 on page 104).

You can also ignore the `.dist` file. It documents the status of the file during delivery by the distributor. As long as you do not modify the "real" configuration files, they remain identical to the `.dist` files.

`quotawarnmsg.example` contains ASCII text, which the administrator can use (by renaming the file as `quotawarnmsg`) to specify a warning message triggered when a quota is exceeded. The `shared` directory is required for the configuration files for shared folders (see section 10.1 on page 153).

7.5.1 Real and "False" Configuration Parameters

The Courier configuration files contain many parameters that come in pairs, for example, `POP3AUTH` and `POP3AUTH_ORIG`. If you are using all of the Courier components including the SMTP server, rather than only Courier IMAP, you can configure the individual programs via a web interface. It reads out the aforementioned `ORIG` variables to determine the options it can make available to the administrator. If you use only Courier IMAP as discussed in this book, the web interface is not available and the `ORIG` variables become superfluous.

They have nothing to do with actual operation. Courier IMAP ignores them and reads out the parameters without the `_ORIG` suffix. The `ORIG` variables can only provide information on the options available. Always make sure to change only the "real" variables, otherwise your changes won't take effect.

By the way, if the variable values contain more than one word and therefore contain spaces, you should enclose them in quotation marks.

7.5.2 POP3 Configuration in `/etc/courier/pop3d`

The parameters listed in the file `/etc/courier/pop3d` influence the way that the POP3 server operates. This section introduces them in their default configuration:

```
PIDFILE=/var/run/pop3d.pid
```

This specifies the file where the ID of the POP3 server process is stored. There is no reason to modify it.

`MAXDAEMONS=40`

This specifies the maximum number of POP3 daemons that may be started simultaneously.

`MAXPERIP=4`

This restricts the number of permitted parallel connections *per IP address*.[4] This prevents denial-of-service attacks by an individual host. Bear in mind that a user may have more than one inbox on your server, and therefore may legitimately create multiple simultaneous connections.

For example, office routers using masquerading/NAT mean that individual IPs (on the router) can create several dozen connections very quickly, which limits the usefulness of this parameter. Do use it in such a situation, but specify a value that is generous while still a lot lower than `MAXDAEMONS`. This way, you can prevent one IP address from using up all the connections, and you can reduce the threat of denial-of-service attacks.

`POP3AUTH=""`

You can use this parameter to specify the password-transfer methods you wish the POP3 server to support. `POP3AUTH_ORIG` lists the following options:

```
POP3AUTH_ORIG="LOGIN CRAM-MD5 CRAM-SHA1"
```

`LOGIN` (and `PLAIN`, which is not listed here), are cleartext methods, whereas `CRAM-MD5` and `CRAM-SHA1` use secure password synchronization. The background to this is described in more detail in section 9.13 on page 147.

`POP3AUTH_TLS=""`

Here you can specify methods that the POP3 server should offer *additionally* for SSL/TLS connections, usually authentication methods without inherent cryptographic protection. `POP3AUTH_TLS_ORIG` permits the values `LOGIN` and `PLAIN`. Further settings for SSL/TLS are described in section 7.6 on page 102.

`POP3_PROXY=0`

If you wish Courier to run in proxy mode for POP3, you have to set `POP3_PROXY=1` (see section 10.3 on page 175).

`PROXY_HOSTNAME`

In proxy mode, you can enter the server's own (!) hostname here, so

---

[4] Did you read this as *Max R.I.P.?* A well-known pun among Courier administrators...

that the proxy can determine whether to forward the connection (see section 10.3 on page 175). This setting is not required if the server is set up properly, as Courier will then use the real system name.

`PORT=110`
This specifies the port(s) that the POP3 daemon should listen to. You can specify multiple ports if you separate them with commas. If the server has more than one IP number, and you wish some ports to be available only on certain IP numbers, you can *not* define them according to the usual `ip:port` format, but have to specify them as `ip.port` instead; for example, `192.168.0.20.110` for port 110 at IP `192.168.0.20`.

`ADDRESS=0`
This specifies the IP address on which the ports will be opened. If you set the value to 0 as shown in this example, the POP daemon will listen on all available IP numbers. You can only specify either one address, or, using 0, all the available addresses.

`TCPDOPTS="-nodnslookup -noidentlookup"`
This contains command-line parameters for calling `couriertcpd`, which manages the TCP/IP connection and reloads the pop3d module.

`-nodnslookup` prevents the reverse lookup for the IP number of the client. This means that the hostname can *not* be listed in the log file, but it also saves time and network traffic.

`-noidentlookup` prevents the server from using the `ident` protocol for queries, which is barely relevant today. Earlier, it was used to ask the client which user created the TCP connection. Who would answer this question nowadays?

`LOGGEROPTS="-name=pop3d"`
The options specified in this parameter are transferred to the `courier logger` program. This is a separate tool that Courier calls to write log entries. The option given in this example specifies the name of the module, so the log file can show what the entry refers to.

`DEFDOMAIN="@example.com"`
The value of `DEFDOMAIN` is automatically attached to every username if the username does *not* contain the first character (usually @). In other words, if a user logs in with the username instead of a complete email address, Courier will add $DEFDOMAIN to the username before authenticating it.

`POP3DSTART=YES`
This parameter is processed by the start script. If you set it to NO, *no* POP3 server will be started.

`MAILDIRPATH=Maildir`
:   This is the location of the directory containing the maildir structure *relative to* the user's home directory (in this case, the emails of the user `tux` can be found in `/home/tux/Maildir`). This parameter is equivalent to the Postfix parameter `home_mailbox` (see section 7.4.1 on page 92) or the entry in the `defaultdelivery` file in QMail (see section 7.4.2 on page 94). Courier does not require a forward slash at the end, so this *must* be a (maildir) directory.

Authentication issues are dealt with not in the POP3 configuration file, but in the configuration file of the `authdaemond` (see section 9.2 on page 122). In versions below 4.1.*x*, the configuration file of pop3d still contains two parameters relevant to authentication:

`AUTHMODULES="authdaemon"`
:   This is the authentication method you wish the POP3 daemon to use for logins. For an overview of possible values, see page 120. In the configuration shown in this book, the server transfers all authentication data to the authentication daemon of the Courier project (see section 9.2 on page 122).

    The new Courier IMAP versions always refer to `authdaemond`, so it is no longer necessary to specify AUTHMODULES in the pop3d file.

`DEBUG_LOGIN=0`
:   This specifies the information that Courier will log. If you specify value 0, only the IP address of the client is logged, whereas the system also logs the username if you specify the value as 1. If you specify `DEBUG_LOGIN=2`, passwords are logged in cleartext (this can be a lifesaver when preparing for migration, see section 6.4 on page 81). No other values are possible here.

    In new versions of Courier IMAP, you specify these parameters in the configuration of the `authdaemond` (see section 9.2 on page 122).

7.5.3 Configuring the IMAP Daemon in `/etc/courier/imapd`

The names and meaning of many parameters for imapd are analogous to ones used by pop3d (e.g., IMAPDSTART corresponds to POP3DSTART; see section 7.5.2 on page 98). Some parameters, such as PORT or MAXPERIP, have exactly the same name. The Courier imapd has the following additional options:

`HEADERFROM=X-IMAP-Sender`
:   If you send emails using IMAP, Courier IMAP adds the email header

listed here to the message (the default value specifies an X-IMAP-Sender: line), and then enters the sender's login name. Yes, that's right: You can use IMAP to *send* emails. For more information, see section 10.5 on page 178.

IMAP_CAPABILITY="IMAP4rev1 UIDPLUS CHILDREN NAMESPACE
    THREAD=ORDEREDSUBJECT THREAD=REFERENCES SORT
    QUOTA IDLE"
: This specifies the IMAP capabilities (see section 2.2.3 on page 33) that the IMAP server will offer the client during login. This parameter shows what Courier IMAP is capable of. Usually, you do not need to change anything. There is one exception: If you want to offer encrypted login methods such as CRAM-MD5 or CRAM-SHA1, you have to add values AUTH=CRAM-MD5 or AUTH=CRAM-SHA1 at this stage. Otherwise, the IMAP server will not be able to inform clients that they can use this method.

IMAP_CAPABILITY_TLS="$IMAP_CAPABILITY AUTH=PLAIN"
: imapd provides these capabilities for SSL/TLS connections. In this example, the server will provide the capabilities defined in IMAP_CAPABILITY, and the additional (usually insecure) PLAIN method for SSL/TLS encryption.

As in shell scripts of Bourne-compatible shells, in Courier configuration files the dollar character prefixed to a variable name expands the value of the variables already defined in the same file.

IMAP_CHECK_ALL_FOLDERS=0
: The IMAP server can actively inform the clients about new emails. New emails are usually expected in the INBOX, which means that Courier does not need to monitor the other IMAP folders. If filter programs are used to sort emails into subfolders, you should activate the IMAP_CHECK_ALL_FOLDERS parameter (i.e., set it to 1), even if this increases the server load slightly.

IMAP_DISABLETHREADSORT=0
: IMAP clients can use the IMAP commands THREAD and SORT from the IMAP extensions with the same name (see section 2.2.3 on page 34) to request the server to sort emails in a folder. This reduces the load on the client, but requires a lot of unnecessary extra work on busy servers. If you set the value to 1 for IMAP_DISABLETHREADSORT, Courier will block this type of request by the client.

IMAP_ENHANCEDIDLE=0
: If you want Courier to support the IDLE command, you have to set this value to 1. Courier can then inform clients actively and in real time when new emails are received, as long as the clients support this function (see section 10.4 on page 176).

`IMAP_IDLE_TIMEOUT=60`
: This specifies how often (in seconds) the server checks for changes to the directories in `IDLE` mode.

`IMAP_KEYWORDS=1`
: This activates support for permanent custom IMAP flags (see section 8.2.1 on page 115).

`IMAP_MOVE_EXPUNGE_TO_TRASH=0`
: If you set this parameter to 1, Courier will move deleted emails to the trash folder instead of actually deleting them. This means that the deletion can be undone.

`IMAP_TRASHFOLDERNAME=Trash`
: This defines the IMAP name of the trash folder if you have specified `IMAP_MOVE_EXPUNGE_TO_TRASH=1`. Courier does not permit folders parallel to the `INBOX`, so the `INBOX` subfolder `INBOX.Trash` is created in this example.

`IMAP_EMPTYTRASH=Trash:7`
: This ensures that Courier deletes *all* emails in the `Trash` folder that have been there for more than seven days. You can specify a different time period for each folder; use commas to separate entries for several folders:

    `IMAP_EMPTYTRASH=Trash:7,Sent:30`

    Courier only checks this option when a user logs in. If a user does not log in for an extended period of time, emails can take up space on the hard disk for longer than specified.

`IMAP_OBSOLETE_CLIENT=0`
: Some email clients used to confuse the IMAP flags `\NoInferiors` (no folders permitted under this folder) and `\HasNoChildren` (subfolders are permitted, but there are none at present). *If* you have problems with subfolders, you can test whether changing this parameter can solve those problems. It is *not* recommended that you set this value to 1 without good reason.[5]

`IMAP_SHAREDINDEXFILE=/etc/courier/shared/index`
: If you want to permit your users to share their IMAP directories with other users (see section 10.1 on page 153), Courier requires a list of the file paths and their shared names. Use `IMAP_SHAREDINDEXFILE` to specify the location of this *index file*. The default file for Courier is `/etc/courier/shared/index`.

---

[5] The authors are not aware of any client that still has the problem mentioned here. If you know of an example, any reports or information would be greatly appreciated.

IMAP_ACL=1
: This activates the ACL IMAP extension. Clients can also configure access permissions to IMAP folders for third parties. Set `IMAP_ACL` if you use shared folders (see section 10.1 on page 153).

UMASK=022
: This replaces the `umask` for the server process with the specified value. This `umask` is used to create files; it can make sense to specify more restrictive values for filesystem-based shared folders (see section 10.1.2 on page 163) than are usually specified for the entire system in `/etc/profile`.[6]

IMAP_ULIMITD=65536
: If Courier is bombarded with work requests, whether coincidentally or on purpose, there is a danger that the server process will need too much RAM and crash; intentionally flooding a system with this goal in mind is often called a *denial-of-service attack*. To prevent this, Courier uses `ulimit -d` to limit the size of the data segments for processes, and it uses `ulimit -v` to limit the size of the virtual memory; both values are limited to the value specified here. This is purely a precaution. The default value is 65,536KB (about 64MB), and should be more than sufficient.

IMAP_USELOCKS=1
: This specifies whether IMAP uses file locking. The maildir directory structure makes this option unnecessary: After all, the maildir format was practically designed to be used via NFS and without file-locking mechanisms (more details on page 108).

  On the other hand, it does no harm to use it, apart from slightly increasing the I/O load of the server. File locking can help prevent some noncritical problems when multiple clients access the same IMAP folder, or even the same email, in parallel. You should therefore set `IMAP_USELOCKS` to 1 if you allow shared folders.

SENDMAIL=/usr/sbin/sendmail
: The Courier IMAP daemon requires the path to the sendmail binary (which can be provided by Postfix or Exim) to send emails.

7.6 The Configuration Files for SSL

Providing encrypted communication paths for users is not complicated and is very much worthwhile. To do so, Courier IMAP starts two additional

---

[6] The values in `umask` do not correspond to the file permissions used for `chmod`! This means that it would be wrong, and even dangerous, to specify UMASK=644.

instances on ports 993 (IMAP via SSL) and 995 (POP3 via SSL). At the same time, it supports the STARTTLS command on standard ports 110 (POP3) and 143 (IMAP). The client can now choose between upgrading a cleartext connection (using STARTTLS) and creating an encrypted connection on one of the specially reserved ports.

The configuration files /etc/courier/pop3-ssl and /etc/courier/imap-ssl control the SSL/TLS encryption. Both contain *additional* parameters; you do not need to repeat the standard POP3 and IMAP settings here. The default file supplied in your distribution or source code package will usually run without requiring configuration.

SSLPORT=995 and SSLPORT=993
: This is the additional port for POP3 and IMAP via SSL. It should be set to the default value 995 in the file pop3-ssl (as specified in /etc/services), and to 993 in imap-ssl.

SSLADDRESS=0
: If you specify 0, SSL/TLS is activated on all of the server's existing IP numbers; alternatively, you can specify *one* IP address from those available.

SSLPIDFILE=/var/run/pop3d-ssl.pid
: The path to the PID file: This is where the program's process ID is stored after it has been started. In the imap-ssl file, for example, you can specify the filename /var/run/imapd-ssl.pid.

SSLLOGGEROPTS="-name=pop3d-ssl"
: Using this parameter you can specify additional options that are transferred to courierlogger. In this example, we specify the component name pop3d-ssl so that the relevant log lines will be uniquely identifiable. In the file imapd-ssl you would specify the name imapd-ssl.

POP3DSSLSTART=YES and IMAPDSSLSTART=YES
: These specify whether the program provides SSL/TLS connections on the port reserved for POP3 and IMAP via SSL and defined in SSLPORT.

POP3DSTARTTLS=YES and IMAPDSTARTTLS=YES
: These specify whether the program provides SSL/TLS connections via STLS and STARTTLS on the standard port reserved for POP3 and IMAP.

POP3_TLS_REQUIRED=0 and IMAPD_TLS_REQUIRED=0
: If you want to prevent all unencrypted connections, specify POP3_TLS_REQUIRED=1. Clients can then only authenticate themselves on port 110 or 143 once they have switched to encrypted mode using STLS or STARTTLS.

COURIERTLS=/usr/sbin/couriertls
: This is the path to the (supplied) program `couriertls`. It assists POP3 and IMAP modules in controlling the SSL/TLS encryption.

TLS_PROTOCOL=SSL3
: This is the SSL/TLS version to be used on the SSL-via-POP3 or SSL-via-IMAP ports. The available values are SSL2, SSL3, and TLS1. Ports 993 and 995 are usually used by older clients, so it seems to pose fewer compatibility problems to configure SSL3 instead of TLS1.

TLS_STARTTLS_PROTOCOL=TLS1
: This is the SSL/TLS version to be used for the STLS or STARTTLS process on ports 110 and 143. Clients that know and use these methods usually understand TLS1.

TLS_CERTFILE=/usr/share/courier-pop3/pop3d.pem
: This is the path to the SSL/TLS certificate. You can use the same certificate for POP3 and IMAP (i.e., specify the same file in both), `imap-ssl`, and `pop3-ssl`.

TLS_VERIFYPEER=NONE
: It is possible to permit SSL/TLS connections only from authorized clients with certificates the server knows to be reliable. NONE switches off these checks entirely, whereas PEER checks any certificates transmitted by the client. REQUIREPEER requires a verifiable certificate from the client and prevents the connection if such a certificate is not received.

TLS_CACHEFILE=/var/run/couriersslcache
: This is the path to a cache file that speeds up SSL/TLS accesses. This file requires no maintenance by the administrator.

TLS_CACHESIZE=524288
: This is the size in bytes of the SSL cache to be created.

If Courier finds no SSL certificate when it starts `pop3d-ssl` or `imapd-ssl`, it will use `mkpop3dcert` or `mkimapcert` to create its own. It uses the entries in files `pop3d.cnf` and `imapd.cnf` for this purpose.

These entries are not relevant to the encryption process, but users can (and should) view the certificate, so it makes sense to use plausible and trustworthy entries for name, city, and country in order to reduce support work. The hostname in the certificate should be the same as the hostname used by the clients, in order to prevent warning messages by the client software as far as possible (see section 13.1.3 on page 209). You should pay attention to the entries marked in italics:

7.6 The Configuration Files for SSL

```
linux: # cat /etc/courier/pop3d.cnf
RANDFILE = /usr/share/courier-imap/pop3d.rand

[ req ]
default_bits = 1024
encrypt_key = yes
distinguished_name = req_dn
x509_extensions = cert_type
prompt = no

[ req_dn ]
C=DE
ST=Berlin
L=Berlin
O=My Company
OU=ICT services
CN=mail.example.com
emailAddress=postmaster@example.com

[ cert_type ]
nsCertType = server
```

Maildir as Email Storage Format

Courier always uses the maildir format to store emails. The server creates a separate maildir hierarchy for each user, consisting of several directories and pure ASCII files. There are no binary files, and everything is easy to read and edit.

Users who have shell access to the email server (i.e., a Unix account in /etc/passwd and a home directory) can have their emails delivered to a maildir directory under their own home directory (e.g., /home/tux/Maildir). Messages are stored with the user's permissions.

Local email programs such as pine or KMail can then read the emails directly from the maildir without involving IMAP. Users who access their emails from a remote host usually do so via TCP/IP.

Ideally, the only system users on mass email servers should be the mail administrators. On these servers, you would store the database of email users in MySQL, LDAP, or a similar repository. The email users do not have

8 Maildir as Email Storage Format

home directories on the server. Instead, you create a separate directory structure (e.g., `/maildir` or `/var/spool/maildir`) with a personal maildir directory (e.g., `/maildir/tux` or `/maildir/geeko`) for each user.

In such settings it is justifiable to use only one user ID which owns all maildir directories. User administration thus becomes easier, as you do not have to take separately managed system login IDs into account, and trouble with data access permissions is avoided.

There are also no real security risks, because there are no shell accounts for ordinary users: As long as mail users cannot work on the server, they do not require protection from one another. The only system users are the user `root` and Courier IMAP, both of which are able to access all directories in any case. The only danger is that an attacker can access the email directories of other users by hacking into Courier IMAP after login, due to the lack of different user IDs. This type of attack does not seem to have occurred so far.

The `maildir` directory of a mail user's mailbox contains at least three subfolders:

```
linux: # ls -la /home/tux/Maildir
drwx------   7 h users 4096 Jul 27 12:07 .
drwxr-xr-x   8 h users 4096 Jul 27 12:04 ..
drwx------   2 h users 4096 Jul 27 12:04 cur
drwx------   2 h users 4096 Jul 27 12:04 new
drwx------   2 h users 4096 Jul 27 12:04 tmp
```

The `cur` directory contains those messages that have been saved and read at least once. `new` contains all messages that were received since the last login, so the server can flag them as `\Recent`. After login, Courier moves these emails into the `cur` directory.

Messages are moved to the `tmp` directory during saving. Once they have been saved successfully, Courier moves them to `new` or to a different location. This prevents the server from delivering an incomplete email to the client if the client downloads the emails in the destination folder in the middle of the save process.

File locking is therefore never used in the maildir format. This makes the use of an NFS-mounted filesystem for mail storage far simpler.

Unlike for POP3, if IMAP users sort their emails into subfolders, these subfolders are saved on the server. The user's maildir contains these subfolders as additional subdirectories.

The names of these directories consist of a dot (.) and the actual folder name. Thus, if the user has folders `INBOX`, `Friends`, and `Company`, the maildir listing would be as follows:

```
linux: # ls -la /home/tux/Maildir
```

```
drwx------   7 h users 4096 Jul 27 12:07 .
drwxr-xr-x   8 h users 4096 Jul 27 12:04 ..
drwx------   5 h users 4096 Jul 27 12:07 .Company
drwx------   5 h users 4096 Jul 27 12:06 .Friends
drwx------   2 h users 4096 Jul 27 12:04 cur
drwx------   2 h users 4096 Jul 27 12:04 new
drwx------   2 h users 4096 Jul 27 12:04 tmp
```

Each IMAP subfolder is an independent directory in the maildir format and therefore contains its own copies of the folders `cur`, `new`, and `tmp`, in which emails for that subfolder are stored:

```
linux:~ # ls -la /home/tux/Maildir/.Friends
drwx------   5 h users 4096 Jul 27 12:06:00 PM .
drwx------   7 h users 4096 Jul 27 12:07 ..
-rw-r--r--   1 h users   17 Jul 27 12:06 courierimapacl
drwx------   2 h users 4096 Jul 27 12:06:00 PM cur
-rw-------   1 h users    0 Jul 27 12:06 maildirfolder
drwx------   2 h users 4096 Jul 27 12:06:00 PM new
drwx------   2 h users 4096 Jul 27 12:06:00 PM tmp
```

The file `maildirfolder` is always empty and its presence signifies a subfolder. `courierimapacl` contains the access permissions for the folder if the user specified any (e.g., in order to share the directory with other users). This subject will be discussed in section 10.1.1 on page 154.

If the `Friends` folder contains further subfolders, Courier will create these subfolders directly under the main maildir directory rather than in the directory `.Friends` (that is, as `Maildir/.Friends.Holiday`, rather than as `Maildir/.Friends/.Holiday`).

Thus, the folder structure is mapped into directory names, with the dot separating levels in the folder hierarchy:

```
linux:~ # ls -la /home/tux/Maildir
drwx------   9 h users 4096 Jul 27 12:09:00 PM .
drwxr-xr-x   8 h users 4096 Jul 27 12:04 ..
drwx------   5 h users 4096 Jul 27 12:07 .Company
drwx------   5 h users 4096 Jul 27 12:06 .Friends
drwx------   5 h users 4096 Jul 27 12:09 .Friends.Orchestra
drwx------   5 h users 4096 Jul 27 12:09 .Friends.Holiday
drwx------   2 h users 4096 Jul 27 12:04 cur
drwx------   2 h users 4096 Jul 27 12:04 new
drwx------   2 h users 4096 Jul 27 12:04 tmp
```

In this manner, an IMAP folder can contain messages as well as additional subfolders.

If an IMAP client is subscribed to individual IMAP folders (see section 2.2.4 on page 41), there is a file named `courierimapsubscribed` that contains the subscription list of the account stored line by line:

8 Maildir as Email Storage Format

```
linux: # ls -la /home/tux/Maildir
drwx------   9 h users 4096 Jul 27 12:09:00 PM .
drwxr-xr-x   8 h users 4096 Jul 27 12:04    ..
drwx------   5 h users 4096 Jul 27 12:07    .Company
drwx------   5 h users 4096 Jul 27 12:06    .Friends
drwx------   5 h users 4096 Jul 27 12:09    .Friends.Orchestra
drwx------   5 h users 4096 Jul 27 12:09    .Friends.Holiday
drwx------   2 h users 4096 Jul 27 12:04    cur
drwx------   2 h users 4096 Jul 27 12:04    new
drwx------   2 h users 4096 Jul 27 12:04    tmp
-rw-r--r--   1 h users  842 Jul 27 12:45    courierimapsubscribed
linux: # cat /home/tux/Maildir/courierimapsubscribed
INBOX
INBOX.Company
INBOX.Friends.Orchestra
```

8.1 The IMAP Namespace

There has been a lot of discussion between the IMAP projects on whether directories may be *parallel* to the INBOX or have to be *under* it. In other words: Can we have directories INBOX, Friends, and Company? Or do they have to be INBOX, INBOX.Friends, and INBOX.Company? IMAP implementations differ according to the developers' preferences. Some IMAP servers permit directories parallel to the INBOX and others do not.

The Courier programmers have decided that private folders may only be located under the INBOX. The only exception is that folders shared by multiple users are not located under the INBOX, but under #shared or shared.

The Courier team has turned down repeated requests for changes and more tolerance. Therefore, no changes to the system configuration can make Courier use folders parallel to the INBOX. The program code just does not support this option, and the Courier developers would have to change the entire folder management system to make this option possible. This means that there is no simple patch to get around this limitation.

As a consequence, there can be problems when migrating from one IMAP system to another. There is more information on this subject in Chapter 6.

Apart from this, there are almost no restrictions when naming IMAP folders. In principle, special characters are permissible in folder names, as are spaces, and there is no reason not to use them. However, in practice, special characters do occasionally cause problems. The switch from ISO-8859 to UTF-8 caused a variety of problems, because afterward, different programs could expect different character sets. This led to complications with filenames containing special characters.

8.2 Filenames of Emails

Unlike Cyrus, for example, Courier does not maintain a database containing information on stored emails apart from the maildir. This makes the server robust and reliable: It is not possible for a database index to be corrupted or for databases to be inconsistent or faulty. Other programs can access the maildir structure without any complicated programming.

On the other hand, emails can contain meta-information that is not saved in the actual email text, such as the IMAP flags \Seen or \Flagged. It is not particularly efficient to gather such information from the individual mail files every time it is needed.

Courier therefore uses a few tricks to speed up the process. Many types of information are coded in the *filename itself* of an individual email. This means that a single directory listing can provide a lot of information about the folder contents very quickly, so that it is not necessary to examine each file individually (which would be time intensive and therefore expensive).

This is best demonstrated using a test email. If your IMAP server is connected to an MTA, you can use email clients such as KMail, Outlook, or Evolution to send the test email. However, the simplest and clearest way to send it is to use the `mail` command directly on the server:

```
linux: # echo Hello World | mail tux@localhost
```

To see whether the email was delivered to user `tux`, go to the `new` folder in the maildir of user `tux`:

```
linux: # ls -la /home/tux/Maildir/new
total 12
drwx------   2 h users 4096 Jul 27 12:40:00 PM .
drwx------  10 h users 4096 Jul 27 12:27:00 PM ..
-rw-------   1 h users  483 Jul 27 12:40 1122460858.V301Ic964.linux
```

The filename of the "Hello World" email consists of a randomly chosen, unique ID (containing, among others things, the date, time, and inode number of the message) as well as the hostname of the server storing the email (in this case, `linux`), so that accidental name conflicts can be avoided on network drives.

Now log on to the IMAP server to access this email:

```
linux: # telnet localhost 143
Trying 127.0.0.1...
Connected to localhost.
Escape character is '^]'.
* OK [CAPABILITY IMAP4rev1 UIDPLUS CHILDREN NAMESPACE THREAD=ORDEREDSUB
JECT THREAD=REFERENCES SORT QUOTA IDLE ACL ACL2=UNION] Courier-IMAP rea
```

8 Maildir as Email Storage Format

dy. Copyright 1998-2004 Double Precision, Inc. See COPYING for distribution information.
a1 login tux password
a1 OK LOGIN Ok.

Use the following IMAP command to access the `INBOX` IMAP folder belonging to user `tux`:

a2 SELECT INBOX
* FLAGS (\Draft \Answered \Flagged \Deleted \Seen \Recent)
* OK [PERMANENTFLAGS (* \Draft \Answered \Flagged \Deleted \Seen)] Limited
* 1 EXISTS
* 1 RECENT
* OK [UIDVALIDITY 1122461011] Ok
* OK [MYRIGHTS "acdilrsw"] ACL
a2 OK [READ-WRITE] Ok

1 RECENT signifies that a new message has been added to this folder since the last login.

You can view this email as follows:

a3 FETCH 1 RFC822
* 1 FETCH (RFC822 {498}
Return-Path: <root@linux.local>
X-Original-To: h@localhost
Delivered-To: h@localhost.linux.local
Received: by linux.local (Postfix, from userid 0)
        id 91F23C46D8; Wed, 27 Jul 2005 12:40:58 +0200 (CEST)
Date: Wed, 27 Jul 2005 12:40:58 +0200
To: h@localhost.linux.local
Message-ID: <42E764BA.mail3U911TA51@linux>
User-Agent: nail 11.4 8/29/04
MIME-Version: 1.0
Content-Type: text/plain; charset=us-ascii
Content-Transfer-Encoding: 7bit
From: root@linux.local (root)

Hello World
)
* 1 FETCH (FLAGS (\Seen \Recent))
a3 OK FETCH completed.

The new folder in the filesystem is now empty, as the email was moved to the cur folder as soon as it was accessed for the first time:

linux: # **ls -la /home/tux/Maildir/new**
total 8
drwx------   2 h users 4096 Jul 27 12:43:00 PM .

```
drwx------   11 h users 4096 Jul 27 12:43:00 PM ..
linux: # ls -la /home/tux/Maildir/cur
total 12
drwx------    2 h users 4096 Jul 27 12:46:00 PM .
drwx------   11 h users 4096 Jul 27 12:43:00 PM ..
-rw-------    1 h users  483 Jul 27 12:40 1122460858.V301Ic964.linux:2,S
```

Abbreviation	IMAP flag	Meaning
R	\Answered	Email was answered
F	\Flagged	Important
S	\Seen	Email has been viewed
P	not implemented in the IMAP protocol	Email was forwarded[1]
D	\Draft	Email is flagged as a draft
T	\Deleted	Email is flagged for deletion (the abbreviation is short for *trashed*)

Table 8.1: Maildir abbreviations for the IMAP system flags

The filename has changed and now contains the flags :2,S at the end. S stands for the IMAP flag \Seen, which Courier set automatically when read access to the email occurred. You can set additional IMAP flags during an IMAP session:

```
a4 STORE 1 +FLAGS (\Flagged \Answered)
* 1 FETCH (FLAGS (\Flagged \Answered \Seen \Recent))
a4 OK STORE completed.
```

\Answered usually appears when an email has been answered, whereas email clients use \Flagged to flag important emails. Courier represents these flags in the filename too, so \Answered becomes R for *Reply*, and \Flagged becomes F:

```
linux: # ls -la /home/tux/Maildir/cur
total 12
drwx------    2 h users 4096 Jul 27 12:54:00 PM .
drwx------   11 h users 4096 Jul 27 12:43:00 PM ..
-rw-------    1 h users  483 Jul 27 12:40 1122460858.V301Ic964.linux:2,FRS
```

The flags *must* appear in the filename in alphabetical order: 2,FRS is correct, but 2,SFR is not permitted. Table 8.1 shows which IMAP flag is represented by each maildir contraction.

[1] If you operate a mailbox with several clients in parallel, this information cannot be synchronized between the clients unless they access the maildir directly via the filesystem and not via IMAP.

The exact filename is not prescribed; standards documents usually use the verb *should* when describing the naming conventions.[2] However, the filename often corresponds to the following pattern:

time.microsecondsPpidVdevIinode.host,S=bytes:2,flags

The exact filename, up to the optional specification of file size (S=*bytes*) or the mandatory colon followed by the flag specification, is not important. The only crucial thing is to avoid identical filenames being created for different messages. For this reason, a number of elements associated with the message are combined, which always results in a unique name, even in cluster operation. These elements include the time, hostname, process ID, hard disk, and inode number involved in the processing of the message. In more detail:

- The time is measured in seconds elapsed since January 1, 1970 (this is 1122460858 seconds for the file 1122460858.V301Ic964.linux:2,FRS mentioned above).

- The placeholder *microseconds* can be replaced with the specification of microseconds. Postfix does not use this.

- One element is the process ID (*pid*) of the process doing the saving. Including this information also helps to prevent filename conflicts. As shown in the example file, Postfix omits this specification, along with the preceding F.

- The placeholder *dev* can be replaced with the device number of the device on which the email file is stored (301 in our example).

- I is followed by the hexadecimal number of the inode containing the beginning of the email file (c964 in this case). The file can be moved to another location (and to other inodes) in the filesystem (for example, by being copied) without harm, since the inode in the filename is only a trick to ensure that the filename is unique.

- Another element is the name of the host saving the email file (linux in this example).

- Many programs do not specify the file size in the S=*bytes* element (the S stands for *size*). Courier adds this information and recalculates the quota load if necessary.

  Although Courier logs the current quota load in a file named maildirsize, it is easier and quicker for the server to calculate the volume of storage used by the mails in a particular folder if the length of each email

---

[2] See http://cr.yp.to/proto/maildir.html and http://www.qmail.org/man/man5/maildir.html.

(in bytes) is stored in its filename. Determining the space occupied by even large directories with thousands of emails will thus not cause any performance problems. For details on quotas, see section 10.2.1 on page 167.

- A colon is used in the filename to specify whether the subsequent flags have been defined in an RFC (`:2,flags`) or are experimental flags (`:1, flags`).

Postfix names stored files slightly differently than Courier does, but this does not cause any problems.

Because emails in the `tmp` directory have not yet been saved to a destination folder, their associated device, inode, and size are not determined; for this reason, the form of their filenames often differs from those of emails saved in regular folders.

If you create a new email file in `cur`, `new`, or an IMAP subfolder with contents conforming to RFC 2822, the file will appear as an email in the user's inbox. When such an email file is deleted, it disappears from the inbox. You can use an ASCII text editor to edit the contents of the file as long as they continue to conform to RFC.

It is only quotas (if used) that may become inexact if the contents of maildir directories are manipulated by hand. This is not a particular problem, as Courier occasionally checks the directories and then recalculates the `maildirsize` files.

8.2.1 Keywords: Custom IMAP Flags

In addition to the five official IMAP flags listed in Table 8.1 on page 113, IMAP clients can use additional custom flags.[3] These are also called *keywords*; they differ from the system flags in that they do not have a preceding backslash in their name: `\Seen` is an official IMAP flag, while `Hello` is a custom flag. Apart from this small detail, custom flags and system flags are treated in the same way.

Like normal IMAP flags, keywords can be temporary (which means they are lost every time a new folder is selected) or saved permanently on the server (so that they are retained after logout).

You have to set the option `IMAP_KEYWORDS` to 1 in `imapd` (see section 7.5.3 on page 101). Only then will Courier save *permanent* flags. If you set `IMAP_KEYWORDS=0`, keywords are still permitted, but they will always be temporary and not be saved in the filesystem.

---

[3] Unfortunately, not many clients support these, and they have mostly been neglected so far.

Once you have activated support for permanent keywords, you can set arbitrary flags via IMAP without further ado:

```
linux: # telnet mail.example.com 143
Trying 127.0.0.1...
Connected to mail.example.com.
Escape character is '^]'.
* OK [CAPABILITY IMAP4rev1 UIDPLUS CHILDREN NAMESPACE THREAD=ORDEREDSUBJ
ECT THREAD=REFERENCES SORT QUOTA IDLE AUTH=CRAM-MD5 AUTH=CRAM-SHA1  ACL
ACL2=UNION XCOURIEROUTBOX=INBOX.Outbox-Test] Courier-IMAP ready. Copy ri
ght 1998-2005 Double Precision, Inc.  See COPYING for distribution infor
mation.
a1 LOGIN tux supersecret
a1 OK LOGIN Ok.
a2 SELECT INBOX.Test
* FLAGS (\Draft \Answered \Flagged \Deleted \Seen \Recent)
* OK [PERMANENTFLAGS (\* \Draft \Answered \Flagged \Deleted \Seen)] Limi
ted
* 3 EXISTS
* 0 RECENT
* OK [UIDVALIDITY 1175900586] Ok
* OK [MYRIGHTS "acdilrsw"] ACL
a2 OK [READ-WRITE] Ok
a3 STORE 3 +FLAGS Hello
* FLAGS (Hello \Draft \Answered \Flagged \Deleted \Seen \Recent)
* OK [PERMANENTFLAGS (Hello \* \Draft \Answered \Flagged \Deleted \Seen)]
  Limited
* 3 FETCH (FLAGS (\Seen Hello))
a3 OK STORE completed.
a4 STORE 2:3 +FLAGS Testtest
* FLAGS (Hello Testtest \Draft \Answered \Flagged \Deleted \Seen \Recent)
* OK [PERMANENTFLAGS (Hello Testtest \* \Draft \Answered \Flagged \Delete
d \Seen)] Limited
* 3 FETCH (FLAGS (\Seen Testtest Hello))
a4 OK STORE completed.
a5 FETCH 1:3 FLAGS
* 1 FETCH (FLAGS (\Seen))
* 2 FETCH (FLAGS (\Seen Testtest))
* 3 FETCH (FLAGS (\Seen Testtest Hello))
a5 OK FETCH completed.
a6 LOGOUT
* BYE Courier-IMAP server shutting down
a6 OK LOGOUT completed
Connection closed by foreign host.
```

Now you should find the directory `courierimapkeywords` in the maildir of this user (or, for this example, in the folder .Test). Courier creates this directory to store flags:

```
linux:/home/tux/Maildir # cd .Test
linux:/home/tux/Maildir/.Test # ls -la
```

8.2 Filenames of Emails

```
total 100
drwx------   6 10000 10000  4096 2007-08-31 00:02 .
drwxr-xr-x  43 10000 root   4096 2007-08-31 08:02 ..
-rw-r--r--   1 10000 10000    43 2007-04-07 01:02 courierimapacl
drwx------   2 10000 10000  4096 2007-09-02 13:23 courierimapkeywords
-rw-r--r--   1 10000 10000   228 2007-08-31 00:02 courierimapuiddb
drwx------   2 10000 10000 69632 2007-08-31 00:01 cur
-rw-------   1 10000 10000     0 2007-04-07 01:02 maildirfolder
drwx------   2 10000 10000  4096 2007-04-07 01:02 new
drwx------   2 10000 10000  4096 2007-09-02 13:45 tmp
```

It contains the file :list, which shows which flags exist and which mails are flagged with these flags. In order to save the flags, Courier simply records the filename and then lists the number of the corresponding flag(s) after it: The first-mentioned flag is assigned number 0, and so on.

In the following example, only flag number 1 (Testtest) has been set for the email that was email number 2 from the listing above. The other email contains flags 0 and 1 (thus, Hello and Testtest). This message is obviously email number 3:

```
linux:/home/tux/Maildir/.Test # cd courierimakeywords
linux:/home/tux/Maildir/.Test/courierimapkeywords # ls -la
total 12
drwx------   2 10000 10000  4096 02.09.07 1:23:00 PM .
drwx------   6 10000 10000  4096 2007-08-31 00:02 ..
-rw-r--r--   1 10000 10000   171 2007-09-02 13:10 :list
linux:/home/tux/Maildir/.Test/courierimapkeywords # cat :list
Hello
Testtest

1175945397.M261049P12647V0000000000000010I00B204AE_1.kjidder,S=1658:1
1175945397.M402948P12647V0000000000000010I00B204B0_2.kjidder,S=1670:1 0
```

If you manually edit this file, do not change the sequence of flags, as the flags are addressed according to their position in the sequence.

This directory may occasionally also contain temporary work files, whose names begin with a dot. These come and go. Courier only creates them temporarily when an email is accessed.

9 Chapter

User Data

Authentication in Courier is a modular affair, so there are many different solutions. Courier supports the use of files, databases, and directory services as repositories for storing information about email users. In order to function correctly, Courier requires the username, the password (in cleartext or as a `crypt` hash),[1] the Unix user ID and group ID for access to the filesystem, and the path to the maildir directory for the mail user. In addition, Courier can also manage *options* for a user account that can be used to tell Courier to change quotas, deactivate IMAP, or set up *shared groups*. For more information, see section 9.12 on page 144.

If the user has a shell account and the emails are stored in the user's `/home` directory, all these specifications (apart from the user options) are located in `/etc/passwd` or `/etc/shadow`. It is therefore not surprising that Courier requires no further configuration for mail users with local Unix system accounts.

---

[1] If you use `CRAM-MD5` or `CRAM-SHA1`, Courier requires a cleartext password. If you use `LOGIN` or `PLAIN`, Courier can use a crypt hash.

On the other hand, shell accounts for ordinary mail users in large systems cause security problems. These are solvable, but beyond a certain number of users the system becomes impossible to administer sensibly. There are also far too many `root` permissions involved in the normal functioning of the system.

As long as the user information mentioned above can be stored in one of the supported databases or in an LDAP directory, Courier allows an unlimited number of *virtual users* to be maintained.

All Courier programs access the `authlib` authentication library, which is specific to the Courier project and supplies the following modules:

authpwd
> This module reads the mail account data with the passwords from /etc/passwd. Now that PAM is so common, `authpwd` is considered obsolete. The module is only created if Courier is `configured` explicitly with the `--with-authpwd` option.

authshadow
> This module is similar to `authpwd`, apart from verifying passwords via /etc/shadow. This module is also only compiled if it is explicitly specified using the `--with-authshadow` option.

authuserdb
> This module supports a mini-database that is made up of cleartext files and is an alternative to /etc/passwd and /etc/shadow (see section 9.4 on 124).

authcram
> This module uses the same mini-database as `authuserdb`, but supports CRAM authentication. `authcram` is now obsolete, as `authuserdb` has taken over the CRAM function.

authpam
> This module transfers authentication requests to PAM (see section 9.3 on page 123).

authvchkpw
> This module transfers authentication requests to QMail's `vchkpw` library.

authmysql
> This module uses MySQL. It is better to use this module via the `authdaemond` for access to the database, instead of using this module directly.

authpgsql
> This module supports PostgreSQL. Again, it is more suitable to use this module via the `authdaemond` than to use it directly.

authldap
: Using LDAP is also supported, but it is recommended that you access LDAP directories using the `authdaemond` for authentication.

authdaemon
: This is not really an authentication module, but rather an authentication proxy called `authdaemond`, which runs in the background and supports all the modules described here.

authcustom
: This module is a (functioning) template for an authentication module; you can complete this module with your own code and implement a custom-built authentication procedure.

authpipe
: This is a module that transfers authentication requests to another program via a pipe. This module can also be used to integrate custom authentication programs.

However, current versions of Courier do not support all the modules mentioned here (see section 9.11 on page 143).

9.1 `authtest` and `DEBUG_LOGIN` for Debugging Assistance

Getting authentication up and running is not a simple matter. The `authtest` tool supplied with Courier IMAP is helpful here; it plays the role of a client and queries the `authdaemond` and the modules that are described in what follows. There are three ways of calling it:

- If you specify the username as the only argument, `authtest` will call up the account data for this user from the corresponding database and display it in a clear manner. This enables you to check whether all data was found and read out correctly. This tool is only available to `root`.

```
linux: # authtest tux
Authentication succeeded.

     Authenticated: tux   (uid 10000, gid 10000)
    Home Directory: /mail/example.com/tux/
           Maildir: Maildir/
             Quota: (none)
Encrypted Password: (none)
Cleartext Password: supersecret
           Options: sharedgroup=example.com
```

- If you also specify a password, `authtest` will check this password, and it will only provide the user data if the password is correct. `authtest` will announce an error message if an incorrect password is provided:

```
linux: # authtest tux  secret
Authentication FAILED: Operation not permitted
```

- If you specify an additional password as the third parameter, `authtest` will attempt to change the password changed using the `authlib` library:

```
linux: # authtest username oldpassword newpassword
[...]
```

This will only work if the old password was specified correctly.

You should also take a look at the `DEBUG_LOGIN` parameter, which is useful for everyday operation (see section 7.5.2 on page 99). Courier versions from 4.1.*x* onward define this value in `authdaemonrc`, which will be described a little later, whereas earlier versions expect this value in `/etc/courier/pop3d` and `/etc/courier/imapd`.

9.2 The `authdaemond`

This is the authentication method that used to be specified in the `pop3d` and `imapd` configuration files, specifically in the `AUTHMODULES` variable (see section 7.5.2 on page 99).

It was possible to specify all of the mentioned modules in this variable, although it has long been advisable to oblige all Courier components to use the `authdaemond`, which could then carry out the actual authentication. New Courier versions are designed to use the `authdaemond` as the central authentication instance.

It runs in the background as a proxy and supports requests destined for all authentication modules from the `authlib`. It caches the authentication requests, which does not happen when these modules are used directly.

This function is essential when authenticating via MySQL, PostgreSQL, or LDAP. The POP3 and IMAP modules are terminated when the POP/IMAP connection is closed, so without the `authdaemond` they would have to connect anew to the SQL or LDAP server at every login. This takes time and is a waste of resources. If 40 IMAP or POP3 sessions run in parallel, this results in 40 module instances running in parallel, which in turn means 40 parallel connections to the database or directory containing the user data.

`authdaemond`, on the other hand, is permanently active and can keep its connections to the database or directory server open. It also requires few connections for parallel requests, as it bundles all the authentication requests of the authentication modules. All in all, it provides important benefits without any drawbacks, and you should not miss out on taking advantage of it.

As already mentioned, older versions of Courier refer explicitly to the `auth` daemond in the `pop3d` and `imapd` configuration files. Newer versions lack this entry, as the `authdaemond` should always be used. The `AUTHMODULES` variable is set automatically and is therefore not included in any configuration files.

Enter the modules to be used in the configuration file of the `authdaemond`, under /etc/authlib/authdaemonrc (sometimes under /etc/courier/authdaemonrc):

```
##NAME: authmodulelist:0
#
# Specifies the authentication modules that will be called.
#
# Remove a module from the list to deactivate it.

authmodulelist="authuserdb authldap authpam"
```

Courier calls the modules in sequence until a module is found that can verify the login request. The login request is refused if the last module does not return a positive reply.

9.3 Authentication via PAM

If you wish to use the *Pluggable Authentication Modules*[2] in your distribution for authentication (and your distribution contains Courier as a complete package), you will usually find a functioning PAM configuration. Most PAM implementations are located in /etc/pam.d and contain separate configuration files for different services. Courier PAM requires both /etc/pam.d/pop3 and /etc/pam.d/imap. These should usually be identical. OpenSuSE 10.2 has prepared these files as follows:

```
linux:/etc/pam.d/ # cat pop3
#%PAM-1.0
auth      include      common-auth
account   include      common-account
password  include      common-password
session   include      common-session
```

The included `common*` files contain the PAM configurations required by PAM for authentication (`auth`), for checking use permissions (`account`),

[2] See http://www.kernel.org/pub/linux/libs/pam/Linux-PAM-html.

for changing the password (`password`), and for adapting the system environment (`session`):

```
linux:/etc/pam.d/ # cat common-auth
auth     required        pam_env.so
auth     required        pam_unix2.so
linux:/etc/pam.d/ # cat common-account
account  required        pam_unix2.so
linux:/etc/pam.d/ # cat common-password
password         requisite       pam_pwcheck.so  nullok cracklib
password         required        pam_unix2.so    nullok use_authtok
linux:/etc/pam.d/ # cat common-session
session  required        pam_limits.so
session  required        pam_unix2.so
session  optional        pam_umask.so
```

The default setting is that Courier verifies only the password login and then uses the PAM system to fetch details such as the home directory and the user ID. It is not possible to change passwords via the IMAP protocol, so it is unnecessary to include `common-password` if Courier IMAP is operated on its own; on the other hand, including it does not cause any problems.[3]

If you have configured your system to verify local shell accounts in sources other than `passwd/shadow`, this should work automatically in Courier or be easy to transfer to the Courier system.

However, there is one tricky aspect: PAM can check the password for Courier, but it cannot return the required user and group IDs or the home directory. Courier must fetch this information from the (readable) file `/etc/passwd`. Nevertheless, it is better to run Courier authentication via `authpam` instead of `authpasswd` or `authshadow`, as the PAM variant is easier to secure, and Courier does not have to access `/etc/shadow` with `root` permissions. If you use `authpam`, you do not need to use `authpwd` and/or `authshadow`.

9.4 The `authuserdb` Module

The `authuserdb` module permits you to create virtual mail accounts outside of `passwd/shadow` without using MySQL or LDAP. Unfortunately, some distributions, such as SuSE, do not contain this module; if this is the case for your installation, you will need to compile your own Courier.

`authuserdb` expects the account information in text file `/etc/authlib/userdb` (sometimes the file is in `/usr/local/authlib/` or wherever the

---

[3] It is possible to implement web frontends that use the `authdaemond` to change email passwords and support such requests. One can also imagine that the `authtest` tool we introduced previously could transfer such requests to the `authdaemond`.

authlib directory is located on the current system). Alternatively, you can create a directory /etc/authlib/userdb/ that contains several text files with the login information. Courier combines these into one single temporary file during operation, but the single files are easier to maintain (for more information, see section 9.4.4 on page 129).

The information saved in userdb does not need to be entered into /etc/passwd. This makes it simple to create email accounts for "virtual users" who do not require a shell account with a Unix login.

The makeuserdb program also converts these userdb files into a GDBM or a DB database, which, for large numbers of mail accounts, enables faster access to account data than reading it from /etc/passwd. The database format is prescribed when Courier is compiled; most distributions use the GDBM format.

The Courier project provides some useful programs for managing the user db databases.

9.4.1 Converting passwd into a userdb

The pw2userdb program writes the data from an existing /etc/passwd into a userdb database. It can only be used if /etc/authlib/userdb is empty and has restrictive file permissions:

```
linux:/etc/authlib # touch userdb
linux:/etc/authlib # chmod 600 userdb
linux:/etc/authlib # pw2userdb > userdb
```

The userdb file then contains the accounts from /etc/passwd, but in a different format:

```
geeko   uid=1000|gid=100|home=/home/geeko|shell=/bin/bash|systempw=$2a$05$
m0WZvfaUKbuvK9BKTPyBKeAblNYKb8PHSPuQ60KEJA4ycK9j/EB4y|gecos=Geeko
1000=   geeko
tux     uid=1001|gid=100|home=/home/tux|shell=/bin/bash|systempw=$2a$10$
8ZWLc9MOH.vB913PJVR9tuluHdzXc9BBcQ2ZJcAqrDJrUsB9jDvZm
1001=   tux
```

Every user ID in the first column is followed by a list of the parameters required by Courier (Unix user ID, Unix group ID, home directory, login shell, and system password as a crypt or MD5 hash), separated from one another by a pipe character (|). The following optional specifications are also possible:

gecos
: This is the real name of the user.[4]

pop3pw, imappw, esmtppw
: Apart from the hashed system password stored in `systempw` and copied automatically by `pw2userdb` from `/etc/shadow`, you can assign separate passwords for POP3, IMAP, and (E)SMTP. If no additional passwords are specified, Courier accesses the `systempw` field.

    By defining separate passwords, you can switch individual services on and off for individual users: If you specify an invalid, arbitrarily chosen `imappw` for an account, the user can log in via POP3 and the `systempw`, but will be unable to log in via IMAP. However, it is cleaner and more elegant to use user options such as `disableimap` and `disablepop3` (see section 9.12 on page 144).

hmac-md5-pop3pw, hmac-sha1-pop3pw, hmac-sha256-pop3w
: There are optional `hmac` variants for the fields `pop3pw`, `imappw`, and `esmtppw`; these variants store the passwords for challenge-response processes (see section 9.4.4 on page 129).

mail
: This specifies the path to the *maildir* (*not* the user's email address).

quota
: This is where you can specify the quota settings for the account; see section 10.2.1 on page 167. This field is only processed if you are using the complete Courier-MTA suite. It is irrelevant if you are using only the Courier IMAP server.

options
: You can also save user options in the `userdb`; this provides a decisive advantage over using traditional shell accounts that are specified in the `/etc/passwd`. For more information, see section 9.12 on page 144.

Courier can deduce email account names from Unix user IDs. To implement this name-from-UID resolution, the `userdb` that arises from a `passwd` converted via `pw2userdb` always contains a separate line after the information for each each account (in this example 1000= geeko):

```
geeko uid=1000|gid=100|home=/home/geeko|shell=/bin/bash|systempw=$2a$05$
m0WZvfaUKbuvK9BKTPyBKeAblNYKb8PHSPuQ60KEJA4ycK9j/EB4y|gecos=Geeko
1000=   geeko
```

---

[4] The term *gecos* is derived from a Unix system from the '70s and is short for *General Electric Comprehensive Operating Supervisor*. This `passwd` field contains information for identifying the account. The information stored there depends on the Unix version. Current Linux systems no longer require it, so the field is usually used to save the real name.

However, this information is currently not evaluated anywhere in the program code, so you do not need to provide it.

You can also create accounts in the `userdb` that contain an at sign (@) in the username; this is not possible if you only use `/etc/passwd`. If you simply use the email address as the account name, you have to refer to the maildir path of the actual account in the `mail` field.

The user can then also log in with his or her email address. The user will be unaware of the shell account the access is readdressed to:

```
tux@example.com    uid=1001|gid=100|home=/home/tux|shell=/bin/bash|syste
mpw=$2a$10$8ZWLc9MOH.vB913PJVR9tuluHdzXc9BBcQ2ZJcAqrDJrUsB9$DvZm|mail=/h
ome/tux/Maildir
1001=    tux@example.com
```

9.4.2 Maintaining Account Data with `userdb`

You can use any ASCII text editor to maintain the `userdb` file. If, however, there are a large number of accounts, or in shell scripts, it is advisable to use the Perl script `userdb`. It saves effort in searching the file and checks that the syntax in the file is correct, which prevents possible errors.

The `set` command

```
userdb account_name set field1=value1 field2=value2 ...
```

sets the specified fields for *accountname* to the specified values. The `unset` command

```
userdb accountname unset feld1 feld2 ...
```

deletes the specified fields. The `del` command

```
userdb accountname del
```

deletes the entire account, though only from the `userdb` and not from `/etc/passwd` and `/etc/shadow`. The `-show` option takes an argument

```
userdb -show accountname
```

and displays the `userdb` entry for *accountname*. If you omit the *accountname* argument, `userdb` will return the data for all user accounts. The script also recognizes option `-f /path/to/file`, which permits a file other than `/etc/authlib/userdb` to be read out and modified.

Thus, if you want to set the maildir directory for account `tux@example.com` to `/home/vmail/tux-example` and the user ID and group ID to 5001, the `userdb` instruction to carry this out runs as follows:

```
linux: # userdb "tux@example.com" set home=/home/vmail/tux-example \
uid=5001 gid=5001
```

If no value is specified for a field, userdb will request one. This means that a password can be changed without including it in the call parameters of the invocation of userdb (which will appear in the process list, which in turn can be examined by all system users). Passwords have to be encrypted and may not be specified in cleartext. The userdbbpw program provides assistance here. It requests a cleartext password from the standard input and puts out the hashed version on the standard output. It is also easy to combine with userdb:

```
linux: # userdbpw | userdb "tux@example.com" set systempw
```

If you make no further specifications, userdbpw uses the classic encrypt() function; if you add the call parameters -md5, -hmac-md5,[5] -hmac-sha1, or -hmac-sha256,[6] it will use other procedures to generate checksums.

9.4.3 Creating a Binary Version of the User Database

Courier does not work on the userdb file; instead, it operates with an indexed binary version stored in userdb.dat and userdbshadow.dat, which is noticeably faster to search: userdbshadow.dat contains the passwords, and userdb.dat contains the other data. The makeuserdb program creates both files from the userdb (Postfix administrators are aware of this technique):

```
linux:/etc/authlib/ # ls -la userdb*
-rw------- 1 root root  3044 Jan 28 17:49 userdb
linux:/etc/authlib/ # makeuserdb
linux:/etc/authlib/ # ls -la userdb*
-rw------- 1 root root  3044 Jan 28 17:49 userdb
-rw-r--r-- 1 root root 14897 Jan 28 18:14 userdb.dat
-rw------- 1 root root 12885 Jan 28 18:14 userdbshadow.dat
```

Changes to the userdb do not affect the running system until makeuserdb converts the account data; this can be done during operation.

Please pay attention to file permissions. userdb and userdbshadow.dat contain passwords, so only root may read these files.

---

[5] See http://en.wikipedia.org/wiki/HMAC.
[6] See http://en.wikipedia.org/wiki/SHA.

9.4.4 Separating the `userdb` into Multiple Files

If you have a large number of accounts, it makes sense to maintain the user data for the `authuserdb` module in small files; that way you can sort the users into independently managed groups—by domain, for example. In addition to specifying an account name directly, all `userdb` commands discussed earlier can also handle a combination that specifies the path to the file containing the data for the specified user. They interpret this path relative to the *directory* /etc/authlib/userdb/.

If you specify example.com/tux as the account name, the commands will apply to user tux in file /etc/authlib/userdb/example.com:

```
linux: # mkdir /etc/authlib/userdb
linux: # chmod 700 /etc/authlib/userdb
linux: # userdb "example.com/tux@example.com" \
set home=/home/vmail/tux.example.com uid=1006 gid=100
linux: # cd /etc/authlib/userdb
linux:/etc/authlib/userdb # ls -la
-rw------- 1 root root   44 Jan 28 20:34 example.com
```

If you specify account domains/example.com/tux, this will refer to /etc/authlib/userdb/domains/example.com and then to the entry tux within this file. The other `userdb` actions function as usual with this address information:

```
linux: # userdbpw | userdb "example-com/geeko@example.com" set imappw
```

A single call to `makeuserdb` combines all data in the files in directory /etc/authlib/userdb/ into the database files userdb.dat and userdbshadow.dat.

CRAM Authentication with `userdb`

The `authcram` module, which has now been integrated into `authuserdb`, also used the `userdb` database. Unlike `authuserdb`, `authcram` also supported the challenge-response procedure (CRAM). However, READMEs and Howtos referring to this module are outdated: The `authcram` module was dissolved, and CRAM support has been integrated into `authuserdb`.

Unlike the other CRAM-capable modules `authmysql`, `authpgsql`, and `authldap`, the password is not saved on the server in cleartext. Instead, `authuserdb` requests a hash corresponding to the CRAM procedure in the user db: HMAC-MD5 for CRAM-MD5, HMAC-SHA1 for CRAM-SHA1, and HMAC-SHA256 for CRAM-SHA256.

Unlike its three colleagues, `authuserdb` can only provide different CRAM procedures in parallel if it has the password hash for all hash procedures.

The hashing method used in the `userdb` also determines the CRAM procedure.

9.4.5 The `atime`

There are detailed explanations of the CRAM procedure and cleartext passwords in section 9.13 on page 147.

If you use the `userdb` and want to offer secure authentication methods, you have to make sure that the user passwords are hashed according to the correct procedure and then saved. As well as the `systempw` field (standard `crypt` hash, which only enables `PLAIN` and `LOGIN`), `userdb` also offers fields `hmac-md5-pw` (HMAC-MD5, enables CRAM-MD5) and `hmac-sha1-pw` (enables HMAC-SHA1), both of which are not very well documented.

When hashing the passwords using `userdbpw`, you must choose the correct hash procedure:

```
linux: # userdbpw -hmac-md5 | userdb "tux@example.com" set hmac-md5-pw
linux: # userdbpw -hmac-sha1 | userdb "tux@example.com" set hmac-sha1-pw
linux: # userdbpw -hmac-sha256 | userdb "tux@example.com" set \
hmac-sha256-pw
```

9.5 Using QMail's `vchkpw` Library for Authentication

The `authvchkpw` module uses the `vpopmail/vchkpw` library of the QMail MTA. If you have set these up so they are operational, authentication requests will be forwarded to this library. For a detailed description, see the QMail documentation.[7]

9.6 Implementing Custom Authentication Methods

The Courier source code contains the `authcustom` module, which is operational except that it does not contain authentication code of its own. As long as you have sufficient knowledge of programming, you can enhance it and compile it with the Courier code; it can then be used for Courier authentication under the name `authcustom`.

---

[7] See http://www.inter7.com/?page=vpopmail.

9.7 Integrating External Authentication Programs

`authpipe` enables you to use any external program for authentication. The `authdaemond` starts this external program and uses the standard input and output to communicate with it.

By default, the `authdaemond` refers to the required program as `/etc/auth lib/authProg`. The name and path are already compiled in and can only be changed by recompiling Courier using the `configure` option `--with-pi peprog`.

To communicate with the external program, `authdaemond` uses the same protocol that it uses for Courier modules. This protocol defines four different requests to the authentication service: PRE, AUTH, PASSWD, and ENUMERATE. `authdaemond` uses the request

```
PRE . service username
```

followed by a newline character to inform the external program which mail service is addressing it; this is indicated by *service*, which can be pop3 or imap. If the requested username exists, the authentication service has to return a list of the account attributes in Table 9.1.

Attribute	Description
USERNAME=*username*	Repeats the name of the requested account
UID=*uid*	Unix user ID of the account
GID=*gid*	Unix group ID of the account
HOME=*directory*	The user's home directory containing the maildir
ADDRESS=*adress*	The email address (not evaluated by POP3 and IMAP)
NAME=*name*	The user's real name (not evaluated)
MAILDIR=*maildir*	Path to the maildir in relation to the home directory
QUOTA=*maxbytes*S,*maxfiles*C	The quota specification: *maxbytes* stands for the upper limit in bytes, and *maxfiles* stands for the maximum number of files (and therefore emails)
PASSWD=*cryptpasswd*	The encrypted password
PASSWD2=*plainpasswd*	The cleartext password
OPTIONS=*option1*=*wert1*,	Possible user options for the account

Table 9.1: Account attributes that the authentication service has to return

continued:

Attribute	Description
`option2=wert2,...`	(see section 9.12 on page 144)

Here, USERNAME, UID, GID, HOME, and ADDRESS are required, along with the trailing dot, which completes the reply:

```
USERNAME=tux
UID=5001
GID=5001
HOME=/home/tux
ADDRESS=tux@example.com
.
```

All other attribute specifications are optional. If an account does not exist, the authentication program has to return FAIL and the newline character. In case of temporary errors (e.g., in the database), the program has to terminate without comment and may not return a reply.

To request the authentication service to verify a login attempt, the authentication daemon uses the AUTH message, which requires the authentication method as an argument. Subsequent individual fields are separated by line breaks, but the initial request message must not end in a line break. This is an example of a verification request for a login using the LOGIN cleartext method:

```
AUTH login
username
password
```

For challenge-response procedures, the authentication daemon transmits the *challenge string* and the *response* returned by the client to the authentication service, which then checks whether they are correct. In the following example of CRAM-MD5, the username and password are coded in *response*:

```
AUTH cram-md5
challenge
response
```

You could also use CRAM-SHA1 or CRAM-SHA256 instead of the CRAM-MD5 procedure.

When a user wishes to change the webmail password for the Courier webmailer from `old_password` to `new_password`, the authdaemond transmits the following request to the authentication service:

```
PASSWD service \t username \t old_password \t new_password
```

Each of the four arguments has to be separated from its neighbor(s) by a *tab*, which is shown here as \t. The PASSWD command and the specification of the service (imap or pop3) making the request (to which the answer is returned) are only separated by a space. The entire request ends in a newline character.

This function is not relevant for POP3/IMAP, as passwords cannot be changed via these protocols. The Courier project only provides this option on the Web interface if all Courier components are working together, and provides an interface for third-party tools.

If the authdaemond issues the ENUMERATE command (which also ends in a line break), the authentication program has to return a list of all accounts. For each account, all of the information is returned in one line, in which the individual fields are separated by tabs (once again shown here as \t). A single dot marks the end of the account list:

```
username \t uid \t gid \t home \t maildir \t option1=val1,option2=val2,
option3=val3
...
.
```

Thus, the last data set is followed by a single line with a lone dot. Such user lists are required to, for example, create shared folders (see section 10.1 on page 153).

9.8 Authentication via MySQL

The data that Courier requires for POP3 and IMAP can also be maintained in an SQL database such as MySQL. You need to set up an SQL table containing a field for each of the following: the username (the account ID), the Linux user ID and group ID, the password, and the path to the user's maildir. The entry in the maildir field is interpreted (as usual) relative to the home directory, which is saved in a separate table field. However, the maildir field can also contain an absolute path, as shown in the example here; in this case, the contents of the home field are irrelevant.

Do not forget to create an index based on the account ID field, so that the table can be searched efficiently.

The following MySQL listing creates database user courier, who is permitted to access the mailbase database locally, and generates the authentication database (see also Figure 9.1):

```
linux: # mysql
mysql> use mysql;
mysql> insert into user (Host, User, Password)
```

9 User Data

```
        values('localhost', 'courier', password('supersecret'));
mysql> insert into db (Host, Db, User, Select_priv)
        values('localhost','mailbase','courier','Y');
mysql> create database mailbase;
mysql> use mailbase;
mysql> CREATE TABLE `mailusers` (
 `id` INT( 11 ) NOT NULL AUTO_INCREMENT,
 `account` VARCHAR( 240 ) NOT NULL ,
 `uid` VARCHAR( 6 ) DEFAULT '5001' NOT NULL ,
 `gid` VARCHAR( 6 ) DEFAULT '5001' NOT NULL ,
 `maildir` VARCHAR( 100 ) DEFAULT '/var/spool/maildirs' NOT NULL,
 `home` VARCHAR( 100 ) NOT NULL ,
 `password` VARCHAR( 255 ) NOT NULL ,
 `created_by` VARCHAR( 60 ) NOT NULL ,
 `created_on` DATE NOT NULL ,
 `memo_txt` VARCHAR( 255 ) NOT NULL ,
 `memo_firstname` VARCHAR( 60 ) NOT NULL ,
 `memo_lastname` VARCHAR( 60 ) NOT NULL ,
 PRIMARY KEY ( `id` ) ,
 UNIQUE ( `account` )
 ) TYPE = MYISAM ;
Query OK, 0 rows affected (0.01 sec)
mysql> quit
linux: # mysqladmin reload
```

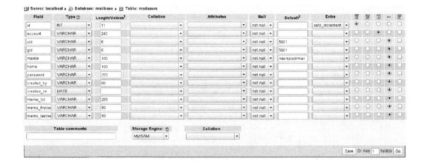

Figure 9.1: The mailusers example table contains the mandatory fields and some additional information for better administration.

In order to use this table, you have to specify in the `authdaemonrc` that the authentication daemon should use the `authmysql` module:

```
authmodulelist="authmysql"
```

For the sake of clarity, the configuration for MySQL access is not located in the `authdaemonrc`, but in the `authmysqlrc`. If you do not have this in your system, it is either in a package that has to be installed separately (and that you have not yet installed), or Courier was compiled without support for MySQL. OpenSuSE, for example, only contains the `courier-authlib-mysql` package starting from version 10.2. If you have an older version, you may have to compile Courier yourself. As a rule of thumb, if your Courier supports MySQL, the `authmysqlrc` will exist.

For each configuration parameter, the desired configuration setting is listed following the parameter and separated from it by spaces or tabs. The following settings are mandatory:

MYSQL_SERVER
> This field specifies the MySQL server to be used, by giving either the hostname or the IP address:
>
> ```
> MYSQL_SERVER     mysql.example.com
> ```
>
> It is not possible to specify more than one server.

MYSQL_USERNAME
> This field contains the username that Courier is to use when logging on to MySQL (`courier` in our current example).

MYSQL_PASSWORD
> This field specifies the corresponding password (`supersecret` in our example).

MYSQL_DATABASE
> This field contains the name of the MySQL database containing the account data (`mailbase` in our example).

MYSQL_USER_TABLE
> This field tells which one of the tables in this database contains the user data (`mailusers` in our example).

MYSQL_CRYPT_PWFIELD
> Which field of this table contains the *encrypted* password? (It is `password` in this example.)

MYSQL_CLEAR_PWFIELD
> This field specifies the field containing the cleartext password. If you do *not* store cleartext passwords, you should remove this option. However, it makes sense to store cleartext passwords, as discussed in section 9.13 on page 147.

MYSQL_UID_FIELD
> This is the field containing the user ID for the account (`uid` in our example).

MYSQL_GID_FIELD
> This is the field containing the group ID for the account (`gid` in our example).

MYSQL_LOGIN_FIELD
: This is the field containing the user's login name (`id` in our example)—the most important field in the table. The MySQL module uses this value to find the data set and read the user ID, group ID, and other parameters.

MYSQL_HOME_FIELD
: This is the field containing the path to the user's home directory (`home` in our example). If the user's maildir is *not* stored under the name `Maildir` directly in the home directory, you have to specify the table field containing the path in MYSQL_MAILDIR_FIELD (see the optional parameters below).

MYSQL_NAME_FIELD
: This is the field containing the actual name of the user (corresponds to the `gecos` field in the `passwd`). This is irrelevant for POP3 and IMAP and is only used for other Courier mail server modules or for the web frontend.

There are also a number of optional parameters:

MYSQL_PORT
: This field specifies the MySQL port if this differs from the default value of 3306.

MYSQL_SOCKET
: This is the path to the MySQL socket if MySQL is operated locally (e.g., /var/mysql/mysql.sock).

MYSQL_OPT
: This field provides additional options for the connection to MySQL. This is for development purposes and is not required for everyday operation.

MYSQL_MAILDIR_FIELD
: By default, Courier searches for a user's emails in the $HOME/Maildir directory. If you wish the user's maildir to be stored in a different subdirectory, use the table field defined here to specify a different directory (relative to $HOME) for each user (`maildir` in our current example).

MYSQL_DEFAULTDELIVERY
: This field defines the default transport method if the SMTP server from the Courier project is used. If you are running the Courier IMAP with a different MTA, this value is irrelevant.

MYSQL_QUOTA_FIELD

This field defines a table field with the quotas for a user (see section 10.2.1 on page 167). This is only available if the entire Courier mail server suite is in use (and not if Courier IMAP is operated alone), so it is irrelevant for us.

MYSQL_AUXOPTIONS_FIELD

This specifies the table field containing additional options for this account (see section 9.12 on page 144). In this field, multiple options have to be separated by commas, and spaces between the comma and the following option are not permitted.

You can also save the options singly in different fields and then use the SQL command `CONCAT` to combine them. Refer to section 9.12.3 on page 147 for instructions.

MYSQL_WHERE_CLAUSE

This field contains a condition that is integrated into the request as a MySQL `WHERE` command:

```
MYSQL_WHERE_CLAUSE server='mailhost.example.com'
```

You can set multiple conditions:

```
MYSQL_WHERE_CLAUSE server='mailhost.example.com' AND status='active'
```

MYSQL_SELECT_CLAUSE

If the username, uid, gid, and path to the maildir do not correspond directly to the database schema—say, if these items are not stored in individual columns of a single table—then this option allows an SQL query to be specified that assembles, in some appropriate fashion, this information from the data in the existing database tables.

For this purpose, the `CONCAT` SQL command can be used to create strings containing elements that are retrieved directly from specified tables and columns. Here we use it to, among other things, calculate the user's maildir path from pieces stored separately in two database tables:

```
MYSQL_SELECT_CLAUSE  SELECT                                       \
   CONCAT(popbox.local_part, '@', popbox.domain_name),            \
   CONCAT('{MD5}', popbox.password_hash),                         \
   popbox.clearpw,                                                \
   domain.uid,                                                    \
   domain.gid,                                                    \
   CONCAT(domain.path, '/', popbox.mbox_name),                    \
   '',                                                            \
   domain.quota,                                                  \
   '',                                                            \
   CONCAT("disableimap=",disableimap,",disablepop3=",             \
```

```
                disablepop3,",disablewebmail=",disablewebmail, \
                ",sharedgroup=",sharedgroup)                  \
    FROM popbox, domain                                       \
    WHERE popbox.local_part = '$(local_part)'                 \
    AND popbox.domain_name = '$(domain)'                      \
    AND popbox.domain_name = domain.domain_name
```

The MySQL command returns the results in the following order and separated by commas:

username, encrypted_password, cleartextpassword, uid, gid, home directory, maildir, quota, complete name, options

MYSQL_ENUMERATE_CLAUSE

This SELECT command is used when the fields for the index file (see section 10.1.1 on page 156) is combined using the authenumerate command (section 10.1.1 on page 160) in order to prepare for shared folders. You only need to prepare this SQL command if the data still needs to be assembled by the CONCAT command. If the data is stored cleanly in separate table fields, this command is not necessary.

```
MYSQL_ENUMERATE_CLAUSE  SELECT                                \
    CONCAT(popbox.local_part, '@', popbox.domain_name),       \
    domain.uid,                                               \
    domain.gid,                                               \
    CONCAT(domain.path, '/', popbox.mbox_name),               \
    '',                                                       \
    CONCAT('sharedgroup=', sharedgroup)                       \
    FROM popbox, domain                                       \

    WHERE popbox.local_part = '$(local_part)'                 \
    AND popbox.domain_name = '$(domain)'                      \
    AND popbox.domain_name = domain.domain_name
```

The complete data set has to be returned as shown and in the following order:

username, uid, gid, home directory, maildir, options

MYSQL_CHPASS_CLAUSE

This MySQL command is executed when a user changes the password. This option is designed for the SqWebMail Courier webmailer and is not relevant if you are only operating Courier IMAP, as users are not able to change their passwords in this case.

DEFAULT_DOMAIN

When a user attempts to log on with a username that is not a complete email address, the domain in this parameter is automatically attached to the request. If the DEFAULT_DOMAIN is example.com, for example, then the login ID `user` is automatically converted into `user@example.com`.

Be careful: This parameter is called `DEFAULT_DOMAIN` and not `MYSQL_DEFAULT_DOMAIN`.

9.9 Authentication via PostgreSQL

If you have the `authpgsqlrc` configuration file, this means that your Courier `authlib` was compiled with PostgreSQL support. You should then specify `authpgsql` in `authdaemonrc` as the module to be used.

```
authmodulelist="authpgsql"
```

There are only a few small differences between using MySQL and using PostgreSQL. Most, though not all, PostgreSQL parameters only differ from their MySQL equivalents in the prefix of the name: `MYSQL_PORT` becomes `PGSQL_PORT`, and the exception to the naming rule, `DEFAULT_DOMAIN`, remains unchanged.

Unfortunately, Sam Varshavchik, the Courier author, has written one small but essential parameter that defies logic and usability and causes annoyance, confusion, and errors: The MySQL parameter `MYSQL_SERVER` is called `PGSQL_HOST` in PostgreSQL.

Why this name change? It creates space for an additional trick that prevents administrators from getting bored: Unlike in MySQL, there is *no* `PGSQL_SOCKET` parameter.

If you want to contact PostgreSQL via a socket instead of the TCP port 5400, you have to set `PGSQL_HOST` to empty and enter the file ending of the PostgreSQL socket in `PGSQL_PORT`. If your PostgreSQL socket is called `/tmp/.s.PGSQL.5400`, you enter the following settings:

```
PGSQL_HOST
PGSQL_PORT 5400
```

If you use the TCP port, the setup is as follows:

```
PGSQL_HOST pgsql.example.com
PGSQL_PORT 5400
```

If you create the `mailusers` table according to the schema shown on page 133 (in the PostgreSQL installation on the computer `pgsql.example.com`), then the `authpgsql` configuration file should look like this:

```
PGSQL_HOST              pgsql.example.com
PGSQL_PORT 5400
PGSQL_USERNAME          courier
PGSQL_PASSWORD          supersecret
PGSQL_DATABASE          mailusers
PGSQL_USER_TABLE        mailusers
PGSQL_CRYPT_PWFIELD     password
PGSQL_UID_FIELD         uid
PGSQL_GID_FIELD         gid
PGSQL_LOGIN_FIELD       account
PGSQL_HOME_FIELD        home
PGSQL_NAME_FIELD        memo_lastname
```

9.10 Authentication via LDAP

Courier can also query an LDAP directory in real time. If your Courier `authlib` was compiled with LDAP support, you will find an already prepared configuration file `authldaprc`, which sets the configuration options discussed here. In the main file `authdaemonrc`, you first specify that authentication is performed by the `authldap` module:

```
authmodulelist="authldap"
```

The following settings can be configured:

LDAP_URI

This is the URL for one or more LDAP servers:

```
LDAP_URI ldaps://ldap.example.com, ldaps://backup.example.com
```

LDAP_PROTOCOL_VERSION

This is the version of the LDAP protocol used:

```
LDAP_PROTOCOL_VERSION 3
```

LDAP_BASEDN

The accounts to be authenticated can be found under the *Distinguished Name (DN)* specified here:

```
LDAP_BASEDN o=example, c=com
```

LDAP_BINDDN

This specifies the DN that Courier uses to log on to the LDAP server:

```
LDAP_BINDDN cn=administrator, o=example, c=com
```

LDAP_BINDPW
: This specifies the password that Courier uses to log on to the LDAP server.

LDAP_TIMEOUT
: This specifies the number of seconds after which Courier should terminate the connection to the LDAP server if the server is not responding. For example:

```
LDAP_TIMEOUT 5
```

LDAP_AUTHBIND
: If you set this variable to 1, Courier verifies the username and password by using them to log on to the LDAP server and checking whether this login is possible ("rebind"). CRAM procedures are not possible, as Courier cannot log on to LDAP without the user's cleartext password. For this reason, this method is usually not used. In this case Courier uses the data from LDAP_BINDDN and LDAP_BINDPW to search the LDAP directory.

LDAP_MAIL
: This is the LDAP attribute in which Courier searches for the login name.

LDAP_DOMAIN
: This automatically adds the specified domain (example.com in this example) to the login name before executing search queries if the client specifies only a username:

```
LDAP_DOMAIN example.com
```

LDAP_FILTER
: This adds the LDAP filter rule mentioned to the search query; this filter rule is placed in parentheses, as is usual for LDAP. You can use this option to query, for example, only accounts of a certain class:

```
LDAP_FILTER (objectClass=AccountMail)
```

Logical conjunctions are also possible. The following filter requires that the accounts belong to the AccountMail class and that their LDAP attribute status is active:

```
LDAP_FILTER (&(objectClass=AccountMail)(status=active))
```

LDAP_ENUMERATE_FILTER
: If this option is set, authenumerate (see section 10.1.1 on page 160) will use LDAP_ENUMERATE_FILTER instead of LDAP_FILTER for LDAP queries:

```
LDAP_ENUMERATE_FILTER (&(objectClass=AccountMail)(!(disableshared=1
)))
```

This example shows how to negate a filter criterion. This query returns all accounts of the `AccountMail` object class whose `disable shared` attribute is *not* 1.

LDAP_HOMEDIR
: This attribute contains the path to the user's home directory. It does not have to be /home/*username*; for a virtual user, it might be /var/maildir/*username* or something similar.

LDAP_MAILROOT
: This attribute can be used to specify the parent of the home directory, if a relative path is entered in the attribute specified by LDAP_HOMEDIR. Courier uses the value of the path expression $LDAP_MAILROOT/$LDAP_HOMEDIR as the home directory. LDAP_MAILROOT is optional and is not usually set.

LDAP_MAILDIR
: This attribute contains the path to the maildir directory in the user's home directory. Courier searches for a user's emails in $LDAP_MAILROOT/$LDAP_HOMEDIR/$LDAP_MAILDIR.

    This attribute is optional. If it is not set, Courier will automatically assume that `Maildir/` is in the user's home directory.

LDAP_DEFAULTDELIVERY
: This corresponds to MYSQL_DEFAULTDELIVERY (see 136). This option only affects the SMTP servers of the Courier project and is irrelevant for Courier IMAP.

LDAP_FULLNAME
: This contains the user's first and last names. This attribute is irrelevant for Courier IMAP.

LDAP_CRYPTPW
: This contains the encrypted password.

LDAP_CLEARPW
: This is the attribute containing the cleartext password. See also the discussion in section 9.13 on page 147.

LDAP_GLOB_UID
: This sets a globally identical user ID for every account:

```
LDAP_GLOB_UID 10000
```

9.11 Obsolete Authentication Modules

`LDAP_UID`
> If `LDAP_GLOB_UID` is empty or has not been set, Courier will consult this attribute for the account's individual user ID.

`LDAP_GLOB_GID`
> This sets a group ID that applies to all users.

`LDAP_GID`
> If `LDAP_GLOB_GID` is empty or has not been set, Courier will consult this attribute for the account's group ID.

`LDAP_AUXOPTIONS`
> This is the attribute containing the user options for the account (see section 9.12 on page 144 and section 9.12.2 on page 146).

`LDAP_DEREF`
> This specifies whether and how any returned LDAP aliases should be resolved. These are LDAP entries that function like a symlink and refer to other entries. LDAP aliases are not usually used.
>
> The possible values correspond to the standard LDAP procedures mentioned in `man 5 ldap.conf`: `never`, `searching`, `finding`, and `always`.

`LDAP_TLS`
> If value 1 is set, the connection to the LDAP server is SSL/TLS encrypted; if value 0 is set, the query data (which could include the user password) is transmitted without encryption.

9.11 Obsolete Authentication Modules

Current versions of Courier no longer support the following modules automatically, as their functions are now carried out by other modules.

9.11.1 The `authpwd` Module

This module reads account information and the password from `/etc/passwd`. It is no longer relevant, as passwords are stored in `/etc/shadow` in the Unix systems used today. If for some reason `/etc/passwd` has to function as the password source, it is advisable to use `authpam`.

9.11.2 The `authshadow` Module

This module corresponds to `authpwd`, except that it reads the password from `/etc/shadow`. There are no advanced configuration settings for this module. However, it is more flexible and secure to use `authpam`, because access permissions can be handled more restrictively; most distributions therefore use PAM.

As `authshadow` and `authpwd` are in direct competition, it makes no sense to use `authshadow` and `authpam` at the same time.

9.11.3 The `authcram` Module

This module no longer exists, as `authuserdb` has taken over its function (see section 9.4.4 on page 129).

9.12 User Options

With Courier IMAP, it is possible to evaluate additional options for individual accounts, in addition to the basic user data. This requires an authentication source that can store the additional fields. If you use shell accounts, for example, user options are not available for authentication based on /etc/passwd and /etc/shadow, but only in conjunction with `authuserdb`, `authmysql`, `authpgsql`, and `authldap`. The following options can be set for a user account:

`disableimap`
: If this flag is set to 1, the user cannot log in via IMAP:

    ```
    disableimap=1
    ```

    The value 0 enables this login. If this flag has not been set, the default setting specified in the `authdaemonrc` file applies (see below).

`disablepop3`
: This option is identical to `disableimap`, but applies to POP3.

`disablewebmail`
: This option is designed for the SqWebMail Courier webmailer. Like `disableimap` and `disablepop3`, it can be used to selectively disable access via SqWebmail. This access restriction does not function for other webmailers, as they do not evaluate this field. It is therefore irrelevant if you are operating only Courier IMAP.

`group`
: This option assigns the account to one or more groups. These can be used for group-based assignment of access permissions (ACLs) to shared email directories (see section 10.1.1 on page 154). An account may belong to multiple groups, and `group` is the only option that can be mentioned multiple times:

```
disableimap=1,group=group1,group=group2,mailhost=mail.example.com
```

Please note: `group` and `sharedgroup` are two different parameters and cannot be interchanged with one another.

`sharedgroup`
: If you want to enable your users to share IMAP folders (see section 10.1 on page 153), you can use this option to assign them to a shared group.

`disableshared`
: When this flag is set to 1, `authenumerate -s` (see section 10.1.1 on page 160) will ignore the corresponding account when generating the list of shared folders, regardless of whether it is assigned to a shared group or not.

`mailhost`
: If you operate Courier IMAP as POP3/IMAP proxy, this option stores the POP3/IMAP server that physically contains the mailbox and to which the proxy should forward the connection. For more information, see section 10.3 on page 175.

Specify the default values for these options in the `authdaemonrc` file for all authentication modules using the `DEFAULTOPTIONS` parameter; separate option-value pairs with a comma and without spaces (!):

```
DEFAULTOPTIONS="disableimap=0,disablepop3=0,disablewebmail=0"
```

Here, access is permitted by default via POP3, IMAP, or SqWebMail, and users are not assigned to a shared group. These default settings are firmly entrenched in the Courier source code, so they apply even if you do not set the `DEFAULTOPTIONS` variable. Because the equal sign is used to specify values for the individual user options as well as to assign the entire list of option settings to the `DEFAULTOPTIONS` variable, you must not forget to include the quotation marks around the list of system-specific default values.

Individual settings in the user data overwrite these default values. There are two ways of specifying who may use IMAP. First, you can set the `disableimap=1` option for users that may not have access. Make no specification in the `DEFAULTOPTIONS` in the `authdaemonrc`, or set `disableimap=0` explicitely (hence "documenting" the default).

Alternatively, you can use the reverse strategy, and specify `DEFAULTOPTIONS="disableimap=1"` in the `authdaemonrc`. This disables IMAP access for all users. You then set option `disableimap=0` in the user data sets of privileged users, which explicitly permits them access.

All authentication modules apart from `authldap` expect these options in a single field, separated by commas and without spaces; this is analogous to the `DEFAULTOPTIONS` setting in the `authdaemonrc` file. In the configuration files of the SQL modules, `MYSQL_AUXOPTIONS_FIELD` (see page 137) or `PGSQL_AUXOPTIONS_FIELD` specify where the options are stored. For the use of LDAP, each option is specified in a separate attribute.

9.12.1 Saving User Options in the `userdb`

It is not possible to store user options in `/etc/passwd`, as there is no free field and the existing fields cannot be used for this purpose. For this reason, it makes sense to use the `userdb` if you do not wish to use SQL databases or LDAP.

The `options` field describes the list of specified options; multiple values are separated by commas and without spaces:

```
tux@example.com    uid=1001|gid=100|home=/home/tux|shell=/bin/bash|
systempw=$2a$10$8ZWLc9MOH.vB913PJVR9tuluHdzXc9BBcQ2ZJcAqrDJrUsB9$Dv
Zm|mail=/home/tux/Maildir|options=disableimap=1,sharedgroup=test,ma
ilhost=mail5.example.com
```

9.12.2 Individual User Options in an LDAP Directory

Unlike the other methods, LDAP stores each individual user option in a separate attribute. If a user's data is in an LDAP directory and that user requires more than the default options, the configuration of the `authldap` module has to assign the relevant attributes to the extra options.

Courier expects the LDAP attribute name to the *left* of the equal sign; this is unfortunately not evident from the examples in the README texts provided by the Courier team, as the names they chose for the attribute and the option are identical. Thus, in the following example, the individual `sharedgroup` value is stored in the `shared` attribute, the `disableimap` option in the `imap` attribute, and the `disablepop3` specification in pop3:

```
#
# LDAP_AUXOPTIONS    LDAP-Attribut=Courier-Option
#
LDAP_AUXOPTIONS    shared=sharedgroup,imap=disableimap,pop3=disablepop3
```

As long as you are aware of which way to read the assignment, there is no reason not to name the attribute after the Courier option. The settings in the `authldaprc` will then be as follows:

```
LDAP_AUXOPTIONS    sharedgroup=sharedgroup,disableimap=disableimap,
disablepop3=disablepop3
```

9.12.3 Storing User Options in Dedicated Fields in an SQL Table

With `authmysql` and `authpgsql`, a separate field in the table can also be specified for each option. In this case, an SQL command should be specified in the file `authmysqlrc` or `authpgsqlrc` that assembles the option settings from all of the relevant fields into a string in which the settings are separated by commas and there are *no spaces*:

```
MYSQL_AUXOPTIONS_FIELD  CONCAT("disableimap=",disableimap,",disablepop3=
",disablepop3,",disablewebmail=",disablewebmail,",sharedgroup=",sharedgr
oup)
```

The following listing is the PostgreSQL equivalent that collects the data from columns `disableimap`, `disablepop3`, `disablewebmail`, and `shared group`:

```
PGSQL_AUXOPTIONS_FIELD  'disableimap=' || disableimap || ',disablepop3='
|| disablepop3 || ',disablewebmail=' || disablewebmail || ',sharedgroup='
|| sharedgroup
```

9.13 Saving Passwords: Cleartext or Hash?

At first, it may seem sensible to store user passwords in the various data stores only in hashed form according to `crypt`, or the MD5 or SHA algorithms, and not in cleartext. Strictly speaking, a hash is not an encryption mechanism, as there is supposedly no way to determine the original value from the result of applying the hash to it.[8]

This has the advantage that neither administrators nor unauthorized third parties can gain access to the cleartext passwords. However, this advantage can become a very serious problem when migrating to different IMAP software (see section 6.4 on page 81).

The `LOGIN` and `PLAIN` transfer methods transfer the password in cleartext, so they should only be used when secured by SSL/TLS. However, only the

---

[8] You could compare a hash value of a password to the sum of the digits of a number. 526 has a digit sum of 13, but the number 526 cannot be recovered from its digit sum of 13 alone. However, a certain sum of digits can arise from an unlimited number of original input values, whereas there is only a probability of 2^{64} that two distinct passwords will give identical MD5 hashes. Of course, there are teams all across the world that are attempting to prove that this might happen much more often. In fact, MD5 has already been undermined in a way that, under certain circumstances, the possibility is less than 2^{64}; hence MD5 must be considered, by and large, cracked. SHA is still viewed as secure.

more secure CRAM procedures (*Challenge-Response Authentication Method*), such as `CRAM-MD5`, `CRAM-SHA1`, `CRAM-SHA256`, or `APOP` (see section 2.1.2 on page 27) make it practically impossible to sniff out the password during transmission.

For these methods, the server generates an individual session key for every login. The client and the server use this key to calculate the hash value of the password; this hash value is only valid for that session. An attacker is not able to use this value at a later stage to log in. However, the server has to know the cleartext password so that it can carry out the same calculations as the client.

In other words: If the password is saved in the supposedly safe hash form, the client can only log in using the insecure methods `LOGIN` and `PLAIN`. Use of safe methods such as `CRAM-MD5`, `CRAM-SHA1`, `CRAM-SHA256`, or `APOP` is only possible if the server can access the cleartext password. This is a basic problem that has nothing to do with Courier.

However, there is one exception that should not exist: Surprisingly, some programs offer `CRAM-MD5` even though they only have the HMAC-MD5 hashes of the passwords.[9]

In this manner, the Courier authentication module `authuserdb` (previously `authcram`) offers `CRAM-MD5`, but only if the passwords are saved in the userdb as HMAC-MD5 hash. This means that the module cannot offer a procedure based on `CRAM-SHA` at the same time.

The explanation is both simple and sobering. The first step of the challenge-response procedure is to hash the password with the standard hash procedure. For `CRAM-MD5`, `secret` becomes the HMAC-MD5 hash `f16f9cd57afad6931bff9508ef68ea2db1b62513b604cf995e4f882bed6d4f1a`, for example. The client then calculates this with the server's *challenge*; this results in the *response*. If `CRAM-SHA1` is used, the client calculates the password hash in the same way using `HMAC-SHA1`.

It *seems* secure if passwords are saved as HMAC-MD5 hashes. However, this is not true. If an attacker gains access to the hash, the attacker can then calculate all other steps of the challenge-response procedure and then log in correctly. This means that the attacker, like the other parties involved, does not require the cleartext password to succeed.

This means that using the HMAC-MD5 hash is just as secure or insecure as saving the password as cleartext. Or to put it another way: The *actual* password used by the client and the server *is* the hash.

This is why we stick with our statement: Challenge-response procedures are only possible if the server knows the cleartext password. Once a HMAC-

---

[9] *HMAC* is short for *Hash Message Authentication Code*; HMAC-MD5 is calculated in a slightly different manner than the standard MD5. These two procedures are not identical, even though they are both often referred to as "an MD5 hash" (see `http://en.wikipedia.org/wiki/HMAC`).

9.13 Saving Passwords: Cleartext or Hash?

MD5 hash has been published, third parties are able to use `CRAM-MD5` to log in.

There is one tiny advantage if only the hash is stored: If an attacker gains access to this data, he or she has to use the challenge-response procedure to log in and is unable to log in using cleartext methods (such as logging on to a web frontend). This may be an advantage for those users that always use the same password, whether for mail servers, FTP accounts, online shops, or social utilities. However, anyone who believes that such multifunction passwords are not available to dozens of others as cleartext passwords is badly mistaken.

In any case, storing the MD5 hash has more drawbacks than benefits, as procedures based on other hashes are no longer possible: CRAM-SHA1 is impossible if the password is not available in cleartext or as an HMAC-SHA hash. This is why the authentication modules `authmysql`, `authpgsql`, and `authldap` always require cleartext passwords in the user data; it is the only way that they can offer all secure CRAM methods in parallel.

According to Courier developer Sam Varshavchik, `authcram` was the first CRAM implementation in the project. He admits that it was a mistake that this module did not store cleartext passwords in the `userdb`. The current `authuserdb` took over this problem from `authcram`. Now, administrators have to decide early on how to hash the passwords in the `userdb`, as it is not possible to switch CRAM authentication methods at a later stage.

Nevertheless, most people feel uncomfortable with saving cleartext passwords. Those who are not aware of the background of CRAM procedures are liable to make the (wrongful) allegation that saving cleartext passwords is irresponsible and endangers security. It is therefore advisable to consider the following arguments:

- The administrator can read all the user's emails anyway, by simply looking at the hard disk; a password is not required.

- If a password is protected from the administrator, it is less protected from about 6 billion other people. It means that the administrator who can access everything anyway cannot read the cleartext password, while any intern or attacker at a large ISP or backbone operator can listen in and record the data when the login data is transmitted. Colleagues or neighbors in an Internet cafe also find it easy to read the password. Last but not least, the administrator can sniff out the password (with a simple `tcpdump`), or the mail server software can log it in the debug mode.

- Users should always be reminded to use different passwords for different providers and services. They may be hard to convince, but they should not get angry just because the administrator now knows the "secret" password used for a dozen other applications ...

Sending a password publicly but hiding it from the administrator is not really logical. The only acceptable argument in its favor is that a successful attacker would have access to the user database containing all the passwords. However, as we demonstrated earlier, it would be just as bad if an attacker gained possession of the MD5 hashes.

What is the actual risk? Is the danger posed by normal password sniffers not a lot more serious and likely? If an attacker gains access to all the user data, won't he or she probably have access to the authentication service or even to the entire set of emails, which means that the passwords are no longer required?

Of course it is a laudable aim to secure a system as well as possible, but it is also important to determine *where* the principal danger comes from. This results from the standard data transport in the Internet, from a sniffing attack from a neighboring computer, or from low password quality.

For all these reasons, it makes sense to grit your teeth, save the passwords in cleartext and then try to explain to the users how this increases (!) security. Do everything in your power to protect the user data from unauthorized access. You have to do this anyway, as even hashed passwords must not fall into the wrong hands.

If you decide to save cleartext passwords, do not forget to configure the `IMAP_CAPABILITY` parameter in `/etc/courier/imap` so that Courier can offer the secure authentication procedures:

```
IMAP_CAPABILITY="IMAP4rev1 UIDPLUS CHILDREN NAMESPACE THREAD=ORDEREDSUBJECT THREAD=REFERENCES SORT QUOTA IDLE AUTH=CRAM-MD5 AUTH=CRAM-SHA1"
```

9.14 Username Selection When Maintaining Multiple Domains

If you have experience with Postfix or other MTAs, you know of the difference between "real" and "virtual" domains. Postfix, for example, distinguishes whether a domain is mentioned in `mynetworks` or in the lookup tables `virtual_maps` or `virtual_alias_domains`.

This procedure is based on the fact that classic shell accounts with user data saved in `passwd` and `shadow` always consist of only a username and lack a domain part. Naturally, this causes problems when you have to map accounts such as `info@` into different domains.

The classic method is to forward these domains to "real" accounts via virtual maps. *Confixx* and *Plesq*, for example, create a vast number of accounts according to the format `web15p3`: 15th domain, 3rd postbox.[10] The

---

[10] This does not necessarily imply high-quality software.

9.14 Username Selection When Maintaining Multiple Domains

user then has to enter this login data in the email client as the username for POP3/IMAP access.

You can name your accounts as you wish; you can even number them, for example, `1234567`, but this is not particularly easy to remember. It is particularly troublesome when you are clearing up and have to delete old domains and mailboxes, unless you maintain an additional database containing the account assignments.

There is an easier way. Even though the at sign (@) was not permitted in the username for POP3/IMAP login in the past, clients have for quite some time now specified complete email addresses as login names. The owner of `info@example.com` can therefore enter `info@example.com` in the email client, and only needs to remember the password.

These usernames cannot be mapped using `passwd` and `shadow`, as the at sign (@) is not permitted there. However, you can create corresponding accounts in MySQL, PostgreSQL, LDAP, and the `userdb`.

The authentication modules use the login name to find the data set in the database or the directory that contains this name in the ID field, and then access the password, the user and group ID, and the path to the email directories. In this case, Courier does not need an account in the traditional sense; it possesses all the information required to check the password and access the files. If you have to administer different domains, MySQL, PostgreSQL, and LDAP are far superior to traditional shell accounts when it comes to storing user information.

Chapter 10

The Work of a Courier Administrator

Once authentication is functioning, setting up a POP3/IMAP server is fairly straightforward. Using a few Courier tricks and features will endear you to mail users and make life easier for the administrator.

10.1 Shared Folders

Courier knows two types of shared folders: virtual shared folders and filesystem-based shared folders.

Virtual shared folders allow users to grant other users access to individual IMAP folders through the IMAP protocol. Users do not require shell access to the mail server, as IMAP directly supports shared folders. All well-known clients have this function.

In order to improve performance, Courier requires a configuration file /etc/courier/shared/index listing all accounts containing shared IMAP folders; this file requires some configuration. It is possible to automate this using shell scripts. If everything is set up properly, the Courier script `authenumerate` (see section 10.1.1 on page 160) will do the work automatically.

Filesystem-based shared folders use symlinks and a number of "dirty" but efficient tricks to integrate individual IMAP folders or entire maildir structures into multiple accounts. This requires manual adjustments at the filesystem level in order to set the required file permissions.

This type of shared folder is therefore not particularly suitable for use with virtualized accounts or Internet service providers, as these mail users do not usually have shell access. It is better suited to mail servers with a user base of technically experienced individuals who are not afraid of (simple) shell commands, for example, on work servers within small companies. As a quick fix, administrators can use them to implement exceptions, provided they have `root` permissions.

10.1.1 Setting Up Virtual Shared Folders

All good email clients allow mail users to grant access to other mail users' IMAP folders using *access control lists (ACLs)*. Other users are identified by their IMAP login name, which does not have to be identical to their email address.

The `courierimapacl` File

If user paul@example.com has granted tux@example.net permission to access the folder Testshare via his own email client, paul's maildir will contain the file courierimapacl:

```
linux:/mail/example.com/paul/Maildir # cd .Testshare
linux:/mail/example.com/paul/Maildir/.Testshare # ls -la
total 24
-rw-r--r--  1 10000 10000     78 18.11.06 11:40:00 PM courierimapacl
drwx------  2 10000 10000   4096 18.10.05 12:56:00 AM courierimapkeywords
-rw-r--r--  1 10000 10000     15 12.01.06 10:39:00 PM courierimapuiddb
drwx------  2 10000 10000   4096 12.01.06 10:39:00 PM cur
-rw-------  1 10000 10000      0 18.10.05 12:56:00 AM maildirfolder
drwx------  2 10000 10000   4096 18.10.05 12:56:00 AM new
drwx------  2 10000 10000   4096 19.11.06  7:48:00 PM tmp
linux:/mail/example.com/paul/Maildir/.Testshare # cat courierimapacl
owner aceilrstwx
administrators aceilrstwx
user=tux@example.net aceilprstwx
```

Table 10.1 shows the *identifiers* that can appear in the first column of this file. By default, two entries for `owner` and `administrators` have to exist in every `courierimapacl` file.

Table 10.1: Assigning permissions through identifiers in the `courierimapacl` file

Identifier	Meaning
`owner`	The owner of this folder
`anyone`	Every user
`anonymous`	Every user (identical to anyone)
`user=loginid`	The user `loginid`
`group=name`	All users in group `name`
`administrators`	All users in group `administrators` (identical to group=administrators)

The `group` user option (see section 9.12 on page 144) makes it possible to associate individual accounts with groups. In this way, members of a group can be assigned shared rights to folders. This is completely different from the `sharedgroup` user option (see section 9.12 on page 145), which is handled differently.

The third line in the example above assigns `tux@example.net` all possible permissions; Table 2.1 on page 36 shows the meanings of these permissions.

It is possible to remove an individual permission from an identifier (that is, to specify "negative permissions") by prefixing a minus sign; this is useful when generous group or `anyone` permissions allow more permissions to a particular user than desired. Courier evaluates all positive permissions and then subtracts the negative permissions, so the order of these entries within the file is irrelevant.

In the following example, all users receive read and write permissions for the affected directory, but write permission is revoked for `tux@example.net`:

```
linux:/mail/example.com/paul/Maildir/.Testshare # cat courierimapacl
owner aceilrstwx
administrators aceilrstwx
-user=tux@example.net w
anyone=lrw
```

However, Courier now has the problem that the permissions are saved in the IMAP folder, but not in `tux@example.net`'s data. In order to determine the folders that this user can access, Courier would have to search through the maildirs of every user.

The `index` File

This is exactly what Courier does. In order to reduce the work involved, the server processes the `index` file. It checks only the accounts listed in this file to see whether they assign to other users permissions for IMAP folders. The number of directories that need to be searched is thereby drastically reduced.

Courier expects this file as `/etc/courier/shared/index`, or, as for individually compiled Courier installations, `/usr/local/etc/courier/shared/index`. This file contains five fields that must be specified, while a sixth field containing user options is optional:

share_name uid gid home_directory maildir options

The `index` file is a partial dump of the user database, whether this database is stored in `passwd`, in an SQL database, or in an LDAP directory. Courier currently requires only the fields *share_name*, *home_directory*, and *maildir*. The columns *uid* and *gid* have to exist but are not evaluated. They set the stage for future extensions.

Every time a user logs in, Courier searches all `courierimapacl` files in the maildir directories mentioned in the `index` file in order to determine the shared folders the user has been given access rights for. Courier uses the *share_name* field only as a label that identifies the folders for the other clients. Therefore, the maildir user's actual login ID is not relevant to the contents of this field, although the username of the corresponding account is usually used. The `index` file on the server containing the accounts of `paul@example.com` and `tux@example.com` looks a bit like this:

```
linux:/etc/courier/shared # cat index
tux     1001 500 /home/tux Maildir/
paul    1002 500 /home/paul Maildir/
```

It could also just as well have had the following contents, though `tux` can *not* log on as `cheffe`:

```
linux:/etc/courier/shared # cat index
cheffe  1001 500 /home/tux Maildir/
paul    1002 500 /home/paul Maildir/
```

There are no complications if some of the directories listed in the `index` file do not exist. Courier simply ignores the corresponding entries and does not display those shares. This means that an `index` file can be used simultaneously on more than one server, even though each server contains only some of the maildir directories.

Courier strictly separates the shared folders available to a user from the user's own IMAP folders. Virtual shared folders are not listed in INBOX, but instead in the #shared.*name_of_share* tree.[1] This prevents mix-ups and name conflicts:

```
#shared.cheffe.Testshare
#shared.cheffe.Holiday
```

But be careful: If the user's login name contains a dot or slash, this destroys the hierarchy of the IMAP namespace when used as a label for folder sharing. Thus, an entry such as

```
linux:/etc/courier/shared # cat index
# Caution: This does *NOT* work
paul.meier   1003 500 /home/paul Maildir/
```

would lead to a shared folder like this:

```
#shared.paul.meier.Testshare
```

The `meier` directory would then be a subfolder of `paul` (instead of `paul.meier` being under `#shared`). Courier tries to solve this problem by replacing each dot and slash with a space (which is permissible in folder names):

```
#shared.paul meier.Testshare
```

The names may no longer be unique in this case. It can also happen that Courier is unable to calculate shared lists properly after such replacements. Large parts of the list will no longer be displayed properly.

Thus, although Courier automatically replaces dots and slashes with spaces in the display name, this replacement can be problematic. Even if the accounts offering shared folders are actually called `paul.meier` or `anna.gerber`, for example, it is advisable to avoid using these two characters in the first column of `index`. Remember that when the `index` file is processed, the important thing is the share name, and not the account names, which can still contain dots.

If you use dots and slashes in your usernames (perhaps because you use complete email addresses for login names), it is a good idea to think of a workaround here and make sure that you have clean labels in the `index` file. `paul.meier` could have the display name `paul-meier`, for example. However, blindly using search-and-replace hacks can run the risk of creating labels that are ambiguous.

---

[1] Filesystem-based shared folders are shown in `shared` and not in `#shared`.

You can also set the IMAP_SHAREDMUNGENAMES parameter to 1 in the configuration file of the imapd. Courier will then replace an invalid . with a \:, and an invalid / with a \;. This may not look nice, but it is a workable solution and therefore worth testing.

Special characters are allowed in IMAP folder names (and in share names). They have to be UTF-8-coded in this file.

Arranging Shared Files

If you are managing a large number of shared folders, the index file containing the shared folders quickly becomes unmanageable, both for the administrator and for the users, to whom the shared folders are displayed in a lengthy list.

In order to avoid this, you can group shared folders and export them into a separate index file. Each of these groups is assigned a special share name of its own that is displayed as an additional hierarchy level.

The main index file index contains the definitions of the group names and references to the index files corresponding to them:

```
groupname   *   indexfilename
```

The asterisk in the second column is a predefined special character and indicates to Courier that this line is not a group definition itself, but gives the name of the file which includes these group definitions. A split index file can contain both:

```
linux:/etc/courier/shared # cat index
employees       *     index-employees
interns         *     index-interns
freelancers     *     index-freelancers
bueroorga    1000 1000 /home/bueroorga Maildir
```

The syntax for permissions in the subfiles is the same as for standard permissions:

```
linux:/etc/courier/shared # cat index-employees
tux          1000 1000 /home/bueroorga Maildir
paul         1000 1000 /home/paul Maildir
geeko        1000 1000 /home/geeko Maildir
```

The shared IMAP folders then have the following hierarchy:

```
#shared.bueroorga.folder
#shared.employees.tux.folder
#shared.employees.tux.folder
#shared.employees.geeko.folder
```

These group definitions are not the same thing as *shared groups*, which we will discuss later. Using the latter, you can ensure that users are unable to see shared folders belonging to groups that they do not belong to. In the groups mentioned above, users in the `employees` group are able to see the shares of users in group `interns` or `freelancers`. Arranging these groups affects the way shared folders appear in the IMAP namespace and makes it possible to assign ACL permissions to groups (see section 10.1.1 on page 154).

Self-Contained Share Groups

If a user can view all share names and IMAP folders in the `index` file, regardless of permissions assigned by other users in the `courierimapacl` files, this can compromise security. The user would then be able to infer the account names from the share permissions, which in turn means that a complete list of users (customers?) is freely available. In addition, the user may be able to tell which users belong to which groups.

This may be irrelevant in a company that has a company-wide address book, but it can be a violation of security in a large organization or an ISP.

Unfortunately, the Courier programmers are refusing to deal with this problem. They claim that it would negatively affect performance if Courier has to parse all `courierimapacl` files. This is rather lame; after all the alternative is *not* using these shared folders at all. This problem will not be dealt with unless someone else writes the patch. ...

Luckily, there is a solution. It is not perfect, but it works. Introduce separate *shared groups* with their own index files by entering a group assignment in the user options (see section 9.12 on page 145). Users are then only able to view the permissions for their own shared groups (their *universe*). However, they will still be able to view all share names and all IMAP folders within the shared group.

Shared groups have another advantage. If the `index` file is large, Courier has to search through a correspondingly large number of directories. This solution is not suitable for several thousand accounts or for overworked servers with many logins. If each shared group has an index file, Courier has to search through far fewer directories.

If, for example, you are managing the email accounts for the three domains `example.com`, `example.net`, and `example.org`, and these belong to different companies and organizations, you could group all users of one domain into a shared group. To do this, set a user option such as `sharedgroup=example.com` for every one of these users. Each user can only belong to *one* shared group.

When a user logs in, Courier determines the `sharedgroup` for that user.

After authentication, the server searches for shared folders in the specific index file for that shared group, instead of searching the global `index` file. The index file for the shared group has a predefined filename, consisting of index and the value of `sharedgroup`. If the `sharedgroup=example.com` option is specified for a user, the file is named `indexexample.com`; for `sharedgroup=developerteam`, the file is named `indexdeveloperteam`.

The index file of the shared group contains the maildir directories and their share names as described in section 10.1.1 on page 156:

```
linux:/etc/courier/shared # cat indexexample.com
info          1000 1000 /mail/example.com/info Maildir/
accounting    1000 1000 /mail/example.com/accounting Maildir/
paul          1000 1000 /mail/example.com/paul.meier Maildir/
geeko         1000 1000 /mail/example.com/geeko Maildir/
```

Every user can only view shared folders for his or her shared group, so it is possible to assign the same share name in different shared groups. The labels `info`, `accounting`, and `paul` are now also permitted for entries in `example.org` accounts:

```
linux:/etc/courier/shared # cat indexexample.org
info          1000 1000 /mail/example.org/info Maildir/
accounting    1000 1000 /mail/example.org/accounting Maildir/
paul          1000 1000 /mail/example.org/paul Maildir/
```

If you do not define the `sharedgroup` option for an account, Courier IMAP will search the global `index` file.

Generating the `index` File Automatically

If you only wish to permit sharing for selected accounts, it makes sense to manage the corresponding `index` files manually. If, however, you wish to permit all or nearly all users to share folders, you can use the `authenumerate` program to generate the `index` file automatically.

`authenumerate` uses the authlib library, which has access to the complete user database, to generate a dump of all user data. You can then redirect this dump to the index file:

```
linux: # authenumerate > /etc/courier/shared/index
```

Unfortunately, almost no documentation exists for this program. It has two call parameters: `-o` tells the program to output the user options for the accounts in the sixth column. This also includes the `sharedgroup`.

`authenumerate -s` lists only those accounts that are permitted to share folders. If the user option `disableshared` is set to 1 for an account, that account is not listed.

Bear in mind that `authenumerate` uses the commands in parameters `MYSQL_ENUMERATE_CLAUSE`, `PGSQL_ENUMERATE_CLAUSE`, and `LDAP_ENUMERATE_FILTER` (see pages 138, 139, and 141) to read out the user data. This command can limit the accounts to be considered or manipulate the data (especially that in the first column).

Automatically Generating Index Files for Shared Groups

If you use shared groups, you require numerous group-specific index files. The `sharedindexsplit` tool can split a global `index` file accordingly. If the index file contains the user options in the sixth column (thanks to `authenumerate -o`), this column will show which user belongs to which shared group. `sharedindexsplit` then automatically prepares a suitable index file for every shared group. You can run the following shell script, for example, as a regular `cron` job:

```
#!/bin/sh
sysconfdir="/etc/courier"
sbindir="/usr/sbin"

# Remove residues from previous run-throughs
rm -rf $sysconfdir/shared.tmp
mkdir $sysconfdir/shared.tmp || exit 1

# Generate temporary index file containing user options
$sbindir/authenumerate -s -o >$sysconfdir/shared.tmp/.tmplist || exit 1

# Split by sharedgroup
$sbindir/sharedindexsplit $sysconfdir/shared.tmp <$sysconfdir/ \
shared.tmp/.tmplist  || exit 1

# Delete temporary file
rm -f $sysconfdir/shared.tmp/.tmplist

# Move the completed files to $sysconf
$sbindir/sharedindexinstall
```

`sharedindexsplit` can also split the shared folders into different index files according to the first *n* characters if you specify this number as the *second* call parameter. It then ignores the `sharedgroup` user option. This is what the shell script would look like:

```
#!/bin/sh
sysconfdir="/etc/courier"
```

10 The Work of a Courier Administrator

```
sbindir="/usr/sbin"

# Remove residues from previous run-throughs
rm -rf $sysconfdir/shared.tmp
mkdir $sysconfdir/shared.tmp || exit 1

# Generate temporary index file containing user options
$sbindir/authenumerate -s >$sysconfdir/shared.tmp/.tmplist || exit 1

# Split by the first character
$sbindir/sharedindexsplit $sysconfdir/shared.tmp 1 <$sysconfdir/ \
shared.tmp/.tmplist   || exit 1

# Delete temporary file
rm -f $sysconfdir/shared.tmp/.tmplist

# Move the completed files to $sysconf
$sbindir/sharedindexinstall
```

The `sharedindexinstall` shell script provided by Courier simply bundles the temporary files and moves them to `/etc/shared`. Make sure that the correct path is specified in `sysconfdir`:[2]

```
linux: # which sharedindexinstall
/usr/sbin/sharedindexinstall
linux: # cat /usr/sbin/sharedindexinstall
#! /bin/sh
# $Id: sharedindexinstall.in,v 1.1 2004/01/11 02:47:33 mrsam Exp $
#
# Copyright 2004 Double Precision, Inc.
# See COPYING for distribution information.
#
# Sample script to safely update shared folder index files.

prefix="/usr"
sysconfdir="/etc/courier"
[...]
```

Subscribing to Shared Folders

Usually IMAP users have to explicitly subscribe to shared folders for their clients to display them (see section 2.2.4 on page 41).

Some email clients, such as KMail (see Figure 10.1), use the IMAP protocol to ask the server for the correct namespace for personal folders (`INBOX.*`) or virtual shared folders (`#shared.*`) in order to display the directories

---

[2] The `prefix` variable was previously used, but it is superfluous in the version used here (1.1 from January 11, 2004), as it is not used in the script.

properly. In that case, you will find the corresponding settings in the IMAP account management.

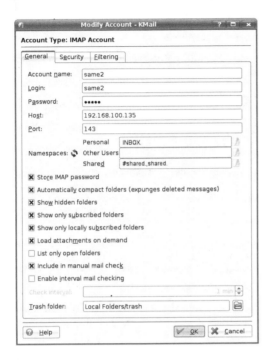

Figure 10.1:
KMail automatically queries the IMAP namespace in order to display the folders properly.

10.1.2 Creating Filesystem-Based Shared Folders

If your users are technically experienced and have shell accounts on the server, you can provide filesystem-based shared folders. In this case, the file access permissions in the maildir directories determine each user's access permissions.

If user `tux` wants to prevent user `geeko` from viewing his maildir, `tux` has to ensure that only he as the owner of the maildir has read and write permissions:

```
tux@linux:~$ ls -lad Maildir/
drwx------  6 tux    users 4096 10. Mar 22:30 Maildir/
```

If he changes the file permissions for his maildir directory or for individual IMAP folders in that directory, other users can access them. You can modify Courier so that it offers the shared maildir directories to other users for subscription via IMAP.

163

A *shareable maildir* is a special maildir with more relaxed access permissions, allowing other users to view it. For this reason, this should not be a user's actual maildir (even though this is technically possible). Instead, a user should create an additional directory in the personal home directory as a *shared maildir*.

Folders in a shareable maildir are called *shared folders*. Other users can subscribe to these folders.

If `tux` wishes to share a folder with colleagues, he uses `maildirmake` to create a separate shareable maildir with open access permissions, without letting other users access his actual maildir. The `-S` parameter tells the program to generate a shareable maildir:

```
tux@linux:~$ maildirmake -S Maildir-Shared
tux@linux:~$ ls -lad Maildir*
drwx------ 7 tux    users 4096 11. Mar 17:31 Maildir
drwxr-xr-x 9 tux    users 4096 11. Mar 17:25 Maildir-Shared
tux@linux:~$
```

The only difference between the maildirs lies in the file permissions. `tux` has now made the shared folder available, and the rest is up to his colleagues.

They can now create a `shared-maildirs` file in their own maildir. This is where they enter the paths to the other available maildirs belonging to other users:

```
geeko@linux:~$ cd Maildir
geeko@linux:~/Maildir$ cat shared-maildir
tux     /home/tux/Maildir-Shared
paul    /home/paul/Maildir2
group   /home/gruppe/Maildir-groupaccess
```

Nothing else needs to be done at file/operating system level. Courier does the rest of the work when somebody subscribes to a folder using the IMAP protocol. When he next logs in, geeko can subscribe to a number of additional folders available in the `shared` namespace.[3] In order to tell them apart, Courier completes the short names of the maildirs in the `shared-maildirs` file:

```
shared.tux.*
shared.paul.*
shared.gruppe.*
```

Courier does all of this in the background using symlinks. To do this, it creates an additional folder named `shared-folders` in geeko's maildir;

---

[3] Virtual shared folders are available from `#shared`.

unlike geeko's normal IMAP folders, this folder does *not* begin with a point.
This shared folder contains the three short names as directories:

```
geeko@linux:~/Maildir$ ls -l
drwx------ 2 geeko users 4096 10. Mar 22:35 courierimapkeywords
-rw-r--r-- 1 geeko users  187 10. Mar 22:19 courierimapuiddb
drwx------ 2 geeko users 4096 10. Mar 22:24 cur
drwx------ 2 geeko users 4096 10. Mar 22:19 new
drwx------ 3 geeko users 4096 11. Mar 17:27 shared-folders
-rw-r--r-- 1 geeko users   27 11. Mar 17:26 shared-maildirs
drwx------ 2 geeko users 4096 11. Mar 19:17 tmp
geeko@linux:~/Maildir$ cat shared-maildir
geeko@linux:~/Maildir/shared-folders$ cd shared-folders
geeko@linux:~/Maildir/shared-folders$ ls -l
drwx------ 6 geeko users 4096 11. Mar 17:27 paul
drwx------ 6 geeko users 4096 11. Mar 17:27 tux
drwx------ 6 geeko users 4096 11. Mar 17:27 group
```

If geeko subscribes to `tux`'s Party folder, Courier creates a maildir named
`tux/Party`. This maildir contains the usual maildir directories `cur`, `new`,
and `tmp`, and also a symlink to `tux`'s actual maildir:

```
geeko@linux:~/Maildir/shared-folders$ ls -l tux/Party
total 24
drwx------ 2 geeko users 4096 11. Mar 5:30:00 PM courierimapkeywords
-rw-r--r-- 1 geeko users  234 11. Mar 5:30:00 PM courierimapuiddb
drwx------ 2 geeko users 4096 11. Mar 5:30:00 PM cur
drwx------ 2 geeko users 4096 11. Mar 5:30:00 PM new
lrwxrwxrwx 1 geeko users   32 11. Mar 17:27 shared -> /home/tux/Maildir-
Shared/.Party
-rw------- 1 geeko users    1 11. Mar 17:30 shared-timestamp
drwx------ 2 geeko users 4096 11. Mar 5:30:00 PM tmp
```

Whenever geeko logs in, Courier compares the contents of `shared/cur` to
those of `cur`; for every file in `tux`'s original directory, it creates a symlink in
geeko's `cur` directory:

```
geeko@linux:~/Maildir/shared-folders$ cd tux/Party
geeko@linux:~/Maildir/shared-folders/tux/Party$ ls -l shared/cur
-rw-r--r-- 1 tux   users 3737 11. Mar 17:30 1173630626.M516761P6734V000
0000000000302I000102C8_6.couriertest,S=3737:2,S
-rw-r--r-- 1 tux   users 3795 11. Mar 17:30 1173630626.M900691P6734V000
0000000000302I000102D0_7.couriertest,S=3795:2,S
-rw-r--r-- 1 tux   users 5052 11. Mar 17:30 1173630627.M359308P6734V000
0000000000302I000102D1_8.couriertest,S=5052:2,S
geeko@linux:~/Maildir/shared-folders/tux/Party$ ls -l cur
total 12
lrwxrwxrwx 1 geeko users 111 11. Mar 17:30 1173630626.M516761P6734V00000
00000000302I000102C8_6.couriertest,S=3737:2, -> /home/tux/Maildir-Shared
```

```
/.groupwrite/cur/1173630626.M516761P6734V00000000000000302I000102C8_6.cou
riertest,S=3737:2,S
lrwxrwxrwx 1 geeko users 111 11. Mar 17:30 1173630626.M900691P6734V00000
00000000302I000102D0_7.couriertest,S=3795:2, -> /home/tux/Maildir-Shared
/.groupwrite/cur/1173630626.M900691P6734V00000000000000302I000102D0_7.cou
riertest,S=3795:2,S
lrwxrwxrwx 1 geeko users 111 11. Mar 17:30 1173630627.M359308P6734V00000
00000000302I000102D1_8.couriertest,S=5052:2, -> /home/tux/Maildir-Shared
/.groupwrite/cur/1173630627.M359308P6734V00000000000000302I000102D1_8.cou
riertest,S=5052:2,S
```

Once this has been done, geeko can treat this IMAP folder like a personal inbox, as long as he has the required file permissions. If tux grants only read permissions, geeko does not have write permissions and may therefore neither delete nor add emails.

Access permissions are defined by the user ID and group ID at system level. The owner of the maildir can only grant read and write permissions for his or her own user group or for all users on the server. It is not possible to grant permissions to individual accounts.

Do not forget that clients may still have to subscribe to these newly available directories.

10.2 Quotas

When asked about the capabilities an IMAP server should have, most administrators name quotas as one of the most important. This is understandable: There is the constant fear that an ever-increasing volume of data will become unmanageable, and too many users treat the technology and infrastructure carelessly. These users often forget that the "couple of GBs" that are unimportant on their personal computer can quickly add up to huge amounts of data on company networks or ISP servers with hundreds or thousands of users; this data is almost unmanageable, and the storage costs in secure environments can be considerable.

On the other hand, it is worth considering whether and how quotas are worth using; sometimes, they do more harm than good. In most cases, the servers have more than enough memory. Quotas are set up to restrict individuals. If everyone *did* use this much space, there would *not* be enough space. This means that emails are preemptively blocked, even though the server could still process them.

Low quota limits also introduce vulnerability to denial-of-service attacks. An account with a restricted quota is flooded on Friday evening, and the problem is only detected on Monday morning, and by then all subsequent legitimate emails (including those from paying customers) have been denied.

As long as the email server has a lot of free memory, lack of quotas is not a problem. Also, with or without quotas, MTAs such as Postfix monitor the free memory and refuse emails before the hard disk is full. Even when quotas have been set, it is still necessary to monitor the server and the free memory: Quotas are usually so generous that the sum of quotas for *all* users exceeds the size of the hard disk, and so offer no protection from filling up server memory.

You can still retain control over disk usage even if you do not use quotas. Simply write a small shell script that determines the inbox size for individual users. All you need to do is enter du -s * in the maildir's main directory; | sort will show the mailboxes with the largest memory consumption. Now you can give a verbal warning and request the user in person to tidy up the directory, or you can automatically send a warning message to the user. This method is often more successful than locking the account, which can create some bad feelings between you and the user.

Another interesting idea is to block SMTP *sending* if a user exceeds his or her quota. You can use the monitoring scripts mentioned to set up this block. While classic quota bounces affect innocent senders, the SMTP block affects the owner of the account. If a user exceeds the quota, he or she is unable to send out new emails.

Not only is this sanction very effective, it also makes sure that users will notice much more quickly when they exceed quotas. If you use traditional quota bounces, users will often only find out that they have exceeded the quota once the senders of (unreceived) emails complain.

The most sensible course is to combine the two quota sanctions: prevent emails from being sent, and only stop accepting new emails once the next limit is reached. This prevents dead accounts from accumulating emails for years.

In the free email sector, quotas can prevent misuse of mailboxes. It makes sense to balance out the benefits and drawbacks: It can be embarrassing for companies if emails are returned to external senders because the employees' mailboxes are full.

10.2.1 Quotas for Courier

Courier permits quotas on two levels. At file level, the server uses the quota capability of the Linux kernel and requires user accounts with an individual user ID. The advantage here is that quotas have nothing to do with the email system; instead, they are enforced because the email server can no longer save new emails, which in turn causes the required bounce.

The maildir++ format permits quotas that Courier can evaluate. Quota files saved in this format also have to be taken into account by the saving Mail

Delivery Agent (MDA); `maildrop`, `procmail`, `local`, and `deliverquota` do this. There are a few MDAs that require an extra patch for these quotas. One of them is the MDA `virtual`, designed by Postfix for MySQL and LDAP users.[4]

Quotas at File Level

As long as you work with real shell accounts rather than with virtual accounts, you can use standard filesystem quotas. As emails are stored under the user ID of the user, they count towards that user's quota. If the quota is exceeded, the system prevents the mail server from saving additional emails.

The mail server usually views such write errors as temporary errors. This means that emails are not lost, but instead remain in the mail server's mail queue; the mail server continues to attempt to deliver them locally to the hard disk. Emails are only returned to the sender as undeliverable if the maximum queuing time has been exceeded. For Postfix, the default of `maximum_queue_lifetime` is five days.

The procedure for setting up quotas at file level differs slightly for different kernel versions, both regarding the names of the commands and the files to be modified. The following version should apply to 2.4.*x* and 2.6.*x*.

First, you have to use the options `usrquota` and `grpquota` to tell the `mount` command that it should activate quotas for the corresponding partition at the user or group level. To do this, complete the appropriate `/etc/fstab` entry:

```
/dev/sda5   /var/maildir   ext3   defaults,usrquota   1   1
```

Please note that the quotas have to be supported by the filesystem. This is the case for Ext2, Ext3, and ReiserFS. After this, you have to remount the partition:

```
linux: # mount -o remount /var/maildir
```

Next, you generate the quota database again so that existing files on all partitions are included if they were mounted using the option `usrquota` or `grpquota`:

```
linux: # quotacheck -avug
```

The top level of the quota partition (in this case, `/var/maildir`) should contain the files `aquota.user` and/or `aquota.group`. For older kernel versions, these files are named `quota.user` and `quota.group`.

[4] See http://vda.sourceforge.net.

10.2 Quotas

Even the best mount options are useless if quotas are deactivated in the kernel. The commands `quotaon` and `quotaoff` switch this function on and off:

```
linux: # quotaon
```

Use the `edquota` command followed by a username to specify the quotas for that user:

```
linux: # edquota geeko
Disk quotas for user geeko (uid 1000):

Filesystem      blocks    soft    hard    inodes    soft    hard
/dev/sda5           74       0       0        23       0       0
```

The second column shows the blocks on this partition currently used by geeko. You can not modify this value, as it is determined by the files stored. The next two columns show the soft and hard limits for the user in blocks. The user may briefly exceed the soft limit, but the hard limit is an absolute restriction.

Like free data blocks, the number of available inodes is limited, so you can also specify quotas for inodes. Column five shows the current consumption, and columns six and seven can be edited and show the soft and hard quotas for inodes.

Simply modify the appropriate columns to change the quotas for a user. 0 means that no quotas have been set. The following example sets a soft limit of 5,000KB and a hard limit of 7,500KB, as the default block size is currently 1,024 bytes.

```
Disk quotas for user geeko (uid 1001):
Filesystem      blocks    soft    hard    inodes    soft    hard
/dev/hda5           74    5000    7500        23       0       0
```

Enter `repquota` to read out all quotas:

```
linux: # repquota -a
*** Report for user quotas on device /dev/sda5
Block grace time: 7days; Inode grace time: 7days
                        Block limits                 File limits
User            used    soft    hard  grace     used  soft  hard  grace
----------------------------------------------------------------------
root        -- 2443081     0       0          99647     0     0
lp          --      55     0       0             18     0     0
mail        --       1     0       0              1     0     0
news        --       1     0       0              6     0     0
uucp        --       1     0       0              2     0     0
```

```
games       --     6993      0      0       179     0     0
man         --     1302      0      0       999     0     0
at          --        1      0      0         3     0     0
wwwrun      --        1      0      0         1     0     0
postfix     --        2      0      0        39     0     0
ntp         --       17      0      0         5     0     0

mdnsd       --        1      0      0         6     0     0
messagebus  --        1      0      0         1     0     0
haldaemon   --        1      0      0         1     0     0
nobody      --        1      0      0         1     0     0
geeko       --       74   5000   7500        23     0     0
```

If your users have shell access to the mail server, they can use the `quota` command to find out the current status:

```
user@linux:~$ quota
Disk quotas for user peer (uid 1001):
    Filesystem  blocks   quota   limit   grace   files   quota   limit   grace
        /dev/hda5    74    5000    7500              23       0       0
```

Quotas through maildir++

Filesystem quotas are often unnecessary, as the maildir format enhanced by Courier contains its own quotas. In addition to the three subdirectories `cur`, `new`, and `tmp`, which are contained in a generic `maildir` directory created by `maildirmake`, there are some Courier-specific files (maildir++ extensions), some of which are used for quotas.

You can use the `maildirmake` call parameter `-q` to activate quotas in an *existing* maildir directory. You can specify a maximum mailbox size in bytes and/or a maximum number of emails: The command `maildirmake -q 10000000S,1000C /path/to/Maildir` sets a quota of approximately 10MB or 10,000,000 bytes (S is short for *size*) and permits up to 1,000 messages (C is short for *count*). The quotas are triggered if one of the two limits is exceeded. As usual, Courier manages the settings in small ASCII files.

```
linux:/home/tux # su tux -c "maildirmake Maildir"
linux:/home/tux # ls -la Maildir
total 20
drwx------  5 tux   users  4096 Jul 28 22:11 .
drwxr-xr-x  8 tux   users  4096 Jul 28 22:11 ..
drwx------  2 tux   users  4096 Jul 28 22:11 cur
drwx------  2 tux   users  4096 Jul 28 22:11 new
drwx------  2 tux   users  4096 Jul 28 22:11 tmp
linux:/home/tux # maildirmake -q 10000000S,1000C Maildir
linux:/home/tux # ls -la Maildir
total 24
```

10.2 Quotas

```
drwx------  5 tux  users  4096 Jul 28 10:12:00 PM .
drwxr-xr-x  8 tux  users  4096 Jul 28 22:11 ..
drwx------  2 tux  users  4096 Jul 28 22:11 cur
-rw-r--r--  1 tux  users    36 Jul 28 22:12 maildirsize
drwx------  2 tux  users  4096 Jul 28 22:11 new
drwx------  2 tux  users  4096 Jul 28 10:12:00 PM tmp
```

You can also create the `maildirsize` file manually for empty maildir directories and edit it at a later stage to change the quota size:

```
linux:/home/tux # cat Maildir/maildirsize
10000000S,1000C
         0           0
```

The `maildirsize` file will look different if the maildir contained emails when the quotas were activated. In this case, `maildirmake` measures the occupied memory and logs this information in the `maildirsize` file.

When new messages are written to the maildir directory, the `maildirsize` file keeps a quota log: The first column contains the changes in occupied memory, and the second column contains the number of new and deleted messages. Courier does not add up the existing values; instead, each software component adds one log line showing how much space and how many emails it has used. Negative values signify that a message has been deleted and the corresponding amount of storage volume has been freed up.

If `tux` has received a few messages in the meantime, the `maildirsize` file would look like this:

```
linux:/home/tux # cat Maildir/maildirsize
10000000S,1000C
         0           0
       523           1
     37909           1
      2039           1
     12976           1
     -2039          -1
```

If a software component wants to check a user's quotas, it reads the valid quota settings from the first line and adds up the values from all other lines. The result shows the occupied memory and the number of files used.

This list naturally increases over time, which means that using this method to calculate quotas would take far too much time once several thousand messages have been received. For this reason, Courier runs through all maildirs from time to time (usually every 15 minutes) and recalculates the `maildirsize` file based on the stored emails. Here is the result after such a file cleanup, when the maildir showed 51,408 bytes in 3 files for `tux`:

```
linux:/home/tux # cat Maildir/maildirsize
10000000S.1000C
     51408             3
```

This quota monitoring method assumes that software components with write access to the maildir understand the `maildirsize` file, process it, and log new emails in it. This means that mail software not only has to be compatible with maildir (which is standard), but also with the maildir++ extensions.

Naturally, Courier is capable of this, but the IMAP server is not the only server with write access to maildirs. The MTA also saves new emails, and if you use shell accounts, even the local email program may access the maildir directly instead of via IMAP—pine, KMail, and other clients can do this. If the `maildirsize` file is not processed during these interactions, quotas can be exceeded without attracting notice.

In principle, this is not a problem, as Courier automatically cleans up the `maildirsize` file, recalculates the quotas using all emails, and collects all the correct data.

One problem remains: The IMAP server is not the most important component for quota monitoring. It can be used to upload emails that increase the data volume, but IMAP sessions usually ensure that messages are deleted and memory is freed up.

The MTA (Postfix, QMail, Exim) is far more important. After all, when quotas are exceeded it is the MTA that has to refuse emails for the account. For this reason, the MTA must recognize and evaluate `maildirsize`, or else the quotas will not be effective. Courier does calculate everything, but who will activate the emergency brake?

10.2.2 Quotas and the MDA

Nearly all MTAs contain their own separate programs that save emails in the filesystem. These programs are Mail Delivery Agents (MDAs). Postfix preferentially uses `local` or `virtual`; the best-known free MDAs are `procmail` (popular for its filters) and `maildrop` (the Courier project MDA). These MDAs are interchangeable.

Not all MDAs support quotas, as this function is not part of the original maildir definition, but is part of the extended maildir++. The free MDAs `local`, `procmail`, and `maildrop` are able to use quotas, whereas `virtual` requires the VDA patch (discussed in the next section).

Check whether the MDA on your MTA can use maildir++ quotas before you use them. You may have to replace the MDA. It is not really important which program saves the file onto the hard disk in the maildir storage format.

Adding Maildir Quotas to `virtual`

Conflicts arise if you need the special capabilities of your original MDA. The Postfix MDA `virtual`, for example, allows user data including maildir paths to be stored in MySQL databases or LDAP directories. `virtual`, however, is not able to use quotas, and often it cannot be replaced with `maildrop`.

Now there is a patch for `virtual`, the VDA patch.[5] You will, however, have to compile Postfix and the `virtual` module yourself. If you do not want to build your own Postfix, you can add a patched `virtual` program to your production system. You can compile this program elsewhere and operate it in *parallel* to the unpatched version in the distribution package, so as not to interfere with the update mechanisms of your distribution. Name the patched version `virtual-quota`, for example, and copy it to the Postfix modules (usually to /usr/lib/postfix). Now change the module call in /etc/postfix/master.cf by replacing the name of the MDA in the line

```
virtual    unix    -    n    n    -    -    virtual
```

with this:

```
virtual    unix    -    n    n    -    -    virtual-quotas
```

The `deliverquota` MDA

The `deliverquota` MDA from the Courier project naturally supports maildir quotas. It expects the email at the standard input; for the call parameter, it requires the absolute or relative path to the directory where the email is to be saved:

```
linux: # cat mail_file | deliverquota /home/tux/Maildir
```

If `deliverquota` serves as an auxiliary program for the MTA, it does not make sense to specify an absolute path to the maildir where the email will be saved, as emails could then only be delivered to one single inbox. Check instead which variable(s) your MTA offers, or use a tilde as placeholder for the home directory.

If you want to have quotas set when the maildir is accessed, `deliverquota` can carry out this task. Simply enter the required quota definition as the last parameter after the maildir path:

```
linux: # deliverquota -c -w 90 ~/Maildir 10000000S,1000C
```

As shown here, the program knows the following call options:

---

[5] See http://vda.sourceforge.net/.

- If you add c (*create*), it will automatically generate any missing maildir directories, and it will even generate parent directories if necessary. This makes a call to `maildirmake` for new users unnecessary, as the first email received will trigger the creation of the maildir.

- `-w percent` will tell `deliverquota` to deliver a quota warning to a user's mailbox as soon as that user has used up more than *percent* of his or her quota limit. You can store this warning as a complete RFC-822 email in /etc/courier/quotawarnmsg, including the mail header and the body. Courier will only update the message ID and the date:

```
linux: # cat /etc/courier/quotawarnmsg
From: Postmaster <postmaster@tux.local>
Reply-To: support@tux.local
To: You;
Subject: Warning: Email quotas exceeded!
Mime-Version: 1.0
Content-Type: text/plain; charset=iso-8859-1
Content-Transfer-Encoding: 7bit

Dear user,

Your mailbox is more than 90% full. Please clean up your mailbox, or
you may be unable to receive new messages.
```

Bear in mind that only 7-bit characters are permitted in the mail header. This means that special characters in the `subject` line are invalid unless they are coded.

`deliverquota` has no interest in your user database; it does not search for the path to the maildir of the recipient, but instead insists on correct call parameters. This has the advantage that `deliverquota` is fairly easy to use as an MDA on different systems, as almost every MTA contains a part in its configuration specifying which program is to save the email. For Postfix, this information is located in the `mailbox_command` parameter in `main.cf`. This parameter is usually empty:

```
linux: # postconf mailbox_command
mailbox_command =
```

At this point we could use `deliverquota` and the call parameters:

```
linux: # postconf -e "mailbox_command = deliverquota -c -w 90 ~/Maildir"
```

As Postfix accepts the user ID corresponding to the mailbox before saving the emails, we can use the tilde (~) to refer to the home directory and thereby specify the maildir path.

Now use a few short test emails to check whether `deliverquota` and your MTA work together properly. Check the following things:

- New emails are recorded in `maildirsize`
- The length of new emails is already coded in their filename by parameter S=

10.3 Building an IMAP Proxy with Courier

Section 3.2 on page 50 discussed whether IMAP proxies are suitable and when. Courier IMAP users have the advantage that they can easily reconfigure their existing IMAP server into a proxy, as all essential questions such as authentication or access to the email storage have already been resolved.

In order to decide where to transfer the client's IMAP connection, Courier evaluates the `mailhost` attribute (see section 9.12 on page 144) when a user logs in. This attribute has to contain the name of the IMAP server that physically contains the IMAP mailbox.

Three parameters are required in the `/etc/courier/imapd` file for the proxy setup:

IMAP_PROXY=1 or POP3_PROXY=1
> These parameters activate the proxy function. Courier searches for the `mailhost` attribute. IMAP_PROXY=0, and POP3_PROXY=0 deactivate the proxy function; the `mailhost` attribute may exist, but it is ignored.

PROXY_HOSTNAME=*hostname*
> If Courier IMAP finds its own hostname in the `mailhost` attribute, it may not transfer the connection (to itself), as this would cause an endless loop. In this case, Courier functions as a normal IMAP server and accesses its local filesystem.
>
> Courier uses the `gethostname()` function to determine its own hostname; `uname -n` will also return this hostname.
>
> If you prefer to specify the name of the IMAP server manually, you can use PROXY_HOSTNAME to do this. This is necessary if the Unix hostname differs from the name stored in the LDAP and Courier is unable to recognize itself.

IMAP_PROXY_FOREIGN=0
> If Courier transfers the IMAP connection to another Courier instance, this setting specifies that Courier does not need to use the IMAP command CAPABILITY to determine the capabilities of the other IMAP server, as it knows its own capabilities. If Courier is to transfer the IMAP connection to some other IMAP software, you should set this parameter to 1.

10.4 Push Instead of Pull: The `IDLE` Command

It is a burden for the mail server if a connected email client searches all IMAP folders for new messages every few minutes. As a large number of clients are constantly connected to the server, this creates constant background activity, and the searches through email folders quickly turn into a basic I/O burden on the hard disk.

The `IDLE` command in the IMAP protocol deals with this problem: The server actively informs the client of changes in the email directories. Unfortunately, not all email clients support it, even though it has a number of benefits:

- The client is informed immediately when a new message is received, instead of finding it during the next routine check made every few minutes.

- It is less work for the server to monitor file changes than for it to let the email client carry out regular searches.

- There is less data traffic (this is why IMAP clients for cell phones in particular support the `IDLE` command).

As new emails are written to the maildir directories by the MTAs/MDAs, Courier is not immediately aware of new emails. For this purpose it can use a *file alteration monitor* such as *FAM*.[6] A prerequisite is that Courier was linked to the FAM during compilation. This is the case for SuSE, for example; SuSE also installs and starts FAM automatically.

Gamin is a second project that claims to be better than the traditional FAM.[7]

Red Hat has already replaced FAM with Gamin. In principle, Courier should work with both tools, as they use identical APIs, according to the Gamin programmers. FAM and Gamin run in the background as daemons; other programs can register directories and files with them, and they will then monitor them for changes and signal when changes occur.

If your distribution allows FAM/Gamin to be used for Courier, you can activate the `IDLE` command in the `IMAP_ENHANCEDIDLE=1` configuration in the imapd file. You should check the following three items:

- Courier has to announce during IMAP login that it supports IDLE. This *capability* should be entered in /etc/courier/imap:

```
IMAP_CAPABILITY="IMAP4rev1 UIDPLUS CHILDREN NAMESPACE THREAD=ORDEREDSU
BJECT THREAD=REFERENCES SORT QUOTA IDLE AUTH=CRAM-MD5 AUTH=CRAM-SHA1"
```

[6] See http://oss.sgi.com/projects/fam/.
[7] See http://www.gnome.org/~veillard/gamin.

10.4 Push Instead of Pull: The IDLE Command

- The `famd` or `gam_server` needs to have been started and must be visible in the process list:

```
linux: # ps ax | grep fam
 2869 ?        Ss    45:21 /usr/sbin/famd -t 240 -T 0 -1 -L
```

- You should also check for communication problems between Courier and FAM/Gamin; they will be visible from the following type of entry in your mail log file:

```
May 28 17:43:10 kjidder couriertcpd: Error: Input/output error
May 28 5:43:11 PM kjidder couriertcpd: Check for proper operation and
configuration
May 28 5:43:11 PM kjidder couriertcpd: of the File Access Monitor daem
on (famd).
```

If you do not have performance problems on your IMAP server, you will not usually need to make any further settings. However, on high-load servers it is advisable to configure FAM to use fewer resources. The following `famd` call parameters are helpful here:

- The FAM daemon terminates by default after five seconds if no client is connected to it. This is not suitable when using it with IMAP servers. Specify `-T 0`; this means that FAM will terminate after 0 seconds (i. e., never).

- If FAM has to monitor an NFS filesystem, it can *not* receive information on file changes from the local Linux kernel. Instead, it uses RPC to connect to the FAM daemon of the NFS server, which then monitors and transfers any changes locally.

  If FAM has not been activated there, the local FAM will check for changes via NFS every few seconds. You can specify this interval using `-t secs`. The default value is 6 seconds, which can result in heavy background activity on busy NFS servers. Usually this parameter is irrelevant, as an FAM daemon typically operates on the NFS server. If you also specify the option `-1`, FAM no longer runs queries via NFS and therefore silently stops operating when the FAM daemon on the NFS server is not running.

- `-L` ensures that FAM accepts only local client queries. This is suitable for the IMAP server, but you should never set `-L` on the NFS server.

You will usually find these configurations in `/etc/famd.conf`. The `idle_timeout` configuration parameter corresponds to `-T`, `nfs_polling_interval` fulfils the same function as `-t`, `no_polling` corresponds to `-1`, and `local_only` is identical to `-L`.

Be careful if you are using SuSE: This distribution contains a `/etc/famd.conf`, but any entries you make have no effect (at least for OpenSuSE 10.2).

Instead, the call parameters are generated from `/etc/sysconfig/fam`, for some strange reason.

10.5 Sending Emails via the IMAP Server

Did you know that IMAP servers can send emails? This function is deactivated by default in Courier. To activate it, simply define a specific outbox folder in `/etc/courier/imapd`:

```
OUTBOX=.Outbox
```

This corresponds to `INBOX.Outbox`; that is, to a subfolder under the inbox, as Courier does not permit directories parallel to the `INBOX` (see section 8.1 on page 110). You should probably use a name other than `Outbox`, as even users unaware of the special meaning of this directory could set up an `outbox` folder, which would then behave in an unexpected manner.

Once you have defined the `OUTBOX` variable, Courier IMAP uses SMTP to send all emails saved in this directory by the client. Courier can add a special X header to specify from which account the email was sent:

```
HEADERFROM=X-IMAP-Sender
```

This results in the following header entry in the sent email:

```
X-IMAP-Sender: tux@linux.local
```

This prevents emails from being sent from an undetectable sender, as the IMAP login name of the sender is added to each outgoing email. You have to judge for yourself whether this is desirable.

For each email in the outbox folder, Courier calls `/usr/bin/sendmail` and transfers the entire email to it. This `sendmail` program contains all well-known MTAs—not only Sendmail, but also Postfix, QMail, and Exim. For this reason, the sending of emails is often controlled from PHP on web servers.

The tool reads the sender and the recipient from the mail header; then the local MTA (installed on the IMAP server) sends the email in the usual fashion.

By default you can only ever send one single email; this is to prevent ricochets when a copying action goes wrong. Imagine if you accidentally moved 20,000 messages from your trash folder to the outbox... You can switch off this safety feature if you add the following line to imapd:

```
OUTBOX_MULTIPLE_SEND=1
```

10.5 Sending Emails via the IMAP Server

This method of sending emails from the IMAP server sounds unusual; indeed, we have only ever used it for test purposes. However, it is not uninteresting. More and more providers, WLAN hotspots, and universities are locking the SMTP port for sending emails. The IMAP outbox solves this problem, as IMAP connections are frequently possible.

In order to use the folder, you should configure the email client so that it temporarily saves emails in the outbox instead of sending them immediately via SMTP. At the same time, you set up a correctly named outbox folder in your IMAP account.

If you can configure your email client to use this new outbox folder as the outbox, the rest will happen automatically. If this does not work, you unfortunately have to drag and drop the messages you wish to send into the outbox folder.

Part III

Cyrus IMAP

Chapter 11

Structure and Basic Configuration

Rumors of the death of the Cyrus IMAP mail server have been greatly exaggerated. For many years it was neglected and developed very little, which led many to consider the project as dead. Four years ago, this changed. The open source project developed by Carnegie Mellon University began to gather momentum.

This mail system is named after Cyrus II (also known as Cyrus the Great), a Persian king who is said to have invented the first postal system in the 6th century.

Cyrus, as it is usually known, grew out of the Andrew mail and bulletin board system, which was developed and used at the university in the early '90s. In the following years the Internet expanded, increasing the requirements for mail systems. The existing bulletin board was no longer enough, and so the Cyrus IMAP project was born.

Cyrus is a system that has grown over time. This is especially noticeable in the configuration files, which often lack consistency, and where options can

11 Structure and Basic Configuration

be switched on and off using a number of values. For more information, see section 12.2 on page 203.

A Cyrus mail server consists of a `master` process and a number of subprocesses. *Subprocesses* are auxiliary programs that control and assist the master process. They are described on page 261. The most important of them are `imapd` (the service for IMAP access), `pop3` for access via POP3, and `lmtpd` and `deliver`, which receive emails from an SMTP server and distribute them to the inboxes.

Figure 11.1 shows the path of an email from delivery by the MTA to delivery to the user's inbox, where it can be accessed using POP3 or IMAP.

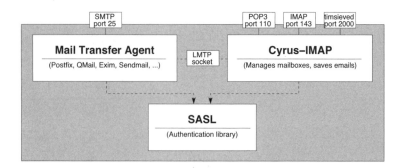

Figure 11.1: Basic structure of a Cyrus mail server

If you want to use a graphical user interface to administer the Cyrus IMAP daemon and the Sieve server, you have to use a web interface such as Webmin[1] with a plugin.[2] Graphical interfaces are also available from Webcyradm[3] and SmartSieve.[4] You should acquaint yourself with the command-line tools and the configuration files, as otherwise you will not get far, even with the help of Webmin & Co.

11.1 Installing Cyrus

The easiest way to install an IMAP server is to use the Cyrus packages of your distribution. In this case, you should be able to rely on the distribution for timely updates in case of security problems. This is why self-compilation, demonstrated in section C.2 on page 325, has considerable advantages.

The packages described here as *optional* contain program modules that you can install if you require them. The distributions do differ in the way they

[1] See http://www.webmin.com/.
[2] See http://www.tecchio.net/webmin/cyrus/.
[3] See http://www.web-cyradm.org/.
[4] See http://smartsieve.sourceforge.net/.

split the packages. For example, only Debian allows you to choose not to install the POP3 server service. SuSE and Red Hat automatically install this service, and you cannot individually deselect it when selecting the packages to install.

11.1.1 OpenSuSE/SuSE Linux Enterprise Server (SLES)

On SuSE distributions, Cyrus SASL is usually already installed from the `cyrus-sasl` package as the standard authentication service. You only have to choose the mechanisms and methods it should support by installing the required packages from the following selection:

- `cyrus-sasl-crammd5` permits challenge-response authentication using the HMAC-MD5-MAC algorithm from RFC 2195 (optional).

- `cyrus-sasl-digestmd5` permits digest-MD5 authentication according to RFC 2831; this method is less susceptible to chosen-plaintext attacks[5] than CRAM-MD5, permits the use of external authentication servers, and optimizes the authentication for clients that have recently logged on (optional).

- `cyrus-sasl-plain` permits cleartext authentication (optional, but required for RFC-compatible servers).

- SASL uses `cyrus-sasl-gssapi` to support the *Generic Security Services Application Programming Interface (GSSAPI)*,[6] a generic API for client-server authentication used specifically in connection with Kerberos (optional).

- `cyrus-sasl-otp` enables one-time passwords (optional).

- `cyrus-sasl-saslauthd` provides the SASL authentication service for Cyrus (optional; see section 13.2.1 on page 212).

- `cyrus-sasl-sqlauxprop` contains the SQL plugin for the `auxprop` SASL authentication module (optional; see section 13.2.2 on page 213).

You require the following packages for the IMAP server itself:

- `cyrus-imapd` provides the POP3 and IMAP server services.

- `perl-Cyrus-IMAP` contains Perl modules required by the additional tools described in section 15.2 on page 263.

[5] See http://en.wikipedia.org/wiki/Chosen_plaintext_attack.
[6] See http://www.faqs.org/faqs/kerberos-faq/general/section-84.html.

- `perl-Authen-SASL-Cyrus` installs Perl modules that are required for controlling SASL using custom Perl scripts (optional).

- `perl-Cyrus-SIEVE-managesieve` provides the `timsieved` Sieve implementation described in section 14.6 on page 240 (optional).

11.1.2 Fedora Core/Red Hat

Before installation, check whether the `imap` package is already installed. This deals with the UW-IMAP server. This service cannot be operated at the same time as the Cyrus IMAP server, so you have to uninstall it if it is there. These are the other packages:

- `cyrus-imapd`

- `cyrus-imap-utils`

- `cyrus-sasl`

- `perl-Cyrus`

- `cyrus-sasl-plain` (optional)

The last package in this list enables cleartext authentication, which you should only use in conjunction with an SSL tunnel.

A source RPM of development version 2.3.8, which you can build in Red Hat, Fedora, and CentOS, is available from http://www.invoca.ch/pub/packages/cyrus-imapd/. However, the distributor does not provide updates and bug fixes for this RPM.

11.1.3 Debian

Debian-DEB package management permits the installation of Cyrus versions 1.5, 2.0, and 2.2 as alternatives. The most up-to-date version, 2.2, is recommended for new installations. Please also note that the system will usually already contain a mail server, the UW IMAP daemon. You must uninstall this before installing Cyrus.

You require the following packages to operate a Cyrus IMAP server in Debian:

- `cyrus-admin-2.2`

- `cyrus-clients-2.2`

- `cyrus-common-2.2`

- `cyrus-imapd-2.2`

- `cyrus-murder-2.2` (optional; if you want to set up a Cyrus cluster, see page 281)

- `cyrus-nntpd-2.2` (optional, if you want to integrate news group services)

- `cyrus-pop3d-2.2` (optional, if you want to offer POP3)

11.2 The Cyrus Hierarchy and Permissions System

The Cyrus IMAP server is organized hierarchically: The email directories, access control via access control lists (ACLs), and storage space restriction quotas are all organized in hierarchies. Any changes to the configuration of a parent directory will automatically affect the descendant directories.

At the filesystem level, every inbox and any other folder is a directory, and every email is a file in that directory. These files are numbered sequentially. Bear this simple principle in mind, and you will soon know how to administer your email accounts.

Let's take user `paul`'s mail directory as an example. When his mailbox is set up, he is automatically assigned an inbox corresponding to a standard directory format, here `/var/spool/imap/user/paul/`. User paul then creates the additional subdirectories `sent`, `draft`, `trash`, and a subdirectory `folders` containing the folders `important` and `unimportant`, in order to organize his emails. At the filesystem level, his inbox now looks like this:

```
linux: #  ls -li /var/spool/imap/user/paul/
115656 -rw------- 1 cyrus mail 3408 Jun 13 13:29 cyrus.cache
115476 -rw------- 1 cyrus mail  184 Jun 10 13:27 cyrus.header
115650 -rw------- 1 cyrus mail  376 Jun 13 13:29 cyrus.index
131128 drwx------ 2 cyrus mail 4096 Jun 13 08:37 folders
115164 drwx------ 2 cyrus mail 4096 Jun 13 08:37 sent
115164 drwx------ 2 cyrus mail 4096 Jun 13 08:37 trash
115164 drwx------ 2 cyrus mail 4096 Jun 13 08:37 drafts
linux: #  ls -li /var/spool/imap/user/paul/folders/
115164 drwx------ 2 cyrus mail 4096 Jun 13 08:37 important
115164 drwx------ 2 cyrus mail 4096 Jun 13 08:37 unimportant
```

When you specify a quota for the directory `user/paul/folders`, this affects the folders `user/paul/folders/important` and `user/paul/folders/unimportant`.

The configuration data of the IMAP server is distributed into two different files. The `/etc/cyrus.conf` file contains the basic settings for the services involved in email delivery. This is where the IMAP and POP3 services are activated and where you specify paths for certain sockets, for example.

The `/etc/imapd.conf` file affects the special functions of the Cyrus server. It contains, among other things, the global values for email and Sieve directories; you also define how virtual domains and SSL certificates are handled, and you specify the Cyrus administrator here.

The interaction with the MTA is specified by the MTA's configuration file(s); in Postfix, these are `/etc/postfix/main.cf` and `/etc/cyrus.conf`. This is discussed in more detail in the following section and in section 14.8 on page 254.

The working directory for Cyrus is located in `/var/spool/imap/`. This is where it creates the users' mailboxes by default. Cyrus stores the emails in the user directories and numbers them sequentially; each email is stored in its own file. The benefit of this method is that an error in the filesystem will only destroy a single message instead of the entire mailbox.

The `/var/lib/imap/` file contains the mailbox index databases and a number of administration files, including status information on the current status of individual mail directories. This dual structure is designed to improve performance when accessing mailboxes, especially when they contain large files or a large number of small emails. These two directories are described in more detail on page 275.

11.3 Features and Functions

Like Courier, Cyrus supports *shared folders*. Using ACLs, it is possible for a mail user to share individual mailbox folders or entire mailboxes with other users or the public; email clients can be used to subscribe to these folders. You can also use these ACLs to assign explicit permissions for individual directories or entire mailboxes.

You can specify memory restrictions through quotas; these can apply in general to all newly generated mailboxes or to all mailboxes, and you can even specify quotas individually for each subdirectory. However, you have to take into account the directory hierarchy. Every subdirectory's quota depends on the quota of the parent directory. However, it is possible to assign more memory to a subdirectory than to its parent directory.

By the way, Cyrus also allows you to display a quota message to users when a certain utilization level is reached, which can be specified in percentages or kilobytes. For more information, see section 14.1.1 on page 226.

When a new mailbox is created, the administrator can assign it in a standard partition or a dedicated directory, or even store it on an individual storage device. The documentation always refers to these as *mail parti-*

tions, whether they are physical partitions or directories. For more information, see section 14.5 on page 239.

Cyrus uses the Cyrus SASL library to authenticate mailbox users.[7] Most distributions contain the required package `cyrus-sasl` and also use it for other services. Cyrus SASL is complicated but versatile, and it implements a large number of authentication mechanisms. Use the option `sasl_pwcheck_method` in the configuration file `/etc/imapd.conf` to specify which of these mechanisms should be used. You can choose from the modules `saslauthd`, `auxprop`, and `authdaemond`. These in turn provide a number of authentication plugins and encryption mechanisms, such as Digest-MD5. Cyrus can use these to call on a number of different data sources.

By default, passwords are transferred in cleartext, but Cyrus naturally enables encryption of login data. The following mechanisms are available, depending on the authentication module used:

- Login, plain (cleartext)

- Digest-MD5 (encrypted)

- CRAM-MD5 (encrypted)

- Kerberos (encrypted)

Section 13.2 on page 211 deals with authentication in more detail.

Users can use the Sieve filter system to make very detailed configuration settings for their mailbox. They can also have emails moved automatically to other directories, set out-of-office notices, and specify other email filters. Sieve email filters directly affect all incoming emails. When Cyrus receives an email, it checks the Sieve definitions and then sorts, answers, or deletes the email. For more information, see section 14.6 on page 240. Cyrus also automatically detects duplicate emails from their ID number and prevents them from being delivered a second time.

Cyrus is innately capable of administering mailboxes for virtual domains. To do this, it simply incorporates the fully qualified domain name (FQDN) when creating the users' mailboxes.

In addition, it is possible to specify domain administrators who can access only the mailboxes within their domain. This function is described in detail in section 14.3.3 on page 237.

---

[7] *SASL* is short for *Simple Authentication and Security Layer*.

11.4 Quick Start

In addition to the Cyrus IMAP daemon, you should also install the following software, which will enable you to operate the Cyrus IMAP server properly:

Cyrus SASL
: Without the SASL library, users cannot authenticate themselves with the IMAP server or receive emails. Cyrus SASL consists of plugins that provide the authentication methods and encryption mechanisms.

    If necessary, you can install these at a later stage, for example, after reading section 13.2 on page 211. In order to enable authentication, `cyrus-sasl-saslauthd` is usually installed by default.

    SuSE installs Cyrus SASL, as it is required for authentication by other services, such as Postfix.

`perl-Cyrus-SIEVE-managesieve` (optional)
: Perl modules required for the operation and control of Sieve email filters.

Perl
: A number of auxiliary programs for Cyrus, such as `arbitronsort.pl` (see section 15.3 on page 269) or `convert-sieve.pl` (see section 15.3 on page 269) are written in Perl. A Perl interpreter is required if you wish to use these modules.

OpenSSL (optional)
: We highly recommend installing OpenSSL for encrypted transmission of user data and emails via TLS/SSL.

MySQL/LDAP/BerkeleyDB (optional)
: You will require a database suitable for administering your mail user information. This database can run on an extra server and does not need to be installed locally.

    These data sources have to be integrated individually. For information on specifying query parameters, see section 13.3 on page 215.

    You can also use Unix system accounts or the `sasldb2` minidatabase provided by Cyrus SASL for user administration.

Postfix or another MTA
: Cyrus requires a separate mail transfer agent to receive the emails that are to be sorted into the IMAP mailboxes. We discuss (and recommend) Postfix; on page 191, we will describe the interaction between Cyrus and Postfix. Postfix is installed on the same computer as Cyrus. However, you can also run the MTA on separate hardware.

The following descriptions are based on the current stable Cyrus version 2.2.12. Experience has shown that they also apply to all other 2.*x* versions.[8]

Select the ports you require from the following list and release them in the firewall protecting the server:

- Select port 25 (SMTP) if the MTA runs on the same computer as Cyrus. For external MTAs, the SMTP port of the IMAP server should only accept packages from the MTA computer.
- Select port 110 (unencrypted POP3 or encrypted POP3) if the TLS tunnel is initiated using STARTTLS.
- Select port 143 (unencrypted IMAP or encrypted IMAP) if the TLS tunnel is initiated using STARTTLS.
- Select port 993 to use IMAP via SSL/TLS.
- Select port 995 to use POP3 via SSL/TLS.

Before Cyrus can provide emails to its users, you first have to set up the interaction between Cyrus and the MTA. After all, the newly installed Postfix and Cyrus servers are not yet aware of each other. Postfix receives emails via SMTP and transfers them to Cyrus for one or more domains; Cyrus then sorts the emails into the user mailboxes.

The most simple and reliable path is an LMTP socket, which both programs can use to communicate using the *Local Message Transport Protocol* (see page 18). A *socket* is a file that only exists while the programs are running, which Postfix uses in this case to transfer the received emails to Cyrus. This requires that both services run on the same system.

If you want to use the LMTP socket, you first have to modify the appropriate configuration files for both mail services. First, you have to explain to Cyrus where the socket for communication between the programs is located. Enter the full path (/var/spool/postfix/public/lmtp in this example) in /etc/cyrus.conf:

```
lmtpunix    cmd='lmtpd' listen='/var/spool/postfix/public/lmtp' prefork=1
```

Use `lmtpunix` to specify that this is a Unix-specific LMTP socket. The option `cmd` specifies how to call the service responsible for the socket, and `listen` tells `lmtpd` the path to the socket. The value following `prefork` specifies the number of Cyrus processes; you do not need to change the default setting.[9] If your email server is very busy and reacts slowly, you can

---

[8] There is an overview of the most up-to-date versions at http://cyrusimap.web.cmu.edu/downloads.html#imap.

[9] The `prefork` value 1 is the default in SuSE.

experiment by increasing this value. In that case, you should also increase the working memory.

Cyrus uses the socket given in this example to "visit" Postfix in its working environment under /var/spool/postfix/. This is generally the best choice of an interface; if Postfix runs from a chroot environment, it cannot leave its working directory and is therefore unable to communicate with Cyrus in a different manner.

Now we have to tell Postfix to be responsible for emails addressed to the required domain(s) and to operate as a relay. To do this, go to the configuration file /etc/postfix/main.cf and define the lookup table relay_domains that contains these domains:

```
relay_domains = hash:/etc/postfix/relay_domains
```

If you want Postfix to accept emails for the domain example.net, enter the following in this file (/etc/postfix/relay_domains in this case):

```
example.net    lmtp:unix:public/lmtp
```

This entry specifies that Postfix should accept emails for domain example.net. At the same time, specify the transport path in the second column: Here, we first define the method lmtp:unix (Unix LMTP socket) and use public/lmtp to specify the path and name of the socket that Postfix should open. This lets Postfix know where to send the emails it receives. Observe here that the default working directory of the Postfix master process is /var/spool/postfix/. This is why you only enter the subdirectory public/lmtp, and not the entire path /var/spool/postfix/public/.

/etc/postfix/relay_domains now contains not only the domain, but also the information on how to transport emails to this domain. Now complete the transport_maps entry in the /etc/postfix/main.cf file so that Postfix will actually use this information:

```
transport_maps = hash:/etc/postfix/transport,hash:/etc/postfix/relay_domains
```

Make sure that you add only the relay_domains file as the transport map. Conversely, do not enter the transport file into the lookup table relay_domains.

If you do this, every manual routing entry in transport causes Postfix to accept emails for this domain without checking, which means that it is an open relay. For this reason, you should continue to maintain *two* files: transport should contain all routing rules for other domains, and relay_domains should contain the domains for which Postfix should accept emails for Cyrus; both should contain the appropriate routing rules.

```
linux:~ # postmap /etc/postfix/relay_domains
```

ensures that Postfix can use the file. The command converts the text file you just edited into a database format that Postfix can read.

Once you have rebooted Cyrus and reloaded Postfix, they can communicate via the LMTP socket. `/var/spool/postfix/public/` should now contain the socket file:

```
linux: # ls -li /var/spool/postfix/public/
total 0
114777 srw-rw-rw- 1 postfix postfix 0 May  9 20:17 cleanup
114815 srw-rw-rw- 1 postfix postfix 0 May  9 20:17 flush
114763 srwxrwxrwx 1 root    root    0 May 22 11:40 lmtp
114774 prw--w--w- 1 postfix postfix 0 May 22 13:08 pickup
114794 prw--w--w- 1 postfix postfix 0 May 22 13:05 qmgr
114848 srw-rw-rw- 1 postfix postfix 0 May  9 20:17 showq
```

If the file is not there, it can mean one of two things: One of the services is not running, or you have entered the wrong path to the socket in one of the configuration files.

Even if everything seems okay so far, some distributions can still cause problems. SuSE, among others, has recently begun to install the AppArmor protection program by default. This program also monitors the way that Postfix behaves. It compares the current server behavior to a predefined profile. AppArmor views the behavior of Postfix as abnormal if it attempts to open the newly created file `relay_domains`. The kernel blocks any attempt by Postfix to open this newly created file with `Permission denied` and logs this in the syslog.

To solve this problem, you have to add rules to the AppArmor configuration that permit Postfix to read this file; unfortunately, describing how to accomplish this task would exceed the scope of this book. Naturally, you can (temporarily) deactivate AppArmor or even remove it completely.

The settings you have made so far cause Postfix to accept all emails for the specified domain and transfer them to Cyrus. Cyrus then checks whether the mailbox of the addressee actually exists. If it does not, Cyrus returns a bounce email to Postfix, and Postfix attempts to deliver it to the sender.

In order to prevent unnecessary load on the email system, the receiving MTA should check the entire email address and refuse to process the email if this is appropriate. This can be achieved with shared user management for Cyrus and Postfix (e. g., with LDAP or MySQL) and with changes to the configuration of the MTA. Go to the `relay_recipient_maps` parameter in Postfix and list all the email addresses for which the MTA should accept emails.

11.4.1 Authentication and Mailboxes

At this point, you should consider how users will be authenticated. The simplest way to separate the email users from the system accounts is to use the minidatabase `sasldb2`. New mail users and their passwords are then listed in a Berkeley database, which Cyrus SASL can query. To use this method, set the authentication method to `auxprop` in the `/etc/imapd.conf` file:

```
sasl_pwcheck_method: auxprop
```

Cyrus SASL now uses the `auxprop` module, which queries the `sasldb2` database by default.

Use the `saslpasswd2` tool to enter user information in the database. This tool requests the passphrase for access to the IMAP server; the phrase may also contain spaces.

First, create the main user `cyrus`; this user is the Cyrus administrator because the value `admins: cyrus` in the `/etc/imapd.conf` file specifies this. Do not confuse this user with the Unix system account `cyrus`. If you prefer, you can also specify a different user. The following example will use the default administrator `cyrus`.

```
linux: # saslpasswd2 cyrus
Password: password for cyrus
Again (for verification): password for cyrus
```

In order to enable Cyrus to read the database, you have to specify the *Unix system user* as the owner of the database, as the server uses the permissions of that user to operate:

```
linux: #  chown cyrus:mail /etc/sasldb2
```

If you forget to do this, the Cyrus administration tool `cyradm` (see section 15.4 on page 271) will return a very cryptic error message during login, which does not mention the problem directly:

```
linux: #  cyradm -auth login localhost -user username
IMAP Password: password for username
          Login failed: user not found at /usr/lib/perl5/vendor_perl
/5.8.8/x86_64-linux-thread-multi/Cyrus/IMAP/Admin.pm line 118
cyradm: cannot authenticate to server with login as username
```

Now, create a small number of user accounts for the initial tests:

```
linux: # saslpasswd2 geeko
Password: secret
Again (for verification): secret
linux: # saslpasswd2 horst
Password: more secret
Again (for verification): more secret
linux: # saspasswd2 paul
Password: most secret
Again (for verification): most secret
```

Now you still need the mailboxes for the individual users. Use the `cyradm` program to create and administer them. Use the following call to log on as an administrator in the command interface and then create the inboxes for the three test users:

```
linux: # cyradm -auth login localhost -user cyrus
IMAP Password: password for cyrus

localhost> cm user.geeko
localhost> cm user.horst
localhost> cm user.paul
localhost> exit
```

At the filesystem level, the new inboxes are located in `/var/spool/imap/user/`. This is defined by the entry `partition-default: /var/spool/imap` in the file `/etc/imapd.conf`. You can modify this path to suit your requirements, and even specify multiple mail partitions, as described in section 14.5 on page 239.

11.4.2 Tests

The simplest way to test whether Cyrus and Postfix work together correctly is to use `telnet` from the command line. If you use this method to deliver an email, you will see any possible errors immediately. Ideally, you should also run `tail -f /var/log/mail` at the same time to track the receipt and delivery of the email.

```
user@linux:$ telnet localhost 25
Trying 127.0.0.1...
Connected to localhost.
Escape character is '^]'.
220 linux.example.net ESMTP Postfix
HELO mail.example.com
250 mail.example.net
MAIL FROM: <test@example.com>
250 Ok
RCPT TO: <geeko@example.net>
```

```
250 Ok
DATA
354 End data with <CR><LF>.<CR><LF>
Subject: A little test email

test test test
.
250 Ok: queued as 46201188B612
quit
221 Bye
```

On the server side, the file /var/log/mail should contain something like this:

```
Apr 26 19:29:45 linux postfix/smtpd[12491]: connect from localhost[127.0
.0.1]
Apr 26 7:30:06 PM linux postfix/smtpd[12491]: 46201188B612: client=local
host[127.0.0.1]
Apr 26 7:30:14 PM linux postfix/cleanup[12548]: 46201188B612: message-id
=<20060426172956.46201188B612@mail.example.de>
Apr 26 7:30:14 PM linux postfix/qmgr[12458]: 46201188B612: from=<test@ex
ample.com>, size=349, nrcpt=1 (queue active)
Apr 26 19:30:14 linux postfix/lmtp[12581]: 46201188B612: to=<geeko@examp
le.net>, relay=public/lmtp[public/lmtp], delay=18, status=sent (250 2.1.5
 Ok)
Apr 26 7:30:14 PM linux postfix/qmgr[12458]: 46201188B612: removed
```

This contains an exact log of the progress of the telnet connection, showing the receipt and delivery of the email: The localhost computer delivers a message created by user account test@example.com and addressed to recipient geeko@example.net. The local Postfix next accepts this message and transfers it to the email server via the LMTP socket; this is confirmed by status=sent (250 2.1.5 Ok). If you entered the wrong recipient or have not created the target mailbox, you will see a log message like this:

```
Sep  3 11:21:38 linux postfix/smtpd[10476]: connect from localhost[127.0
.0.1]
Sep  3 11:22:18 AM linux postfix/smtpd[10476]: 4D49B1C187: client=localh
ost[127.0.0.1]
Sep  3 11:22:23 linux postfix/cleanup[10487]: 4D49B1C187: message-id=<20
070903092218.4D49B1C187@mail.heinlein-support.de>
Sep  3 11:22:23 linux postfix/qmgr[6383]: 4D49B1C187: from=<test@example
.com>, size=368, nrcpt=1 (queue active)
Sep  3 11:22:23 linux postfix/lmtp[10488]: 4D49B1C187: to=<achim@example
.com>, relay=mail.heinlein-support.de.de[public/lmtp], delay=17, delays=
17/0.02/0.02/0.19, dsn=5.1.1, status=bounced (host mail.heinlein-support
.de.de[public/lmtp] said: 550-Mailbox unknown.  Either there is no mailb
ox associated with this 550-name or you do not have authorization to see
 it. 550 5.1.1 User unknown (in reply to RCPT TO command))
Sep  3 11:22:23 linux postfix/cleanup[10487]: 8C2001C1AC: message-id=<20
```

```
070903092223.8C2001C1AC@mail.heinlein-support.de.de>
Sep  3 11:22:23 linux postfix/qmgr[6383]: 8C2001C1AC: from=<>, size=2548
, nrcpt=1 (queue active)
Sep  3 11:22:23 linux postfix/bounce[10490]: 4D49B1C187: sender non-deli
very notification: 8C2001C1AC
Sep  3 11:22:23 linux postfix/qmgr[6383]: 4D49B1C187: removed
Sep  3 11:22:23 linux postfix/lmtp[10488]: 8C2001C1AC: to=<test@example.
com>, relay=mail.heinlein-support.de.de[public/lmtp], delay=0.03, delays
=0.01/0/0/0.02, dsn=5.1.1, status=bounced (host mail.heinlein-support.de
[public/lmtp] said: 550-Mailbox unknown.  Either there is no mail
box associated with this 550-name or you do not have authorization to se
e it. 550 5.1.1 User unknown (in reply to RCPT TO command))
Sep  3 11:22:23 linux postfix/qmgr[6383]: 8C2001C1AC: removed
Sep  3 11:22:24 AM linux postfix/smtpd[10476]: disconnect from localhost
[127.0.0.1]
```

The delivery attempt ended in the `removed` status, which means that the email was removed and not delivered. Instead, a bounce message was returned to the sender.

If you did everything properly, the test email can be viewed in the mailbox of user geeko@example.net. Take a look at the mailbox directory to confirm this:

```
linux: #   ls -li /var/spool/imap/user/geeko/
total 44
115481 -rw------- 1 cyrus mail 1529 May 12 17:35 1.
115232 -rw------- 1 cyrus mail 5068 May 22 13:40 cyrus.cache
115144 -rw------- 1 cyrus mail  184 Nov 23 23:43 cyrus.header
115218 -rw------- 1 cyrus mail  376 May 22 13:40 cyrus.index
```

The file 1. contains the first email received in this mailbox. In order to view it with an email client, the following data is required for IMAP user geeko:

- The FQDN of the IMAP server (`localhost` is sufficient for local access)
- The username geeko
- The password `secret`

Even if email collection now works for the email client, the email server is still rather rudimentary. You need to change this. After all, what good is an email server that cannot provide additional functions, safeguards, and comfort?

Chapter 12

A Closer Look at the Configuration Files

The Cyrus server is controlled by two files: `cyrus.conf` and `imapd.conf`. The first file controls the behavior of the auxiliary programs delivered with Cyrus, which assist the mail servers and are used by Cyrus for a number of other tasks. The second configuration file controls the behavior of the Cyrus master process, which in turn influences Cyrus subprocesses such as Sieve and `notifyd`. This means that `imapd.conf` controls `imapd` as well as `master` and the subprocesses.

12.1 /etc/cyrus.conf

This configuration file consists of three sections enclosed in curly brackets: `START{}`, `SERVICES{}`, and `EVENTS{}`. Many distributions, such as Open-

SuSE and SLES, contain a configuration like that described below, whereas you have to create it manually for other distributions (such as Debian and Gentoo). Use a hash mark (#) as a comment character to deactivate entries that you do not need.

12.1.1 The `START{}` Section

The `START{}` section specifies services and auxiliary programs that are to be run when Cyrus is started and before the (email) services are started. The `recover` entry `ctl_cyrusdb -r`, for example, defines a command that tidies the Cyrus database when the program is started and restores it in case of a crash:

```
START {
  # Do not delete this entry
  recover       cmd='ctl_cyrusdb -r'

  # Only required when using idled for IDLE
  # (default: activated)
  idled         cmd='idled'
}
```

`idled` informs the email client of changes to the user mailbox, for example, when a new message is received. In order to do this, it uses the IDLE IMAP command. You can deactivate this service, but then the email client has to query the mailbox at regular intervals, regardless of whether it contains new messages. For more information on this subject, see section 10.4 on page 176.

12.1.2 The `SERVICES{}` Section

This section defines services that Cyrus uses to communicate with the outside world. You can specify, for example, which services should receive, send, or filter emails. Use the `listen` option to specify a port or socket that a service should use to exchange data.

```
SERVICES {
    imap        cmd='imapd' listen='imap' prefork=1
 #  imaps       cmd='imapd -s' listen='imaps' prefork=1
    pop3        cmd='pop3d' listen='pop3' prefork=1
 #  pop3s       cmd='pop3d -s' listen='pop3s' prefork=1
    sieve       cmd='timsieved' listen='sieve' prefork=1

 # You require one of the two LMTP types to receive emails from the MTA
 #  lmtp        cmd='lmtpd' listen='lmtp' prefork=0
    lmtpunix    cmd='lmtpd' listen='/var/spool/postfix/lmtp' prefork=1
```

```
# Only required if the notifyd notification service is used
# (The contents of the following two commented-out lines should be
# in one single line.)
#   notify  cmd='notifyd' listen='/var/lib/imap/socket/notify' proto='udp'
#   prefork=1
}
```

The `imap` entry starts the IMAP service used by the email client to manage the mailboxes. The service is to wait for client queries on the `imap` port (i.e., port 143) and should only run on one single instance (`prefork=1`). The same applies to `imaps`, with the difference that `imapd` uses the `-s` switch to create a secure SSL/TLS connection. For this purpose, you have to configure Cyrus with TLS/SSL as described in section 13.1 on page 208. The entries for unencrypted and encrypted POP3 access have the same structure, but they use the `pop3` command instead of the `imapd` command. `sieve` starts the `timsieved` email filter service, which is discussed in detail in section 14.6 on page 240.

`lmtp` defines the service that accepts emails from the MTA. It can do this on the `lmtp` port or the `lmtp` socket. If the socket is used, the service is started with `lmtpunix`. If you run LMTP via a port, you first have to define it in the `/etc/services` file, as there is no predefined port for LMTP. Port 24 is the port designed for this purpose, so the additional entry in `/etc/services` should look like this:

```
linux: # cat /etc/services
[...]
lmtp               24/tcp     any private mail system
lmtp               24/udp     any private mail system
[...]
```

Once activated, the `notify` entry calls the Cyrus information service (see section 14.7 on page 252), which notifies the user or administrator when messages are received in a mailbox. The data protocol is set to `udp` for this service.

If you want to test Cyrus and another email server simultaneously on the same computer, you can replace the standard ports `pop3`, `pop3s`, `imap`, and `imaps` with other port numbers or names (as defined in the `/etc/services` file) after the `listen` attribute.

12.1.3 The EVENTS{} Section

The last section of the configuration file lists services and tools that are executed at regular intervals by default. These are mainly services that carry out regular maintenance tasks. This area could also be described as the "crontab" for Cyrus. These are the standard Cyrus maintenance programs that are entered here:

```
EVENTS {
  # Always required
  checkpoint    cmd='ctl_cyrusdb -c' period=30

  # Only required if you want to activate the suppression of duplicate
  # emails
  delprune      cmd='cyr_expire -E 3' at=0400

  # Only required if the TLS cache should be deleted regularly
  tlsprune      cmd='tls_prune' at=0400

  # Only comment out the following entry if Cyrus
  # should regularly delete old messages for EVERY (!) user. In
  # this example, the ipurge service is called every 60 minutes and then
  # deletes all messages older than 30 days.
  # 'man 8 ipurge' provides more details on this service

  # cleanup     cmd='ipurge -d 30 -f' period=60
}
```

The `ctl_cyrusdb` command after `checkpoint` checks the Cyrus index databases regularly (every 30 minutes in this example) and attempts to remove any problems (thanks to option `-c`).

The `delprune` entry uses the `cyr_expire` command to prevent duplicate emails from being delivered (in our example, this is done every day at 4 AM). An email could be duplicated, for example, because the sender has sent it both to the list address *and* Cc:'d it to the user's personal address. The `-E 3` switch in the example above ensures that only entries older than 3 days are affected.

Cyrus can "remember" TLS sessions so that it does not need to create a new TLS encryption for every contact of that same client. The `tls_prune` command entered after `tlsprune` cleans the TLS session cache, if it is in use, at the time specified by `at` (every morning at 4 AM in our example).

The `ipurge` command in the `cleanup` entry automatically deletes all emails at specified intervals (every 60 minutes in our case). The `-d 30` option in the example above ensures that only entries older than 30 days are affected. You can also filter emails by size in bytes (`-b`), kilobytes (`-k`), and megabytes (`-m`), with each switch followed by a space and the desired value. The `-f` switch means that emails are deleted not only from the inbox, but also from all email directories underneath the inbox. You can use the `-i` option to invert the specified filter value: thus, the `-i -d 30` option only affects emails *newer* than 30 days. You should only activate the `cleanup` entry if you and your users require this cleanup, as emails cannot be restored once they have been deleted.

12.2 `/etc/imapd.conf`

The IMAP server's main configuration file contains key-value pairs separated by a colon, for example, `configdirectory: /var/lib/imap`. Multiple values are separated from each other with spaces.

Use one of the following values to activate an option: `1`, `yes`, `on`, `t`, or `true`. Conversely, `0`, `no`, `off`, `f`, and `false` deactivate an option. Unfortunately, the preconfigured `imapd.conf` files are inconsistent in the use of these values. The examples in this book also stem from production servers that use inconsistent values, which mirrors the chaotic manner in which the original configuration files developed; this is something you learn to deal with.

`admins`
:   This option defines the admin accounts for mailbox administration. The default administrator is the user `cyrus` (see also section 14.3.3 on page 237):

    `admins: cyrus`

`allowanonymouslogin`
:   If this option is set to a positive value such as `yes`, it permits visitors to log in. By default, this is not permitted. It can make sense to activate this option if, for example, you provide shared folders on your mail system and want them to be accessible to users who do not have an email account on your server.

    These users then create an account for user `anonymous` on their email clients, and this user can access the IMAP server with any password. This account does not have an inbox, but visitors can use it to subscribe to all shared folders available to the Cyrus user `anyone`.

`autocreatequota`
:   If you enter a value other than 0, Cyrus will automatically create mailboxes for new users when they first log in, and then limit the memory available to these mailboxes to the quota value you specify here (see section 14.1.1 on page 226). This only works if an account name and password have been defined for that user account. If these have not been defined, no mailbox is created. A negative value (-1, for example) for `autocreatequota` removes the quota. This option only affects newly created mailboxes, not existing ones.

`configdirectory`
:   This option specifies the storage location for the Cyrus administration directory. In SuSE, the default value is `/var/lib/imap`.

`defaultdomain`
:   This option defines the domain for email accounts without an explicit domain definition; these user mailboxes are *unqualified* user

mailboxes. This option is required if your server handles virtual domains (see page 232).

`hashimapspool`
If you activate this switch, Cyrus generates a hash value for every mailbox directory. This improves performance, but it only affects inboxes with widely branching subdirectory structures.

`lmtp_overquota_perm_failure`
When this switch is activated and a user's mailbox is full, Cyrus refuses to accept emails via the LMTP socket and returns a permanent error. This entry is only useful if you have set quotas.

`lmtp_downcase_rcpt`
If this switch is activated, it ensures that Cyrus automatically converts the recipient's email address into lowercase characters. Even though the local section of an email should be case sensitive according to the RFC, it can reduce the number of support requests if you only allow lowercase characters.

`maxmessagesize`
If you specify a value for this option (in bytes), Cyrus refuses all emails via the LMTP socket that exceed this value. However, this task should really be carried out by the MTA operating as MX for the domain, and not by Cyrus, so as to prevent the emails from getting into the email system in the first place. This reduces the workload and thereby improves performance.

`partition-default`
This option defines the storage location for mailboxes, usually `/var/spool/imap` (see also section 14.5 on page 239).

`poptimeout`
This option specifies the time period (in minutes) after which an inactive POP3 connection to an email client is terminated. The minimum permitted value is 10 minutes.

`quotawarn`
This value (in percent of allowed maximum quota) specifies when a quota message is sent to the client during login. You can also use quotawarnkb to send a quota message when a certain mailbox size in kilobytes is reached (see section 14.1.1 page 226).

`reject8bit`
If this switch is activated, Cyrus rejects emails if they have eight-bit character sets in the email header instead of the standard seven-bit character sets. If this option is deactivated, Cyrus replaces eight-bit characters in the email header with an X.

`sievedir`
> This option specifies the working directory for the Sieve email filter service (see section 14.6 on page 240); for SuSE, it is

> `sievedir: /var/lib/sieve`

> This directory contains the filter settings for the alphabetically sorted user mailboxes that the Sieve daemon manages. It is usually not necessary to access it manually.

`sasl_pwcheck_method`
> This option specifies the method that Cyrus SASL uses to authenticate users. You can use `auxprop`, `saslauthd`, and `authdaemond`. Section 13.2 on page 211 deals with authentication in more detail.

`timeout`
> After how many minutes should the IMAP server terminate an inactive connection to an email client? The minimum value is 30 minutes, and there is no upper limit. Cyrus will ignore any values lower than the minimum.

`unixhierarchysep`
> This is an important switch if you use virtual domains (see also section 5 on page 235). Usually, Cyrus uses a dot as the separator when mapping mailbox structures. However, if you use mailboxes containing the users' first and last names, you should use the *Unix separator*, a forward slash (/), instead. To do this, activate `unixhierarchysep`.

`username_tolower`
> If this option is active, all usernames are automatically converted to lowercase. This makes authentication less prone to errors, but it is only possible if the authentication source (LDAP, for example) is *not* case sensitive.

`virtdomains`
> If this switch is activated, Cyrus can handle virtual domains. For more information on this subject, see section 14.3 on page 232.

If you wish to use SSL/TLS to encrypt the connection, you also have to specify the paths to the SSL certificates and SSL keys:

`tls_cert_file`
> This option specifies the path to the email server's certificate:

> `tls_cert_file: /usr/ssl/certs/servercert.pem`

`tls_key_file`
> This option specifies the path to the email server's key:

```
tls_key_file: /usr/ssl/certs/serverkey.pem
```

tls_ca_file
: This option specifies the path to the certificate of the certification authority (CA):

```
tls_ca_file: /usr/ssl/CA/CAcert.pem
```

tls_ca_path
: This option specifies the path to the directory containing the CA certificate and the file with its hash value:

```
tls_ca_path: /usr/ssl/CA
```

If you use option `tls_ca_file` to explicitly specify the CA certificate, you do not need to set `tls_ca_path`.

For more information on SSL certificates, see section 13.1 on page 208.

The following two options are only mentioned because SuSE writes them to `/etc/imapd.conf`, though they have no effect on their own even when activated. They activate *Dynamic Relay Authorization Control (DRAC)*,[1] a technology enabling *POP/IMAP before SMTP* (also known as *SMTP after POP*):

dracinterval
: If you enter a value other than 0, you activate POP/IMAP before SMTP. This value specifies how many minutes the client has to send emails via SMTP after POP3 or IMAP login.

drachost
: This is the hostname of the server providing the DRAC service. With the exception of specific setups, this is always `localhost`.

Cyrus has to be patched manually for these options to have any effect, as DRAC is not part of the official suite and is hardly ever used anymore. SuSE distributions contain the patch; it is available under `/usr/share/doc/packages/cyrus-imapd/contrib/drac_auth.patch`, along with the documentation. For more information, go to `http://mail.cc.umanitoba.ca/drac/`.

There are other options that are required only for special scenarios; these include the integration of authentication sources such as LDAP and MySQL servers, as described in section 13.2 on page 211, and cluster setups, which are described in more detail in section 17.1 on page 281.

---

[1] See `http://mail.cc.umanitoba.ca/drac/`.

13

Authentication and Safeguards

You have cleared the first hurdle and the email server works. After a quick breather, you should next consider the subject of safeguards. In principle, you can transmit email data across the network in cleartext, but nowadays every responsible postmaster should safeguard such an important means of communication and protect users' data as well as possible. This chapter deals with two basic security measures: encrypting the data stream and safeguarding the authentication process. You should always offer these options to your users, or even require them.

Administrators also need to know how to protect the communication of the servers in their own network if not all system services, such as email servers and authentication sources, operate on the same computer. In this case, without additional measures, user and authentication data is sent across a more or less unsafe network, and should therefore not be transmitted in cleartext if at all possible.

13.1 Encrypting with SSL/TLS

Authentication data from mail clients and the transmission of emails should always be treated in a highly confidential manner. For the email server, this means encrypting the data stream used by the clients to send authentication data and emails. This then permits the use of authentication mechanisms that transmit passwords in cleartext.

Nearly all email servers and clients meet the requirements for building up encrypted connections via SSL/TLS, as does the Cyrus daemon. The following practical example shows how to integrate OpenSSL into Cyrus.

13.1.1 SSL Transmission Types

The Cyrus IMAP server supports two implementations of *Transport Layer Security*: with STARTTLS and as an SSL wrapper. The difference between these methods is the point in time when encryption begins.

In the first case, the client connects to the normal IMAP port 143 and executes the STARTTLS command. The client and server then encrypt the data stream. This also applies for POP3 connections via port 110, but in that case the command is STLS.

The SSL wrapper is an additional mode in which Cyrus listens on a port dedicated to IMAP via SSL (port 993) or POP3-SSL (port 995). When the client connects to one of these ports, the data stream is encrypted before the IMAP session begins. Cyrus supports this function automatically if it was compiled with OpenSSL support. Both of these methods require a key infrastructure.

13.1.2 Real and Fake Certificates

The technical functioning of data stream encryption is not affected by your choice of certificate; you can use a certificate from a commercial certificate authority (CA) or create your own SSL certificate. This is a cosmetic decision as long as you do *not* permit cleartext authentication. However, if clients transmit user passwords to the server in unencrypted form, the users should be able to check that they are sending their sensitive data to the *correct* server. This only works properly if the server certificate has been certified by a trustworthy certificate authority or issued by a trustworthy member of a *trust network*.

Most email clients contain a prepared list of *trustworthy* certificate authorities. When a client connects to an email server that sends its public SSL key, it checks its local list of trustworthy certificate authorities. If you use a certificate from a "real" certificate authority, the client finds the corresponding entry and is satisfied.

However, if you use a "fake" certificate or one you created yourself, the client will not find it in this list. The user then receives a warning message that the email server may not be trustworthy. Security-conscious users will terminate the connection immediately and call up the support hotline. If you do create your own certificates, you should inform your users in advance about the certificate your server uses, or provide a sample certificate on your website that users can download.

In this case, even security-conscious users will usually accept the certificate (once they have checked it), and the email client will trust your email server from this point onward. There are clients that do not save this information permanently and display the warning message to their users every time; examples include older versions of Outlook and TheBat.

Unfortunately, free certificates such as those provided by OpenCA[1] or CaCert[2] can also cause problems: Although open source clients such as Mozilla Thunderbird accept these certificates, Outlook and others insist on commercial certificates, which are not cheap and pour money into the coffers of the CA companies. If you use a free certificate, it is advisable to inform your users that more and more people are joining together to form an alternative trust network that provide real and free certificates for everyone.

13.1.3 Creating and Integrating SSL Certificates

You can create your own certificate with OpenSSL for *test operation*, even if you plan to use a real certificate with a public key from a CA for actual operation.

You can store the certificate in a directory (e. g., /usr/ssl); if it does not exist, use `mkdir /usr/ssl/` to create it before calling `openssl`. The following command creates an SSL certificate according to the X.509 standard. This certificate is valid for 1,460 days (4 years); use the `openssl-req` option `-nodes` to store it in unencrypted form in directory /usr/ssl/, along with the corresponding private key:

```
linux:/usr/ssl # openssl req -new -x509 -nodes -out /usr/ssl/server.pem \
 -keyout /usr/ssl/server.pem -days 1460
Generating a 1024 bit RSA private key
....................++++++
.........................................................++++++
writing new private key to '/usr/ssl/server.pem'
-----
You are about to be asked to enter information that will be incorporated
into your certificate request.
What you are about to enter is what is called a Distinguished Name or a
```

[1] See http://www.openca.org/.
[2] See http://www.cacert.org/.

```
DN.
There are quite a few fields but you can leave some blank
For some fields there will be a default value,
If you enter '.', the field will be left blank.
-----
Country Name (2 letter code) [AU]:DE
State or Province Name (full name) [Some-State]:Berlin
Locality Name (eg, city) []:Berlin
Organization Name (eg, company) [Internet Widgits Pty Ltd]:My company
Organizational Unit Name (eg, section) []:Email sending department
Common Name (eg, YOUR name) []:mail.example.com
Email Address []:peer@example.com
```

You *have* to enter the name of the email server in the Common Name field. The users enter that name in their email clients as the email server name. If these entries do not match, the clients will display a warning that the connection is probably not trustworthy.

The /usr/ssl/server.pem file contains the private server key as well as the public certificate, so only the root user may have read access to this file. Use chmod 400 /usr/ssl/server.pem to change the permissions.

The current Cyrus IMAP version supports OpenSSL by default, whereas you may have to add this support in older versions. For information on how to do this, see section C.2.4 on page 329. Enter the following values in the /etc/imapd.conf file to activate SSL support:

```
tls_cert_file: /usr/ssl/server.pem
tls_key_file: /usr/ssl/server.pem
```

Enter the path to the certificate file in tls_cert_file and the path to the private key file in tls_key_file. If you use a certificate from a real CA, you should activate the following options so that the email server can evaluate the correct CA certificate:

```
tls_ca_file: /usr/ssl/CA/CAcert.pem
tls_ca_path: /usr/ssl/CA
```

This is where you enter the file containing the CA certificate and the path to the directory containing the CA certificate as a hash value. This ensures that the CA certificates have not been modified.

If authentication is done through a secure SSL tunnel, you can use authentication methods that transmit the password in cleartext. In this case, you should only permit encrypted connections via SSL. To make the necessary settings in the /etc/cyrus.conf file, open the corresponding ports for IMAP/IMAPs and POP3/POP3s in the Services section, or close them by prefixing them with a comment character:

```
# UNIX sockets start with a slash and are put into /var/lib/imap/socket
SERVICES {
  # add or remove based on preferences
  imap            cmd="imapd" listen="imap" prefork=0
  imaps           cmd="imapd -s" listen="imaps" prefork=0
  pop3            cmd="pop3d" listen="pop3" prefork=0
  pop3s           cmd="pop3d -s" listen="pop3s" prefork=0
  [...]
}
```

This setting permits login via SSL and without encryption.

You can also configure the server so that cleartext passwords are only permitted if the client has built a TLS/SSL tunnel. For more information, see section 13.2 on page 211.

You have to restart the IMAP daemon before your Cyrus IMAP server will provide data stream encryption via TLS/SSL to the clients. Use `lsof -i` to view the open IMAPs and POP3s ports:

```
[...]
master    10895   cyrus    5u   IPv6   35505      TCP *:imap  (LISTEN)
master    10895   cyrus   11u   IPv4   35509      TCP *:imap  (LISTEN)
master    10895   cyrus   14u   IPv6   35513      TCP *:imaps (LISTEN)
master    10895   cyrus   17u   IPv4   35515      TCP *:imaps (LISTEN)
master    10895   cyrus   20u   IPv6   35519      TCP *:pop3  (LISTEN)
master    10895   cyrus   23u   IPv4   35521      TCP *:pop3  (LISTEN)
master    10895   cyrus   26u   IPv6   35525      TCP *:pop3s (LISTEN)
master    10895   cyrus   29u   IPv4   35527      TCP *:pop3s (LISTEN)
master    10895   cyrus   32u   IPv6   35531      TCP *:sieve (LISTEN)
master    10895   cyrus   35u   IPv4   35533      TCP *:sieve (LISTEN)
[...]
```

It is advisable to read `/var/log/messages` and `/var/log/mail` when you modify or add configuration settings. This will enable you to detect errors that are not mentioned when the program is started. You can also use a packet sniffer such as `tcpdump` to check that the login is really encrypted and that no user information is visible in the TCP packages.

13.2 Cyrus SASL

The makers of the Cyrus IMAP server also provide a library that implements the Simple Authentication Security Layer (SASL). The Cyrus IMAP daemon is not the only program to use `libsasl`, or *Cyrus SASL*, as it is also known; third-party programs use it to access the modules it controls, which in turn provide access to a number of authentication sources.

13.2.1 Cyrus SASL Modules

The `sasl_pwcheck_method` entry in the `/etc/imapd.conf` file specifies which module is used.

The `saslauthd` Authentication Service

`saslauthd` is not actually a module, but rather an independent authentication service that Cyrus addresses like a module. It simply receives cleartext passwords and compares them to a number of data sources using plugins:

getpwent
: This module permits access to passwords in the `passwd` configuration file in Unix systems.

shadow
: This module permits access to the user data in the complementary Unix configuration files `passwd` and `shadow`.

kerberos4
: This module permits access to Kerberos-4 servers.

kerberos5
: This module permits access to Kerberos-5 servers.

pam
: This module uses Pluggable Authentication Modules.

rimap
: This module sends authentication requests to an IMAP server. This plugin is only useful in conjunction with third-party programs such as Postfix, which use the authentication sources set up for the IMAP server.

ldap
: This module queries the user data on an LDAP server.

`saslauthd` is an independent service, so it is controlled from its own configuration file. You only need to specify in /etc/imapd.conf that sasl authd is to be used. Specify which plugin should be used in /etc/syscon fig/saslauthd:[3] SASLAUTHD_AUTHMECH=pam, for example, means that the PAM plugin will be used. If you do *not* specify a plugin in the saslauthd configuration file, shadow is used automatically.

[3] This is a SuSE-specific path; in Debian and other distributions, you can often specify this directly in /etc/saslauthd.

PAM is an exception among plugins. It is not a method that directly queries *one* data source, but a system that transfers this task to a real authentication service. This makes the setup more complex, but this detour means that all PAM data sources are available to the Cyrus mail server, including fingerprints and iris scans. You can find such a module at http://www.kernel.org/pub/linux/libs/pam/modules.html, among other sites.

13.2.2 The `auxprop` Module

The `auxprop` module also uses a collection of plugins for authentication. It can use the following plugins to access data sources:

sasldb
: This module permits access to the minidatabase `sasldb2`.[4]

ldapdb
: This module queries an LDAP server.

sql
: This module obtains the authentication data from an SQL server.

Unlike the `saslauthd` module, `auxprop` attaches great importance to security and permits authentication by methods such as CRAM or DIGEST-MD5. Both procedures transmit hash values instead of user passwords, and they check these hash values during authentication. DIGEST-MD5 is newer and is viewed as more secure.

If you do not specify a plugin in the /etc/imapd.conf configuration file, `sasldb` will be used automatically.

Using the `authdaemond`

Cyrus SASL can also use the `authdaemond` module to call the Courier IMAP authentication service (see section 9.2 on page 122) and thereby access MySQL, LDAP, and PostgreSQL data. This is only suitable as an authentication source for a Cyrus IMAP server in special circumstances, such as migrating from Courier to Cyrus or adding a Cyrus IMAP server to an existing Courier IMAP server. This module is only capable of handling cleartext passwords. The following is an example of a suitable entry in /etc/imapd.conf:

```
sasl_pwcheck_method: authdaemond
sasl_authdaemon_path: /var/run/authdaemon.courier-imap/socket
sasl_mech_list: PLAIN LOGIN
```

---

[4] The predecessor, `sasldb`, is only used in very old versions of Cyrus-SASL 1.*x* and is no longer relevant for current Cyrus IMAP versions.

First specify the module. Then tell `authdaemond` where the socket for the Courier authdaemon is located. Then specify the password encryption method; in this case, it has to be cleartext, as the module is not capable of encryption.

The Outdated `pwcheck` Module

This authentication service was used until Cyrus version 1.5; it can only read the files `passwd` and `shadow`. It was replaced by `saslauthd` and is only supported for reasons of backward compatibility. This service only operates with cleartext passwords.

There are a number of patches by other providers for all authentication modules, but these are *not* officially supported. One of these[5] modifies `pwcheck` so that this service can query an LDAP database.

13.2.3 The Authentication Process

As soon as an IMAP client contacts the Cyrus server, the server offers the client all the supported authentication mechanisms. Depending on the module, these can be as follows:

- `PLAIN` is the method used by Unix systems to transmit cleartext passwords, and `LOGIN` is the method adapted for Microsoft Outlook.

- `CRAM-MD5` and `DIGEST-MD5` both encrypt the user password and compare the calculated value during authentication. `DIGEST-MD5` is newer and more secure than `CRAM-MD5`.

- `KERBEROS_V4` and `GSSAPI` (Kerberos 5) are two methods that can be used.

- `EXTERNAL` enables the integration of additional mechanisms (not discussed here).

When choosing a module, you should only make cleartext mechanisms available to your users if the cleartext passwords are transmitted on a connection encrypted with TLS/SSL.

The mechanisms provided by the client must also be available and supported by the authentication module. Only enter those mechanisms in the `/etc/imapd.conf` file that are actually available, for example, `sasl_mech_list: PLAIN LOGIN` for transmission of passwords in cleartext. If you want to provide more than one mechanism, simply write one after the other and separate consecutive mechanisms with a space.

---

[5] See http://www.surf.org.uk/downloads/.

The client can then choose its favorite mechanism (usually the safest) from that list and send a corresponding request to the email server. If you offer authentication mechanisms that are not provided by the authentication service and the data source, the system may not be able to authenticate the user.

The Cyrus IMAP daemon uses `libsasl` to transfer the query from the client to the authentication service configured with `sasl_pwcheck_method` in the `/etc/imapd.conf` file. This service consults the appropriate data source and returns the result to the daemon.

13.3 Calling Different Data Sources

If you wish to use the Cyrus IMAP daemon in a larger environment, you will probably already have a central data source containing user data for other services. Cyrus can access many of these once it has been configured to do so.

13.3.1 Standard Authentication Methods for Unix

In its default state, the Cyrus email server uses the `saslauthd` authentication method with the `shadow` plugin, which means that it uses Unix system accounts. In this case, you have to use the usual tools to create a new system user for every new mailbox, for example:

```
linux: # useradd zoidberg
linux: # passwd zoidberg
Changing password for zoidberg.
New Password: zoidbergs_password
Reenter New Password: zoidbergs_password
Password changed.
```

This command creates a Unix account for user `zoidberg`, which means that it generates the required entries in `/etc/passwd` and `/etc/shadow`. Once you have done this, Cyrus can authenticate the new user.

However, creating a new Unix system account for *every* new Cyrus user is not only superfluous but also a potential security risk.

In general, it is advisable to use a different authentication mechanism, as this method becomes unwieldy if you have more than a few hundred users. It is also quicker to search databases if they are text files, which in turn improves the email server performance.

13.3.2 `sasldb2`

`sasldb2` is a quick, easy, and relatively secure method for authenticating users. This method uses the authentication module `auxprop` with the `sasldb2` plugin. The required configuration for the Cyrus IMAP daemon is described in section 11.4.1 on page 194.

However, this miniature user database quickly reaches its limits if, for example, you want to map groups as well as usernames and passwords. `sasldb2` is not capable of this or of central user management for multiple services. This is only possible with a real database management system (such as MySQL) and with LDAP.

13.3.3 Cyrus and MySQL

When Cyrus was first conceived, it was not designed to be connected to a MySQL database, but this connection works thanks to PAM. MySQL is now easier to set up and connect than other external data sources such as LDAP.

The `auxprop` plugin

You can now use the SASL plugin `sql`, which connects to MySQL via the `libsasl` authentication library. Make sure that Cyrus SASL is compiled with support for MySQL. The prepared packages of current distributions have already done this.

If you compile Cyrus SASL yourself, you have to set the `configure` parameter `--with-mysql=/usr/local/mysql` (see section C.2.3 on page 326).

In order to connect Cyrus to a MySQL database using the `auxprop` plugin `sql`, you have to go to the `/etc/imapd.conf` file and define the access data for the database and the SQL command that compares the transmitted user data to that in the database:

```
sasl_pwcheck_method: auxprop
sasl_auxprop_plugin: sql
sasl_sql_engine: mysql
sasl_sql_hostnames: localhost
sasl_sql_user: sqlusername
sasl_sql_passwd: sqlpassword
sasl_sql_database: cyrus
sasl_sql_verbose: no
sasl_sql_select: SELECT password FROM cyrus_email WHERE username = '%u'
AND active='1'
sasl_sql_usessl: 0
```

You can specify multiple SQL servers in `sasl_sql_hostnames`. Separate them with commas. You can also specify a port:

```
sasl_sql_hostnames: localhost, 192.168.0.33:3306
```

Set `sasl_sql_verbose` to yes for debugging in order to make the log messages in the syslog more explicit.

`sasl_sql_usessl`: 0 specifies that the connection to the database server will *not* be made via an SSL tunnel. Use the value 1, for example, to activate this function.

In this example, the SQL command defined in `sasl_sql_select` searches the `cyrus_email` database table for the password matching the username specified during login (%u), but only if the value for `active` is set to 1 in the table. Defining such a table column is a simple way to activate or deactivate a user account.

You can use the following SQL command, among others, to generate a MySQL table suitable for the SQL query specified in `sasl_sql_select`:

```
CREATE TABLE "cyrus_email"(
  "id" int(11) NOT NULL auto_increment,
  "username" varchar(50) NOT NULL default ,
  "password" varchar(50) NOT NULL default ,
  "real_name" varchar(150) NOT NULL default ,

  "active" tinyint(4) NOT NULL default "1",
  PRIMARY KEY  ("id"),

  UNIQUE KEY "id_2" ("id"),
  KEY "id" ("id")
);
```

You can also use the more convenient web interface from phpMyAdmin to create this database. When Cyrus is restarted, it compares the data transmitted during user authentication to the contents of the MySQL database table that was just generated. If a queried value is not found, perhaps because a user account has not yet been created, MySQL returns an error message, and Cyrus SASL does not permit the user to log in. You can test this using the `imtest` tool, for example. This tool enables you to test entire IMAP logins and the behavior of the IMAP server:

```
linux: # imtest -m login -a zoidberg localhost
* OK linux Cyrus IMAP4 v2.2.12 server ready
C01 CAPABILITY
* CAPABILITY IMAP4 IMAP4rev1 ACL QUOTA LITERAL+ MAILBOX-REFERRALS NAMESP
ACE UIDPLUS ID NO_ATOMIC_RENAME UNSELECT CHILDREN MULTIAPPEND BINARY SOR
T THREAD=ORDEREDSUBJECT THREAD=REFERENCES ANNOTATEMORE IDLE AUTH=DIGEST-
MD5 AUTH=CRAM-MD5 SASL-IR X-NETSCAPE
C01 OK Completed
Please enter your password: zoidbergs_password
```

13 Authentication and Safeguards

```
L01 LOGIN zoidberg {5}⁶
+ go ahead
<omitted>
L01 NO Login failed: user not found
Authentication failed. generic failure
Security strength factor: 0
Q01 LOGOUT
Connection closed.
```

If the command is called with the -m login switch, this forces the use of the SASL password-transfer method LOGIN. If you do not specify a switch, imtest will automatically choose the safest mechanism. The last argument after the username is the hostname. If you do not enter a hostname, imtest will automatically use localhost.

The key to the problem is the line L01 NO Login failed: user not found. It means that the specified user, zoidberg, does not exist.

This is what a successful login process looks like:

```
linux: # imtest -a zoidberg localhost
WARNING: no hostname supplied, assuming localhost
* OK linux Cyrus IMAP4 v2.2.12 server ready
C01 CAPABILITY
* CAPABILITY IMAP4 IMAP4rev1 ACL QUOTA LITERAL+ MAILBOX-REFERRALS NAMESPA
CE UIDPLUS ID NO_ATOMIC_RENAME UNSELECT CHILDREN MULTIAPPEND BINARY SORT
THREAD=ORDEREDSUBJECT THREAD=REFERENCES ANNOTATEMORE IDLE STARTTLS AUTH=C
RAM-MD5 SASL-IR X-NETSCAPE
C01 OK Completed
A01 AUTHENTICATE CRAM-MD5
+ PDQwMjE1MDUzMjUuNDA0MzU4N0BndWNreT4=
Please enter your password: zoidbergs_password
cGF1bCBiMTM5Y2NjMmMxYTU4ZjYyMmI5Y2JkYjNkOTY4OTUwYg==
A01 OK Success (no protection)
Authenticated.
Security strength factor: 0
Q01 LOGOUT
Connection closed.
```

In this example, no password encryption mechanism was specified (using -m), so it is nice to see that imtest uses the secure CRAM-MD5 mechanism: A01 AUTHENTICATE CRAM-MD5.[7]

---

[6] When imtest calls the LOGIN command in this case, the command does not list the password directly in cleartext as the second argument; instead, it uses {5} to tell the server to enter a five-character string in a separate line (zoidberg's password, which is entered in reply to the request Please enter your password:). For more information on this syntax, see section A.4 on page 305.

[7] For information on the AUTHENTICATE command, see section A.2 on page 297.

The Detour via PAM

The SASL plugin may be much more convenient, but in some setups you may still want to use the older method of connecting via PAM. To do this, make the following entries in the `/etc/pam.d/imap` file:

```
auth sufficient pam_mysql.so user=mail passwd=secret host=localhost db=cy
rus table=cyrus_email usercolumn=username      passwdcolumn=password crypt=
1 logtable=log logmsgcolumn=msg logusercolumn=user loghostcolumn=host log
pidcolumn=pid logtimecolumn=time

auth sufficient pam_unix_auth.so

account required pam_mysql.so user=mail passwd=secret host=localhost db=c
yrus table=cyrus_email usercolumn=username passwdcolumn=password crypt=1
logtable=log logmsgcolumn=msg logusercolumn=user loghostcolumn=host logpi
dcolumn=pid logtimecolumn=time

account  sufficient  pam_unix_acct.so
```

The entries in this file are organized in columns separated by spaces. The first column contains the module type that is to be used, the second column contains the control flag, and the third column contains the name of the PAM module to be used, followed by optional arguments. To connect to MySQL, you must require the module types `auth` and `account`. The first module is responsible for authentication, whereas `account` is responsible for any restrictions.

The `sufficient` control flag signifies that no additional modules of the specified type will be called if the specified module has carried out its service successfully.

The `pam_mysql.so` module requires access parameters to the MySQL database as its arguments. In this example, you access the `cyrus_email` table in the `cyrus` database and specify that the password can be found in the `password` column and the username in the `username` column of that table.

If authentication via MySQL fails, a second attempt is made using module `pam_unix_auth.so`, which queries the Unix files `passwd` and `shadow`.

If, in addition to the IMAP server, you want other Cyrus services to fetch information from the MySQL database, copy the PAM configuration file and rename it correspondingly:

```
linux: # cp /etc/pam.d/imap /etc/pam.d/pop
linux: # cp /etc/pam.d/imap /etc/pam.d/sieve
linux: # cp /etc/pam.d/imap /etc/pam.d/smtp
```

Now you only have to "explain" to Cyrus that it should use PAM as the authentication module. To do this, set the `sasl_pwcheck_method` parameter

13 Authentication and Safeguards

in /etc/imapd.conf to saslauthd and use SASLAUTHD_AUTHMECH=pam to specify the access plugin in /etc/sysconfig/saslauthd.

When Cyrus calls saslauthd, this module contacts PAM, which in turn contacts the backend specified for PAM: In this case, the PAM module pam_mysql.so authenticates the users via the MySQL database. You can use PAM for other backends by applying this method as well.

13.3.4 Cyrus and LDAP

This is another way to authenticate users through their username and password. You can also map groups, but not ACL and quota settings for mailboxes. You have to use cyradm for this purpose.

Communication with the LDAP server can be local (via an LDAP socket) or remote by TCP via port 389 or 636 (LDAP via SSL). For access to a remote LDAP server, you have to ensure that the required ports are activated in the firewall.

You should install OpenLDAP on the LDAP server, OpenSSL on the LDAP client (i.e., the Cyrus server), and the LDAP server, and *phpLDAPAdmin*[8] on the LDAP server. It is far easier to manage and oversee LDAP trees on this web interface than on the console.

Configuring the LDAP Server

First, you have to set up a schema on the LDAP server that can map the usernames and passwords. Once you have set up the LDAP schema, you can administer it using the phpLDAPAdmin web interface, for example.

In most cases, the LDAP server already provides authentication data to other services, so you only need to adapt the parameters on the client.

LDAP via auxprop

The auxprop SASL module can be used for querying an LDAP server, as it has a suitable plugin (ldapdb) and uses shared-secret mechanisms for encrypted password transmission. This means that the authentication data will never be transmitted in cleartext.

Specify the following values in the /etc/imapd.conf file:

```
sasl_pwcheck_method: auxprop
sasl_auxprop_plugin: ldapdb
sasl_ldapdb_uri: ldap://ldap.example.com
```

[8] See http://phpldapadmin.sourceforge.net/.

```
sasl_ldapdb_id: ldap-username
sasl_ldapdb_pw: ldap-password
sasl_ldapdb_mech: DIGEST-MD5
```

You can use `DIGEST-MD5` as the password encryption method, as it is safer than cleartext. In this case, the user passwords have to be stored as MD5 hashes instead of as cleartext in the LDAP directory. However, you should try to encrypt the data stream to the LDAP server via SSL, as SASL is unaffected by this method and continues to log on to the LDAP server in cleartext.

Now you only need to specify the search path that will be used to read the data from LDAP. To do this, make an entry in the `/etc/slapd.conf` file on the LDAP server:

```
sasl-regexp uid=(.*),cn=.*,cn=auth ldap:///ou=training,o=example,c=com??
sub?(&(objectclass=inetOrgPerson)(mail=$1))
```

Now, when Cyrus SASL connects to the LDAP server, SASL attempts to log in with the username and the password stored in the `example.com` domain in the `inetOrgPerson` LDAP object. If this works, the user is authenticated and may log in.

LDAP via `saslauthd`

`saslauthd` can also access LDAP. However, you should use TSL/SSL to secure the data stream in this case, as `saslauthd` only sends cleartext passwords. Secure the connection between the email client and the email server and the connection between the email server and the LDAP server if these are on different computers.

To connect Cyrus to an LDAP server that is set up properly and has a suitable schema, you should begin by configuring the `saslauthd` in the `/etc/sysconfig/saslauthd` file:

```
## Path:              System/Security/SASL
## Type:              list(getpwent,kerberos5,pam,rimap,shadow,ldap)
## Default:           pam
## ServiceRestart:    saslauthd
#
# Authentication mechanism to use by saslauthd.
# See man 8 saslauthd for available mechanisms.
#
SASLAUTHD_AUTHMECH=ldap
```

You can also make this entry in the `/etc/imapd.conf` file, from which it is transmitted to the `saslauthd`.

13 Authentication and Safeguards

saslauthd requires an additional configuration file containing the parameters for the LDAP query. On most systems, you will have to create /etc/saslauthd.conf:

```
ldap_servers: ldap://ldap.example.com/
# Path to the LDAP server

ldap_version: 3

ldap_search_base: ou=schulung, o=example, c=com
# Entry into the LDAP search path

ldap_bind_dn: cn=root, o=example, c=com
# Path to the login user

ldap_bind_pw: xxxxx

# Password of the login user

ldap_filter: (uid=%u)
# Value that is being searched for:
# %u = evaluates the entire UID
# %U = only evaluates up to the @ character

ldap_scope: sub
# sub searches recursively to the end from the point of entry.
# Alternatives: base (non-recursive), one (only one element down)

######################
# If you want the connection between SASL and the LDAP server to be
# encrypted, you should enter the TLS certificate data here.

# In this case, you have to configure the LDAP server with TLS support
# as well.

# ldap_tls_check_peer: yes
# ldap_tls_cacert_file: /usr/ssl/cacert.pem
# ldap_tls_cacert_dir: /usr/ssl/
# ldap_tls_cert: /usr/ssl/servercert.pem
# ldap_tls_key: /usr/ssl/serverkey.pem
```

The `ldap_tls_check_peer:  yes` switch ensures that the certificates of the client and the server are checked for authenticity. The other parameters specify the paths to the SSL certificates of the server and the certificate authority (as described in section 13.1 on page 208).

Now you have to restart both saslauthd and Cyrus so that the modified configuration files are loaded. Once you have done this, Cyrus will query the LDAP server for authentication information. You can use the testsaslauthd tool to check whether all of this worked:

```
linux: # testsaslauthd -u zoidberg -p zoidbergs_password
0: OK "Success."
```

-u specifies the username, and -p is followed by the password.

Once you have stored information on each user's group in the LDAP tree in some other attribute, you can use separate parameters to query this group affiliation in the `saslauthd.conf` file. `ldap_group_search_base` specifies the LDAP path where the search is done. If none is specified, the path specified in `ldap_search_base` is used. `ldap_group_attr` specifies which attributes should be queried. `ldap_group_match_method` defines the LDAP method that will be used to search for the result. `ldap_group_filter` specifies the search filter that will be used. The following is an example of a definition of a group query:

```
ldap_group_search_base: cn=gruppen,dc=example,dc=com
ldap_group_attr: memberUid
ldap_group_match_method: filter
ldap_group_filter: (memberUid=%D)
```

You will find all other functions and switches in the `/usr/share/doc/packages/cyrus-sasl/LDAP_SASLAUTHD` file, but these are irrelevant for group affiliation queries using Cyrus.

13.3.5 Cyrus and Kerberos

PAM or `saslauthd` is required for authentication on a Kerberos-5 server. The latter is the only SASL module containing a plugin for querying a Kerberos server. To use it, set the `sasl_pwcheck_method` parameter in `/etc/imapd.conf` to `saslauthd`, and set the variable SASLAUTHD_AUTHMECH in `/etc/sysconfig/saslauthd` to `kerberos5`:

```
## Path:           System/Security/SASL
## Type:           list(getpwent,kerberos5,pam,rimap,shadow,ldap)
## Default:        pam
## ServiceRestart: saslauthd
#
# Authentication mechanism to use by saslauthd.
# See man 8 saslauthd for available mechanisms.
#
SASLAUTHD_AUTHMECH=kerberos5
```

Now, all you need to add is the Kerberos identity for accessing the Kerberos server. To do this, enter the host key of the IMAP server in the file `/etc/krb5.keytab`. Use the command-line tool `kadmin` to do this. Before calling it, you have to modify the parameters for access to the Kerberos server in the `/etc/krb5.conf` file:

```
[libdefaults]
        default_realm = EXAMPLE.COM

[realms]
        EXAMPLE.ORG = {
                kdc = kerberos.example.com
                admin_server = kerberos.example.com
        }

[logging]
    kdc = FILE:/var/log/krb5/krb5kdc.log
    admin_server = FILE:/var/log/krb5/kadmind.log
    default = SYSLOG:NOTICE:DAEMON
```

The section `libdefaults` specifies the *realm* for which this Kerberos server is responsible (unless otherwise specified). Specify the *key distribution center* (`kdc`) and the Kerberos server in `realms` to define the realm in more detail. Use `logging` to specify the parameters for logging on the key and the Kerberos servers.

Now change the file permissions so that user `cyrus` can read the `/etc/krb5.keytab` file.

A functioning Kerberos system (server and client) is a prerequisite for this scenario. This also means that you have to have installed the Kerberos utilities and the Kerberos client on the Cyrus computer.

Advanced Cyrus Configuration

By now you have seen the basic functions of Cyrus and its overall structure, which is admittedly confusing at first. Once you've become familiar with the material in the previous chapters, you should be able to set up an operational email server, but it will still be missing the more interesting aspects and functions that make the Cyrus IMAP daemon worth using in the first place. The next section will describe these special features, which ease (and, in some cases, enable) the administration of multiple mailboxes and domains.

14.1 Mailbox Quotas

One convenience—at least for administrators—is the ability to restrict the amount of memory available to mail users. You should carefully consider how much storage to allocate to user accounts; after all, people send Power-

Point files and entire photo albums via email. Hard disks have become less expensive, but as the amount of data that people send by email increases, these trends almost cancel each other out.

Filesystem quotas, like those provided by Linux, are only helpful for managing storage use if you create a system user account for each mailbox. One of Cyrus's advantages is that it is independent of system-level user accounts. In particular, it includes its own quota system, which is also independent from operating system quotas.

Even if you have sufficient storage space, for example, on an SAN server, it is advisable to use quotas with Cyrus, as the files containing administrative information grow along with the mailboxes. If the partition containing the mailboxes fills up, the mail system's database files may become corrupted, and in that case they cannot always be properly restored. The Cyrus email server is unfortunately quite a delicate structure to troubleshoot.[1]

14.1.1 Automatic Quotas

The `autocreatequota` switch in the `/etc/imapd.conf` file is used to activate and deactivate quotas. It is easy to make mistakes while doing this, as the documentation provided by Cyrus does not describe the option clearly. There are three different configurations:

`autocreatequota: 0`
> Users may not create new mailboxes. Instead, the administrator has to create mailboxes and set up quotas manually.

`autocreatequota: number_larger_than_0`
> A mailbox structure is created automatically for new users. The mailbox is only created automatically when a user first logs in if the username and password are already stored in the authentication data source. The user may save email in this mailbox until the capacity (in kilobytes) specified by the value is reached.

`autocreatequota: number_smaller than_0`
> Cyrus creates a mailbox structure when a new user logs in for the first time, as long as the username and password already exist in the authentication data source. However, specifying a negative value (-1, for example) means that no quota is set, and the user has unlimited storage space.

The `quotawarn` option allows a parameter to be specified that tells Cyrus when to send a warning message to the user's email client if the user is about to use up his or her quota. For example, `quotawarn: 62` causes

---
[1] For arguments *against* using quotas, see section 10.2 on page 166.

the warning to appear when 62 percent of the user's quota has been used up. Figure 14.1 illustrates this using Mozilla Thunderbird.

The `quotawarnkb` option works similarly, but specifies the amount of space (in kilobytes) that is still *available* in the account when the email client first shows the warning that the quota will be exceeded soon. For example, `quotawarnkb: 1024` alerts users that space is running low when 1,024KB or less remains in the account.

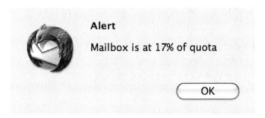

Figure 14.1: Once the other 83 percent of memory has been filled, the IMAP server refuses to accept emails for this account.

Cyrus uses the `GETQUOTA`[2] IMAP command to inform the client how much of the available memory has been used (in percent or kilobytes). The client can decide how (and, indeed, whether) to present this information to the user (see Figure 14.2).

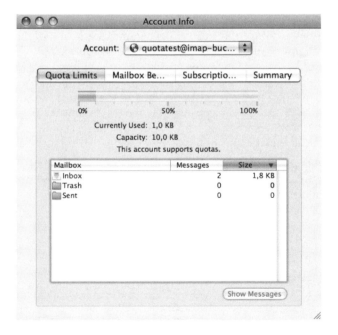

Figure 14.2: The email client (Mozilla Thunderbird in this case) displays activated quotas with the mailbox information.

---

[2] This command is part of the `QUOTA` extension described in RFC 2088 and implemented by Cyrus.

14.1.2 Manual Quotas

The `cyradm` configuration tool, described in section 15.4 on page 271, can be used to create and modify quotas. When reducing a quota, make sure that the new quota value specified is greater than the amount of memory currently used by the mailbox. Otherwise, user data is lost, and the mailbox index will be damaged.

The following example shows how to manually specify a quota of 10,000KB for user `paul`'s mailbox and all of its subdirectories:

```
linux: # cyradm -auth login localhost -user cyrus
IMAP Password: password for cyrus
localhost> listmailbox
user.paul (\HasNoChildren)
user.geeko (\HasNoChildren)
localhost> lq user.paul

localhost> sq user.paul 10000
quota:10000
localhost> lq user.paul

 STORAGE 0/10000 (0%)
localhost> exit
```

`lq` is an abbreviation of the `listquota` command and shows the existing quotas and current utilization: `paul` currently has only empty mailboxes, which means that the entire quota is still available to him. Use `setquota`, or `sq` for short, to set the quota. This command expects the *quotaroot* as its first argument, that is, the mailbox or mailbox subdirectory to whose children the quota applies. The second argument is a number specifying the amount of available memory in kilobytes or the value `none`, which removes a previously set quota. It is not possible to specify percentages here.

The following example shows how to set a quota for all mailboxes and subdirectories underneath the Cyrus root directory `user`, list all the quotas using `lq`, and then delete them all again:

```
localhost> sq user 100000
quota:100000
localhost> lq user
 STORAGE 0/100000 (0%)
localhost> sq user none
remove quota
```

If you specify a quota for the entire Cyrus root directory in this manner, all mailboxes in that directory will be codependent. Once the quota limit has been reached, none of the subordinate mailboxes can receive emails, and the email clients of all the users receive a message like that shown in Figure

14.3. Anyone who tries to send a message to one of the users also receives a bounce email, as can be seen by examining the mail log of the email server:

```
Jun 10 12:04:37 linux postfix/smtpd[3540]: connect from plasma.jpberlin.de[213.203.238.10]
Jun 10 12:04:37 linux postfix/smtpd[3540]: 1AAB21C3B3: client=plasma.jpberlin.de.de[213.203.238.10]
Jun 10 12:04:37 linux postfix/cleanup[3543]: 1AAB21C3B3: message-id=<466BCCAE.9040904@heinlein-support.de>
Jun 10 12:04:37 linux postfix/qmgr[2486]: 1AAB21C3B3: from=<p.hartleben@heinlein-support.de.de>, size=4541, nrcpt=1 (queue active)
Jun 10 12:04:37 linux postfix/smtpd[3540]: disconnect from plasma.jpberlin.de[213.203.238.10]
Jun 10 12:04:37 linux postfix/lmtp[3544]: 1AAB21C3B3: to=<paul@example.com>, relay=public/lmtp[public/lmtp], delay=0, status=deferred (host public/lmtp[public/lmtp] said: 452 4.2.2 Over quota (in reply to RCPT TO command))
```

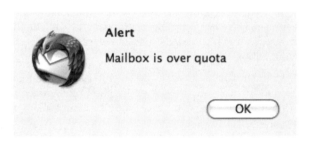

Figure 14.3:
Email clients such as Mozilla Thunderbird inform the user when a quota limit is reached.

You can see that the external email server `plasma.jpberlin.de` is attempting to deliver an email to local user `paul@exaple.com`, but this attempt is refused with `452 4.2.2 Over quota`.

`listquotaroot`, or `lqr` for short, shows the amount of available memory used in a mailbox or directory hierarchy. You can use it to detect quota dependencies between a superdirectory and a subdirectory.

Let's take a look at a mailbox with one quota. As no explicit quota is specified for the `Trash` subdirectory, `lq` does not return any results:

```
localhost> lq user.quotatest.Trash

localhost> lqr user.quotatest.Trash
user.quotatest STORAGE 6/10 (60%)
```

Nevertheless, the quota settings for the entire mailbox apply; the `lqr` command displays these quota settings. It is possible to allocate more memory to a mailbox subdirectory than is specified for the entire mailbox.

The `quota` tool in the /usr/lib/cyrus/bin/ directory provides a complete overview of all quotas in the system. Invoke it as Unix user `cyrus`:

```
cyrus@linux:$ /usr/lib/cyrus/bin/quota
   Quota  % Used    Used Root
   10000       0       8 user/quotatest@example.com
                       0 user/quotatest/Trash@example.com
                       0 user
      10       0       0 user/cyrus
   10000       0       0 user/paul
```

It displays the quotas that are set for each mailbox, and the utilization in percent and kilobytes. Section 14.9.2 on page 257 describes how to use `quota` to repair defective quotas.

14.2 Shared Folders and ACLs

Cyrus is capable of handling shared directories and mailboxes. Access to such shared folders is handled by the *access control lists*, or *ACLs*. These contain user permissions for files. By default, every user has access only to his or her own mailbox.

For example, suppose you want `anna` the secretary to have read access to the `Invoices` subdirectory in the boss's mailbox. Both users have to be set up correctly on the system, and the user `boss` has to have created the `Invoices` subdirectory.

Now use the `cyradm` tool to make the required settings. The `cyradm` command `setaclmailbox` (`sam` for short) sets the permissions, and `listacl mailbox` or `lam` displays them:

```
linux: # cyradm -auth login localhost -user cyrus
IMAP Password: password for cyrus
localhost> setaclmailbox user.boss.Invoices anna lr
localhost> listaclmailbox user.boss.Invoices
boss lrswipcda
anna lr
```

Now `anna` can subscribe to the boss's `Invoices` directory and read it. The `l` permission makes a mailbox visible for a user. However, any subdirectories will not become visible.

The `r` permission is required to read the contents of a mailbox. `r` only refers to the specified directory. If, for example, `Invoices` contains a further subdirectory, `anna` will not be able to access it.

In some cases, it is necessary for several colleagues to have access to a shared directory. In this case, Cyrus enables you to work with *groups*, which

14.2 Shared Folders and ACLs

avoids the trouble of having to share the subdirectory with each user individually. If you assign multiple users to a group and then assign r permission for a certain directory to that group, all members of the group will be able to subscribe to and read the directory.

You need to use an authentication source that can map groups and members. The simplest choice is the Unix permissions system, with the `passwd`, `shadow`, and `groups` files. LDAP and MySQL databases are slightly more complicated to set up. `sasldb2` cannot map groups and is therefore not suitable for this purpose. The following example shows how to share a mailbox in such a case:

```
linux: # cyradm -auth login localhost -user cyrus
IMAP Password: password for cyrus
localhost> setaclmailbox user.information_board group:sharedreader lr
localhost> exit
```

Now, all the members of the `sharedreader` group can view and read the `information_board` mailbox.

Shared folders and shared mailboxes are simply mailboxes and subdirectories with an extended user group, so quotas apply here just like they do for personal mailboxes.

Table 2.1 on page 36 lists all the permissions you can assign. Unlike Courier, Cyrus only knows the permissions lrswipcda, and not e, t, and x.

Please also note that some permissions, such as l (*list* mailbox name) and r (*read* mailbox), are codependent. If a user wishes to subscribe to a shared folder and is only given the read permission, he or she will be unable to find that shared folder, as this requires the list permission. If a user has r but not l, Cyrus will not display the contents of the corresponding shared folder.

The Cyrus admin user needs to have the d permission in order to delete a mailbox:

```
localhost> lam user.horst
horst lrswipcda
localhost> dm user.horst
deletemailbox: Permission denied
localhost> sam user.horst cyrus all
localhost> lam user.horst
horst lrswipcda
cyrus lrswipcda
localhost> dm user.horst
```

You can find aliases for the most common permission combinations in Table 14.1. However, these combinations cannot be combined with additional

231

permissions, so you have to choose between aliases and permission combinations.

Table 14.1: Abbreviations for common permission combinations

Alias	Meaning
none	Removes all permissions for a mailbox from a user
read	Sets permissions `lrs`
post	Sets permissions `lrsp`
append	Sets permissions `lrsip`
write	Sets permissions `lrswipcd`
all	Sets all permissions (`lrswipcda`)

14.3 Virtual Domains

Cyrus creates a subdirectory for every user in the `/var/spool/imap/user/` directory in accordance with the default settings in `/etc/imap.conf`. This goes smoothly as long as every username is unique. However, simple namespaces cause problems as soon as there are two users with the same name, for example, `paul@example.net` and `paul@example.com`. Many administrators set up creatively named directories like these:

```
example_net_paul/
example_net_geeko/
example_com_paul/
```

In extreme cases, domain names can be turned into sequential numbers, or some other naming scheme can be used that has no relation to the actual email addresses. This can work well for a while (and may even secure the position of the mail administrator), but handling subdirectories becomes more difficult.

Why choose complicated methods when there is an easy way? With *virtual domains*, Cyrus provides a concept for managing extended namespaces.

14.3.1 The Underlying Concept

The Cyrus IMAP server considers every user as part of a domain, even though we have only worked with simple user accounts without a domain part. It assigns users, such as `paul`, `geeko`, and `horst`, to a domain, such as the Postfix relay domain `example.net` in our example in section 11.4 on page 192, for which the MTA accepts emails that it then forwards to Cyrus.

14.3 Virtual Domains

In this case, Cyrus jargon refers to *unqualified users* located in a *default domain*. This domain is not mentioned explicitly in Cyrus, and all emails addressed to the domain are sorted into the appropriate user account in the /var/spool/imap/users/ directory. Figure 14.4 shows what this looks like at the directory level.

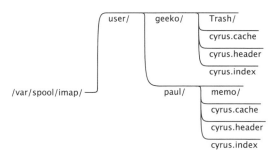

Figure 14.4:
The structure of the mailbox directory without virtual domains

Cyrus only shows its full ability when more than one domain has to be managed. It then works with *qualified users* and an extended namespace, that is, with multiple *virtual domains*. Figure 14.5 shows the structure of the email directories in this case.

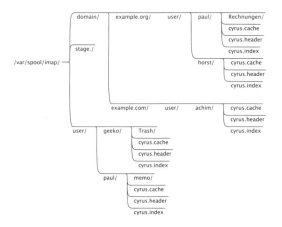

Figure 14.5:
Far more complex: an email directory when virtual domains are used

Every user now has a personal email directory in his or her own domain. This means the same username paul can be associated with accounts in different domains. The username for authentication is then the complete email address.

In order to implement this, Cyrus first needs to know that it is dealing with multiple virtual domains. Use the virtdomains parameter in the /etc/imapd.conf file to tell it so:

233

14 Advanced Cyrus Configuration

```
virtdomains: yes
```

Cyrus will now process virtual domain entries and create *new* user mailboxes within the domain structure. If you want the server to manage both unqualified and qualified user mailboxes, you have to specify a *default domain*:

```
defaultdomain: example.net
```

The server will now assign unqualified mailboxes in the `user/` directory to the `example.net` domain. Unfortunately, Cyrus makes it impossible to use symbolic links to match these unqualified names to their new qualified names at the file level: Cyrus stores the entire directory structure in parallel in administration databases, so it will crash at the latest during a recovery. Hard links are also not possible, as they are not permitted for directories.

When switching from a single-domain configuration to a multiple-domain configuration, you should always assign existing user mailboxes to the default domain. Otherwise, existing users will no longer be able to log on to the email server using their unqualified usernames, and the email server will be unable to deliver email correctly.

Restart Cyrus with `rccyrus restart` so that it will use the modified configuration.

Assuming that users are authenticated via `sasldb2`, create new users for the `example.com` domain as follows:

```
linux: #   saslpasswd2 paul@example.com
Password: password for paul@example.com
Again (for verification): password for paul@example.com
linux: #   chown cyrus:mail /etc/sasldb2
```

The mailboxes for Cyrus are created as follows:

```
linux: # cyradm -auth login localhost -user cyrus
IMAP Password: password_for_cyrus
localhost> cm user.paul@example.com
localhost> exit
```

After this command, the new directory should look like this:

```
linux: #   ls -la /var/spool/imap/domain/example.com/user/paul/
total 20
drwx------ 2 cyrus mail 4096 2006-07-14 13:06 .
drwx------ 3 cyrus mail 4096 2006-07-14 13:06 ..
-rw-------   1 cyrus mail    4 2006-07-14 13:06 cyrus.cache
-rw-------   1 cyrus mail  146 2006-07-14 13:06 cyrus.header
-rw-------   1 cyrus mail   76 2006-07-14 13:06 cyrus.index
```

The uppermost directory level contains the user/ subdirectory with the mailboxes of the unqualified users, and a domain/ subdirectory for all of the virtual domains:

```
linux: #  ls -l /var/spool/imap/
total 8
drwx------ 4 cyrus mail 4096 2006-07-14 13:06 domain
drwx------ 5 cyrus mail 4096 2006-07-13 15:23 user
```

There is one more small hurdle: Imagine that user `paul` wants to use an email address containing his first and last names, of the form `paul.meier@example.com`. In this case, there is a problem. If you use `cyradm` to create such a mailbox, this tool interprets the dot between the first and last names as a *netnews separator* and therefore creates an additional subdirectory, `/var/spool/imap/domain/example.com/user/paul/meier/`. In `cyradm`, it will look like this:

```
localhost> cm user.paul@example.com
localhost> cm user.paul.meier@example.com
localhost> lm
user.paul@example.com (/HasChildren)
user.paul.meier@example.com (HasNoChildren)
```

In the email client, `meier` will appear as a subdirectory of the `INBOX` of user `paul`.

To avoid this, go to the `/etc/imapd.conf` file and enter `unixhierarchy sep:  1` to prevent Cyrus from using dots as the default level separator. The positive value (1 in this example) ensures that Cyrus ignores the dot and instead, like Unix, uses the slash (/) as a separator. If you now create users `paul@example.com` and `paul.meier@example.com` in `cyradm`, this will lead to the following result:

```
localhost> cm user/paul@example.com
localhost> cm user/paul.meier@example.com
localhost> lm
user/paul@example.com (HasNoChildren)
user/paul.meier@example.com (HasNoChildren)
```

`user.paul@example.com` and `user.paul.meier@example.com` are entirely independent mailboxes. This change also has an effect at the filesystem level:

```
linux: #  ls -l /var/spool/imap/domain/example.com/user/
total 4
drwx------ 4 cyrus mail 4096 May 22 20:02 paul
drwx------ 3 cyrus mail 4096 May 22 20:02 paul^meier
```

The dot in the mailbox name is represented by a caret (^). When creating mailboxes, you must now make sure to use the slash rather than the dot as the separator between hierarchical levels. If, from habit, you continue to use the previous syntax when creating new mailboxes, the `user.paul.meier.Trash@example.com` subdirectory created by the command `cm user.paul.meier.Trash@example.com` will appear on one level on the hard disk:

```
linux: #  ls -li /var/spool/imap/domain/example.com/
[...]
drwx------ 2 cyrus mail 4096 Nov 26 12:29 user^paul^meier^Trash
[...]
```

In order to avoid mistakes, you should only create qualified mailboxes once you have activated the `virtdomains` parameter. Otherwise, the result will be top-level mailboxes with a domain part that cannot be edited, and can only be deleted when you temporarily deactivate `virtdomains`.

Make sure that you always use the `user` prefix when creating mailboxes, because otherwise they cannot be addressed correctly. If such an error occurs, you have to deactivate support for virtual domains, delete the faulty mailbox, reactivate support for virtual domains, and then create the mailbox again.

14.3.2 Effects on ACLs

If Cyrus is used solely for unqualified user accounts, you can assign permissions for all mailboxes with `cyradm`, using the administrator account `cyrus`. Every user can also assign permissions for his or her own directories to other users.

Things are slightly different if Cyrus is using virtual domains. The unqualified admin user `cyrus` can still assign permissions globally, but all other users can only assign permissions within their own domain (for unqualified users, this is the default domain).

Cyrus does not allow permissions to be assigned between domains. Thus, user `paul@example.net` is unable to assign read permission for his memo mailbox folder to user `geeko@example.com`, either using the `cyradm` command `sam` or in the email client, as `paul` is in a different domain than `geeko`. In this case, `cyradm` terminates the call with the following error message:

```
localhost> sam user/paul/memo@example.net user/geeko@example.com lr
setaclmailbox: user/geeko@example.com: lr: Invalid identifier
```

Within a domain, this can be done:

```
localhost> lam user/paul/memo@example.net
paul@example.net lrswipcda
localhost> sam user/paul/memo@example.net geeko@example.net lr
localhost> lam user/paul/memo@example.net
paul@example.net lrswipcda
geeko@example.net lr
```

14.3.3 Domain Administrators

Naturally, separate administrator accounts can be designated for each virtual domain. These domain administrators have the same permissions as the global administrator, but their scope is restricted to their own domain. To set up domain administrators, add the qualified usernames to the `admins` entry in the `imapd.conf`:

```
admins: cyrus paul@example.net geeko@example.com
```

In this case, `cyrus` receives global administrator permissions, whereas `paul @example.net` and `geeko@example.net` can only carry out administrator tasks for their respective domains: `paul` for `example.net` and `geeko` for `example.org`.

In general, if you enter a username without a domain part, this user will receive general Cyrus administrator permissions. Usernames with a domain part are assigned these privileges only for their own domain. If you enter a name with a domain section for which Cyrus is not responsible, the user receives no permissions and can only see an empty `cyradm` console. If the global Cyrus administrator is deleted, it is no longer possible to carry out administrative tasks, but the email server continues to run.

Be careful when assigning administrator permissions, as a user with a global administrator account can affect the entire Cyrus system and therefore cause considerable damage.

If you loaded Sieve scripts onto the server before implementing virtual domains, you will have to adapt these scripts. For more information, see section 14.6.6 on page 252.

14.4 Sorting Emails into Subdirectories

One of the benefits of IMAP is that users can sort their emails into different subdirectories on the server, which means they do not have to download them and manage them locally. Most clients create these subfolders under the `INBOX`.

14 Advanced Cyrus Configuration

If you want to automatically sort emails into subdirectories when they arrive at the server, this usually requires the email client to have corresponding functionality. The p permission (see Table 2.1 on page 36) is required for all directories to which a filter script should move emails. In newly created directories, the user automatically has this permission. You must be given the p permission if you subscribe to another user's mail directories.

There are no problems if a user only uses one client. If, however, a user often changes computers or only has access via web clients from Internet cafes, the user has to set up and synchronize the filter settings on every email client that he or she will use. Luckily, the Cyrus email server provides support here.

The *sender* must address the email in such a manner that the email server can sort it into the correct subdirectory. The manner of address in turn depends on the configuration of the directory separator, specified in the unixhierarchysep parameter (see page 235).

If you use netnews separators, Cyrus separates the directory levels with a dot. The sender can then directly address the target subdirectory in the email address of the recipient by using a dot to separate it from the recipient name. For example, if you want to send an email to paul@example.com, and the email is to be sorted directly into the Invoices subdirectory of the INBOX, you would address the email to paul.Invoices@example.com.

If, on the other hand, Cyrus uses Unix separators, a slash separates levels in the directory hierarchy. As discussed earlier, this is necessary, for example, when email addresses consist of first and last names separated by dots. In this case, an email for the Invoices subdirectory of the INBOX for email address paul.meier@example.com should be addressed to paul.meier/Invoices@example.com. If you address the email to paul.meier.Invoices@example.com (with a dot instead of a slash), you will get the following error message:

```
<paul.meier.Invoices@example.com>: host public/lmtp[public/lmtp]
    said: 550-Mailbox unknown.  Either there is no mailbox associated
    with this 550-name or you do not have authorization to see it.
    550 5.1.1 User unknown (in reply to RCPT TO command)
```

In this case, Cyrus searches for a mailbox named paul.meier.invoices@example.com, but this mailbox does not exist.

This is not really a practical solution, as most senders will not know whether Cyrus is in use, what the correct subdirectory is called, or even which separator the server uses. Automatic mail filtering only makes sense in conjunction with Sieve scripts (see section 14.6 on page 240).

14.5 Email Partitions

Enter the `partition-default` parameter in `/etc/imapd.conf` to specify the location where Cyrus creates and expects the mailboxes by default. This implies, however, that other locations could be specified for the storage of user mailboxes. Cyrus calls these storage locations *partitions*, regardless of whether these are physical partitions or directories.

In some cases additional mail partitions are advisable, for example, once your system has reached a certain size and the default partition is running out of memory, or if the hard disk system is no longer able to process queries effectively. I/O bottlenecks are one of the most common causes of slow systems, ahead of CPU overloads. In this case, you should consider placing new mailboxes on other hard disks or partitions. You can define these as follows:

```
partition-default: /var/spool/imap
partition-mail1: /var/spool/mail1
partition-mail2: /var/spool/mail2
partition-mail3: /var/spool/mail3
defaultpartition: mail3
```

Every *mail partition* receives a separate name. The name of the parameter defining the mail partition consists of the character string `partition-` followed by the name of the partition as the suffix. The `partition-mail1` entry in the example specifies that directory `/var/spool/mail1` forms mail partition `mail1`. For reasons of clarity, it is advisable to give the physical email directory or mount point the same name as the mail partition, but this consistency is not mandatory. If you do not specify a partition when creating new mailboxes, Cyrus will create the mailboxes in the mail partition specified by `defaultpartition`, here `mail3`.

In order to create a new mailbox in a partition, enter the name of the mailbox as an additional parameter for the `cyradm` command `createmailbox`:

```
localhost> createmailbox user.achim mail1
```

The command in this example creates a mailbox for user `achim` in mail partition `mail1`. If `cyradm` returns the error message `createmailbox: System I/O error` in response to this command, you should have a look at the system log: You probably forgot to give write permissions to Cyrus for the new mail partition. To do this, use `chown cyrus:mail /var/spool/mail1`, for example, to assign ownership of the directory to the Cyrus system user and his or her group.

If you do not specify a mail partition when creating the mailbox, it will automatically be created in the location specified in `partition-default:`.

If even this partitioning of email storage no longer suffices to provide the necessary performance, you should build a cluster to relieve your email server. For instructions, see page 281.

14.6 The Sieve Email Filter

Its speed and operation may be matters of debate, but many administrators choose Cyrus as their email server because of the server-side email filtering it allows, using scripts written in a specially developed language, *Sieve*. Many other email servers now have a Sieve interface, and email clients such as KMail or Squirrelmail allow the creation and management of Sieve filter scripts.

The Sieve script language has fewer functions than `procmail`, for example, but seems to be much more intuitive to many users for exactly that reason. Unlike `procmail`, users can place Sieve scripts on the server without having to have a shell account. They only need to be able to log on as Cyrus users.

14.6.1 The Email Filter Daemon `timsieved`

The email filter daemon `timsieved` has been in development at Carnegie Mellon University since 1994, along with the Cyrus IMAP daemon. It imports filter scripts created by users for managing their mailboxes and uses them to control the Cyrus master process. By default, it listens on port 2000. Tim Showalter, after whom the service is named, works at CMU and is responsible for integrating the service into Cyrus. In addition to this particular Sieve implementation for Cyrus, which is also known as *Managesieve*, there are Sieve implementations for other servers.

`timsieved` allows emails to be forwarded, refused, and moved to specific mailbox directories, and it also allows the sending of out-of-office notices. The `notifyd` service allows notification messages to be sent when specific emails are received.

When Cyrus receives emails, `timsieved` applies the existing rules to these emails. Emails can be deleted by sender or spam tag, moved to subdirectories, forwarded, or automatically replied to, for example, when the user is away from the office.

14.6.2 Configuring and Testing

The required package has to be installed in order for the email filter service to work. The package name usually contains `sieve`; in SuSE, for example, it is called `perl-Cyrus-SIEVE-managesieve`.

14.6 The Sieve Email Filter

Specify the working directory for `timsieved` in `/etc/imapd.conf`:

```
sievedir: /var/lib/sieve
```

This is where the Sieve scripts uploaded by users are stored, sorted into subdirectories A to Z by the first letter of the username.

By including the Sieve daemon in `cyrus.conf` in the SERVICES section, you integrate it as a process in the Cyrus process chain:

```
sieve    cmd="timsieved" listen="sieve" prefork=0
```

The first part is the name by which the service is known within Cyrus. `cmd` indicates that the service will be provided by the `timsieved` program. `listen` defines the port where the service should listen for commands. The `prefork` switch specifies how often the service is started in order to wait in idle mode. The default value is sufficient here.

`sivtest` is an aid that allows you to test the Sieve function after Cyrus has been restarted.

This little program simulates a user login on the Sieve server. The output shows whether the server has been configured correctly and whether the authentication works:

```
linux: # sivtest -a paul localhost
"IMPLEMENTATION" "Cyrus timsieved v2.2.12"
"SASL" "DIGEST-MD5 PLAIN CRAM-MD5 LOGIN"
"SIEVE" "fileinto reject envelope vacation imapflags notify subaddress re
lational comparator-i;ascii-numeric regex"
OK
AUTHENTICATE "DIGEST-MD5"
{236}
bm9uY2U9ImV3Q2lQOHkzU3dwYU9lbFJOMmNxbjRZOHJmS2o5ODcrSnJHS3dhdEtvQUU9IixyZ
WFsbT0iZ3Vja3kiLHFvcD0iYXV0aCxhdXRoLWludCxhdXRoLWNvbmYiLGNpcGhlcj0icmM0LT
QwLHJjNC01NixyYzQsZGVzLDNkZXMiLGlheGJ1Zj00MDk2LGNoYXJzZXQ9dXRmLTgsYWxnb3J
pdGhtPW1kNS1zZXNz
Please enter your password: most secret
{344+}
dXNlcm5hbWU9InBhdWwiLHJlYWxtPSJndWNreSIsbm9uY2U9ImV3Q2lQOHkzU3dwYU9lbFJOM
mNxbjRZOHJmS2o5ODcrSnJHS3dhdEtvQUU9Iixjbm9uY2U9InI3ZHlrMlJ4Mzg2UFZjRm5KQU
1YRzUwVjhQYjlOa1ZkdmhEOCsvekdqLzA9IixuYz0wMDAwMDAwMSxxb3A9YXV0aCljb25mLGN
pcGhlcj1yYzQsbWF4YnVmPTEwMjQsZGlnZXN0LXVyaT0ic2lldmUvbG9jYWxob3N0NOIixyZXNw
b25zZT1kZTViY2E3MTFmYzRmYTQ1YjBmZGQ4ZGQ2ZTNhNGJkNA==
OK (SASL "cnNwYXV0aD01ZmY5YjhkYzV1ZTA4MmZjMTBiZWUxNmE3ODUxNzRkZQ==")
Authenticated.
Security strength factor: 128
logout
OK "Logout Complete"
Connection closed.
```

This test shows that `paul` has logged in successfully. `-a` is used to transfer the username for authentication. If you do not specify this option, `sivtest` will automatically use the name of the system user who is logged on. `localhost` is used if you do not specify a hostname.

The server returns the name of the Sieve service and its version number, the name of the password-transfer mechanisms available on the responsible authentication service, and the functions available in Sieve (see section 14.6.4 on page 246).

In this case, the user is authenticated using a challenge-response procedure (`DIGEST-MD5`) based on the password. If the password digest calculated by the server matches the value calculated for the password entered (`dXNlcm5hbWU9...`), the server confirms the action with `authenticated`. If not, the login test terminates with `NO "Authentication Error"`.

14.6.3 The `sieveshell` Administration Tool

Users can use `sieveshell` to upload, delete, activate, and deactivate filter scripts on the server from a command line. They can write the scripts in any text editor (see section 14.6.4 on page 246) and then store them in a directory. They then call `sieveshell` in interactive mode in that directory.

As the argument, the command expects the name of the server that is to be addressed. If the email user's name does not correspond to that of the Unix user who is currently logged on, the user uses the option `-a name` or `--authname=name` to specify that name:

```
user@linux:$ sieveshell -a paul -u paul localhost
connecting to localhost
Please enter your password:
>
```

Usually, the authentication name (Who am I?) transferred by `-a` is automatically used for authorization (What may I do?). However, this only works in systems that use Kerberos for logging in. The `sieveshell` documentation states succinctly that for every other login service, you should transfer the name once again using `-u`. Otherwise, the user has to enter the password three times in a row in order to log in.

If Kerberos is used for authentication, you can use the option `-rrealm` or `--realm=realm` to specify the realm you are logging into.

You can place commands that you would usually enter at the `sieveshell` prompt into a script file. If you call the program with option `-e script` or `--exec=script`, it will process these commands non-interactively. This process is suitable for automatically importing Sieve scripts.

The following commands are permitted in `sieveshell` scripts and at the `sieveshell` prompt:

`help`
> This is the help function for the program.

`list`
> This command lists the Sieve scripts that are currently loaded.

`put` *file name*
> This command places the specified Sieve script on the server. `sieve shell` does not display the filename suffix. Thus, `vacation.script` becomes `vacation`. You can also use a second argument to specify a name that `sieveshell` should use. Make sure not to use special characters or spaces in your script names. Such characters can cause problems when the scripts are imported.

`get` *name*
> This command displays the specified script on the console. If you enter a filename as a second argument, `sieveshell` will store the script under this name in the filesystem.

`delete` *name*
> This command deletes the specified script from the server.

`activate` *name*
> This command activates the specified script on the server:

```
linux: # sieveshell -a paul -u paul localhost
connecting to localhost
Please enter your password: most secret
> put vacation.script
> put atwork.script
> activate vacation
> list
vacation   <- active script
atwork
```

> In this example, two Sieve scripts called `vacation.script` and `atwork.script` were loaded onto the Sieve server, but only `atwork` was activated. The `list` command shows the loaded scripts: `vacation` is active, `atwork` inactive.

`deactivate`
> This command deactivates the script that is currently active.

`quit`
> This command ends the program.

It is not possible to overwrite an existing script on the server with a script having the same name. If you want to change a script, you have to delete it from the server and then upload and activate the new version. Each user may upload a maximum of five scripts, but only one of these may be active. For this reason, it makes sense to put all rules into a single script.

Most users will probably be overwhelmed by a command-line tool such as `sieveshell`, especially since they have to enter the server address and their email username explicitly. For this reason, it is advisable to offer web interfaces such as `smartsieve`[3] (see Figure 14.6) or `websieve`,[4] which can be operated without a Linux command line.

Figure 14.6: Filter rules are easy to set up with the web interface from smartsieve.

The `smartsieve` project seems as though it will be successful, as it is both more convenient to use and under active development. When we went to press, there was a first release candidate of the stable version, whereas the most recent beta version of `websieve` was published in July 2004.

The popular webmail client Squirrelmail[5] also has more capabilities than simply interacting with IMAP servers. The plugin `avelsieve`[6] makes it possible to edit filter criteria conveniently in a browser. It can also be used to control the `notifyd` information service (see section 14.7 on page 252), which provides information when certain emails are received.

The Webmin Cyrus plugin (see page 184) also allows Sieve scripts to be managed on the server. However, only administrators should use this plugin, as a lot of fine tuning is required to secure this web interface for use by normal users.

Some email programs, such as KMail (see Figures 14.7 and 14.8), can also be used to control a Sieve server. Where possible, you should recommend

---

[3] See http://smartsieve.sourceforge.net/.
[4] See http://sourceforge.net/projects/websieve/.
[5] See section 5.1 on page 68.
[6] See http://email.uoa.gr/projects/squirrelmail/avelsieve.php.

such an email client to your users. It is much more convenient than using a web interface. If you do this, you should remember to activate the Sieve port 2000 (TCP) in your firewall.

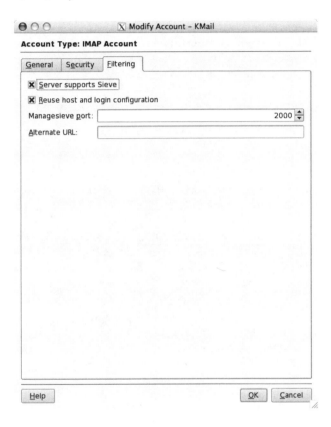

Figure 14.7:
You can activate Sieve script administration in the account settings of the KMail client.

Figure 14.8:
KMail displays existing Sieve scripts in a clear manner. Right-click an email account to create a new script.

14.6.4 The Sieve Script Language

The Sieve script language is similar to C or PHP. When a Sieve script is uploaded with `sieveshell`, it is checked and then written to the working memory.

The script contains the filter criteria and the actions to be taken when each criterion applies; these actions are placed in curly brackets. Instructions have to end with a semicolon:

```
require "fileinto";
if address :is "from" "test@example.com" {
        fileinto "INBOX.Testmails";
        stop;
}
```

In this example, the emails from `test@example.com` (as determined by the From: header) are automatically placed in the `INBOX.Testmails` of the recipient, thanks to the `fileinto` operation. If, as in this case, an instruction ends with `stop`, no other rules within the curly brackets are processed for this email. In this way, any succeeding actions in the same block can be temporarily deactivated. The `stop` command is also used preemptively to stop an action safely. Here, if the `fileinto` command in the example fails, the email is automatically forwarded to the `INBOX`.

For some actions, you may have to load additional modules using the `require` operation. This applies to the functions `fileinto`, `reject`, `vacation`, and `envelope`. Multiple modules are separated by commas and enclosed in square brackets:

```
require ["fileinto", "vacation"];
```

Most rules in Sieve scripts are conditional queries that begin with `if`. After the keyword come *test commands*.

The `address` test command is always used when you want to explicitly check address fields in the email header (such as From:, To:, Cc:, and Bcc:):

```
if address :is ["to", "cc"] "paul@example.com"
```

searches the To: and Cc: address fields for the specified address. Multiple entries are combined in square brackets. If you do not specify anything between the `:is` operator and the address, all address entries in the header are checked.

If you want to evaluate the email envelope, load the `envelope` module, which provides this function. The following, for example, deletes all emails addressed to `toeveryone@example.com` in the SMTP dialog:

14.6 The Sieve Email Filter

```
require "envelope";
if envelope :all :is "to" "toeveryone@example.com" {
        discard;
}
```

Header contents (often `Date:` or `Subject:`) can be evaluated using `header`. This command can filter more exactly than `address`. You also use this function if you want to use only a part of an address field (such as the `To:` header) as a filter criterion:

```
require "fileinto";
if header :contains "To" "paul@example" {
        fileinto "INBOX/memo";
}
```

This rule moves all emails that contain "paul@example" in a recipient address into the `memo` directory; this includes emails addressed to paul@example.com and to paul@example.net. The `address` function does not have this ability.

The relational operators for `header` and for `address` are `:is`, `:contains`, and `:matches`. A rule is satisfied when one of the following holds:

- The header matches the specified pattern exactly (`:is`).

- The header contains the specified pattern (`:contains`).

- The placeholder specified for `:matches` matches the header. The following rule, for example, filters emails where the `To:` or `Cc:` header contains an email address with user part `finances` and any domain part with the top-level domain `.com`.

    ```
    if header :matches [ "To", "Cc" ] "finances@*.com" {
          discard;
    }
    ```

If you want to use POSIX2-style regular expressions for comparison, you would use `:regex` instead of `:matches`. For example,

```
require "regex";
if header :regex "Subject" "^\*\*\*EROTIC" {
        discard;
}
```

prevents emails whose subject line begins with "***EROTIC" from being delivered.

If you want to check whether a header exists, use the `exists` command. To find out whether a header does not exist, use `not exists`.

Use `size` if you want to use the size of an email with attachments as a filter criterion. The condition `if size :over 10M` in a rule, for example, stipulates that it applies to all emails larger than 10MB. For kilobytes and gigabytes, specify `K` or `G` instead of `M`; if you want to filter by number of bytes, you would specify only the number. Use `:under 1M` to search for emails smaller than 1MB. It is not possible to directly determine whether an email's size corresponds *exactly* to a certain value.

If a rule applies, you can do the following with the filtered emails:

discard
: This command deletes the email.

fileinto *directory*
: This command moves the message to the specified directory. If the directory does not yet exist, the email is placed in the INBOX.

keep
: This command places the email in the INBOX, unless the recipient address specifies a suitable subdirectory (see section 14.4 on page 237).

redirect *email_address*
: This command returns the email to the MTA, which then redirects it to the specified address. The recipient in the email envelope is then only the address the email is redirected to. You can use this function to formulate the most simple Sieve script possible:

```
redirect "paul@example.com";
```

This script forwards all emails addressed to the mailbox to paul@example.com.

reject *text*
: This command returns the email to the sender, together with a message.

```
require "reject";
reject "Spam not wanted";
```

This command returns all messages addressed to this mailbox to the sender with the following comment in the email body:

```
Your message was automatically rejected by Sieve, a mail
filtering language.

The following reason was given:
Spam not wanted
```

vacation *text*
> The sender receives an out-of-office notification. The :days *number* parameter prevents the sender from receiving an out-of-office reply to *every* email addressed to this recipient. If you do specify the number of :days between notifications, the sender will receive the notification no more often than every seven days:
>
> ```
> require "vacation"; vacation "Am away on business until 6.20.";
> ```
>
> You can also add the :addresses option followed by recipient addresses:
>
> ```
> require "vacation"; vacation :days 2 :addresses ["geeko@example.co
> m", "horst@example.com"] "Am away on business until 6.20.";
> ```
>
> In this case, Sieve only sends an out-of-office reply to the sender if the recipient is one of the addresses in the square brackets. :days 2 ensures that this reply is not sent out for every email to geeko@example.com and horst@example.com, but is only sent every two days. The recipient's address can be specified not only in the To: header, but also the Cc: or Bcc: headers; the email can even be a forwarded email. It is not possible to create out-of-office replies for third parties, as the rule only refers to the user's own email account.

Conditional queries offer additional options:

if anyof (*condition1, condition2* ...){*instructions*;}
> The instructions in the curly brackets are executed if at least *one* of the specified conditions applies.
>
> ```
> require "fileinto";
> if anyof (header :is "From" "listadmin@example.com",
>          header :is "To" "user@list.example.com",) {
>    fileinto "INBOX/mailinglist";
> }
> ```
>
> For Sieve to sort an email into the mailinglist directory, the email header must contain either the From: address listadmin@example.com or the To: address user@list.example.com (or both).

if allof (*condition1, condition2* ...){*instructions*;}
> This condition is like if anyof, but here *all* conditions have to apply:
>
> ```
> if allof (address :is "listadmin@example.com", size :over 10M ){
>    [...]
> }
> ```

14 Advanced Cyrus Configuration

In the example, the email address `listadmin@example.com` must be in one of the header address fields, and the message has to be larger than 10MB.

`elseif allof (conditions){instructions;}`
Alternative rules apply when the `if` condition is not met. You can use `anyof` instead of `allof`.

`else {instructions;}`
Instructions are carried out when the `if` conditions and `elseif` conditions are not met.

An example that uses these features is the following script, which requires the modules `fileinto` and `vacation` containing the functions `fileinto` and `vacation`.

```
require ["fileinto", "vacation"];
if address :is "paul.meier@example.com" {
  fileinto "INBOX.Important";
}
elseif address :is "paul@example.com" {
  keep;
}
else {
  vacation :addresses ["admin-team@example.com", "support@example.com"]
  "I'm on vacation ...";
}
```

Emails containing `paul.meier@example.com` in one of the header address fields are sorted into the `Important` email directory, which is a subdirectory of the `INBOX`. If the address is `paul@example.com`, the email is delivered directly into the `INBOX`.

In all other cases, the `vacation` function evaluates the recipient. If the recipient is `admin-team@example.com` or `support@example.com`, the sender receives an out-of-office reply. This makes sense, for example, if your email address is listed on email distribution lists or as a forwarding address.

When creating your filter script, remember that the first applicable rule is executed and any rules that follow may no longer be applied.

There are other sample scripts that you can adapt to your own requirements, not only in the Sieve RFC 3028, but also on http://wiki.fastmail.fm/index.php/SieveExamples, http://en.wikipedia.org/wiki/Sieve_(mail_filtering_language), and http://www.bath.ac.uk/bucs/email/sieve.shtml.

14.6.5 Setting Up Sieve Scripts Automatically for New Accounts

There is very little documentation for a highly useful function that allows Sieve scripts to be set up automatically for every newly created mailbox. This function is very useful for fighting spam, for example. Activate it in file /etc/imapd.conf using the switch `autocreate_sieve_script`, followed by the path to the script to install:

```
autocreate_sieve_script: /var/lib/sieve/global/script-name
```

Make sure that the directory permissions in this directory allow the user cyrus to access it.

Remember that the `autocreatequota` switch must have a value other than 0 for Cyrus to create a mailbox automatically when a new user first logs on (see section 12.2 on page 203). The authentication data of the new user must already be available.

Once Cyrus is restarted, it translates the specified script into byte code for each new mailbox that is created automatically. You can follow this process in the syslog:

```
Aug 27 07:52:14 linux imap[32729]:
 login: [10.0.41.2] auto1@example.com
 plaintext User logged in
Aug 27 07:52:14 linux imap[32729]: autocreateinbox: User auto1@example.
com, INBOX was successfully created in partition default
Aug 27 07:52:14 linux imap[32729]: autocreate_sieve: autocreate_sieve_c
ompiledscript option is not defined. Compiling it
Aug 27 07:52:14 linux imap[32729]: entered bc_action_emit with filelen:
 16
Aug 27 07:52:14 linux imap[32729]: entered bc_action_emit with filelen:
 200
Aug 27 07:52:14 linux imap[32729]: autocreate_sieve: User auto1@example
.com, default sieve script creation succeeded
```

When user `auto1@example.com` first logs on to the email server, the server automatically creates a mailbox structure with an `INBOX` for that user. Then, the global Sieve script (named `redirect` in this example) is compiled into byte code suitable for Sieve and saved in the Sieve directory of the mailbox in both byte code (`redirect.bc`) and cleartext:

```
linux: # ls -l /var/lib/sieve/domain/e/example.com/a/auto1/
total 8
lrwxrwxrwx 1 cyrus mail  12 Aug 27 07:52 defaultbc -> redirect.bc
-rw------- 1 cyrus mail 220 Aug 27 07:52 redirect.bc
-rw------- 1 cyrus mail 162 Aug 27 07:52 redirect.script
```

The Sieve directories for the individual mailboxes are stored in `/var/lib/sieve/`, sorted alphabetically by the first letter of the domain and mailbox name.

The user never sees this script and cannot edit it. It is still executed automatically when emails are received for that user.

If you subsequently change the global script, this does not affect existing mailboxes, only newly generated ones. If you want to update the Sieve script for all mailboxes, you have to replace it manually in the Sieve directory for every user.

14.6.6 Adapting Sieve Scripts

When you migrate older Cyrus servers or introduce virtual domains, you have to adapt the Sieve scripts that are on the server. To do this, call the tool `translatesieve`, which you will find in `/usr/share/doc/packages/cyrus-imapd/tools/` in the tool collection:[7]

```
linux:/usr/share/doc/packages/cyrus-imapd/tools # ./translatesieve
you are using /var/lib/sieve as your sieve directory.
translating sievedir /var/lib/sieve... a b c d e f g h i j k l m n o p q
r s t u v w x y z done
```

14.7 The `notifyd` Daemon

"I don't think I've ever seen that in use," "Does it even work?", "I think that daemon might be out of date, is it even included anymore?"... You usually get answers like these when you try to tell people about the mysterious Cyrus notification service. However, it is not true that this SERVICES entry in the `cyrus.conf` file (see section 12.1.2 on page 201) is left over from the early days and nobody remembered to delete it; the notify daemon really works.

It operates in the background and receives its commands from the Cyrus master process, if either the master process informs the information service when new emails are received or a Sieve script provides notification that a certain email has been received. The second option is also available to normal users.

---

[7] For some distributions, such as Debian or Fedora, you have to install the separate package `cyrus-tools`.

14.7.1 Drums or Smoke Signals?

To activate the notify service, simply enable the corresponding line in the /etc/cyrus.conf file:

```
# this is only necessary if using notifications
notify cmd="notifyd" listen="/var/lib/imap/socket/notify" proto="udp" pr
efork=1
```

Now you can decide whether you want to receive notifications and by what mechanisms. The variables sievenotifier and mailnotifier in the /etc/imapd.conf file determine whether you receive notifications, and you assign the required delivery method as a value to one of these variables.

The mailnotifier parameter, if enabled, ensures that the notify daemon sends out a notification every time an email is received. sievenotifier specifies the type of notification for emails that correspond to a Sieve rule.

You can specify the values of these two options to make a global default setting for the entire Cyrus system. You can override the default setting for Sieve scripts with a :method specification, as shown in an example below. If you do not set either option, the information service is disabled.

You can choose among the following delivery methods:

null
: This method disables notifications. You can also leave out the entire entry in the global configuration file. This value is useful in Sieve scripts if you want to disable individual notification requests temporarily without having to rewrite the entire script.

log
: This method writes the message into the syslog. This setting is mainly useful as a value for mailnotifier in the /etc/imapd.conf file and can assist you when you track down errors. The logfile then contains entries like this:

    ```
    May 12 18:15:33 linux notifyd[13779]: do_notify using method 'log'
    May 12 18:15:33 linux notifyd[13779]: MAIL, , paul@example.com, IN
    BOX, "From: Peer Hartleben <mail@peer2peer.it> Subject: Tuesday T
    o: paul@example.com "
    ```

    Do not forget to set mailnotifier back to null (or to comment it out) as soon as you have found the error, as logfiles can fill up quickly.

mailto
: This delivery method is only available in Sieve scripts. It ensures that the notify daemon sends an information email when an event occurs:

14 Advanced Cyrus Configuration

```
require "notify";
if header :contains "from" "boss@example.com" {
    notify :method "mailto" :options ["paul@example.com"]
            :message "The boss has sent a new email";
}
```

When an email is received from boss@example.com, this Sieve filter rule sends a message to paul@example.com; the body of the email contains the text The boss has sent a new email. The subject line is always [SIEVE] New mail notification.

You can also enter the address of an SMS gateway[8] after :options if you want the notify daemon to send you a text message.

zephyr, sms, xmpp

There is no Cyrus documentation for these methods, and even forums and Internet drafts cannot provide an exact description. They only mention that an appropriate "environment" is required for the delivery of Zephyr, text message, or XMPP-(Jabber) notifications.

Zephyr is an ancient instant messaging system that was developed by MIT between 1983 and 1993, but it is hardly ever used any more. If you are interested, http://www.volker-wegert.de/node/455 provides instructions on how to install it on current Linux systems.

14.8 Cyrus and Other MTAs

Section 11.4 on page 191 explained how to dock Cyrus onto the Postfix Mail Transfer Agent. However, you can use any MTA with this IMAP server. The major difference from the Courier IMAP server is that Cyrus stores and manages emails in own databases. For this reason, it is not enough for the delivering MTAs to place the emails somewhere on the hard disk for Cyrus to collect them.

Far too much work would be required to modify MTAs so that they store emails in a format that Cyrus understands. Instead, the best solution is to set up direct communication between Cyrus and the MTA. If both services are running on the same computer, it makes sense to use a Unix socket for the connection. If the MTA and the IMAP server run on different computers, a TCP socket is more suitable. You can also use a TCP socket locally, but this will only incur unnecessary overhead, as the emails will have to be assembled into TCP/IP packages.

Define the selected interface in the /etc/cyrus.conf file, in the SERVICES section:

---

[8] Your SMS gateway operator will provide this address.

```
# at least one LMTP is required for delivery
# lmtp      cmd="lmtpd" listen="lmtp" prefork=0
lmtpunix   cmd="lmtpd" listen="/var/spool/postfix/public/lmtp" prefork=1
```

The LMTP socket, which is used when the MTA runs on a different computer, has been commented out here. From Cyrus's point of view, the `listen` entry in the active definition of the Unix socket specifies the end of the socket from which Cyrus receives the emails. Now you have to tell the MTAs that they should use this socket to deliver emails.

If the MTA is unable to handle LMTP, it is also possible to deliver the emails via the Cyrus `deliver` service. This is only possible if the MTA permits external commands for email delivery. Usually, only the Cyrus master process uses the `deliver` service to sort the emails into mailboxes, but the service can also be externally controlled.

In Exim, for example, you can do this with `/usr/lib/cyrus/bin/deliver -m $local_part`. The `-m` switch ensures that the mailbox name is specified; in Exim 4 it is read out of the `local_part` variable. You should only use this method if you really have to, as delivery via `deliver` does not always work properly.

When any other error occurs, simply read the logfiles and observe which service logs an error, so that you can determine where your troubleshooting should begin. Experience has shown that most errors are caused by faulty paths, especially when Cyrus and the MTA are connected via the LMTP socket, or by missing permissions—even if the error messages are not always specific.

14.9 Backing Up and Restoring Data

Even though Cyrus email servers are rather stable, problems can still occur, for example, when an error happens in the filesystem or when data is not written correctly after a computer crashes. Cyrus then requires a lot of work, as its data cannot simply be restored from a backup; this is due to the fact that, in addition to storing emails on the hard disk, Cyrus also manages index databases and status information. The mail store and administrative databases must always agree, and only Cyrus can ensure this. If you do have to make repairs, you can use the `reconstruct` program.

14.9.1 Using `reconstruct` to Repair Mailboxes

`reconstruct` searches for intact header files in the `/var/spool/imap/` directory and then attempts to restore the status information and databases in the `/var/lib/imap/` directory. This tool only works properly for complete mailboxes with complete index and header files. The program is in the `/usr/lib/cyrus/bin/` directory, and you start it as user cyrus.

If the database index is faulty, or if directories or mailbox contents have been deleted from the command line, `reconstruct` will compare the index of each mailbox with the existing data in the mailbox directory (if you call `reconstruct` without options):

```
cyrus@linux:/usr/lib/cyrus/bin/$ ./reconstruct
user/paul@example.com
user/paul/Drafts@example.com
user/paul/Sent@example.com
user/paul/Test@example.com
user/paul/Trash@example.com
user/paul/mailclient@example.com
user/paul/memo@example.com
user/paul.hartleben@example.com
user/paul.hartleben/schrott@example.com
user/quotatest@example.com
user/quotatest/Sent@example.com
user/quotatest/Trash@example.com
user/geeko@example.com
user/cyrus
user/paul
user/pwtest
user.achim.Invoices
```

The command's output simply shows that all mailboxes are being scanned. You will only know that the repair has been successful if the mailbox is once again available.

If you know where the error occurred, you can repair only the affected mailbox in order to save time. Please note that you have to enter the mailbox names using the appropriate separators. If `unixhierarchysep:yes` is set in virtual domain environments, the call should look like this:

```
cyrus@linux:/usr/lib/cyrus/bin/$ ./reconstruct -r user/paul
```

When the `-r` switch is activated, `reconstruct` will recursively scan all the mailboxes on the system, including the subdirectories, and will make any required corrections. This takes quite a lot of time.

If a large number of index databases in `/var/lib/cyrus/` are destroyed, the `-f` option restores the mailboxes. You should only use this switch in an emergency, as `reconstruct` will then search for `cyrus.header` files in the `/var/spool/imap/` directory and create a new mailbox for every file it finds. All other information, such as quotas, is lost, and you have to enter it again.

When loading backups onto a Cyrus system, you should proceed as follows:

- Stop Cyrus.

- Load the backup.

- Run `reconstruct` over the backup you just loaded.

- Restart Cyrus.

14.9.2 Restoring Quotas

If quotas are defective or are missing after loading the backup, you can use the `quota` tool to repair them. Call it as Unix user `cyrus`:

```
cyrus@linux:/usr/lib/cyrus/bin/$ ./quota -f mailboxname
```

If the `-f` switch is active, the tool repairs defective or inconsistent mailboxes.

Sometimes the quota information for a mailbox will be missing after you have loaded a backup. If you cannot restore them using the `cyradm` tool, the only option is to delete the quotaroot file. It is stored in `/var/lib/imap/quota/` in the subdirectory of the mailbox. If a different `configdirectory` is specified in `/etc/imapd.conf`, you should look for it there. Don't forget to use `quota -f mailboxname` at the end to make the index database and mail directory consistent with one another. Once you have done this, you can use `cyradm` to set the quota again for that mailbox.

14.10 Performance Tuning

Thanks to indexes and minidatabases, Cyrus is known as a fast IMAP server. However, this is usually a subjective assessment, as there are very few comparisons against other email servers.[9]

If you have enough time, you could have a detailed look at the system to see if you can improve performance a little, as the state in which it is delivered is usually far from the ideal state. Before fiddling with the workings, you should bear the following in mind:

- Always work with a safety net—the key word is *backup*.

---

[9] Carnegie Mellon University publishes many live statistics concerning Cyrus at `http://graphs.andrew.cmu.edu/`, but as there are no comparisons to other mail servers, these do not really serve as the basis for valid arguments.

- Design your test scenario so it fits everyday situations. Ready-made test programs such as mstone[10] can provide comparable results.

- Never change more than one value at a time, and test your system after each change.

- And don't forget the backup.

The (positive) effects of tuning always depend directly on the performance resources of your computer. These are disk I/O, CPU performance, and, the most important of all, RAM. Cyrus shows off to advantage if there is a lot of RAM. Mail servers are slowed down most by their searching of email directories. For this reason, Cyrus saves all data required for the search in small index databases. As the number of databases in the RAM increases, the reaction time decreases.

14.10.1 Parameters in /etc/imapd.conf that Influence Performance

The following options in the /etc/imapd.conf file affect the performance of Cyrus:

berkeley_cachesize
: This value specifies how much RAM each Cyrus index database may use. You can specify a value between 20KB and 4GB, but you must always specify the value in kilobytes. The default value is 512KB. You should only increase this value cautiously, as it depends directly on the following switch.

berkeley_txns_max
: This is where you can specify how many simultaneous transactions are permitted per database. You should be careful when making changes here, and keep the system under careful observation; if you set the value too high, busy computers can quickly be overloaded. The default value is 100.

maxmessagesize
: Use this to determine the maximum size of emails that can be transferred to Cyrus via the LMTP socket. The default value is 0, which permits all emails to be transferred. Restrictions do not increase performance directly, but they can help if your system is overloaded. But be careful: You have to specify the value in bytes. (Can't programmers ever agree on a single unit to use, at least for the same product?)

---

[10] See http://mstone.sourceforge.net/.

14.10 Performance Tuning

poptimeout
: By default, inactive POP3 connections are kept open for 10 minutes. You can enter a shorter time (in minutes) to relieve the demand on server resources.

partition-name
: You can distribute new mailboxes to additional mailbox partitions in order to relieve the load on your RAID system, or if you are running out of memory. For more information, see section 14.5 on page 239.

You can improve performance slightly by changing the format of the index databases.

berkeley
: Databases in this format react to queries fairly quickly and support binary contents. They are often slightly unstable, which is usually due to locking errors when accessed a lot.

berkeley-nosync
: This option is identical to berkeley, but data is held in the cache before being written. This increases the speed of write accesses. Unfortunately, it also reduces data security: If the cache is deleted for some reason (a power outage, for example), the data is lost.

skiplist
: This format was developed by the Cyrus programmers. If offers good write and read access, supports binary contents, and is known to be relatively stable. If locking problems occur with Berkeley databases, skiplist is the next best option.

flat
: Databases in this format are relatively easy to handle, as their contents are text based. They are also fairly stable, but the speed for write accesses is comparatively poor.

If you change the format of a database backend, it is *not* enough simply to enter it in the /etc/imapd.conf file. You also have to convert the database into the required format with the cvt_cyrusdb tool described on page 267. Please also note that not every format is suitable for every Cyrus database:

seenstate_db
: This is where you can specify the format of the index database for the "read" status. The developers of Cyrus recommend skiplist, but you can also use berkeley and flat.

annotation_db
: This option specifies the format of the annotation database. This

contains server metadata, such as system information or the email address of the server administrator. You can use `berkeley` and `skip list`.

`duplicate_db`

In this database, Cyrus stores information that it requires to suppress duplicate emails. This function is activated by default, but you can deactivate it in the `/etc/cyrus.conf` file in the `EVENTS{}` section (see section 12.1.3 on page 202).

You can use `berkeley`, `berkeley-nosync`, and `skiplist`. If you use `berkeley-nosync`, Cyrus keeps changes in the cache and only writes them into the database when the server is less busy. This value is recommended here.

`ptscache_db`

This option specifies the format of a database that is used to optimize the working memory management. You can use `berkeley` and `skiplist`.

`quota_db`

The quota database contains the currently valid mailbox quotas. You can use `flat`, `berkeley`, `skiplist`, and `quotalegacy`. The latter option was developed specifically for managing quotas in Cyrus and is therefore recommended.

`subscription_db`

The subscription database contains information on the mailboxes that are currently in use. You can use `flat`, `berkeley`, and `skiplist`.

`tlscache_db`

The TLS cache memorizes TLS connection information. You can use the database formats `berkeley`, `berkeley-nosync`, and `skiplist`. We recommend `berkeley-nosync`, as caching information does not have to be written immediately, and the I/O load on the disk is reduced.

You can also improve performance by using faster hard disks and choosing an appropriate filesystem (see page 53). It is advisable to use a filesystem that performs well when handling multiple small files. ReiserFS gets the best results in most benchmark tests. However, we have found that ReiserFS is not always stable and requires a lot of work and patience when problems occur. Reiser4 makes an even better impression where speed is concerned, but due to its beta status, it should be used carefully. When making your decision, you should also check the repair tools available for your choice of filesystem and take your skills with these tools into account.

Chapter 15

Internal Structure and Modules

You do not necessarily need to know which modules a Cyrus IMAP server is composed of and which internal auxiliary programs it uses, but this background information is important for troubleshooting. Cyrus is built according to the classic Unix concept of "one service—one function," which means that it has a modular structure (as shown in Figure 15.1) and is controlled by a master process, just like Postfix. The individual components of Cyrus are listed in the `/usr/lib/cyrus/bin/` directory.

Nearly all the programs listed there are started exclusively by the Cyrus master process and not manually. If you have to call any of them manually, for example, when repairing a faulty mail server, you have to make each call as the user `cyrus`.

The names can vary in different distributions; some Cyrus packages provided by distributions do not contain some of these tools, while others contain additional special tools.

15 Internal Structure and Modules

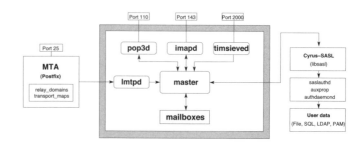

Figure 15.1:
The most important
Cyrus processes and
their functions

15.1 The Cyrus Daemons

The following programs are daemons that provide specific services in the background. They are all started by the `master` process. This master process is at the heart of Cyrus. It and all its dependent services run under the `cyrus` Unix account, which provides additional security for the system. Should an attacker hack into the IMAP server, he or she will only have the permissions of `cyrus`.

`idled`
: This service can be used to inform the mail client when new messages have been received. Usually, mail clients check mailboxes regularly, without knowing whether new emails have been received. The idle daemon evaluates the signals from the LMTP daemon and forwards this information to the mail client.

`imapd`
: This daemon provides the IMAP function and opens the IMAP ports.

`lmtpd`
: This service provides the LMTP socket and manages it according to the configuration in `/etc/cyrus.conf`. It is the interface between Cyrus and the delivering MTA.

`lmtpproxyd`
: The LMTP proxy service is used in cluster setups and transfers the emails received from the MTA to the backend server.

`mupdate`
: This is the Cyrus Murder server service. It is required by Cyrus clusters, where it synchronizes the information with that from the Cyrus backend servers (see page 281).

`nntpd`
: This daemon downloads messages via the Net News Transfer Protocol.

`notifyd`
: The Cyrus notification service (see section 14.7 on page 252) processes the notification requests from the master process when an email is delivered via LMTP. Depending on the configuration, it either creates a log entry or sends a message (e. g., via email) when a new email is received.

`pop3d`
: This service provides the Cyrus POP3 function.

`pop3proxyd`
: The POP3 proxy server is only used in cluster setups and transfers the POP3 requests from mail clients from the frontend to the backend server.

`smmapd`
: Cyrus uses the *Sendmail Socket Map Daemon* to check whether a mailbox exists and whether it is within its quota. If the mailbox does not exist, or if it has reached its quota, `smmapd` provides this information to the master process.

`timsieved`
: This is the Sieve email filter service (see section 14.6.1 on page 240).

15.2 Tools for Analysis, Maintenance, and Repairs

Cyrus uses some of the following auxiliary programs internally; in many distributions, they are already integrated in `/etc/cyrus.conf`. They can also be called manually for analyses or repairs.

15.2.1 Statistics and Analysis

`arbitron`
: This tool provides statistical information on all mailboxes, or on individual mailboxes if specified:

```
cyrus@linux:~/bin$  ./arbitron
Loading Mailboxes...Done
Loading Users........................
example/net!user/quotatest 0 0
user.achim 0 0
example/com!user/paul/Trash 0 0
```

```
example/com!user/paul.meier 0 0
example/com!user/paul/memo 0 0
example/com!user/paul 0 0
example/com!user/paul.meier/schrott 0 0
```

For each mailbox, this tool creates one line with the following information: the mailbox name and the number of accounts that have read this mailbox within the past 30 days, followed by the number of subscribers to this mailbox directory.

The -d switch restricts the time period for which the statistical information is supplied (-d 20, for example, will limit the statistical time period to the past 20 days). The -p switch allows statistical evaluation for more than one month (-p 10 provides statistical information for the last ten months, for example).

`chk_cyrus`

This tool checks the consistency of the Cyrus databases by synchronizing them with the email directories:

```
cyrus@linux:~/bin$  ./chk_cyrus
Examining partition: ALL PARTITIONS
checking: example.com!user.paul (/var/spool/imap/domain/example.com/user/paul)
  -> 5 records
checking: example.com!user.paul.Trash (/var/spool/imap/domain/example.com/user/paul/Trash)
  -> 0 records
checking: example.com!user.paul.memo (/var/spool/imap/domain/example.com/user/paul/memo)
  -> 3 records
checking: example.com!user.paul^meier (/var/spool/imap/domain/example.com/user/paul^meier)
  -> 2 records
checking: example.com!user.paul^meier.schrott (/var/spool/imap/domain/example.com/user/paul^meier/schrott)
  -> 2 records
checking: example.com!user.quotatest (/var/spool/imap/domain/example.com/user/quotatest)
  -> 1 records
checking: sommer.top!user.geeko (/var/spool/imap/domain/sommer.top/user/geeko)
  -> 0 records
checking: user.paul (/var/spool/imap/user/paul)
  -> 0 records
checking: user^horst (/var/spool/mail1/user^horst)
  -> 0 records
```

The list shows all existing mailbox directories, together with their path in the filesystem and the number of emails found. If this information does not match the information in the Cyrus databases,

15.2 Tools for Analysis, Maintenance, and Repairs

the tool returns an inconsistency warning message. You should then use `reconstruct` to repair the inconsistent mailbox.

`mbexamine`

This tool examines the mailbox, index, and header files and transfers this information to another process, to the screen, or to a file. It is useful if you need a detailed overview of the mailboxes.

If you call this command without a switch, it will provide information on all mailboxes. You can also specify an individual mailbox:

```
cyrus@linux:~/bin$ ./mbexamine user/paul/memo@example.com
Examining user/paul/memo@example.com...
 Mailbox Header Info:
  Path to mailbox: /var/spool/imap/domain/example.com/user/paul/memo
  Mailbox ACL: paul@example.com  lrswipcda        quotatest@example.org   lrs
  Unique ID: 1a9e415d4564f279
  User Flags: $NotJunk $Junk JunkRecorded

 Index Header Info:
  Generation Number: 58
  Format: NORMAL
  Minor Version: 6
  Header Size: 76 bytes  Record Size: 60 bytes
  Number of Messages: 1  Mailbox Size: 1499 bytes
  Last Append Date: (1186641337) Thu Aug  9 08:35:37 2007
  UIDValidity: 1164243577  Last UID: 12
  Deleted: 0  Answered: 0  Flagged: 0
  POP3 New UIDL: 1
  Last POP3 Login: (0) Thu Jan  1 01:00:00 1970

 Message Info:
000001> UID:00000012   INT_DATE:1184694344 SENTDATE:1184666400 SIZE:1499
       > HDRSIZE:1497   LASTUPD :1186641337 SYSFLAGS:00000000   LINES:1       CACHEVER:2
       > USERFLAGS: 00000000 00000000 00000000 00000001
 Envel>{278}("Tue, 17 Jul 2007 19:46:30 +0200" "Testtt" (("Peer Hartleben" NIL "mail" "peer2peer.it")) (("Peer Hartleben" NIL "mail" "peer2peer.it")) (("Peer Hartleben" NIL "mail" "peer2peer.it")) ((NIL NIL "paul" "example.com")) NIL NIL NIL "<200707171946.30885.mail@peer2peer.it>")
BdyStr>{81}("TEXT" "PLAIN" ("CHARSET" "us-ascii") NIL NIL "7BIT" 21 NIL ("INLINE" NIL) NIL)
  Body>{58}("TEXT" "PLAIN" ("CHARSET" "us-ascii") NIL NIL "7BIT" 21)
CacHdr>{188}User-Agent: KMail/1.9.6
Content-Type: text/plain;
  charset="us-ascii"
Content-Transfer-Encoding: 7bit
```

15 Internal Structure and Modules

```
Content-Disposition: inline
Message-Id: <200707171946.30885.mail@peer2peer.it>

  From>{33}peerhartleben <mail@peer2peer.it>
    To>{25}<paul@example.com>
    Cc>{0}
   Bcc>{0}
Subjct>{8}"testtt"
```

This result shows the header information from the `memo` subdirectory of `paul@example.com`'s mailbox; among other things, the header information shows the paths, the permissions, and the number, size, and headers of the messages the mailbox contains. In the example, the subdirectory contains a message with `testtt` in the subject line.

mbpath
: This tool returns the path to the storage location in the system of the specified mailbox's contents (`paul@example.com`'s mailbox, in this example):

```
cyrus@linux:~/bin$ ./mbpath user/paul@example.com
/var/spool/imap/domain/example.com/user/paul
```

15.2.2 Maintenance and Repair

The tools described here are useful aids for maintenance work on Cyrus. Some applications can be run automatically, for example, as a `cron` job.

ctl_cyrusdb
: This tool maintains and repairs all Cyrus databases. If you call the program with the `-r` switch, it tidies up the database and attempts to repair defects. This tool is executed automatically every 30 minutes and whenever Cyrus is started. You can find it in the `/etc/cyrus.conf` file in the sections START and EVENTS.

ctl_deliver
: This tool carries out checks and maintenance on the deliver database `deliver.db`. It is usually operated by Cyrus, but you can also use it manually to read out the deliver database. This is done by calling `ctl_deliver -d`, which lists the emails that were most recently delivered.

ctl_mboxlist
: This tool carries out internal checks and maintenance on the `mailboxes.db` database. This tool can also return the contents of that mailbox if the `-d` switch is activated. The database contains a list of all mailboxes and the permissions that have been assigned:

```
cyrus@linux:~/bin$ ./ctl_mboxlist -d
example.com!user.paul            default paul@example.com lrswipcda
example.com!user.paul.Drafts     default paul@example.com lrswipcda
example.com!user.paul.Sent       default paul@example.com lrswipcda
example.com!user.paul.Test       default paul@example.com lrswipcda
example.com!user.paul.Trash      default paul@example.com lrswipcda
```

cvt_cyrusdb

This tool converts Cyrus databases into different database formats. When called without a switch, it shows the database formats that can currently be converted. The conversion is done by issuing a command of the following form:

```
cvt_cyrusdb name_of_old_db old_db_format name_of_new_db \
new_db_format
```

The following example converts `annotations.db` from the `skiplist` format to the `flat` format (see section 14.10.1 on page 259):

```
cyrus@linux:~/bin$ ./cvt_cyrusdb /var/lib/imap/annotations.db \
skiplist /tmp/TEST-db flat
Converting from /var/lib/imap/annotations.db (skiplist) to /tmp/TE
ST-db (flat)
Warning: apparently empty database converted.
```

Make sure that you always enter the absolute paths to the databases, as the tool will otherwise terminate with an error message.

cyrdump

This tool returns the contents of a mailbox on the standard output, where the emails are shown one after another. You have to specify the mailbox or subdirectory as the argument:

```
cyrus@linux:~/bin$ ./cyrdump user/paul@example.com > paul_dump
```

creates a dump for `paul@example.com`'s mailbox and saves it in a file named `paul_dump`.

quota

This tool manages and repairs the mailbox quota (see section 14.9.2 on page 257).

reconstruct

This tool initializes and repairs the Cyrus database directory (see section 14.9.1 on page 255).

squatter

This program creates a squat fulltext index for every mailbox. It lists all existing emails in this index so that they are easier to find for the

15 Internal Structure and Modules

mail client. Please note that the index can only account for existing emails. When new emails are received, you have to run `squatter` again. For this reason, it makes sense to activate this program as a regular event in the `/etc/cyrus.conf` file, for example, by adding the following line in the EVENTS section:

```
squatter  cmd="/usr/bin/nice -n 19  /usr/lib/cyrus/bin/squatter" period=120
```

`squatter` now runs every two hours with a `nice` value of 19. After activating `squatter`, you should observe your system load. If there are a large number of large mailboxes, creating the index can take some time and slow down the system. For this reason, you should only start this service with a high `nice` value, so as not to put too much unnecessary strain on your server.

15.2.3 Internal Tools

There are also service programs that only Cyrus can use and that are useless for administrators.

`compile_sieve`
: This tool translates Sieve scripts into byte code so they can run in the Sieve daemon. It is almost identical to `sievec` and is used when Sieve scripts are created automatically. There is more information on this subject in section 14.6.5 on page 251.

`cyr_expire`
: This tool marks messages as obsolete, thereby flagging them for deletion. It has been entered as a regular command in the `/etc/cyrus.conf` file in the EVENTS section (see section 12.1.3 on page 202).

`deliver`
: This tool sorts delivered emails into the correct inboxes. It is usually used only by the master process, but other MTAs can use it to deliver emails (see section 14.8 on page 254).

`fetchnews`
: This tool receives news from news servers approved as peering partners and transfers these news messages to the Cyrus master process.

`fud`
: This tool delivers master process information on the status of mailboxes and the emails they contain.

`ipurge`
: This tool deletes emails from inboxes according to their age and expiration date (see section 12.1.3 on page 202).

sievec
: Like `compile_sieve`, this tool translates Sieve scripts into binary code so they can be executed by the Sieve daemon. It is executed by default when Sieve scripts are uploaded.

tls_prune
: This tool deletes expired TLS sessions from the `tls_sessions.db` database (see section 12.1.3 on page 202).

15.3 Other In-House Tools

Some distributions contain additional Cyrus tools in the documentation directory in `/usr/share/doc/packages/cyrus-imap/tools/`. This is a collection of mostly undocumented scripts that can be used for additional tasks.

arbitronsort.pl
: This tool sorts the output of the `arbitron` statistics tool (see section 15.2.1 on page 263) according to the number of users that have selected and subscribed to a mailbox.

config2header
: This tool is used to compile and patch the Cyrus source code; it is called automatically during compilation.

config2man
: This tool is also used to compile the source code and called automatically during compilation.

convert-sieve.pl
: This tool is required when upgrading Cyrus versions up to and including 2.1.12. It adapts Sieve scripts to the namespace Cyrus uses for virtual domains.

dohash
: This tool is required for upgrading Cyrus versions up to and including 1.6.1. This tool creates a hash value for faster mailbox indexing.

masssievec
: This upgrade tool for Cyrus versions up to and including 2.2.0 adapts existing Sieve scripts to the modified byte code format.

mkimap
: This tool creates the directory structure that Cyrus requires, which consists of mailboxes and an index/administration section; it is usually only required when Cyrus is installed manually from the source

code. During startup, the tool imports the working paths from the parameters `configdirectory` and `partition-default` in the `/etc/imap.conf` file and creates the mailbox structure in these locations in the filesystem:

```
linux:/usr/share/doc/packages/cyrus-imapd/tools #   ./mkimap
reading configure file...
i will configure directory /var/lib/imap.
i saw partition /var/spool/imap.
i saw partition /var/spool/mail1.
done
configuring /var/lib/imap...
creating /var/spool/imap...
creating /var/spool/mail1...
done
```

`mknewsgroups`
This tool creates a Usenet newsgroup directory structure used to map newsgroups in Cyrus. If the command is called with the `-h` switch, it returns a list of all kinds of parameters.

`mupdate-loadgen.pl`
This Perl script creates load on the mupdate server in a Cyrus Murder cluster (see page 281) by sending multiple requests:

```
linux:doc/packages/cyrus-imapd/tools #   ./mupdate-loadgen.pl
0 RESERVE "test.mupdate-load.3830.0" "borked.andrew.cmu.edu"
1 FIND "test.mupdate-load.3830.112"
2 FIND "test.mupdate-load.3830.101"
3 FIND "test.mupdate-load.3830.82"
4 FIND "test.mupdate-load.3830.20"
5 RESERVE "test.mupdate-load.3830.1" "borked.andrew.cmu.edu"
6 FIND "test.mupdate-load.3830.25"
7 FIND "test.mupdate-load.3830.40"
8 FIND "test.mupdate-load.3830.101"
9 FIND "test.mupdate-load.3830.87"
10 FIND "test.mupdate-load.3830.141"
11 RESERVE "test.mupdate-load.3830.2" "borked.andrew.cmu.edu"
12 FIND "test.mupdate-load.3830.9"
13 FIND "test.mupdate-load.3830.25"
[...]
```

It is an important tool when testing Murder clusters.

`rehash`
If you activate the `fulldirhash: 1` function in `/etc/imapd.conf`, all mailbox directories are given a hash value of the entire username for faster indexing. Use `rehash` to generate a new hash value.

translatesieve
: When Cyrus is reconfigured to handle virtual domains, the namespace settings change. If you want to continue using the Sieve scripts already on the server, you call `translatesieve` to adapt these scripts to the modified namespace.

undohash
: This tool removes hash values that have been set for mailboxes.

upgradesieve
: In more recent versions of Cyrus, the Sieve directories have to be adapted to a new structure. The following Perl script carries out this task:

    ```
    linux:/usr/share/doc/packages/cyrus-imapd/tools # ./upgradesieve
    you are using /var/lib/sieve as your sieve directory.
    upgrading sievedir /var/lib/sieve...a b c d e f g h i j k l m n o p
     q r s t u v w x y z
    done
    ```

    If you need to upgrade, you can find more detailed information in the change log of the new version.

15.4 The `cyradm` Administration Tool

The `cyradm` tool is the central point for administrators. It uses some of the internal tools mentioned above and is controlled with the following commands:

help
: This lists all available commands.

listmailbox (lm for short)
: This command lists the names of all mailboxes with reference to subdirectories (*children*):

    ```
    localhost> lm
    user/paul (\HasNoChildren)
    user/paul.meier/schrott@example.com (\HasNoChildren)
    user/paul.meier@example.com (\HasChildren)
    user/paul/Drafts@example.com (\HasNoChildren)
    user/paul/Sent@example.com (\HasNoChildren)
    user/paul/Test@example.com (\HasNoChildren)
    user/paul/Trash@example.com (\HasNoChildren)
    user/paul/mailclient@example.com (\HasNoChildren)
    user/paul/memo@example.com (\HasNoChildren)
    user/paul@example.com (\HasChildren)
    ```

```
user/pwtest (\HasNoChildren)
user/quotatest/Sent@example.com (\HasNoChildren)
user/quotatest/Trash@example.com (\HasNoChildren)
user/quotatest@example.com (\HasChildren)
```

createmailbox (cm for short)
: This command creates a top-level mailbox or a mailbox subdirectory:

    ```
    localhost> cm user.exampleuser
    localhost> cm user.exampleuser.Trash
    localhost> lm
    user.exampleuser (\HasNoChildren)
    user.exampleuser.Trash (\HasNoChildren)
    ```

deletemailbox (dm for short)
: This command recursively deletes a mailbox (see section 14.2 on page 231).

renamemailbox (renm for short)
: This command renames a mailbox:

    ```
    localhost> lm
    user.exampleuser (\HasNoChildren)
    localhost> renm user.exampleuser user.testuser
    localhost> lm
    user.testuser (\HasNoChildren)
    ```

setaclmailbox (sam for short)
: This command sets ACLs for a mailbox (see section 14.2 on page 230).

deleteaclmailbox (dam for short)
: This command removes all entries from the mailbox ACL. As parameters you have to specify the mailbox name and the user whose ACL is to be removed:

    ```
    localhost> lam user.testuser
    anyone lrs
    localhost> dam user.testuser anyone
    localhost> lam user.testuser
    localhost>
    ```

    In this example, the lrs ACL of user anyone was removed.

listaclmailbox (lam for short)
: This command lists all active ACLs for a mailbox:

    ```
    localhost> lam user.testuser
    anyone lrs
    ```

    The output shows that user anyone has permissions lrs for mailbox user.testuser (see Table 2.1 on page 36).

setquota (sq for short)
: This command sets a quota for a mailbox or a subsidiary element (see section 14.1.2 on page 228).

listquota (lq for short)
: This command shows the active quota for a mailbox or a subsidiary element (see section 14.1.2 on page 228).

listquotaroot (lqr for short)
: This command shows how much of the quota of a mailbox hierarchy has been used (see page 229).

setinfo
: This command creates information messages that the mail client displays to the user when the user logs on, sets metadata that can be read out with special commands, and activates a variety of functions. It is called according to the syntax setinfo *type value*. The command knows the following functions:

- motd creates an information text that the mail client can display during login:

    ```
    localhost> setinfo motd "Have fun with Cyrus"
    ```

- comment allows the administrator to store a short description of the server.

- admin sets the email address of the server administrator. This information can be read out with the GETMETADATA IMAP command, but so far this has only been specified as an Internet draft.[1] Mail clients that support it can show information on the server. However, the authors are not aware of any commonly used programs that carry out this task for comment and admin. It is highly likely that this will change, especially for clients that support the *Lemonade* profile,[2] which has been much discussed lately. It will especially apply to mobile clients such as cell phones.

- shutdown makes it possible to specify a text that the user's mail client can show during login. The server then terminates the connection immediately. This is very useful during maintenance, for example.

- expire followed by a number specifies the number of days after which an email is considered obsolete. You can use cyr_expire to delete such emails. However, you should only call this function if you really want to use it, as emails cannot be restored once you have deleted them.

---

[1] See http://tools.ietf.org/html/draft-daboo-imap-annotatemore.
[2] See http://tools.ietf.org/html/draft-ietf-lemonade-profile-bis-05.

15 Internal Structure and Modules

- squat makes sure that all mailboxes receive a squat index (see section 15.2.2 on page 267).

version

This function outputs the versions of the Cyrus server and the programs involved:

```
localhost> version
name        : Cyrus IMAPD
version     : v2.2.12 2005/02/14 16:43:51
vendor      : Project Cyrus
support-url : http://asg.web.cmu.edu/cyrus
os          : Linux
os-version  : 2.6.16.21-0.15-xen
environment : Built w/Cyrus SASL 2.1.21
              Running w/Cyrus SASL 2.1.21
              Built w/Sleepycat Software: Berkeley DB 4.3.29: (November 10, 2006)
              Running w/Sleepycat Software: Berkeley DB 4.3.29: (June 16, 2006)
              Built w/OpenSSL 0.9.8a 11 Oct 2005
              Running w/OpenSSL 0.9.8a 11 Oct 2005
              CMU Sieve 2.2
              DRAC
              TCP Wrappers
              mmap = shared
              lock = fcntl
              nonblock = fcntl
              auth = unix
              idle = idled
```

xfermailbox (xfer for short)

This function moves a mailbox from one backend server to another in a Murder cluster. It is called according to the syntax xfer *mailbox_name target_mail_server*.

```
localhost> xfer user.testuser mail.example.net
```

moves the user.testuser mailbox from the local computer to the mail server mail.example.net.

quit

This function ends cyradm.

Have a look at the manual page for cyradm on your system, as the central administration tool is given new functions in nearly every new Cyrus version.

Chapter 16

Cyrus at the Filesystem Level

If you want to see how Cyrus manages the emails it receives, it is worth having a look at the pertinent directories in the filesystem. This knowledge will be useful when creating backups, for example (see section 14.9 on page 255). Try not to change anything here. Cyrus manages its directories autonomously, so manual changes can quickly lead to inconsistent mailboxes and operational problems.

The Cyrus mail server stores and manages emails in two separate working directories.

16.1 The Email Directory

Cyrus creates user mailboxes in the /var/spool/imap directory, and it also stores the emails here. The directory contains the two main directories

16 Cyrus at the Filesystem Level

user/ and domain/. All *unqualified* mailboxes for users whose account names do not have a domain part are stored in the first directory. The second directory contains all *qualified* mailboxes belonging to user accounts with a domain part (if virtual domains are in use). Upon receipt of the first email, Cyrus creates an additional directory called stage./, where it buffers all newly received emails before sorting them into the appropriate user directories.

Mailboxes created by cyradm or created automatically always contain the files cyrus.header, cyrus.cache, and cyrus.index, which are used to manage the directory they are in. They have a binary format specific to Cyrus.

```
linux: # ls -al /var/spool/imap/user/paul/
total 32
drwx------ 2 cyrus mail 4096 Nov 21 17:35 ./
drwx------ 3 cyrus mail 4096 Nov 21 16:29 ../
-rw------- 1 cyrus mail 1989 Nov 21 17:10 1.
-rw------- 1 cyrus mail 1988 Nov 21 5:35:00 PM 2.
-rw------- 1 cyrus mail 1988 Nov 21 5:35:00 PM 3.
-rw------- 1 cyrus mail 2864 Nov 21 17:35 cyrus.cache
-rw------- 1 cyrus mail  169 Nov 21 16:29 cyrus.header
-rw------- 1 cyrus mail  256 Nov 21 17:35 cyrus.index
drw------- 2 cyrus mail 4096 Nov 21 16:35 memo/
```

cyrus.cache contains caching information that speeds up the display of emails in this directory by the client, while cyrus.index saves index and status information on the individual emails.

Figure 16.1: View of a mailbox in Thunderbird with altnamespace activated

Cyrus stores the readable ACLs for the directory in cyrus.header:

```
linux:/var/spool/imap/user/paul/ # strings cyrus.header
Cyrus mailbox header
"The best thing about this system was that it had lots of goals."
        --Jim Morris on Andrew
```

```
user.paul       7ab084d44544a02f
paul    lrswipcda       cyrus   lrswipcda
```

In this case, users `paul` and `cyrus` have all permissions for this directory, which is the `user.paul` mailbox. The character string following the mailbox name uniquely identifies this mailbox.

Apart from administration files, the mailbox shown above contains a `memo` subdirectory for user `paul`. If you enter the `altnamespace` option in the `imapd.conf` file and activate it with value 1, for example, `memo` will appear on the *same* level as the `INBOX` (thus, in the `paul` directory itself) in the user's email program (see Figure 16.1). Otherwise, all subdirectories are arranged *under* the `INBOX`, and `memo` is then displayed in the client as a subdirectory of the `INBOX` (see Figure 16.2). The `altnamespace` setting only has a cosmetic effect for the user interface, and does not affect the structure or processing of emails on the server.

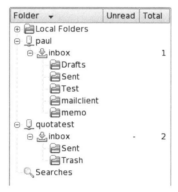

Figure 16.2: View of mailbox without altnamespace

The three numbered files show that `paul`'s mailbox has already received three messages. Cyrus stores all emails as sequentially numbered files, and the server adds a dot to the end of the name.

16.2 The Administration Directory

Cyrus creates all status information, databases, and index files for mailbox administration under the `/var/lib/imap/` path. This is an extremely sensitive area and should only be modified by Cyrus.

The contents of this directory are directly connected to the contents of the mailbox directory. When a change is made to a mailbox, this change has to be synchronized with the administration directory. This task is reserved for the mail server, and may only be done manually with `cyradm` or `reconstruct`. Making manual changes at the filesystem level nearly

16 Cyrus at the Filesystem Level

always causes administration information to become inconsistent; in the worst case, this can cause loss of emails.

/var/lib/imap/ contains the following individual files and directories:

annotations.db
: This database contains internal information for Cyrus affecting the mailboxes and the entire server, such as the email address of the postmaster entered with the setinfo[1] cyradm command, or text used to store additional information concerning the server.

backup/
: This directory contains automatically created backups of the mailboxes.db database.

db/
: This directory contains the current index database while the system is running. These directories are newly generated every time the server starts.

db.backup1/
: This directory contains a copy of the annotations.db and mailboxes.db databases currently in use.

deliver.db
: This file is required for filtering and rejecting duplicate emails. It contains a sender-recipient list of all delivered emails along with their email ID. This information can be used to suppress duplicate emails. This function is activated and deactivated in the /etc/cyrus.conf file (see section 12.1.3 on page 202).

log/
: This is where the IMAP server stores supplementary logging information for entries in the syslog. The name of the logfile always corresponds to the process ID of the IMAP server process.

mailboxes.db
: This file is Cyrus' main database, and contains information for all mailboxes and their subdirectories, such as the mailbox name, user, permissions, and so on.

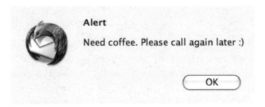

Figure 16.3: This is how Mozilla Thunderbird displays the contents of the msg/motd file.

[1] See section 15.4 on page 273.

16.2 The Administration Directory

`msg/`
: If the administrator saves a file called `motd` in this directory, the user will see the text in this file when he or she logs in (see Figure 16.3). The file could contain warning messages or information on using the email system. Please note that only the text from the first line is displayed, and that you may not use special characters.

`proc/`
: This is a directory of the login processes of the email clients. This is where Cyrus takes care of all active connections from IMAP clients. Each of them gets an individual process ID which is used as a filename in this directory. Among other things, these files contain the IP address of the mail client, the username, and the name of the mailbox accessed by the client:

    ```
    [10.0.41.2]     paul@example.com example.com!user.paul
    ```

`quota/`
: This directory contains files specifying the user quotas, which are stored separately for each mailbox directory. The `p/` subdirectory, for example, contains the `user.paul` file, which in turn contains the currently active mailbox quota.

`socket/`
: This file contains the socket files that the Cyrus master process uses to communicate with the subprocesses.

`shutdown`
: If this file exists, Cyrus terminates all login attempts by clients and requests the clients to display the first line of this text file as an alarm message in the email client. This can be useful, for example, if you want to prevent users from logging on during maintenance work on the server, but still want to inform the users how long the server will be down.

    This function is supported by, among others, Thunderbird, Apple's Mail program, and even Microsoft Outlook email clients. Other programs, for example, KMail, do not display this information, but simply refuse to give the user access without providing an explanation.

`tls_session.db`
: This database contains the session data of the SSL/TLS connections. Once Cyrus has built a TLS connection to a client, it memorizes it in this file and can therefore connect more quickly the next time that same client logs in.

`user/`
: This directory contains information on messages flagged as `seen` as

well as a list of subscribed mailboxes. Cyrus stores them per mailbox in subdirectories. Each subdirectory contains two files: `userid.seen` contains the seen emails, while `userid.sub` contains the subscription information.

Cyrus in a Cluster

As user mailboxes grow, but before the mail server reaches the limits of its capacity, you should consider extending the system. For ways of doing this, have a look at page 43.

For a long time, there was no stable solution that allowed Cyrus to be operated in a cluster. In the past three years, more work has been done on this subject, as a good mail server has to be extendable.

The official answer to the problem is a *Cyrus Aggregator* or *Cyrus Murder*. The term *murder* is another word for *swarm*, and refers to *a murder of crows*, rather than to homicide.

17.1 The Cyrus Aggregator

This extension makes it possible to deal with load peaks by operating Cyrus with frontend and backend mail servers. The Cyrus Aggregator is a type of load balancer that forwards requests to other Cyrus backend servers. The required auxiliary programs have been part of the Cyrus distribution from version 2.1. In some distributions, such as Debian, for example, it is necessary to install the `cyrus2x-murder` package on all cluster computers.

According to the Cyrus programmers, this extension is still "relatively young in the grand scheme of things," and users deploy it at their own risk. The authors know a few setups where the Murder clusters run smoothly and stably; one of these setups is at Carnegie Mellon University.

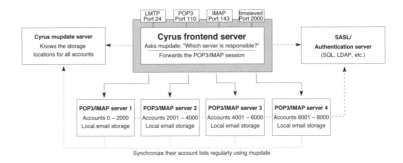

Figure 17.1: A Cyrus cluster setup with two backend servers

17.1.1 The Aggregator Concept

A Cyrus cluster distributes administrative tasks onto three different server types. During the first extension phase this increases performance as the load of a large mail server is distributed to several small ones. Users will not even notice this, as they still contact one mail server, just as before.

You require at least one frontend computer, one backend computer, and one *mupdate* server (short for *murder update*) as the interface where mailbox information is exchanged (see Figure 17.1).

The frontend server provides the interface with the clients and the MTA. It is the first point of contact in the chain, and is responsible for receiving user requests and balancing the load. It is also the direct point of contact for the MTA. Users are authenticated on the frontend server, which also reduces the computing load on the backend server. If the frontend server fails, the entire system is brought to a standstill, as the mail clients then cannot contact the mail server. In order to prevent this, you should operate multiple frontend servers in parallel and regulate access to them with a load balancer that distributes the user requests to different computers. Cyrus itself does not do any load balancing here.

Backend servers are independent POP3/IMAP servers, as in our previously described setups. Each of them manages a number of mailboxes and provides a list of these mailboxes to the mupdate server. A backend server usually knows only one external "user": the frontend server that collects and delivers emails and has to be authenticated for this purpose. If one of the backend servers fails, the mailboxes on this computer are unavailable, but the other backend servers are unaffected.

The mupdate server, on the other hand, is essential. It functions as the memory of the cluster, as it manages the lists showing which mailboxes are stored on which backend server. The frontend servers require this information so that they know which backend server to address. The mupdate server synchronizes the lists regularly with the backend servers. If this computer fails, the frontend servers are left in the dark and none of the users are able to access their mailboxes. For this reason, you should always have a reserve mupdate computer that is ready for operation.

When a user wishes to look at his or her mailbox, the mail client contacts the frontend server. The frontend server checks the access data. If this is correct, it attempts to determine the backend server where it will find this user's mailbox. It asks the mupdate server for this information. If the requested mailbox exists, the frontend server contacts the corresponding backend server and calls up the mailbox for the user.

17.1.2 The Cluster Setup

Before setting up a cluster, you should consider the mail partitions and the required memory reserves (see also section 14.5 on page 239). Every backend server can have its own hard disk space or be connected to a central storage system, which should be redundantly secured. The following setup assumes that the backend servers use their own hard disk space.

Create additional Cyrus user accounts on the mupdate and backend servers to enable the frontend, backend, and mupdate servers to authenticate one another. You could use the same data source as that used for normal users, but then you would have to (for example) connect the mupdate server to an LDAP server, and this would make the setup even more complicated and more difficult to troubleshoot. For this reason, it is advisable to store the *Cyrus update users* in the `sasldb2` database on the backend computers and the mupdate server, and to use that database as an additional authentication source (see section 11.4.1 on page 194).

The Frontend Server

To enable the frontend server to authenticate mail clients making requests, simply enter the data source you currently use in the `/etc/imapd.conf` file. The following `imapd.conf` entries inform the frontend server of the name of the mupdate server and how to log on to it.

```
servername: cyrus-frontend.example.com
```

specifies the *fully qualified domain name (FQDN)* of the frontend server, which is to be used for communication between the individual cluster servers. To specify the FQDN of the mupdate server, use the following:

```
mupdate_server: mupdate.example.com
```

The `mupdate_port` parameter specifies the port on which the mupdate server listens:

```
mupdate_port: 3905
```

You have to enter the username twice, as Cyrus SASL authenticates the user and then checks whether the user is authorized to communicate with the mupdate server:

```
mupdate_username: cyrus-backend
mupdate_authname: cyrus-backend
```

You can use the same username as for the backend server—no additional user entry for the frontend server is required. Unfortunately, you have to enter the password in cleartext:

```
mupdate_password: secret
```

After the frontend server has logged on to the mupdate server, the mupdate server tells the frontend server which backend server contains the mailbox of the requesting client. The frontend server now logs on to the appropriate backend server. The following `imapd.conf` entries specify how it does this:

```
proxy_authname: cyrus-frontend
```

This entry specifies the name the frontend server uses to log on to the backend servers. You can specify a separate password for each backend server:

```
cyrus-backend_password: secret
cyrus-backend2_password: secret
```

The part of the parameter name before the `_password` suffix *has to* correspond to the host part of the FQDN of the corresponding backend server (`cyrus-backend` and `cyrus-backend2` in this case). This means that the different backend servers must have different hostnames.

Now you have to instruct the frontend server to forward all IMAP commands to the appropriate backend server, as they cannot be processed locally anymore. To do this, set the following value in the `/etc/imapd.conf` file:

```
proxyd_disable_mailbox_referrals: 1
```

The frontend server now has access to all cluster components involved and is able to answer client requests.

If you use Sieve email filtering, Sieve now only runs on the backend servers; the frontend server has to transfer Sieve commands from the user to the proper backend server. As a single machine in a non-cluster (single-server) setup, it would be responsible itself for redirecting Sieve requests to the local Sieve server. For cluster operation, you have to switch this function off in the `/etc/imapd.conf` file:

```
sieve_allowreferrals: 0
# Deactivates referrals to the local Sieve service.

sieveuserhomedir: no
# Deactivates the use of Sieve user directories
# on the local computer.

sievedir: /var/lib/sieve
# The directory containing the Sieve scripts on the
# corresponding backend server.
```

To configure the additional services that communicate with the mupdate server, go to the `/etc/cyrus.conf` file and add the following to the section SERVICES:

```
mupdate cmd="mupdate" listen="mupdate" prefork=1
```

This line activates the mupdate service that listens on port 3905 and makes sure there is always a a running instance.

```
fud cmd="fud" proto="udp" listen ="4201" prefork=0 maxchild=10
```

This line collects and evaluates the information on the user mailboxes provided by the mupdate server. Fast UDP is used as the protocol here. The service runs on port 4201 and may start a maximum of 10 subprocesses. This is a suitable default value. If your clients have to wait for a long time, you can increase this value step by step. If you do this, make sure to use `top` to monitor the load on your system.

When you restart Cyrus, it will import and apply this configuration.

The Backend Server

A backend server is an independent Cyrus mail server without an authentication source for the users. The configuration differs from the standard configuration in that the computer informs the mupdate server regularly about its mailboxes and has to allow the frontend server to log in.

Make the following entry in the `/etc/imapd.conf` file so that the frontend can be authenticated in the `sasldb2` database:

```
sasl_pwcheck_method: auxprop
```

Now that backend server will use the `auxprop` module for authentication. This module reads the `sasldb2` database by default in distributions such as SuSE; on other systems you may have to enter this information:

```
sasl_auxprop_plugin: sasldb
```

You can also use `ldapdb` or `sql` instead of the `sasldb` plugin (for more information, see section 13.2.1 on page 212).

To initialize this database, create the Cyrus user that the frontend server will use for authentication on the backend server. In this example, we have used `cyrus-frontend`:

```
linux: #  saslpasswd2 cyrus-frontend
Password: secret
Again (for verification): secret
```

Now check whether the `cyrus` system user owns the database you have just created and whether it is part of the `mail` group. If this is not the case, issue `chown cyrus:mail /etc/sasldb2` at the command line to correct this.

You have to carry out this process once on every backend server *and* on the mupdate server. The frontend server does not require this data source because no other server from the cluster needs to be authenticated on the frontend server. Only the frontend server needs to be able to log on to the mupdate server and the backend servers.

To inform the backend server which mupdate server it should provide information on its mailboxes to, and to instruct it how to communicate with that mupdate server, enter the following in the `/etc/imapd.conf` file:

```
mupdate-server: cyrus-mupdate.example.com
# The FQDN where the server can reach the mupdate server

mupdate_port: 3905
# The port where the server can communicate with the mupdate server
```

```
mupdate_username: cyrus-backend
mupdate_authname: cyrus-backend
mupdate_password: secret
# The access data for authentication on the mupdate server.
# You have to enter the password in cleartext.
```

Now you have to specify which frontend servers may access the backend server:

```
proxyservers: cyrus-frontend
# Hostname of the frontend server. You can specify more than one,
# and separate them with spaces.
```

Use the `admins` parameter to specify the Cyrus users that have administrator permissions for the backend server:

```
admins: cyrus cyrus-frontend
```

Give these permissions to the `cyrus` Cyrus administrator and to `cyrus-frontend`, so that the frontend server can process the mailboxes.

If you want to move user mailboxes from one backend server to another, you have to use `allowusermoves` explicitly to permit the frontend server to begin the moving process:

```
allowusermoves: yes
```

The `xfermailbox cyradm` command will only function properly if you have set this value on the backend server (see section 15.4 on page 274).

Users can only subscribe to IMAP directories on a backend server other than their own if you permit this explicitly:

```
allowsubscribes: yes
```

Activate the cluster services in the `/etc/cyrus.conf` file. Go to the START section and enter the following line:

```
mupdatepush cmd="ctl_mboxlist -m"
```

This will ensure that the `ctl_mboxlist` program starts when the server starts, and the `-m` switch ensures that the program synchronizes the local mailboxes with the list on the mupdate server. If the mailboxes change, the program will contact the mupdate server during regular operation. The

```
fud cmd="fud" proto="udp" listen="4201" profork=0 maxchilds=10
```

entry in the SERVICES section activates the service that manages the mailbox information; the same applies for the frontend server.

The mupdate Server

The mupdate server is the link between the frontend and backend servers, so it has to be able to communicate with both of them and always have an up-to-date list of the mailboxes on the individual backend servers.

Set up the authentication in the `/etc/imapd.conf` file as you did for the backend server:

```
sasl_pwcheck_method: auxprop
sasl_auxprop_plugin: sasldb
```

You also have to create the user that the backend server will use for authentication on the mupdate server (using `saslpasswd2 cyrus-backend` in this example). Do not forget to assign read permissions for the database containing the login information to user `cyrus` with `chown cyrus:mail /etc/sasldb2`.

The following configuration entries in `/etc/imapd.conf` will put Cyrus in the mupdate mode:

```
admins: cyrus-backend
# Cyrus account used by the backend server for authentication.
# The backend server receives administrative permissions for this account.

servername: cyrus-mupdate.example.com
# The hostname used by the mupdate server when communicating
# with the other servers.
```

To activate the mupdate service, go to the `SERVICES` section in the `/etc/cyrus.conf` file and add the following line:

```
mupdate    cmd="mupdate -m" listen="mupdate" prefork=1
```

The `-m` switch starts the mupdate service as the master that listens on port 3905.[1] This service always keeps an instance on idle so that it can react immediately to a request. You have to restart Cyrus to activate the mupdate setup.

Testing

Once you have set up all of the three types of cluster machines, you should observe the email and system logs (using `tail -f /var/log/messages` and `tail -f /var/log/mail`, for example) so that you can detect any errors immediately. If everything looks good, deliver an email to the frontend server:

---

[1] Without this option, mupdate will start as the slave, which is the case on the backend servers.

17.1 The Cyrus Aggregator

```
cyrus-frontend # telnet localhost 25
Trying 127.0.0.1...
Connected to localhost.
Escape character is '^]'.
220 cyrus-frontend.example.com ESMTP Postfix
HELO mail.heinlein-support.de
250 cyrus-frontend.example.com
MAIL FROM: <p.hartleben@heinlein-support.de>
250 Ok
RCPT TO: <paul@example.com>
250 Ok
DATA
354 End data with <CR><LF>.<CR><LF>
Subject: This is a test email

Test
.
250 Ok: queued as 835281C3C2
quit
221 Bye
Connection closed by foreign host.
```

If this email reaches the mailbox on the backend server, you will know that this part of operation works. Now check a user mailbox. The easiest way is to check the mailbox on the frontend server with `telnet`:

```
linux: # telnet localhost 143
Trying 127.0.0.1...
Connected to localhost.
Escape character is '^]'.
* OK linux Cyrus IMAP4 v2.2.12 server ready
a001 LOGIN paul@example.com secret
a001 OK User logged in
a002 SELECT inbox
* FLAGS (\Answered \Flagged \Draft \Deleted \Seen $NotJunk $Junk JunkRec
orded)
* OK [PERMANENTFLAGS (\Answered \Flagged \Draft \Deleted \Seen $NotJunk
$Junk JunkRecorded \*)]
* 6 EXISTS
* 0 RECENT
* OK [UNSEEN 2]
* OK [UIDVALIDITY 1164122999]
* OK [UIDNEXT 66]
a002 OK [READ-WRITE] Completed
a003 fetch 2 body[header]
* 2 FETCH (FLAGS (\Seen $NotJunk JunkRecorded) BODY[HEADER] {1520}[2]
Return-Path: <paul@example.com>
```

[2] This listing is also interesting because it shows the use of custom IMAP flags: Here, a spam filter on the client flags all incoming emails as `JunkRecorded` and as `$NotJunk` or `$Junk`.

```
Received: from gucky.heinlein-support.de ([unix socket])
         by linux (Cyrus v2.2.12) with LMTPA;
         Tue, 17 Jul 2007 19:47:58 +0200
X-Sieve: CMU Sieve 2.2
[...]
From: Peer Hartleben <p.hartleben@heinlein-support.de>
To: paul@example.com
Subject: testttt
Date: Tue, 17 Jul 2007 7:48:49 PM +0200
User-Agent: KMail/1.9.6
MIME-Version: 1.0
Content-Type: text/plain;
  charset="us-ascii"
Content-Transfer-Encoding: 7bit
Content-Disposition: inline
Message-Id: <200707171948.49989.paul@example.com>

)
a003 OK Completed (0.000 sec)
```

Should you encounter any trouble, one of the following hints will usually help you solve your problems:

- *All* operations have to run on the frontend server. This applies to sending and receiving emails and to creating and managing mailboxes. Do not access the backend servers directly, as you will otherwise risk inconsistencies in your system.

- All Cyrus features in use must be active on the frontend and backend servers. If, for example, you use `altnamespace` or `virtdomains`, you have to enter these parameters identically in `/etc/imapd.conf` on all computers apart from the mupdate server. Otherwise the users will be unable to access their mailboxes or will only see a part of them.

- Make sure the hostnames are consistent. Unless you specify otherwise, SASL will use the hostname of the machine for authentication on the mupdate server, for example. If you change the hostname, the computer can no longer log on. To be on the safe side, you should define the computer name using the `servername` option in the `/etc/imapd.conf` file. Cyrus will then use the name specified here instead of the actual hostname.

- Mailboxes are no longer created automatically in a cluster. On single-server systems, Cyrus automatically creates mailboxes for new users if the users' authentication data is available; in Murder clusters, you have to create the mailboxes manually. Developers are currently working on making this feature automatic in the Murder setup.

17.2 Cyrus Replication

As we indicated previously, frontend servers can be cloned and addressed through a load balancer, but we have not mentioned redundancy in connection with backend servers. Every backend server contains different mailboxes. This means there is no backup for any of them: If one of these backend computers is unavailable, the affected users will not be able to access their mailboxes by any other means.

A replication mechanism exists in Cyrus version 2.2 and higher, but it is still in the beta stage. This is why Carnegie Mellon University has provided a warning: *Deploy at your own risk*. Fearless administrators who wish to be beta testers and use it should read the official how-to guide.[3] This replication mechanism can be used for backend servers in a Murder setup or for independent Cyrus mail servers.

The only other alternative is to regularly copy the data on a Cyrus backend to an identical system that can be activated if necessary and take over the Cyrus tasks of that machine. This process is similar to the backup described in section 14.9 on page 255.

17.2.1 Replicating the Authentication Data

Because authentication data is managed separately by the Cyrus system, it also has to be replicated separately. You have to do this yourself, and you can use the mechanisms of the data sources involved to help you where possible. In the simplest case, where authentication is done via Unix system accounts, you only need a cron job that uses `rsync` to regularly save `/etc/passwd`, `/etc/shadow`, and `/etc/groups`, if required, or you can use central user management with the *Network Information Service (NIS)*. For LDAP and MySQL databases, it is advisable to use the synchronization mechanisms of these systems, but a description would exceed the scope of this book. Starting from version 5, MySQL has an integrated replication mechanism that is described in more detail on `http://dev.mysql.com/doc/refman/5.0/en/replication.html`.

For LDAP databases you can use the `slurpd` service, which enables a master-slave replication of LDAP servers and can therefore provide redundancy for an authentication backend. For more information on operation and implementation, go to `http://www.bind9.net/manual/openldap/2.2/replication.html`.

---

[3] See `http://cyrusimap.web.cmu.edu/imapd/install-replication.html`.

Appendixes

IMAP Command Reference

IMAP is a complex protocol with a complex and versatile definition. In addition to RFC 3501,[1] which defines IMAP in version 4rev1, the version valid since March 2003, there are huge numbers of other RFCs and Internet drafts containing numerous *IMAP extensions*.

This variety is not surprising, as the `CAPABILITY` command in the IMAP protocol was intentionally designed as a foundation that servers can build upon to provide flexible optional extensions and specialized functions that the inventors of IMAP could never have imagined.

Unfortunately, a list of these innumerable extensions would exceed the scope of this book, and many of the more recent extensions are not yet included in current software versions. There are many wonderful extensions:

---

[1] See http://www.faqs.org/rfcs/rfc3501.

URLAUTH (RFC 4467[2]) allows the specification of an IMAP server, login data, IMAP folder, and messages in this style: `imap://tux@example.com/INBOX/;uid=425`. This makes it possible to reference individual messages, and to pass this reference to third parties. Other RFCs extend existing standards: RFC 4731[3] was published in November 2006 and provides additional functions for the SEARCH commands.

The following reference introduces IMAP4rev1 and the main IMAP extensions currently supported by Courier and Cyrus.

Some IMAP commands are only available during specific periods of an IMAP session. For this reason, the commands are sorted according to the statuses described in section 2.2.2 on page 31. IMAP commands and subcommands are not case sensitive.

In the IMAP protocol, lengths are measured in *octets*, or units containing eight bits. Nearly all current systems use eight bits per byte, so *octet* and *byte* can be used synonymously: 120 octets correspond to 120 bytes.

A.1 Commands Always Available to Clients

CAPABILITY

This command queries the capabilities of the server (see also section 2.2.3 on page 33). The server returns an *untagged* reply line that starts with `CAPABILITY IMAP4rev1`. Every server has to support the capabilities STARTTLS, AUTH=PLAIN, and LOGINDISABLED:

```
a001 CAPABILITY
* CAPABILITY IMAP4rev1 STARTTLS AUTH=GSSAPI LOGINDISABLED
a001 OK CAPABILITY completed
```

The server uses LOGINDISABLED to announce that it cannot receive an authentication request from this client at this time. In the example, the server will most probably not permit authentication until the client uses STARTTLS to switch into encrypted mode.

NOOP

As in many other protocols, this command is short for *no operation*. The client can use this command to keep the connection open and reset any autologout timers:

```
a002 NOOP
a002 OK NOOP completed
```

When replying to NOOP, many servers provide the current message status, which informs the client if new emails have been received:

---

[2] See http://www.ietf.org/rfc/rfc4467.txt.
[3] See http://www.ietf.org/rfc/rfc4731.txt.

```
a003 NOOP
* 22 EXPUNGE
* 23 EXISTS
* 3 RECENT
* 14 FETCH (FLAGS (\Seen \Deleted))
a003 OK NOOP completed
```

LOGOUT

If a client logs out using LOGOUT, the server sends an *untagged* BYE and then closes the connection:

```
a004 LOGOUT
* BYE IMAP4rev1 Server logging out
a004 OK LOGOUT completed
```

A.2 Commands Available in the Not-Authenticated Status

AUTHENTICATE

This command starts the authentication of the client. The client and the server then exchange additional information, depending on the authentication method used. In *challenge-response procedures*, the server sends the session key (the *challenge* to the client) in a line marked with a plus sign (+), and the client uses the challenge, the username, and the password to calculate the corresponding login string (the *response*).

```
a001 AUTHENTICATE CRAM-MD5
+ PDUwNjZGNEVFNDNGM0NCQzIzODI1MEVERTc3ODg4Qjg4QGtqaWRkZXI+
cC5oZWlubdVpbiBlZjlkZdQ5YjIxYzk3ZekzNzQ4MzUhMmQ2NDYzZjlhOA==
a001 OK LOGIN Ok.
```

LOGIN

This command requests a simple login in cleartext; according to the RFC, every server must support this type of login. For security reasons, it should only be available in SSL/TLS mode, as the username and password are transmitted without protection, which means they are easy to detect during transmission unless further steps are taken to secure the communication channel:

```
a001 LOGIN tux secret
a001 OK LOGIN completed
```

STARTTLS

The client uses this command to initiate the switch to SSL/TLS-encrypted communication. It continues to use the existing connection:

```
a001 CAPABILITY
* CAPABILITY IMAP4rev1 STARTTLS LOGINDISABLED
a001 OK CAPABILITY completed
a002 STARTTLS
a002 OK Begin TLS negotiation now
```

The server is now able to return other CAPABILITY replies in SSL/TLS-encrypted connections. It can offer a larger variety of login mechanisms:[4]

```
a003 CAPABILITY
* CAPABILITY IMAP4rev1 AUTH=PLAIN
a003 OK CAPABILITY completed
a004 LOGIN tux secret
a004 OK LOGIN completed
```

A.3 Commands Available in the Authenticated Status

SELECT

This command selects a folder to function as the context for later commands that operate on messages, and deletes the emails flagged as \Deleted from the previous working folder. The server replies to this command with a number of untagged lines that may be returned in an arbitrary sequence; these lines provide information to the client on the status of the folder:

```
a005 SELECT INBOX
* FLAGS (\Answered \Flagged \Deleted \Seen \Draft)
* 172 EXISTS
* 1 RECENT
* OK [UNSEEN 12] Message 12 is first unseen
* OK [UIDVALIDITY 3857529045] UIDs valid
* OK [UIDNEXT 4392] Predicted next UID
* OK [PERMANENTFLAGS (\Deleted \Seen \*)] Limited
a005 OK [READ-WRITE] SELECT completed
```

The server uses FLAGS to provide information on the flags it is currently storing in the RAM (see section 2.2.3 on page 35), while OK [PERMANENTFLAGS (*flag1 flag2* ...)] specifies all flags that the client can change permanently. If the server does not provide this information, the client can assume that it may change all flags during the session, but that the server will not store any of these changes.

---

[4] Because the communication between client and server is encrypted, it cannot be carried out as shown here in a session initiated via telnet; instead, you have to use a tool such as openssl.

The number preceding the word EXISTS indicates how many messages the folder contains, while RECENT follows the number of messages flagged as \Recent or the new emails received since the last login; the client is the first to view these emails. The server uses OK [UNSEEN *number*] to return the sequence number of the first unread message (not the number of unread messages).

OK [UIDNEXT *unique-id*] informs the client of the next *Unique ID*; OK [UIDVALIDITY *unique-id-value*] returns the *Unique ID Value* that is currently valid (see section 2.2.1 on page 29).

The server uses tagged reply *tag* OK [READ-WRITE] SELECT comp lete to indicate that it has finished executing the SELECT command. If the client has write permissions for the folder, the server *should* add the information [READ-WRITE] to the OK reply. If the client only has read permissions, the server *must* return [READ-ONLY].

EXAMINE

This command corresponds to the SELECT command, but the client selects the folder only for *reading*. The server returns the same reply as that it returns to the SELECT command, but specifies [READ-ONLY] in the concluding OK line:

```
a006 EXAMINE Test
* 17 EXISTS
* 2 RECENT
* OK [UNSEEN 8] Message 8 is first unseen
* OK [UIDVALIDITY 3857529045] UIDs valid
* OK [UIDNEXT 4392] Predicted next UID
* FLAGS (\Answered \Flagged \Deleted \Seen \Draft)
* OK [PERMANENTFLAGS ()] No permanent flags permitted
a006 OK [READ-ONLY] EXAMINE completed
```

Access via EXAMINE may not alter the \Recent flag of new messages, as that would be a change to the directory by the server.

LIST

The LIST command returns a list of all directories available to the client. The server also specifies the folder attributes and the applicable *hierarchy delimiter* in its untagged replies:

```
a016 LIST "" "*"
* LIST (\HasNoChildren) "." "INBOX.Private.Holiday"
* LIST (\HasNoChildren) "." "INBOX.Private.Orchestra"
* LIST (\HasChildren)   "." "INBOX.Private"
* LIST (\HasNoChildren) "." "INBOX.ToDo"
* LIST (\HasNoChildren) "." "INBOX.Test"
* LIST (\HasChildren)   "." "INBOX.Book stuff"
* LIST (\HasNoChildren) "." "INBOX.Book stuff.LPIC-1"
* LIST (\HasNoChildren) "." "INBOX.Book stuff.Postfix 3"
```

```
* LIST (\HasNoChildren) "." "INBOX.Book stuff.Snort"
* LIST (\HasNoChildren) "." "INBOX.Book stuff.IMAP"
* LIST (\Unmarked \HasChildren) "." "INBOX"
a016 OK LIST Completed
```

The LIST command has two parameters: the second consists of the mailbox name or a wildcard pattern. The first is called a *reference*, and it specifies the context in which the mailbox name is interpreted in relation to the reference:

```
a017 LIST "INBOX.Private" "*"
* LIST (\HasNoChildren) "." "INBOX.Private.Holiday"
* LIST (\HasNoChildren) "." "INBOX.Private.Orchestra"
a017 OK LIST completed
```

The reference is important if the IMAP server allows access to a filesystem or a news server in accordance with RFC 3501. As neither Courier nor Cyrus permit this, the subject would exceed the scope of this book.

During normal email operation, the reference argument remains empty, as shown in the command tagged as a016. The mailbox name is then exactly the same as the folder name used in the SELECT command (see section A.3 on page 298).

The asterisk (*) wildcard can traditionally represent any character. On the other hand, the percent sign (%) represents any character apart from the hierarchy separator:

```
a018 LIST "" "INBOX.Private*"
* LIST (\HasNoChildren) "." "INBOX.Private.Holiday"
* LIST (\HasNoChildren) "." "INBOX.Private.Orchestra"
* LIST (\HasChildren)   "." "INBOX.Private"
a018 OK LIST completed
a019 LIST "" "INBOX.Private%"
* LIST (\HasChildren)   "." "INBOX.Private"
a019 OK LIST completed
```

If you specify an empty mailbox name as the second argument, the LIST command simply returns the hierarchy separator:

```
a020 LIST "" ""
* LIST (\Noselect) "." ""
a020 OK LIST completed
```

CREATE

This command creates a new folder on the server. For subdirectories, the client has to specify the complete path, including the hierarchy delimiter specified by the server (this is a dot in the following example). Should intermediate directories not exist, the server has to create them automatically:

```
a021 CREATE PRIVATE
a021 OK CREATE completed
a022 CREATE PRIVATE.FRIENDS.HOLIDAY
a022 OK CREATE completed
```

The server decides whether folders PRIVATE and Private can exist at the same time, and it makes this decision for each directory. Only the INBOX may not be case sensitive.

Unfortunately, the client cannot simply query the rules on case sensitivity applied by the server to a folder, and instead has to rely on trial and error.

DELETE

This command deletes the specified directory from the server. If it contains subdirectories (as the new directory PRIVATE in the previous example contains the subfolder PRIVATE.FRIENDS.HOLIDAY), the server may *not* delete these subdirectories automatically.

If you delete the PRIVATE directory along with all its messages, it will continue to appear in the listings, but will be marked with the \Noselect flag. The server uses this flag to show that the directory can only map the name structure, but cannot contain actual messages.

This means that directories flagged as \Noselect cannot be deleted using DELETE, as they have already been deleted.

RENAME

This command renames a folder on the server. If the folder contains subfolders, their path will also be modified. If the parent directory of the new folder does not yet exist, the server will create it automatically:

```
a023 LIST "" *
* LIST () "/" Test
* LIST (\Noselect) "/" foo
* LIST () "/" foo/bar
a023 OK LIST completed
a024 RENAME Test bla
a024 OK RENAME completed
a025 RENAME foo zowie
a025 OK RENAME Completed
a026 LIST "" *
* LIST () "/" bla
* LIST (\Noselect) "/" zowie
* LIST () "/" zowie/bar
a026 OK LIST completed
```

If the INBOX folder is renamed, the INBOX directory *must* continue to exist as an empty folder; the emails are moved into the new directory. If the INBOX contains subdirectories, these also continue to exist:

```
a027 LIST "" *
* LIST () "." INBOX
* LIST () "." INBOX.bar
a027 OK LIST completed
a028 RENAME INBOX old-mail
a028 OK RENAME completed
a029 LIST "" *
* LIST () "." INBOX
* LIST () "." INBOX.bar
* LIST () "." old-mail
a029 OK LIST completed
```

SUBSCRIBE

This command places the specified directory onto the list of directories subscribed to by the client (or the user); the client can access it in a targeted manner using the LSUB command (see below). See section 2.2.4 on page 41 for the advantages of this procedure.

The server may check whether the directory exists at the time the SUBSCRIBE command is executed. It may not delete directories from the subscription list of a client, even if these directories cease to exist. It is therefore possible to keep a subscription to directories that no longer exist, in case they are later recreated.

UNSUBSCRIBE

This command removes a directory from the list of subscribed directories.

LSUB

The parameters and server replies correspond to those of the LIST command (see page 299), but LSUB (short for *list subscribed*) only returns the directories subscribed to by the client.

STATUS

This command allows targeted querying of status information without the server selecting the appropriate directory (for example, by using EXAMINE, see page 299). This command is useful for determining the status of directories that are currently not selected.

STATUS queries often take some computing time, and Courier and other servers find it hard to evaluate a directory in addition to the selected mailbox, so RFC 3501 prohibits the use of the STATUS command for directories that have already been selected.

The client specifies the parameters it requires in parentheses:

```
a030 STATUS Test (UIDNEXT MESSAGES)
* STATUS Test (MESSAGES 231 UIDNEXT 44292)
```

APPEND

This command inserts a new email into the current folder. This email has to correspond to RFC 2822 (that is to say, it has to consist of an email header and an email body separated by a blank line). The server has to obey the following rules:

- If the email contains a `Date:` header line, the server will use the date in that row to denote the time the email was received.
- If the target folder does not exist, the server may not create this directory. Instead, it can add [TRYAGAIN] to the reply, which signifies to the client that it has to use CREATE to create this folder.
- If the client adds flags such as \Seen or \Answered in parentheses, the server *should* save these flags:

  ```
  a031 APPEND saved-messages (\Seen) {310}
  + Ready for literal data
  Date: Mon, 7 Feb 1994 21:52:25 -0800 (PST)
  From: Tux <tux@example.com>

  Hi Paul, can we meet tomorrow at 3.30?

  a031 OK APPEND completed
  ```

  If this information is missing, the server should not save any flags, and simply show the \Recent flag to the client. The client must also include the length of the new email in curly brackets (310 in this case) so the IMAP server can detect the end of the transmission.
- If the server is unable to insert the email for some reason, it has to restore the directory to its previous state so that it seems as if no action had taken place.

A.4 Commands Available in the Selected Status

CHECK
: The CHECK command allows programmers to debug their own IMAP implementation. It does not provide any default return values. This allows the software to reply with any debug output, or to return an OK without carrying out any other action. Clients should always use NOOP to keep the connection open.

CLOSE
: This command physically deletes all emails flagged as \Deleted from a folder. The affected folder is then deselected. The IMAP connection then switches to the authenticated status.

  If the client uses SELECT or EXAMINE to select a different folder, or if it logs out with LOGOUT, the server implicitly executes a CLOSE so that all emails flagged as \Deleted are deleted.

EXPUNGE

EXPUNGE also deletes all messages flagged as \Deleted, but it keeps the folder in the selected status and returns an untagged message for each deleted email.

Be careful: When emails are deleted, this naturally affects the sequence numbers of the messages. As servers delete each email individually, they renumber the emails after each deletion to close the gap. In the following example, messages 3, 4, 7, and 11 are deleted, but the server returns the IDs of messages 3, 3, 5, and 8:

```
a032a STORE 3,4,7,11 +FLAGS (\Deleted)
* 3 FETCH (FLAGS (\Deleted \Seen))
* 4 FETCH (FLAGS (\Deleted))
* 7 FETCH (FLAGS (\Deleted \Flagged \Seen))
* 11 FETCH (FLAGS (\Deleted \Seen))
a032a OK STORE completed
a032b EXPUNGE
* 3 EXPUNGE
* 3 EXPUNGE
* 5 EXPUNGE
* 8 EXPUNGE
a032b OK EXPUNGE completed
```

If the client does not require a list of deleted messages, it should use CLOSE instead of EXPUNGE.

SEARCH

This command orders the server to search through all messages in the selected folder. The server returns an untagged list of the sequence numbers of all emails corresponding to the search criteria. A number of rules apply here:

- The text search is *case insensitive*.
- A text search is considered to be successful as soon as the search pattern is found as a substring in an email.
- The search criteria are always linked by a logical AND unless the client explicitly demands an OR.
- The search pattern can be a list of several search terms enclosed in brackets if required by the logical combination with OR or NOT.

The order of search criteria is irrelevant.

The following search criteria are available:

sequencenumber1,sequencenumber2,...

If you specify the sequence number(s) of one or more emails, the server will only search the specified email(s). You can use enumerations such as (24,90,30) or segments such as (80:100), or you can combine these two options:

```
a033 search TEXT "yesterday" 24,90,30,80:100
* SEARCH 24 90
a033 OK done
```

Here, the word `yesterday` appears in emails 24 and 90.

ALL
> This option selects all emails in the mailbox.

ANSWERED
> This option selects all messages flagged as \Answered.

BCC *string*
> This option selects emails containing the specified *string* in the Bcc: field of the email header.[5]

BEFORE *date*
> This option selects emails with an internal date previous to *date*. This does not take the time into account. *date* has to be specified in this format: 29-Sep-2007.

BODY *string*
> This option selects messages containing the specified *string* somewhere in the email body:
>
> ```
> a034 SEARCH BODY "yesterday evening"
> * SEARCH 218 587 1232 1421 2258 3696 4123
> a034 OK SEARCH done.
> ```
>
> You can also use the following alternative syntax for this command:
>
> ```
> a034 SEARCH BODY {13}
> + OK
> yesterday evening
> * SEARCH 218 587 1232 1421 2258 3696 4123
> a034 OK SEARCH done.
> ```
>
> If you enter the length of the character string in bytes (13 in this case) and end the command with a line break (CR/LF), the server will then request the search string (Courier uses + OK in this case). You can now enter the search string without enclosing it in quotation marks, as shown.
>
> You can use this method to search for special characters, such as characters with a byte value above 127; these characters are not permitted in the command itself. You have to specify the character set with CHARSET:
>
> ```
> a035 SEARCH CHARSET iso-8859-1 BODY {7}
> + OK
> München
> ```

---

[5] Most email clients delete the Bcc: field from the email header because it is designed for recipients who are to remain unknown by the other recipients. It is very likely that a mailbox will not contain any emails with this information.

```
4412 4416 4420 4427 4429 4430 4434 4435 4438 4440
a035 OK SEARCH done.
```

This command will search all email parts coded according to ISO-8859-1, and will search for the München character string, which is 7 bytes long (in this coding).

CC *string*
: This command searches for messages containing the specified *string* in the `Cc:` field of the email header.

DELETED
: This command selects all messages flagged as `\Deleted`.

DRAFT
: This command selects all messages flagged as `\Draft`.

FLAGGED
: This command selects all messages flagged as `\Flagged`.

FROM *string*
: This command searches for messages that contain the *string* in the `From:` field of the email header.

HEADER *fieldname string*
: This command searches messages with the specified header field (in accordance with RFC 2822) for messages containing the given *string*:

```
036 SEARCH HEADER X-Virus-Scanned amavisd
* SEARCH 90 194
036 OK done
```

If *string* is empty, the query will apply to all messages that contain the header field, no matter what the contents are:

```
037 SEARCH HEADER X-Virus-Scanned ""
* SEARCH 24 29 90 98 194
037 OK done
```

KEYWORD *flag*
: This command searches for messages containing the specified flag.

LARGER *n*
: This command selects emails larger than *n* bytes. A line break corresponds to exactly *two* bytes, as emails conclude with CR/LF instead of only CR or LF, in accordance with RFC 2822.

NEW
: This command searches for all messages flagged as `\Recent` but not as `\Seen`.

NOT *search_option*
: This command selects emails that do *not* correspond to the search option:

A.4 Commands Available in the Selected Status

```
a038 SEARCH FLAGGED BEFORE 1-Jan-2007 NOT FROM "geeko"
* SEARCH 3 6 7 9 10 11 12 15 16  20 21 22 24 25  29 31 32 33
a038 OK SEARCH completed.
```

OLD
: This command selects all messages not flagged as \Recent.

ON *date*
: This command slects emails whose internal date is the same as *date*. This does not take the time into account.

OR *searchoption1 searchoption2*
: This command selects messages that match *searchoption1* or *searchoption2*:

```
039 SEARCH OR FROM tux@ FROM paul@
* SEARCH 25 29 31 32 33 55 64
039 OK done
040 SEARCH (OR FROM tux@ FROM paul@) BEFORE 1-Jan-2007
* SEARCH 25 29 31 32 33
040 OK done
```

RECENT
: This command selects all messages flagged as \Recent.

SEEN
: This command selects all messages flagged as \Seen.

SENTBEFORE *date*
: This command selects messages with a date in the Date: header that lies before the *date*. This does not take the time into account.

SENTON *date*
: This command selects messages with a date in the Date: header that matches the specified *date*. This does not take the time into account.

SENTSINCE *date*
: This command selects messages with a date in the Date: header that lies after the specified *date*. This does not take the time into account.

SINCE *date*
: This command selects emails with an internal date stamp that is the same or later than the *date*. This does not take the time into account.

SMALLER *n*
: This command selects emails smaller than *n* octets.

SUBJECT *string*
: This command returns messages with *string* in the Subject: field of the email header.

A IMAP Command Reference

TEXT *string*
: This command selects emails containing the *string* in both, the header or body:

    ```
    a041 SEARCH TEXT "Holiday"
    * SEARCH 4 23
    a041 OK SEARCH completed.
    ```

    TEXT usually searches the raw data on standard servers. In raw data, special characters are usually coded as =FC or =C3=BC.[6] For this reason, it makes more sense to use the SEARCH sub-command BODY (see section A.4 on page 305).

TO *string*
: This command selects messages containing the *string* in the To: field of the email header.

UID *uid1,uid2,...*
: This command selects messages with a unique identifier that contains one of the numbers specified as search criteria.

UNANSWERED
: This command selects all messages not flagged as \Answered.

UNDELETED
: This command selects all messages not flagged as \Deleted.

UNDRAFT
: This command selects all messages not flagged as \Draft.

UNFLAGGED
: This command selects all messages not flagged as \Flagged.

UNKEYWORD *flag*
: This command selects all the emails that do *not* contain the specified flag.

UNSEEN
: This command selects all messages not flagged as \Seen.

FETCH
: This command requests the specified message(s). The client can use concluding keywords to retrieve specific parts of an email. If, for example, it wants to create a table of contents, it can retrieve only the email headers required for the index, as the email body is not required at that stage. The following keywords are available in FETCH:

    BODY or BODYSTRUCTURE
    : This command fetches the MIME structure of the email:

---

[6] Both strings are equivalent to the German umlaut ü.

```
a042 FETCH 8 BODYSTRUCTURE
* 8 FETCH (BODYSTRUCTURE (("text" "plain" ("charset" "iso-8859
-1") NIL NIL "quoted-printable" 721 22 NIL ("inline" NIL) NIL)
("image" "jpeg" ("name" "Bild1_anse_gaulettes1.jpg") NIL NIL))
a042 OK FETCH completed.
```

This example email contains 22 lines and is 721 octets (or bytes) in length. Depending on interpretation, `NIL` is either short for *not in list* or for *nothing* (Latin: *nihil*), and serves as a placeholder for empty fields in the MIME structure.

BODY[] or RFC822

This command retrieves the entire specified email(s). When these two commands are used, the server automatically sets the \Seen flag. To prevent this, you should use `BODY.PEEK[]` instead of `BODY[]`, which is also capable of all the extensions discussed here.

BODY[HEADER]

This command retrieves the entire header of a message in accordance with RFC 2822:

```
a043 FETCH 30 BODY[HEADER]
* 30 FETCH (BODY[HEADER] {1458}
Return-Path: <p.heinlein@heinlein-support.de>
X-Original-To: tux@example.com
Delivered-To: tux@example.com
[...]
Message-Id: <200706062304.5047.p.heinlein@heinlein-support.de>

)
a043 OK FETCH completed.
```

The untagged reply line contains the length of the server reply in curly brackets (1458 octets, or bytes, in this case).

`RFC822.HEADER` is a synonym for `BODY.PEEK[HEADER]`.

BODY[HEADER.FIELDS (*field1 field2 ...*)]

This command only retrieves the specified fields from the message header:

```
a044 FETCH 30 BODY[HEADER.FIELDS (Message-ID)]
* 30 FETCH (BODY[HEADER.FIELDS ("Message-ID")] {67}
Message-Id: <200706062304.5047.p.heinlein@heinlein-support.de>

)
a044 OK FETCH completed.
a045 FETCH 30 BODY[HEADER.FIELDS (Message-ID Date)]
* 30 FETCH (BODY[HEADER.FIELDS ("Message-ID" "Date")] {105}
Date: Wed, 6 Jun 2007 23:04:04 +0200
Message-Id: <200706062304.5047.p.heinlein@heinlein-support.de>

)
a045 OK FETCH completed.
```

BODY[HEADER.FIELDS.NOT (*field1 field2* ...)]
: This command retrieves the header *without* the specified fields.

BODY[*level*.MIME]
: Complex messages consist of several parts: the actual email text, some binary attachments, and sometimes even an additional message as an attachment. All this is held together by the MIME structure.

    You can use MIME to retrieve the technical details of the different encapsulated levels of the message. The actual email text is on level 1:

    ```
    a046 FETCH 8 BODY[1.MIME]
    * 8 FETCH (BODY[1.MIME] {127}
    Content-Type: text/plain;
      charset="iso-8859-1"
    Content-Transfer-Encoding: quoted-printable
    Content-Disposition: inline

    )
    a046 OK FETCH completed.
    ```

    The first attachment is on level 2:

    ```
    a047 FETCH 8 BODY[2.MIME]
    * 8 FETCH (BODY[2.MIME] {159}
    Content-Type: image/jpeg;

      name="Image1.jpg"
    Content-Transfer-Encoding: base64
    Content-Disposition: attachment;
            filename="Image1.jpg"

    )
    a047 OK FETCH completed.
    ```

BODY[TEXT] or RFC822.TEXT
: This command retrieves the entire contents of the email without the header:

    ```
    a048 FETCH 7040 BODY[TEXT]
    * 7040 FETCH (BODY[TEXT] {843}
    Dear all,

    I would like to setup Debian Women for Indonesian
    But I dunno What should I do=20
    The first thing that in my mind is translating Debian Women =
    site to Indonesian language
    The other things are waiting Debian Women Bug Squashing and =
    Debian package tutorial.

    any suggestion ?=20
    ```

A.4 Commands Available in the Selected Status

```
Thanks in advance=20
[...]

)
a048 OK FETCH completed.
```

It is possible to restrict the output. In the following example, we restrict it to the first 200 characters:

```
a049 FETCH 7040 BODY[TEXT]<0.200>
* 7040 FETCH (BODY[TEXT]<0> {200}
Dear all,

I would like to setup Debian Women for Indonesian
But I dunno What should I do=20
The first thing that in my mind is translating Debian Women =
site to Indonesian language
The other t)
a048 OK FETCH completed.
```

Do *not* insert a space between the last square bracket and the first angle bracket. If you want to see the mail body between characters 100 and 200, change the contents of the angle brackets to <100.200>. However, RFC822.TEXT is not capable of this extension to the syntax.

ENVELOPE

When it receives this command, the server generates a listing of the most important data in the RFC 2822 header of the email; this data can be used to display a message overview (subject, date, sender, message ID). This has nothing to do with the SMTP envelope used to deliver the email, as this ceases to exist when the email is saved.

```
a050 FETCH 7040 ENVELOPE
* 7040 FETCH (ENVELOPE ("Thu, 28 Feb 2008 21:56:28 -0800 (PST)
" "Debian Women Indonesia" (("Nur Aini Rakhmawati" NIL "khaula
h_tc" "yahoo.com")) NIL NIL (("Debian Women" NIL "debian-women
" "lists.debian.org")) NIL NIL NIL "<178623.17300.qm@web38005.
mail.mud.yahoo.com>"))
a050 OK FETCH completed.
```

FLAGS

This command lists all the flags set for the specified message(s).

INTERNALDATE

This command returns the internal date of the message:

```
a051 FETCH 45,46 INTERNALDATE
* 45 FETCH (INTERNALDATE "30-Apr-2006 15:57:48 +0000")
* 46 FETCH (INTERNALDATE "30-Apr-2006 15:57:48 +0000")
a051 OK done
```

RFC822.SIZE

This command returns the size of the message according to RFC 2822 (with CR/LF at the end of the lines) in bytes:

```
a052 FETCH 42 RFC822.SIZE
* 42 FETCH (RFC822.SIZE 3649)
a052 OK done
```

UID

This command returns the unique ID of the message:

```
a053 FETCH 42 UID
* 42 FETCH (UID 43)
a053 OK done
```

This shows that the sequence number and the UID are not usually the same.

It is possible to combine multiple keywords in parentheses:

```
a054 FETCH 56 (FLAGS INTERNALDATE RFC822.SIZE)
* 56 FETCH (RFC822.SIZE 3731 FLAGS (\Seen) INTERNALDATE "30-Apr-200
6 15:57:49 +0000")
a054 OK done
```

There are abbreviations for typical combinations:

ALL

This abbreviation is the same as (FLAGS INTERNALDATE RFC822.SIZE ENVELOPE).

FAST

This abbreviation is the same as (FLAGS INTERNALDATE RFC822.SIZE).

FULL

This abbreviation is like the combination (FLAGS INTERNALDATE RFC822.SIZE ENVELOPE BODY).

STORE

This command adds flags to one or more messages. The server replies with one or more untagged FETCH replies in which it sums up the flags that apply to the affected messages. The client can prevent this FETCH reply (to save transmission volume and transmission time, for example), by using the FLAGS.SILENT STORE option, which also has three versions.

FLAGS (*flag1 flag2* ...)

This command sets all flags specified here. Any existing flags not mentioned here are deleted. The exception is the \Recent flag, which is not deleted.

+FLAGS (*flag1 flag2* ...)

This command adds all the flags specified here:

A.4 Commands Available in the Selected Status

```
a055 STORE 2:4 +FLAGS (\Deleted)
* 2 FETCH (FLAGS (\Deleted \Seen))
* 3 FETCH (FLAGS (\Deleted))
* 4 FETCH (FLAGS (\Deleted \Flagged \Seen))
a055 OK STORE completed
```

Custom flags (or *keywords*) are set like system flags, but there is one difference: there is no preceding \ in custom flags:

```
a056 STORE 100 +FLAGS (project)
100 FETCH (UID 102 FLAGS (\Seen project))
a056 OK done
```

-FLAGS (flag1 flag2 ...)
This command removes all flags specified here.

COPY

This command copies the specified message(s) to another folder. The server *should* preserve flags, and it *should* set the \Recent flag, as the emails are recent for the new location:

```
a057 COPY 2:4 MEETING
a057 OK COPY completed
```

As for the APPEND command (see page 302), the server *should* not simply create missing folders, but instead return a NO reply to the client along with [TRYCREATE], which in turn encourages the client to create the directory.

If the COPY command fails for some reason, the server has to restore the directory to its previous status.

UID

You can prefix this special command to COPY, FETCH, and STORE. It signifies to these commands that the figure specified as the argument refers to unchanging unique IDs rather than sequence numbers.

Thus, the following command copies the messages with sequence numbers 2 to 4 into the INBOX.Private folder:

```
a058 COPY 2:4 INBOX.Private
a058 OK COPY completed
```

whereas the following command copies the messages with unique IDs 400 to 403 (this does not imply that the folder necessarily contains more than 400 messages):

```
a059 UID COPY 400:403 INBOX.Private
a059 OK COPY completed
```

313

If you want to limit the range of emails to be processed to the highest unique ID in this folder, you can use the wildcard asterisk (*) as follows: 403:*. Even if the highest unique ID is lower than the starting value of 403, the server will still return one message (the message with the highest unique ID), unless the folder is entirely empty.

The following example shows that unique IDs are not necessarily sequential:

```
a060 UID FETCH 4827313:4828442 FLAGS
* 23 FETCH (FLAGS (\Seen) UID 4827313)
* 24 FETCH (FLAGS (\Seen) UID 4827943)
* 25 FETCH (FLAGS (\Seen) UID 4828442)
a060 OK UID FETCH completed
```

The server ignores nonexistent unique IDs. If none of the specified UIDs exist, the server will reply OK even though it did nothing. Sequence numbers are always sequential and without gaps, so this problem cannot occur for normal COPY, FETCH, and STORE commands.

If the client prefixes the UID command to a SEARCH command, this informs the server that it should show the results as unique IDs (and not as sequence numbers). The server still regards the message IDs delivered by the client as sequence numbers:

```
a061 UID SEARCH 1:100 FROM "Smith"
* UID SEARCH 80 242 882
a061 OK SEARCH done.
```

Naturally you can continue to use the unique ID as a search criterion. In the following example, the client is searching messages 1 to 100 for emails with a UID that is equal to or higher than 403. The server returns the unique IDs in an untagged reply:

```
a062 UID SEARCH 1:100 UID 403:*
* SEARCH 6924 8697 16600 16908 19373 19374
a062 OK SEARCH done.
```

A.5 IMAP Extensions

A large number of additional IMAP extensions have been defined over the course of time, but they are unfortunately spread across a variety of RFCs. This development is still ongoing, and additional extensions are under discussion; such extensions could offer additional translation or multilingual options.

A.5 IMAP Extensions

The client can use the `CAPABILITY` command to determine which IMAP extensions are supported by the server:

```
a CAPABILITY
* CAPABILITY IMAP4rev1 UIDPLUS CHILDREN NAMESPACE THREAD=ORDEREDSUBJECT
THREAD=REFERENCES SORT IDLE AUTH=CRAM-MD5 AUTH=CRAM-SHA1 ACL
a OK CAPABILITY completed
```

Many extensions provide exactly one new eponymous command, while others provide no commands or a variety of differently named IMAP commands. The following overview shows the most important IMAP extensions.

UIDPLUS
: The server sends extended replies according to RFC 4315 (previously RFC 2359) that contain the unique IDs of the emails.[7] The client has to send fewer queries, and the extension provides the foundation for *offline IMAP* (also known as *cached* or *disconnected IMAP*).

CHILDREN
: When servers return directory listings, they include the attributes \HasChildren and \HasNoChildren.[8] The client once again requires fewer queries, as it no longer needs to check whether an IMAP folder contains additional subdirectories.

NAMESPACE
: The IMAP namespace is not precisely defined, so the client can use this command to query the supported name schema of the server.[9]

SORT
: The server supports search commands using SORT.[10]

THREAD=*algorithm*
: The server supports the specified THREAD search method.[11]

IDLE
: The server supports push email via the IDLE command (see pages 176 and 200).[12]

AUTH=*method*
: This extension lists the login methods available in addition to LOGIN and PLAIN.[13]

---

[7] See http://www.ietf.org/rfc/rfc4315.txt.
[8] See http://www.ietf.org/rfc/rfc3348.txt.
[9] See http://www.ietf.org/rfc/rfc2342.txt.
[10] See http://www.ietf.org/internet-drafts/draft-ietf-imapext-sort-18.txt.
[11] See http://www.ietf.org/internet-drafts/draft-ietf-imapext-sort-18.txt.
[12] See http://www.ietf.org/rfc/rfc2177.txt.
[13] See http://www.ietf.org/rfc/rfc2060.txt.

ACL
: This extension supports ACLs (*access control lists*) via IMAP, so that one user can share individual IMAP folders with other users; see section 10.1 on page 153 (Courier) and section 14.2 on page 230 (Cyrus).[14]

QUOTA
: If quotas have been set for an account, the client can use this extension to query the permitted maximum limit and the current utilization.[15]

A.6 Experimental Commands

Commands beginning with X are not defined in standards; they are considered to be experimental or proprietary. The server may not send X-replies unless a client has explicitly attempted to use such a command.

If a server supports proprietary X-commands, it provides this information in reply to the CAPABILITY command. One example is the XCOURIEROUTBOX Courier feature, which can be used to send emails via IMAP (see section 10.5 on page 178):

```
a CAPABILITY
* CAPABILITY IMAP4rev1 UIDPLUS CHILDREN NAMESPACE THREAD=ORDEREDSUB
JECT THREAD=REFERENCES SORT IDLE AUTH=CRAM-MD5 AUTH=CRAM-SHA1 ACL
XCOURIEROUTBOX=INBOX.Outbox-Test
a OK CAPABILITY completed
```

---

[14] See http://www.ietf.org/rfc/rfc4314.txt.
[15] See http://www.ietf.org/rfc/rfc2087.txt.

Appendix B

POP3 Command Reference

POP3 also has different connection statuses, but these statuses are simple and logical:

Authorization State
  The connection has been created, but the user has not yet logged in. This means the user can ask the server to list its extensions, request an SSL encryption, and execute the authentication commands USER, PASS, AUTH, and APOP.

Transaction State
  The user is logged in and can view emails; authentication commands are no longer available.

Update State
> The client has logged out with QUIT. The server now deletes the messages that were marked as deleted and then closes the connection.
>
> If the connection between the client and the server was closed without QUIT, the server does not go into the update state. Emails marked for deletion therefore remain on the server.

B.1 An Overview of All Commands

USER *username*
> This command transfers the username during login.

PASS *password*
> This command transfers the cleartext password during login.

STAT
> This command lists the number of emails in the INBOX and the overall size in bytes.

LIST
> This command returns a numbered list of all emails and the size of each email in bytes. If you enter one of these email numbers as an argument, the server replies with the size of the email.

RETR *n*
> This command fetches email number *n* from the email server.

DELE *n*
> This command marks (!) email number *n* for deletion on the email server.

NOOP
> This command (the name stands for *no operation*) assists the client in staying connected to the server even when the client is inactive. You can also use it to see whether a connection exists.

RSET
> This command removes the deletion mark from any email deleted during the current POP3 session, so it could be described as an *undelete* command.

QUIT
> This command ends the POP3 session. All emails marked for deletion are deleted at this time.

There are also a number of commands that are not mandatory for servers:

AUTH *method*
: The client can suggest an authentication method to the server. If the server supports this method, it will begin the appropriate protocol. If not, the server will return an error code:

```
AUTH KERBEROS_V4
-ERR Authentication failed.
```

APOP
: This command initiates login with an encrypted password.

CAPA
: This command asks the server which POP3 extensions are available:[1]

    ```
    CAPA
    +OK Here's what I can do:
    SASL CRAM-MD5 CRAM-SHA1 LOGIN
    STLS
    TOP
    USER
    LOGIN-DELAY 10
    PIPELINING
    UIDL
    IMPLEMENTATION Courier Mail Server
    ```

    In this case, the server provides the following extensions:

    STLS
    : STLS is actually the POP3 STARTTLS extension. This command allows clients to request TLS encryption while in the authorization state (see STARTTLS-RFC 2595).

    TOP
    : This command uses syntax TOP *n* *x* to query the header and the first *x* lines of email number *n*.

    USER
    : This command indicates that cleartext login with the USER command is available.

    LOGIN-DELAY *n*
    : This command tells the client how long it must wait between logins.

    PIPELINING
    : This command allows clients to give several POP3 commands in direct succession without waiting for the reply from the server after each one. The server has to return the replies in the sequence in which the commands were sent, as they cannot be correlated properly otherwise.

---

[1] See RFC 2449, http://www.ietf.org/rfc/rfc2449.txt.

UIDL
: This command calls up the unique ID of the email specified by the client by number. The unique ID must remain the same for all POP3 sessions, as it is used by the client to synchronize the mailbox.

IMPLEMENTATION
: This capability allows the server to identify itself with a personalized ID text specified in the argument, but it does not provide any new POP3 commands.

Installing from the Source Code

If the version of the mail server supplied in your distribution is out of date, if you urgently require a new feature, or if you want to modify the server to suit your environment, you will have to compile your own executable from the source code. However, when you build your own server, you are responsible for finding and preventing security holes, since your installation is no longer covered by the updates provided by the official distribution.

C.1 Courier

When compiling the Courier IMAP server from the source code, it is helpful to know about potential problems in advance. The following example

C Installing from the Source Code

shows how to set up a minimal installation for OpenSuSE 10.2. The process is usually the same for other distributions, though the names of the packages can vary.

If you have not done so already, you should first install the following packages:

- Tools required for compiling the source code: make, gcc, gcc-c++, and all packages that these depend on
- The GDBM databases from packages gdbm and gdbm-devel
- openssl for SSL/TLS-encrypted connections.

Depending on the authentication backend(s) you require, you will also require the dev(el) packages for MySQL (mysql-devel), PostgreSQL (postgresql-devel), and/or OpenLDAP (openldap2-devel). It is possible to compile Courier without the appropriate C/C++ header files, but then you will lack the configuration files and support for authentication methods.

Go to the official download page of the Courier project,[1] download the most recent versions of the packages courier-imap and courier-authlib, and then unzip them. But be careful: For security reasons, you cannot compile Courier with root permissions. For this reason, you must carry out the following tasks with a normal user account:

```
user@linux:$ cd src
user@linux:src$ wget http://prdownloads.sourceforge.net/courier/ \
courier-imap-4.1.3.tar.bz2
[...]
user@linux:src$ wget http://prdownloads.sourceforge.net/courier/ \
courier-authlib-0.59.3.tar.bz2
[...]
user@linux:src$ tar -xvjf courier-authlib-0.59.3.tar.bz2
courier-authlib-0.59.3/
courier-authlib-0.59.3/README
courier-authlib-0.59.3/configure.in
courier-authlib-0.59.3/aclocal.m4
[...]
user@linux:src$ tar -xvjf courier-imap-4.1.3.tar.bz2
courier-imap-4.1.3/
courier-imap-4.1.3/packaging/
courier-imap-4.1.3/packaging/suse/
courier-imap-4.1.3/packaging/suse/courier-imap.init.in
[...]
```

Compile the package courier-authlib first. Make sure that you have normal user permissions when compiling the source code, but install it after completion with root permissions.

[1] See http://www.courier-mta.org/download.php.

```
user@linux:src$ cd courier-authlib-0.59.3
user@linux:src/courier-authlib-0.59.3$ ./configure
[...]
checking for strchr... yes
configure: creating ./config.status
config.status: creating Makefile
config.status: creating config.h
config.status: executing depfiles commands
user@linux:~/src/courier-authlib-0.59.3$ make
[...]
Compiling authpasswd.c
Linking authpasswd
CONFIG_FILES=authlib.3 CONFIG_HEADERS= /bin/sh ./config.status
config.status: creating authlib.3
config.status: executing depfiles commands
make[2]: Leaving directory '/home/user/src/courier-authlib-0.59.3'
make[1]: Leaving directory '/home/user/src/courier-authlib-0.59.3'
user@linux:src/courier-authlib-0.59.3$ su -c "make install"
Passwort: root-password
[...]
/usr/bin/install -c -m 644 -m 660 authdaemonrc.tmp /usr/local/etc/authl
ib/authdaemonrc.dist
rm -f authdaemonrc.tmp
chown daemon /usr/local/etc/authlib/authdaemonrc.dist
chgrp daemon /usr/local/etc/authlib/authdaemonrc.dist
:
make[4]: Leaving directory '/home/user/src/courier-authlib-0.59.3'
```

Now proceed to package `courier-imap`:

```
user@linux:src$ cd courier-imap-4.1.3
user@linux:src/courier-imap-4.1.3$ ./configure
[...]
config.status: creating imapd.cnf
config.status: creating pop3d.cnf
config.status: creating config.h
config.status: executing depfiles commands
user@linux:~/src/courier-imap-4.1.3$ make
[...]
cp imap/pop3d-ssl.dist .
cp imap/imapd.cnf .
cp imap/pop3d.cnf .
cp -f ./maildir/quotawarnmsg quotawarnmsg.example
make[2]: Leaving directory '/home/user/src/courier-imap-4.1.3'
make[1]: Leaving directory '/home/user/src/courier-imap-4.1.3'
user@linux:src/courier-imap-4.1.3$ make check
[...]
INFO: LOGIN, user=confmdtest, ip=[127.0.0.1], protocol=SMAP1
INFO: LOGOUT, user=confmdtest, ip=[127.0.0.1], headers=0, body=0, rcvd=
2491, sent=6164, time=0
INFO: LOGIN, user=confmdtest, ip=[127.0.0.1], protocol=SMAP1
INFO: LOGOUT, user=confmdtest, ip=[127.0.0.1], headers=0, body=0, rcvd=
```

C Installing from the Source Code

```
26, sent=610, time=0
make[2]: Leaving directory '/home/user/src/courier-imap-4.1.3/imap'
make[1]: Leaving directory '/home/user/src/courier-imap-4.1.3/imap'
make[1]: Entering directory '/home/user/src/courier-imap-4.1.3'
[...]
make[1]: Leaving directory '/home/user/src/courier-imap-4.1.3'
user@linux:src/courier-imap-4.1.3$ su -c "make install"
[...]
test -z "/usr/lib/courier-imap/share" || mkdir -p -- "/usr/lib/courier-
imap/share"
 /usr/bin/install -c 'mkimapdcert' '/usr/lib/courier-imap/share/mkimapd
cert'
 /usr/bin/install -c 'mkpop3dcert' '/usr/lib/courier-imap/share/mkpop3d
cert'
make[2]: Leaving directory '/home/user/src/courier-imap-4.1.3'
make[1]: Leaving directory '/home/user/src/courier-imap-4.1.3'
user@linux:src/courier-imap-4.1.3$ su -c "make install-configure"
[...]
  TLS_CERTFILE: new
  TLS_TRUSTCERTS: new
  TLS_VERIFYPEER: new
  TLS_CACHE: new
  MAILDIRPATH: new
make[1]: Leaving directory '/home/user/src/courier-imap-4.1.3'
```

The procedure shown will ensure that program directories and configuration files are all installed under /usr/local. Where /etc/courier/imapd is mentioned in the book, you will now find the file under /usr/local/etc/courier/imapd. This is advisable so that your own builds are separated from the standard packages provided by the distributions. If you nonetheless want to install your self-compiled Courier directly in the root hierarchy, you should add the --prefix="" parameter to the configure commands:

```
user@linux:src/courier-authlib-0.59.3$ ./configure --prefix=""
[...]
user@linux:src/courier-imap-4.1.3$ ./configure --prefix=""
[...]
```

Do not forget to install the start and stop scripts. You can either move them to the correct location or integrate them with a symlink. You require root permissions for this step:

```
linux: # cd /etc/init.d
linux:init.d # ln -s ../../usr/lib/courier-imap/libexec/imapd.rc .

linux:init.d # ln -s ../../usr/lib/courier-imap/libexec/imapd-ssl.rc .
linux:init.d # ln -s ../../usr/lib/courier-imap/libexec/pop3d.rc .
linux:init.d # ln -s ../../usr/lib/courier-imap/libexec/pop3d-ssl.rc .
```

C.2 Cyrus

It is only possible to compile the Cyrus IMAP server from the source code (as demonstrated below) if Cyrus SASL has already been installed. This is the case on many Linux systems, as this library is used almost as a default authentication mechanism for a variety of applications (such as Postfix). If you cannot install it from the package management of your distribution, you will have to compile it manually (as shown below). In some distributions (such as SuSE Linux 9.3), you may encounter problems with the distribution's default settings when linking a custom-built Cyrus to a SASL library installed by package management.

To perform the compilation, you will need the C/C++ compiler (contained in packages `gcc` and `gcc-c++` for SLES), `make` (from the `maketools` package), and the header files from packages `glibc-devel` and `libstdc++-devel`.

C.2.1 Cyrus Sources

The best place to download the program sources for the IMAP server and the SASL library is the Cyrus website of Carnegie Mellon University:[2]

```
user@linux:$ wget ftp://ftp.andrew.cmu.edu/pub/cyrus-mail/ \
cyrus-sasl-2.1.22.tar.gz
[...]
user@linux:$ wget ftp://ftp.andrew.cmu.edu/pub/cyrus/ \
cyrus-imapd-2.2.12.tar.gz
[...]
```

Other sources are available on the Internet, but they usually differ from the original and contain very specific modifications. You should always use stable versions for production systems. If you want to experiment, you can use the beta versions marked as *unstable*, but you do so at your own risk.

`tar -xvzf` unzips the source text archives into two separate subdirectories, `cyrus-imapd-2.2.12` and `cyrus-sasl-2.1.22`.

C.2.2 Creating a System User

Make sure that the user `cyrus` and the group `mail` exist on your system, because your compiled programs will not function properly otherwise. Like nearly every other important service, Cyrus IMAP and Cyrus SASL operate with the permissions of a special-purpose user and a separate group.

---

[2] See http://cyrusimap.web.cmu.edu/downloads.html.

C Installing from the Source Code

```
linux: # grep mail /etc/group
maildrop:!:59:
linux: # grep cyrus /etc/passwd
```

Here, the user `cyrus` and group `mail` do not yet exist, so you have to create them as follows:

```
linux: # groupadd mail
linux: # useradd -d /usr/lib/cyrus -g mail cyrus
linux: # passwd cyrus
Changing password for cyrus.
New Password: password-for-cyrus
Reenter New Password: password-for-cyrus
Password changed.
```

The `useradd` command shown above assigns the working directory `/usr/lib/cyrus` to user `cyrus`, and then assigns the user to the `mail` group.

C.2.3 Installing Cyrus SASL

Use the `configure` option to determine which Cyrus SASL functions are activated and which ones should remain inactive:

```
linux: # cd cyrus-sasl-2.1.22/
linux:cyrus-sasl-2.1.22 # ./configure \
--with-saslauthd=/var/run/saslauthd \
--with-plugindir=/usr/local/lib/sasl2 \
--with-mysql=/usr/local/mysql \
--with-openssl=/usr/local/ssl \
--with-bdb-incdir=/usr/local/bdb/include \
--with-bdb-libdir=/usr/local/bdb/lib \
--with-dblib=berkeley \
--enable-anon \
--enable-login \
--enable-plain \
--enable-sql \
--enable-cram \
--enable-digest \
--disable-krb4 \
--disable-otp
configure: creating cache ./config.cache
checking build system type... x86_64-unknown-linux-gnu
checking host system type... x86_64-unknown-linux-gnu
checking target system type... x86_64-unknown-linux-gnu
checking for a BSD-compatible install... /usr/bin/install -c
checking whether build environment is sane... yes
checking for gawk... gawk
checking whether make sets $(MAKE)... yes
checking for gcc... gcc
```

```
checking for C compiler default output... a.out
checking whether the C compiler works... yes
[...]
Configuration Complete. Type 'make' to build.
```

`--with-saslauthd=/var/run/saslauthd` specifies the path to the process directory of the SASL authentication service.

`--with-plugindir=/usr/local/lib/sasl2` specifies the directory that will contain the SASL plugins.

`--with-mysql=/usr/local/mysql` activates support for MySQL (via PAM). You have to enter the path to the required PAM modules as the value for the switch. The `--enable-sql` switch ensures that the compilation process creates the SQL plugin which Cyrus SASL will later use to query a MySQL database.

`--with-openssl=/usr/local/ssl` requests support for OpenSSL and determines the path to the OpenSSL installation directory.

You can only use `sasldb2` after you have specified the path to the Berkeley database header files (using `--with-bdb-incdir=/usr/local/bdb/include`) and used `--with-bdb-libdir=/usr/local/bdb/lib` to specify the path to the Berkeley database libraries. You also have to use `--with-dblib=berkeley` to request support for the Berkeley database.

SASL uses `--enable-anon` to allow anonymous login and `--enable-login` to allow passwords to be transferred in cleartext compatible with Windows. `--enable-plain` activates authentication using the `PLAIN` mechanism (also in cleartext). `--enable-cram` ensures that SASL accepts CRAM-MD5 passwords; `--disable-digest` ensures that Digest-MD5 passwords are refused. `--disable-krb4` deactivates support for Kerberos-4, while `--disable-otp` deactivates one-time passwords.

For additional ways of influencing library functions, see the documentation in the `doc/` directory of the unzipped source code or call `./configure --help`.

If you activate functions that use other services, these services have to exist on the system when you call `configure`. If, for example, you specify `--enable-sql` and MySQL is not installed on your system, `configure` will terminate with an error message.

In that case, you should take a close look at the last error message. In most cases, a program required for compilation is missing; in the example shown here, it is the compiler:

```
linux:cyrus-sasl-2.1.22 # ./configure
configure: loading cache ./config.cache
checking build system type... (cached) x86_64-unknown-linux-gnu
checking host system type... (cached) x86_64-unknown-linux-gnu
```

C Installing from the Source Code

```
checking target system type... (cached) x86_64-unknown-linux-gnu
checking for a BSD-compatible install... (cached) /usr/bin/install -c
checking whether build environment is sane... yes
checking for gawk... (cached) gawk
checking whether make sets $(MAKE)... (cached) yes
checking for gcc... (cached) gcc
checking for C compiler default output... configure: error: C compiler
cannot create executables
See 'config.log' for more details.
```

Simply install `gcc` and `g++`, and `configure` will run properly. If this works, you can now begin the compilation and installation process:

```
linux:cyrus-sasl-2.1.22 # make && make install
```

You should set a symbolic link to the directory containing the library files you have just created, because some programs expect the SASL library in the `/usr/lib/` directory:

```
linux:cyrus-sasl-2.1.22 # ln -s /usr/local/lib/sasl2 /usr/lib/sasl2
```

Depending on your distribution and the architecture of your system, the library location for SASL may have a different name. Common names are `/usr/lib/sasl2` in 32-bit systems and `/usr/lib64/sasl2` in 64-bit systems.

To be on the safe side, you should compile the `testsaslauthd` test program delivered along with the source code, and then copy it to the `/usr/local/bin` directory. This does not take long, as you do not have to create a makefile:

```
linux:cyrus-sasl-2.1.22 # cd saslauthd/
linux:saslauthd # make testsaslauthd
linux:saslauthd # cp testsaslauthd /usr/local/bin/
```

Call `/usr/local/bin/testsaslauthd` to test the `saslauthd` SASL plugin. By default, it queries PAM on SuSE systems, and PAM then queries the Unix system accounts. For this purpose, it is advisable to use an existing Unix system user:

```
linux: # testsaslauthd -u username -p password -f /var/run/sasl2/mux0
OK "Success."
```

`-u` specifies the username, `-p` the password, and `-f` specifies the path to the socket used to communicate with SASL.

C.2.4 Installing the Cyrus IMAP Server

The installation of the Cyrus IMAP server follows the same principle as that of Cyrus SASL:

```
linux: # cd /usr/local/src/cyrus-imapd-2.2.12
linux:cyrus-imapd-2.2.12 # export CPPFLAGS="-I/usr/include/et"
linux:cyrus-imapd-2.2.12 # ./configure \
--with-sasl=/usr/local/lib \
--with-perl \
--with-auth=unix \
--with-dbdir=/usr/local/bdb \
--with-bdb-libdir=/usr/local/bdb/lib \
--with-bdb-incdir=/usr/local/bdb/include \
--with-openssl=/usr/local/ssl \
--without-ucdsnmp
checking build system type...
[...]
```

Cyrus requires the `com_err.h` header file that belongs to the Common Error library and is missing from many systems. You therefore are likely to have to install it; in Debian and Ubuntu you will find it in the `comerr-dev` package. The header file is usually located in the /usr/include/et/ directory, and you can use the CPPFLAGS environment variable to specify this.

`--with-sasl=/usr/local/lib` ensures that Cyrus uses the Cyrus SASL library installed in /usr/local/lib. `--with-perl` allows the server to support Perl scripts, which are used for the majority of Cyrus scripts and modules. `--with-auth=unix` sets unix as the default authentication method. This means that Cyrus evaluates the files /etc/passwd and /etc/shadow when email users log on.

Use `--with-dbdir=/usr/local/bdb` to specify the path to the subtree for the Berkely database files; the files are now activated and you can use them to store user data in an `sasldb2` database. However, you have to use `--with-bdb-libdir=/usr/local/bdb/lib` and `--with-bdb-incdir=/usr/local/bdb/include` to explicitly specify the path to the Berkeley database libraries and header files. `--with-openssl=/usr/local/ssl` activates support for OpenSSL and specifies the path to the SSL installation folder.

`--without-ucdsnmp` disables SNMP support. Even though this has not been officially documented, you can monitor Cyrus using SNMP. If you want to find out more, you should have a look at http://osdir.com/ml/mail.imap.cyrus/2003-01/msg00517.html.

./configure --help lists all the options you can use to adapt Cyrus to your own needs during compilation.

Once ./configure has run successfully, you should use make && make install to initiate the compilation and installation process. Once instal-

C Installing from the Source Code

lation is complete, you have to use the `mkimap` program to create the working directories for Cyrus. The paths are stored in the `/etc/imapd.conf` configuration file, which is processed by `mkimap`:

```
linux: # /usr/local/cyrus/bin/mkimap
reading configure file...
i will configure directory /var/lib/imap.
i saw partition /var/spool/imap.
done
configuring /var/lib/imap...
creating /var/spool/imap...
done
```

Now check that user `cyrus` has read and write permissions for these directories and files, and that the `mail` group has read permissions.

C.2.5 Convenient Starting and Stopping

A start-and-stop script for simple activation and termination will provide the finishing touch to the Cyrus IMAP daemon:

```bash
#!/bin/bash
#
# Cyrus-Startup-Skript

case "$1" in
start)
    # Cyrus-SASL starten
    /usr/local/sbin/saslauthd -c -a shadow &

    # Cyrus-IMAP-Daemon starten
    /usr/cyrus/bin/master &
    ;;
stop)
    # Cyrus-SASL beenden
    killall saslauthd

    # Cyrus-IMAP-Server beenden
    killall /usr/cyrus/bin/master
    ;;
*)
    # Ausgabe der möglichen Optionen
    echo "Usage: $0 start|stop"
    exit 1
    ;;
esac
```

Naturally, you can modify the more complex start and stop scripts provided by the distributions so that they will run with the Cyrus you have compiled.

Index

Symbols
*, in server reply 31
*, wildcard for LIST 300
., as mailbox separator (Cyrus) 205, 235, 238
/, as mailbox separator (Cyrus) 205, 235, 238
% (wildcard), for LIST 300
8-bit characters *see* eight-bit characters

A
a (permission) 37
access permissions *see* ACLs
access time, of a file *see* atime
account options *see* user options (Courier)
ACLs 34, 36, 37, 154
    Cyrus 231, 232
    group-based (Courier) 144
    identifier 154
    IMAP extension 34, 316
        activating (Courier) 102
    listing (Cyrus) 272
    manipulating (Courier) *see* maildiracl (tool)
    negative permissions 155
    removing (Cyrus) 272
    saving in Courier *see* courierimapacl (file)
    setting (Cyrus) 272
    switching off at filesystem level 58
    for virtual domains (Cyrus) 236, 237
active directory with user data 81
ADDRESS (Courier parameter) 98
address (Sieve command) 246
administration directory (Cyrus) 203
administrator, creating (Cyrus) 194
admins (Cyrus option) 203, 287, 288
aggregator 51, 281–290
    backend server 282, 286–287
    frontend server 282–285
allowanonymouslogin (Cyrus option) 203
allowsubscribes (Cyrus option) 287
allowusermoves (Cyrus option) 287
altnamespace (Cyrus option) 277
annotation database (Cyrus) 259
annotation_db (Cyrus parameter) 259
annotations.db (file) 267, 278
\Answered (flag) 35
    in the filename (maildir) 113
    searching for 305
APOP 27, 28, 148
    POP3 command 317, 319
AppArmor 193
APPEND (IMAP command) 302
Apple Mail 279
aquota.user (file) 168
arbitron 263
arbitronsort.pl (tool) 190, 269
atime, switching off 57–58, 64
attachments, retrieving individually (IMAP) 310
AUTH (IMAP extension) 315
AUTH (POP3 command) 317, 319
AUTH=PLAIN (capability) 296
authcram (Courier) 120, 129, 144, 148
authcustom (Courier) 121, 130
authdaemond (Courier)
    activating 99
    configuration file *see* authdaemonrc
    starting 88
    daemon 20, 121–123
        configuration file *see* authdaemonrc
        custom authentication modules *see* authcustom
    using with Cyrus SASL 189, 213

Index

authdaemonrc (Courier configuration file) 95, 123, 134, 145
AUTHENTICATE (IMAP command) 218, 297
Authenticated (IMAP status) 32
    available commands 298–303
    switching to 303
Authenticated Post Office Protocol *see* APOP
authentication *see* logging in
    by fingerprint 213
    by hash values instead of passwords 213
    by iris scan 213
    Cyrus 207–224
        via Kerberos 212, 214, 223–224
        via LDAP 212–214, 220–223
        via MySQL 213, 216–220
        via PAM 219–220
        via SQL database 213
    daemon (Courier) *see* authdaemond
    choosing method (POP3) 319
    choosing method (Courier) 99, 122
    IMAP commands 297
    library (Courier) *see* Courier Authlib
    password in cleartext 210
    POP3 commands 317
    programs, custom (Courier) 121
    proxy (Courier) *see* authdaemond
authenumerate 160
    tool 138, 145
authldap (authentication module for Courier) 121, 140–146
    caching requests 122
authldaprc (file) 95, 140
authlib 120–144
AUTHMODULES (Courier parameter) 99, 122, 123
authmysql (authentication module for Courier) 120, 133–139, 144, 147
    caching requests 122
authmysqlrc (file) 134–139
authorization state (POP3) 317
authpam (Courier) 120, 123–124
authpgsql
    authentication module for Courier 120, 139, 140, 144, 147
        caching requests 122
    file 139
authpipe (Courier) 121, 131–133

authProg (authentication tool) 131
authpwd (authentication module for Courier) 120, 143
authshadow (authentication module for Courier) 120, 143
authtest (tool) 121–122
authuserdb (authentication module for Courier) 120, 124–129, 144
authvchkpw (authentication module for Courier) 120
autocreate_sieve_script (Cyrus option) 251
autocreatequota (Cyrus option) 203, 226, 251
autologout timer, resetting 296
auxprop (Cyrus SASL module) 189, 194, 213
    LDAP connection via 220, 221
    MySQL connection via 216
availability 19, 43–51
avelsieve (Squirrelmail plugin) 244

B

backup (IMAP folders) 29
backup (main Cyrus database) 278
backup/ (directory) 278
BALANCE (iptables) 47
Bcc header, searching in 305
benchmark tools 55
berkeley (Cyrus database format) 259
berkeley-nosync (Cyrus database format) 259
berkeley_cachesize (Cyrus parameter) 258
berkeley_txns_max (Cyrus parameter) 258
block size, for NFS 64
body
    retrieving (IMAP) 310
    retrieving partially (IMAP) 311
    retrieving partially (POP3) *see* TOP (POP3 command)
    searching in 305
bonnie 55
byte-octet conversion 296

C

c (permission) 37
CA *see* certificate authority (CA)
cache proxy 51, 73–74
cached IMAP *see* offline IMAP
CAPA (POP3 command) 319
capabilities 33

Index

for encrypted communication (IMAP) 297
   polling (IMAP) 296
   polling (POP3) 319
   specifying for Courier 100
CAPABILITY (IMAP command) 175, 295, 296, 314
   for encrypted communication 297
case sensitive
   folder names 301
   search 40
Cc header, searching in 306
cell phone (and IMAP) 176, 273
certificate authority (CA) 208
   list in email clients 208
   trustworthy 208
certificates *see* SSL certificates
challenge-response procedure 129, 148, 242, 297
change time, of a file *see* ctime
character encoding, considering during a search 305
character set, considering during a search 305
CHECK (IMAP command) 303
CHILDREN (IMAP extension) 34, 315
chk_cyrus 264
chmod, influence on c and mtime 57
cleartext
   login *see* LOGIN (IMAP command)
   passwords 81
client, workaround for faulty 101
CLOSE (IMAP command) 32, 303
cluster 20
   Cyrus 281, 291
Cluster filesystem, as email repository 45
CLUSTERIP (iptables) 47
cm *see* createmailbox
com_err.h (Common Error library) 329
compile_sieve (tool) 268
compiling
   Courier 321, 324
   Cyrus 325, 330
CONCAT (SQL command) 137
conditional query (Sieve) *see* if (Sieve)
Cone 85
config2header (tool) 269
config2man (tool) 269
configdirectory
   Cyrus option 203
   Cyrus parameter 270

configuration parameters
   Courier 96–105
   reading out (Courier) 100
connection
   information, caching (SSL) 260
   keeping open *see* NOOP
   terminating
      automatically for POP3 (Cyrus) 259
      with IMAP *see* LOGOUT (IMAP command)
      with POP3 *see* QUIT (POP3 command) 318
      unintended (IMAP) 32
   testing *see* NOOP
contents, of an email *see* body
convert-sieve.pl (tool) 190, 269
COPY (IMAP command) 313
   using the Unique ID 313
Courier 18, 85–179
   configuration 95–105
   configuring SSL encryption 102–105
   crashing 93
   vs. Cyrus 20–21
   downloading 322
   IMAP proxy 50, 145
   installation 86–87
   installing from the source code 321, 324
   migration problems 110
   misleading reply to LIST (POP3) 25
   MTA 85
   paths 87
   project 85
Courier Authlib 85
Courier team
   reaction to bug reports 93
   reaction to change requests 110
courierimapacl (file) 109, 154–155
courierimapkeywords (directory) 116
courierimapsubscribed (file) 109
courierlogger (tool) 98, 103
couriertcpd 88
   specifying command-line parameters 98
COURIERTLS (Courier parameter) 104
couriertls (tool) 87, 104
CPU *see* processor
CRAM 129
CRAM-MD5 100, 119, 148, 214

Index

using with Cyrus 213
when testing the login with imtest 218
CRAM-SHA1 100, 119, 148
CRAM-SHA256 148
crash, Courier 93
CREATE (IMAP command) 300
createmailbox
    cyradm command 239
    cyradmin command 272
creating users
    Cyrus 194
    with saslpasswd2 194
Crispin, Mark 33
crypt
    hash, instead of cleartext password 119
    as password hash algorithm 147
ctime 57
ctl_cyrusdb (tool) 266
ctl_deliver 266
ctl_mboxlist 266
cur
    for creating directories 88
    for listing contents of a directory 108, 112
    for listing purpose of a directory 108
cvt_cyrusdb 267
cyr_expire (tool) 202, 268
cyradm (tool) 21, 194, 271–274, 277
    setting quotas 228
    setting up shared folders 230
cyrdump (tool) 267
Cyrus 18, 183–291
    activating SSL support 210
    administration information 277–280
    as administration tool *see* cyradm, (tool)
    allowing anonymous users 203
    connecting to MySQL 213, 216–220
    connecting to PostgreSQL 213
    vs. Courier 20–21
    creating an administrator 194
    creating users 194
        with saslpasswd2 194
    directory hierarchy 187
    downloading 325
    encrypting access data 189
    and firewalls 191, 220
    function test 195–197
    IMAP proxy 51
    installation 184–187
        under Debian 186
        under Red Hat 186
        from source code 325, 330
        under SuSE 185
    LMTP *see* LMTP
    location in the filesystem 204
    lowercase addresses 204
    maximum email size 204
    Murder cluster 51, 281–290
    ports 191
    and Postfix 191–197
    project origins 183
    Red Hat source RPM for 186
    refusing to accept email (quota) 204
    SASL authentication methods 205
    Sieve directory 205
    SSL certificates 205
    user vs. Unix system account 215
    working directory 188
Cyrus (IMAP server)
    data security 255, 257
    domain administrators 237
    notify daemon 252
    operating with other MTAs 254, 255
    sorting email 237
    specifying a timeout 205
    virtual domains 232
Cyrus Aggregator *see* aggregator
Cyrus SASL *see* libsasl
    library 190
cyrus-admin-2.2 (Debian package) 186
cyrus-clients-2.2 (Debian package) 186
cyrus-common-2.2 (Debian package) 186
cyrus-imap-utils (Red Hat package) 186
cyrus-imapd
    Red Hat package 186
    SuSE package 185
cyrus-imapd-2.2 (Debian package) 187
cyrus-murder-2.2 (Debian package) 187
cyrus-nntpd-2.2 (Debian package) 187
cyrus-pop3d-2.2 (Debian package) 187
cyrus-sasl
    package 189
    Red Hat package 186
cyrus-sasl-crammd5 (SuSE package) 185
cyrus-sasl-digestmd5 (SuSE package) 185

Index

cyrus-sasl-otp (SuSE package) 185
cyrus-sasl-plain
    Red Hat package 186
    SuSE package 185
cyrus-sasl-saslauthd (SuSE package) 185
cyrus-sasl-sqlauxprop (SuSE package) 185
cyrus.cache (file) 276
cyrus.conf 188, 199–202, 266
    checkpoint 202
    cleanup 202
    configuring
        the mupdate server 288
        the murder backend 287
        the murder frontend 285
    defining the LMTP socket 191
    delprune 202
    EVENTS{} section 201–202, 260, 268
    idled 200
    imap 201
    listen 200, 201
    lmtp 201, 254
    lmtpunix 254
    notify 201, 253
    pop3d 201
    recovering 200
    SERVICES{} section 200–201, 210, 241, 254, 285, 288
    sieve 201, 241
    specifying nice values for events 268
    START{} section 200
    structure 199
    tlsprune 202
cyrus.header (file) 256, 276
cyrus.index (file) 276

D

d (permission) 37
dam see deleteaclmailbox
data (Squirrelmail directory) 70
data loss, through ReiserFS 54
data protection 159
data segment, limiting size of (Courier) 102
database format
    annotation database (Cyrus) 259
    berkeley-nosync (Cyrus) 260
    converting (Cyrus) 267
    duplicate database (Cyrus) 260

    possible (Cyrus) 259
    quota database (Cyrus) 260
    quotalegacy (Cyrus) 260
    subscription database (Cyrus) 260
date
    as search criterion 305, 307
    determining the internal (IMAP) 311
    format in IMAP commands 305
db.backup1/ (directory) 278
db/ (directory) 278
DEBUG_LOGIN (Courier parameters) 81, 99, 122
debugging, an IMAP implementation 303
default domain (Cyrus) 234
DEFAULT_DOMAIN (Courier parameter) 138, 139
defaultdelivery (QMail configuration file) 94
defaultdomain (Cyrus option) 203, 234
DEFAULTOPTIONS (Courier parameter) 145
defaultpartition (Cyrus option) 239
DEFDOMAIN (Courier parameter) 98
DELE (POP3 command) 26, 318
DELETE (IMAP command) 301
delete permission see ACLs
deleteaclmailbox (cyradmin command) 272
\Deleted (flag) 31, 32, 35, 303, 304
    searching for email with 40, 306
    number of 31
deletemailbox (cyradmin command) 272
deleting
    email (IMAP) 39, 298, 303, 304
    email (POP3) 26, 318
    folders (IMAP) see DELETE (IMAP command)
    undoing the deletion of email (POP3) 26, 318
deliver
    Cyrus service 255
    tool 268
deliver databases (Cyrus) 266
deliver.db (file) 266, 278
deliverquota
    MDA 173
    tool 87
denial-of-service attack 166
    preventing (Courier) 97, 102
dialup, and IMAP 29
DIGEST-MD5 (password-transfer method) 214
    using with Cyrus 213, 242
    when using an LDAP server 221
dir_index (mount option) 58–60

Index

Direct Routing (LVS) 47
directory *see* folders
    permissions 163
disableimap (user option) 126, 144
disablepop (user option) 144
disablepop3 (user option) 126
disableshared (user option, Courier) 145, 161
disableweb (user option) 144
discard (Sieve command) 248
disconnected IMAP *see* offline IMAP
.dist file (Courier) 96
dm *see* deletemailbox (cyradmin command)
DNAT (iptables) 46–47
DNS 46
dohash (tool) 269
domain administrators (Cyrus) 237
domains, in the login name 150
DoS *see* denial-of-service attack
dot (.), as mailbox separator (Courier) 109
downloading
    Courier 322
    Cyrus 325
    Cyrus SASL 325
DRAC, using with Cyrus 206
drachost (Cyrus option) 206
dracinterval (Cyrus option) 206
\Draft (flag) 35
    in the filename (maildir) 113
    searching for 306
dump, of a mailbox (Cyrus) 267
duplicate database (Cyrus) 260, 278
duplicate emails, avoiding (Cyrus) 260, 278
duplicate_db (Cyrus parameter) 260

E

e (permission) 37
edquota 169
eGroupWare 18
eight-bit characters, in headers, rejecting email with 204
email
    addressing to subfolders 36, 237, 238
    copying 39, *see* COPY (IMAP command)
    deleted (number of) 31
    deleting
        IMAP 39
        obsolete automatically 268

POP3 26, 318
    Sieve *see* discard (Seive command)
determining the MIME structure of 308
determining the size of (IMAP) 311
determining the Unique ID for 312
drafts *see* \Draft (flag)
envelope *see* envelope
fetching from server
    IMAP *see* FETCH (IMAP command)
    POP3 25, 318
file size in the filename (maildir) 114
filenames (Courier) 111–117
format, RFC 306
ID, Unique *see* Unique ID
informing the client of new 100, 101
inode of file 114
meta-information 111
moving
    instead of deleting (Courier) 101
    in Sieve *see* fileinto (Seive command)
new (number of) 31, 112, 299
placing in folder *see* APPEND (IMAP command)
reading
    number of 31
    offline 24
redirecting (Sieve) *see* redirect
rejecting (Sieve) *see* reject
remaining on the server 24
repository, central 45
saving *see* backup
searching *see* searching, in email
sending a test *see* test email, sending
sending via IMAP 99
sequence number 29
    of the first unread 299
size as search criterion 306, 307
sorting into inboxes (Cyrus) 268
storage location
    Courier 99
    Exim 94
    Postfix *see* home_mailbox
    QMail 94
suppressing duplicates in Cyrus 260, 278
Unique ID 299
unread 40, 299
viewing *see* FETCH (IMAP command)

Index

email addresses
    as login IDs 157
    as login names 150
    storing server administrator's 273
    as usernames for shell accounts 127
email clients *see* client
    and certificates 208
encryption
    activating with SSL/TLS (Courier) 103
    and certificates 208
    configuring with SSL/TLS (Courier) 102–105
    forcing (Courier) 103
    of the database connection (Cyrus) 217
    with SSL/TLS 102, 208, 211
envelope
    evaluating (Sieve) 246
    querying data in (IMAP) 311
    Sieve command 246
/etc/authlib/ 95
/etc/cyrus.conf *see* cyrus.conf
/etc/fstab *see* fstab
/etc/groups *see* groups (file)
/etc/imapd.conf *see* imapd.conf
/etc/passwd *see* passwd
/etc/shadow *see* shadow (file)
/etc/userdb *see* userdb
Evolution 17
EXAMINE (IMAP command) 32, 299
    and CLOSE 303
exchange, migrating 81
Exim 18
    connecting to Cyrus 255
    integration into Courier 94–95
exim.conf 94
exists (Sieve command) 247
EXPUNGE (IMAP command) 32, 304
Ext2/Ext3
    as email data storage 54–62
    journal mode 60–62
    speeding up *see* dir_index (mount option)
Ext4, as email storage medium 56
extensions *see* IMAP, extensions

F

FAM (File Alteration Monitor) 176
famd (daemon) 177
FETCH (IMAP command) 37, 112, 308, 312
    using the Unique ID 313
fetchnews (tool) 268
File Alteration Monitor (FAM) 176
file locking, activating (Courier) 102
fileinto (Sieve command) 246, 248
filenames, for email (Courier) 111, 117
filesystem
    performance 55–57
    selecting 53, 57
    tuning the performance of 57, 62
filter settings
    for mailboxes 205
    migrating 80
    removing from Squirrelmail 80
fingerprint, authentication by 213
firewall, Sieve ports 245
fishing, for passwords 82
\Flagged (flag) 35
    in the filename (maildir) 113
    searching for 306
flags 29
    \Answered *see* \Answered (flag)
    \Deleted *see* \Deleted (flag)
    \Draft *see* \Draft (flag)
    \Flagged *see* \Flagged (flag)
    \Recent *see* \Recent (flag)
    \Seen *see* \Seen (flag)
    abbreviation in the maildir 113
    activating custom (Courier) 101
    adding 312
    custom 35, 75, 87, 115–117, 289, 313
    excluding in a search 308
    modifiable by client 36
    permanent 29, 36, 101, 115, 298
    permitted in the email folder 35, 298
    querying in a message 311
    removing 313
    save type 36
    searching for 306
    session-based 29, 115
    setting *see* STORE (IMAP command)
    temporary *see* flags, session-based
flat (Cyrus database format) 259
folders
    adapting names during migration 78
    case-sensitive names of 301
    creating *see* CREATE (IMAP command)

deleting see DELETE (IMAP command)
    after a specified period (Courier) 101
leaving see UNSELECT (IMAP command)
listing subscribed see LSUB (IMAP command)
moving during migration 78
naming 110
parallel to the INBOX 78, 79, 110
permissions for see ACLs
permitted flags 35
renaming 79–80
    IMAP see RENAME (IMAP command)
selecting see SELECT (IMAP command)
selecting to read see EXAMINE (IMAP command)
spaces in names of 110
special characters in names of 110, 158
sub- see subfolders (Courier)
subscribed (Cyrus) 280
subscribing see SUBSCRIBE (IMAP command)
    to folders on different backends 287
synchronizing continuously 76
unsubscribing see SUBSCRIBE (IMAP command)
format
    for an annotation database see annotation_db
    for a duplicate database see duplicate_db
    for a quota database see quota_db
    for a subscription database see subscription_db
From header, searching in 306
fsck.reiserfs 54
fstab
    command, activating quotas 168
    optimizations 62
fud (tool) 268
fulldirhash (Cyrus option) 270
fulltext index 267

G

gam-server (tool) 177
Gamin 176
gecos 126, 136
GETMETADATA (IMAP command) 273
getpwent (saslauthd plugin) 212
GETQUOTA (IMAP command) 227
GID see group ID

group (user option) 155
group management with Courier via 144
group affiliation (of a user) 155
group ID
    field in a MySQL table (Courier) 135
    field in a PostgreSQL table (Courier) 139
groups (file), Cyrus group management via 231
groupware 18
    Horde see Horde
grpquota (mount option) 168
GSSAPI 185
    using with Cyrus 214

H

HA see availability
Haberland, Juri 79
hard disk I/O see I/O
\HasChildren (folder flag) 34
hash procedure, for password transmission 148
hashimapspool (Cyrus option) 204
\HasNoChildren (folder flag) 34
    error in the client 101
header lines
    calling individual (IMAP) 39, 309
    searching in 306
header rows, evaluating (Sieve) 247
HEADERFROM (Courier parameter) 99, 178
headers
    refusing eight-bit characters in 204
    retrieving (IMAP) 309
    retrieving (POP3) see TOP (POP3 command)
    Sieve command 247
hierarchy separators
    Courier 109
    Cyrus 235, 238
    determining 35, 300
HMAC-MD5 (hash procedure) 148
home_mailbox (Postfix variable) 92
Horde 70–73
hostname, logging the client's (Courier) 98

I

i (permission) 36
I/O, as limiting factor 44, 65
ident lookup (Courier) 98
IDLE (IMAP command) 34, 100, 101, 176–178, 200, 315

Index

idled 200, 262
if (Sieve) 246
IMAP 18, 28, 41, 295, 316
    daemon
        configuration (Courier) 99–102
        configuration (Cyrus) *see* imapd.conf
        Courier 87
        Cyrus 262
        exporting data set to mbox files 76
        mode of operation 19
        starting (Courier) 88
    disabling login (Courier) *see* disableimap
    email sending via 99, 316
    experimental commands 316
    extensions 33, 295, 314
    functions 19
    offline *see* offline IMAP
    proxy *see* proxy
    Proxy (project) 51, 73–74
    RFC 33
    separate password for (Courier) 126
    session, process 31–33
imap (Red Hat package) 186
imap.conf (file) 258, 260
IMAP4rev1 (RFC) 295
IMAP_ACL (Courier parameter) 102
IMAP_CAPABILITY (Courier parameter) 100, 150
IMAP_CAPABILITY_TLS (Courier parameter) 100
IMAP_CHECK_ALL_FOLDERS (Courier parameter) 100
IMAP_DISABLETHREADSORT (Courier parameter) 100
IMAP_EMPTYTRASH (Courier parameter) 101
IMAP_ENHANCEDIDLE (Courier parameter) 100
IMAP_IDLE_TIMEOUT (Courier parameter) 101
IMAP_KEYWORDS (Courier parameter) 101, 115
imap_migrate 76
IMAP_MOVE_EXPUNGE_TO_TRASH (Courier parameter) 101
IMAP_OBSOLETE_CLIENT (Courier parameter) 101
IMAP_PROXY (Courier parameter) 175
IMAP_PROXY_FOREIGN (Courier parameter) 175
IMAP_SHAREDINDEXFILE (Courier parameter) 101
IMAP_SHAREDMUNGENAMES (Courier parameter) 157
imap_tools 76
IMAP_TRASHFOLDERNAME (Courier parameter) 101
IMAP_ULIMITD (Courier parameter) 102
IMAP_USELOCKS (Courier parameter) 102
imapcopy 76
imapd *see* IMAP, daemon
    Courier configuration file 95, 99–102, 115, 122, 123
    Cyrus daemon *see* IMAP, daemon
imapd-ssl (Courier configuration file) 95, 103
imapd.cnf (Courier configuration file) 88, 96, 104
imapd.conf 188, 189, 203–206
    admins 203, 237, 287, 288
    allowanonymouslogin 203
    allowsubscribes 287
    allowusermoves 287
    altnamespace 277
    annotation_db 259
    authentication via sasldb2 (Cyrus) 194
    autocreate_sieve_script 251
    autocreatequota 203, 226, 251
    berkeley_cachesize 258
    berkeley_txns_max 258
    configdirectory 203, 270
    configuring the mupdate server 288
    configuring the murder backend 286–287
    configuring the murder frontend 283–285
    connecting to MySQL 216
    defaultdomain 203, 234
    defining the directory for mailboxes 195
    drachost 206
    dracinterval 206
    duplicate_db 260
    fulldirhash 270
    hashimapspool 204
    lmtp_downcase_rcpt 204
    lmtp_overquota_perm_failure 204
    mailnotifier 253
    maxmessagesize 204, 258
    mupdate-port 286
    mupdate-server 286
    mupdate_authname 284, 286
    mupdate_password 284, 286
    mupdate_port 284
    mupdate_server 284
    mupdate_username 284, 286

Index

partition-default 204, 239, 270
partition-name 259
poptimeout 204, 259
proxy_authname 284
proxyd_disable_mailbox_referrals 285
proxyservers 287
ptscache_db 260
quota_db 260
quotawarn 204, 226
quotawarnkb 204, 227
reject8bit 204
sasl_mech_list 214
sasl_pwcheck_method 205, 215, 219
sasl_sql_hostnames 216
sasl_sql_select 217
sasl_sql_usessl 217
sasl_sql_verbose 217
seenstate_db 259
servername 283, 288, 290
sieve_allowreferrals 285
sievedir 205, 241, 285
sievenotifier 253
sieveuserhomedir 285
structure 203
subscription_db 260
timeout 205
tls_ca_file 206, 210
tls_ca_path 206, 210
tls_cert_file 205, 210
tls_key_file 205, 210
tlscache_db 260
unixhierarchysep 205, 235
username_tolower 205
virtdomains 205, 233
IMAPD_TLS_REQUIRED (Courier parameter) 103
IMAPDSSLSTART (Courier parameter) 103
IMAPDSTART (Courier parameter) 99
IMAPDSTARTTLS (Courier parameter) 103
imaplogin (Courier) 87
imapsync 76–78
    tool 76, 81
IMP 70–73
IMPLEMENTATION (POP3 capability) 320
important emails *see* \Flagged (flag)
imtest (tool) 217–218
in.imapproxyd *see* IMAP, Proxy (project)
INBOX

folders parallel to 78, 79, 110
    renaming 301
index (file) 153, 156–158
    generating automatically 160
    on multiple servers 156
    for a shared group 159
    for shared folders (Courier) 88, 101, 138
    splitting 161
index databases (Cyrus) 259, 260, 278
    changing format of 267
    maximum RAM consumption 258
initscript, Courier 88–89
inode, of an email file 114
installing
    Courier 86–87
    from the source code
        Courier 321, 324
        Cyrus 325, 330
Internet interface
    for Cyrus administration 184
Internet Message Access Protocol *see* IMAP
iozone 55
IP address
    limiting the number of connections per 97
    logging the client's (Courier) 98, 99
    of the POP3/IMAP server (Courier) 98
iptables, load distribution via 46, 47
ipurge (tool) 202, 268
iris scan, authentication by 213

J

Jabber notification (Sieve) 254
journal mode 60–62

K

keep (Sieve command) 248
Kerberos 185
    support for Cyrus 212
    using with Cyrus 214, 223–224
    using with Sieve 242
Kerberos Post Office Protocol *see* KPOP
kerberos4 (saslauthd plugin) 212
kerberos5 (saslauthd plugin) 212
key, for challenge-response 148
keywords *see* flags, custom
KMail 17, 279
    and Sieve 244

Kolab 18
KPOP 28

L

l (permission) 36
lam *see* listaclmailbox
Lamiral, Gilles 76
laptops, subscribing to folders and 41
LDAP
    configuration file (Courier) *see* authldaprc
    replication 291
    using with Courier *see* authldap, 140–146
    using with Cyrus 212–214, 220–223, 231
ldap (saslauthd-Plugin) 212
LDAP_AUTHBIND (Courier option) 141
LDAP_AUXOPTIONS (Courier option) 143, 146
LDAP_BASEDN (Courier option) 140
LDAP_BINDDN (Courier option) 140, 141
LDAP_BINDPW (Courier option) 141
LDAP_CLEARPW (Courier option) 142
LDAP_CRYPTPW (Courier option) 142
LDAP_DEFAULTDELIVERY (Courier option) 142
LDAP_DEREF (Courier option) 143
LDAP_DOMAIN (Courier option) 141
LDAP_ENUMERATE_CLAUSE (Courier parameter) 161
LDAP_ENUMERATE_FILTER (Courier option) 141
LDAP_FILTER (Courier option) 141
LDAP_FULLNAME (Courier option) 142
LDAP_GID (Courier option) 143
LDAP_GLOB_GID (Courier option) 143
LDAP_GLOB_UID (Courier option) 142
ldap_group_attr (Cyrus option) 223
ldap_group_filter (Cyrus option) 223
ldap_group_match_method (Cyrus option) 223
ldap_group_search_base (Cyrus option) 223
LDAP_HOMEDIR (Courier option) 142
LDAP_MAIL (Courier option) 141
LDAP_MAILDIR (Courier option) 142
LDAP_MAILROOT (Courier option) 142
LDAP_PROTOCOL_VERSION (Courier option) 140
ldap_search_base (Cyrus option) 223
LDAP_TIMEOUT (Courier option) 141
LDAP_TLS (Courier option) 143
ldap_tls_check_peer (Cyrus option) 222
LDAP_UID (Courier option) 143

LDAP_URI (Courier option) 140
ldapdb (auxprop plugin) 213
Least Connection (LVS) 49
legal situation 20
Lemonade 273
libsasl 211–215
    compiling MySQL support 216
Linux Virtual Server *see* LVS
LIST (IMAP command) 34, 41, 299
LIST (POP3 command) 24, 25, 318
    misleading Courier reply 25
listaclmailbox
    cyradm command 230
    cyradmin command 272
listmailbox (cyradmin command) 271
listquota
    cyradm command 228
    cyradmin command 273
listquotaroot
    cyradm command 229
    cyradmin command 273
lm *see* listmailbox
LMTP 18
    between Cyrus and Postfix 191–192
    Cyrus 254
    daemon (Cyrus) *see* lmtpd (daemon)
    maximum email size (Cyrus) 258
    proxy (Cyrus) *see* lmtpproxyd (daemon)
    socket, defining (Cyrus) 191
    specifying port for 201
lmtp_downcase_rcpt (Cyrus option) 204
lmtp_overquota_perm_failure (Cyrus option) 204
lmtpd (daemon) 262
lmtpproxyd (daemon) 262
lmtpunix (definition) 191
load balancer 44–49
    combining with proxy 50
    Cyrus 282, 291
load distribution 43–51
load test, on the mupdate server 270
local (MDA) 172
Local Message Transfer Protocol *see* LMTP
log files (Cyrus) 278
log information (Courier) *see* DEBUG_LOGIN
LOGGEROPTS (Courier parameter) 98
logging in
    Courier 119, 151

341

Index

disabling (SqWebMail) *see* disableweb
via external authentication programs (Courier) 131–133
IMAP 31, 34, 297
    disabling (Courier) *see* disableimap
    encrypting 210
methods *see* authentication method
via MySQL database (Courier) *see* authmysql
via MySQL database (Cyrus) 213, 216–220
via PostgreSQL database (Courier) *see* authpgsql
POP3 24, 318
    disabling (Courier) *see* disablepop
    encrypting 27
via PostgreSQL database (Cyrus) 213
via shell account *see* shell account
via SQL database (Cyrus) 213
testing (Cyrus) *see* imtest (tool)
testing on the Sieve server 241
logging out
    IMAP status 32
    POP3 *see* QUIT (POP3 command)
logging tool (Courier) *see* courierlogger
LOGIN (IMAP command) 31, 34, 297
LOGIN (password transfer method) 81
LOGIN (password-transfer method) 34, 97, 119, 147, 214
    forcing with imtest 218
login data, determining via SQL query
    Courier 137
    Cyrus 217
login ID (email address) 157
LOGIN-DELAY (POP3 command) 319
LOGINDISABLED (capability) 296
LOGOUT (IMAP command) 32, 297
    and CLOSE 303
lq *see* listquota
lqr *see* listquotaroot
lsof, testing the POP/IMAP function 89
LSUB (IMAP command) 41, 302
LVS 47–49

M

mail *see* email
mail contents *see* body
Mail Delivery Agent *see* MDA
mail partitions 189, 239
    default partitions 239
    defining 239
mail repository
    overloaded 50
mail server 17
Mail Transfer Agent *see* MTA
mail_spool_directory (Postfix variable) 92
mailbox contents
    listing (Cyrus) *see* listmailbox
    listing (IMAP) 34, 299
    listing (POP3) 24, 318
mailbox_command (Postfix) 174
mailboxes
    creating (Cyrus) *see* createmailbox
    creating directories 17
    Cyrus, listing 266
    deleting (Cyrus) *see* deletemailbox
    location in the filesystem (Cyrus) 195, 204
    moving in a cluster *see* xfermailbox
    moving to another murder backend 287
    partitions (Cyrus) 259
    putting out on the standard output 267
    querying 17
    renaming (Cyrus) *see* renamemailbox
    repairing (Cyrus) 255, 257
    saving *see* backup
    searching *see* searching, in email
mailboxes.db 278
    file 266, 278
maildir 107–117
    creating directories 88
    creating from mbox 78–79
    location (Courier) 99
    vs. mbox 91
    and NFS 63, 108
    operating Exim with 94, 95
    operating Postfix with 92
    specifying in a MySQL table (Courier) 136
    specifying in userdb 126
maildir+ 172
maildiracl (tool) 87
maildirfolder (file) 109
maildirkw (tool) 87
maildirmake 164, 174
    tool 88
MAILDIRPATH (Courier parameter) 99
maildirsize (file) 114, 115, 170

Index

Maildrop 85
maildrop (MDA) 172
mailheader *see* header
mailhost
    user option 145
               Courier 175
mailnotifier (Cyrus option) 253
main.cf (Postfix configuration file) 92
maintenance, announcing 279
makeuserdb (tool) 125, 128, 129
Managesieve 240
masssievec (tool) 269
MAXDAEMONS (Courier parameter) 97
maxmessagesize
    Cyrus option 204
    Cyrus parameter 258
MAXPERIP (Courier parameter) 97
mb2md.pl 79
mbexamine 265
mbox files 91–92
    converting to the maildir format 78–79
    importing to an IMAP server 76
mbpath (tool) 266
MD5, as password hash algorithm 147
MDA 18
    of the Courier project *see* Maildrop
    with quota capability *see* deliverquota
message text *see* body
meta-information, for email 111
migration 75–82
    the exchange 81
    filter settings 80
    problems with Courier 110
MIME
    attachment *see* attachments
    structure, determining for an email 308
mirroring *see* RAID
mkfs.ext3 59
mkimap (tool) 269
mkimapdcert (tool) 88, 96, 104
mknewsgroups (tool) 270
mkpop3dcert (tool) 88, 96, 104
modification time
    of a file *see* mtime
    of file permissions *see* mtime
    of ownership *see* mtime
motd (file) 279

mount (command), activating quotas 168
Mozilla Thunderbird *see* Thunderbird
msg/ 279
MTA 17, 18
    connection to Courier 90–95
    of the Courier project 85
mtime 57
mupdate
    daemon 262
    server 282, 286, 288
            load test 270
            port 284, 286
mupdate-loadgen.pl (tool) 270
mupdate-port (Cyrus option) 286
mupdate-server (Cyrus option) 286
mupdate_authname (Cyrus option) 284, 286
mupdate_password (Cyrus option) 284, 286
mupdate_port (Cyrus option) 284
mupdate_server (Cyrus option) 284
mupdate_username (Cyrus option) 284, 286
Murder cluster *see* aggregator
MySQL
    creating table for user management 133
    replication 291
    specifying authentication server (Courier) 135
    support for Courier (OpenSuSE) 86, 134
    table, for user data (Courier) 135
    using with Courier 147, *see* authmysql
    using with Cyrus 231
MYSQL_AUXOPTIONS_FIELD (Courier parameter) 137, 146
MYSQL_CHPASS_CLAUSE (Courier parameter) 138
MYSQL_CLEAR_PWFIELD (Courier parameter) 135
MYSQL_CRYPT_PWFIELD (Courier parameter) 135
MYSQL_DATABASE (Courier parameter) 135
MYSQL_DEFAULTDELIVERY (Courier parameter) 136
MYSQL_ENUMERATE_CLAUSE (Courier parameter) 138, 161
MYSQL_GID_FIELD (Courier parameter) 135
MYSQL_HOME_FIELD (Courier parameter) 136
MYSQL_LOGIN_FIELD (Courier parameter) 136
MYSQL_MAILDIR_FIELD (Courier parameter) 136

Index

MYSQL_NAME_FIELD (Courier parameter) 136
MYSQL_OPT (Courier parameter) 136
MYSQL_PASSWORD (Courier parameter) 135
MYSQL_PORT (Courier parameter) 136
MYSQL_QUOTA_FIELD (Courier parameter) 137
MYSQL_SELECT_CLAUSE (Courier parameter) 137
MYSQL_SERVER (Courier parameter) 135
MYSQL_SOCKET (Courier parameter) 136
MYSQL_UID_FIELD (Courier parameter) 135
MYSQL_USER_TABLE (Courier parameter) 135
MYSQL_USERNAME (Courier parameter) 135, 139
MYSQL_WHERE_CLAUSE (Courier parameter) 137

N

NAMESPACE
    IMAP command 315
    IMAP extension 34
naming
    IMAP folders 110
    emails (Courier) 111–117
NAS, as email repository 20
negation *see* NOT (search link)
NetApp filer 55
netnews separators 238
new
    contents of directory 111
    creating directories 88
    directories 94, 108
    messages *see* \Recent (flag)
        number of 31, 299
NFS
    and Cyrus 63
    as email repository 45, 63–65
    for email storage 21
    FAM tuning 177
    and IDLE 177
    and maildir 63, 108
    and mbox 91
nfsvers (mount option) 64
nice value, specifying for events (cyrus.conf) 268
NIL (definition) 309
nntpd (daemon) 263
noacl (mount option) 58
noatime (mount option) 57, 64

\NoInferiors (folder flag) 101
NOOP
    IMAP command 31, 296
    POP3 command 27, 318
\Noselect (flag) 301
NOT (search link) 306
Not Authenticated (IMAP status) 31
    available commands 297–298
notify (daemon) 252, 254
notifyd 240
    daemon 263
numbering, emails 29

O

obsolete email, deleting automatically 268
octet, definition 296, 309
octet-byte conversion 309
offline IMAP 29, 30, 315
old email, deleting automatically 268
one-time passwords (Cyrus) 185
OpenGroupware 18
OpenLDAP *see* LDAP
OpenSSL
    integrating in Cyrus 208
    support in older Cyrus versions 210
openssl 298
ordered (journal mode) 60, 61
_ORIG variables (Courier) 96
out-of-office notices *see* vacation (Sieve command)
outbox 178
OUTBOX (Courier parameter) 178
OUTBOX_MULTIPLE_SEND (Courier parameter) 178
Outlook 17, 209, 279

P

p (permission) 36, 238
PAM
    support in Courier *see* authpam
    support in Cyrus 212, 219–220
pam (saslauthd plugin) 212
partition-default (Cyrus)
    option 204, 239
    parameter 239, 270
partition-name (Cyrus parameter) 259
partitions (Cyrus) *see* mail partitions

Index

PASS (POP3 command) 24, 317, 318
passwd
   converting into userdb *see* pw2userdb
   file
         authentication via (Courier) 119, 120, 143
         authentication via (Cyrus) 212, 214, 219
         restrictions on usernames 151
passwords
   additional SSL transfer methods for Courier POP 97
   changing 138
   checking as hash 148
   cleartext 81
   cleartext transmission vs. hashing 147–150
   determining in cleartext 81
   encrypting (POP3) 27
   entering in userdb 128
   entry (IMAP) *see* LOGIN (IMAP command)
   entry (POP3) *see* PASS (POP3 command)
   field in a MySQL table (Courier) 135
   field in a PostgreSQL table (Courier) 139
   fishing, as a migration method 82
   logging (Courier) 99
   separate for different services 126
   sniffing 149
   transfer methods
         cleartext 97
         as crypt hash 119
         Courier POP server 97
         in plaintext 34, 119, 210
Perdition 51
performance 19
   of filesystems 55–57
   influencing the Cyrus performance 215, 257, 260
   of RAID 63
   shared folders 159
   tuning, of the filesystem 57–62
perl-Authen-SASL (SuSE package) 186
perl-Cyrus (Red Hat package) 186
perl-Cyrus-IMAP (SuSE package) 185
perl-Cyrus-SIEVE-managesieve 190
   SuSE package 186
permanent flags 29, 36, 298
   activating (Courier) 101

permissions *see* ACLs
persistence 45
PGSQL_AUXOPTIONS_FIELD (Courier parameter) 146
PGSQL_CRYPT_PWFIELD (Courier parameter) 139
PGSQL_DATABASE (Courier parameter) 139
PGSQL_ENUMERATE_CLAUSE (Courier parameter) 161
PGSQL_GID_PWFIELD (Courier parameter) 139
PGSQL_HOME_PWFIELD (Courier parameter) 139
PGSQL_HOST (Courier parameter) 139
PGSQL_LOGIN_PWFIELD (Courier parameter) 139
PGSQL_NAME_PWFIELD (Courier parameter) 139
PGSQL_PASSWORD (Courier parameter) 139
PGSQL_PORT (Courier parameter) 139
PGSQL_UID_PWFIELD (Courier parameter) 139
PGSQL_USER_TABLE (Courier parameter) 139
phpLDAPAdmin (tool) 220
PID
   file (Courier) 97
   of the saving process 114
PIDFILE (Courier parameter) 97
PIPELINING (POP3 command) 319
PLAIN (password-transfer method) 34, 81, 97, 100, 119, 147, 214
Pluggable Authentication Modules *see* PAM
POP/IMAP before SMTP, using with Cyrus 206
pop2imap 76
POP3 18, 23, 28
   connection status 317
   disabling login (Courier) *see* disablepop
   email remains on the server 24
   extensions 319
   migrating to IMAP 76
   problems during migration 78
   providing for Debian (Cyrus) 187
   separate password for (Courier) 126
   server *see* POP3 daemon
   specifying a timeout (Cyrus) 259
POP3 daemon 18
   configuration (Courier) 96–99
   Courier 87
   Cyrus 263

345

Index

mode of operation 19
number simultaneously started (Courier) 97
PID file (Courier) 97
preventing from starting (Courier) 98
starting (Courier) 88, 98
POP3_PROXY (Courier parameter) 97, 175
POP3_TLS_REQUIRED (Courier parameter) 103
POP3AUTH (Courier parameter) 96, 97
POP3AUTH_ORIG (Courier) 96
POP3AUTH_TLS (Courier parameter) 97
pop3d *see* POP3 daemon 87
pop3d (Courier configuration file) 95–99, 122, 123
pop3d-ssl (Courier configuration file) 95, 103
pop3d.cnf (Courier configuration file) 88, 96, 104
POP3DSSLSTART (Courier parameter) 103
POP3DSTART (Courier parameter) 98
POP3DSTARTTLS (Courier parameter) 103
pop3login (Courier) 87
pop3proxyd (daemon) 263
poptimeout
    Cyrus option 204
    Cyrus parameter 259
PORT (Courier parameter) 98
ports
    IMAP 33, 89
        via SSL 103, 208
    IMAP via SSL 87
    LDAP 220
        via SSL 220
    monitoring 89
    mupdate server 284, 286
    in the murder cluster 285
    POP3 18, 23, 89
        via SSL 87, 103
    PostgreSQL 139
    Sieve 245
    specifying for MySQL
        Courier 136
        Cyrus 216
    specifying for POP3/IMAP server (Courier) 98
    specifying SSL for Courier 103
    to be released for Cyrus 191
PosgreSQL table
    for user data (Courier) 139
Post Office Protocol *see* POP3
Postfix 18
    configuring as a relay 192

integration into Courier 92–94
naming for email in maildirs 114
PostgreSQL
    contacting via the socket (Courier) 139
    using with Courier *see* authpgsql, 139–140, 147
    using with Cyrus 213
postmark 55
process ID *see* PID
    Cyrus 279
processor, requirements (IMAP) 44
procmail (MDA) 172
profile files (Squirrelmail) 80
proxy
    caching for IMAP 51, 73–74
    Courier as 175
    IMAP server as 44, 50, 51
    mode of the Courier POP3 server 97
proxy_authname (Cyrus option) 284
PROXY_HOSTNAME (Courier parameter) 97, 175
proxyd_disable_mailbox_referrals (Cyrus option) 285
proxyservers (Cyrus option) 287
ptscache_db (Cyrus parameter) 260
pull procedure (IMAP) 32
push procedure (IMAP) 32
pw2userdb (tool) 125
pwcheck (Cyrus SASL module) 214

Q

QMail 18
    integration into Courier 94
    using the vchkpw library with Courier 120, 130
qualified users (Cyrus) 233, 276
quit (cyradm command) 274
QUIT (POP3 command) 27, 318
quota
    Cyrus tool 257
    tool 230
QUOTA (IMAP extension) 316
QUOTA extension 227
quota.user (file) 168
quota/ (directory, Cyrus) 279
quota_db (Cyrus parameter) 260
quotacheck (tool) 168
quotaoff (command) 168

Index

quotaon (command) 168
quotaroot 228, 257
quotas 20, 166, 167, 267
   and MDAs 172
   calculating (Courier) 115
   Courier 167, 175
      calculating 114
      specifying in MySQL 137
      specifying in userdb 126
      warning message when exceeded 96
      when manually storing email 115
   Cyrus 225, 230, 279
      automatic 226
      checking 263
      listing 273
      manual 228
      restoring 257
      setting 273
      showing utilization 273
      warning message when exceeded 204
   database, Cyrus 260
   filesystem 168
   maildirsize 170
   monitoring 167
   via maildir+ 170
   warning 174
quotawarn (Cyrus option) 204, 226, 227
quotawarnkb (Cyrus option) 204
quotawarnmsg
   Courier configuration file 96
   file 174

R

r (permission) 36
RAID 62–63
RAM consumption
   Cyrus index database 258
   IMAP 43
rccourier-authdaemon (script) 88
rccourier-imap (script) 88
rccourier-imap-ssl (script) 88
rccourier-pop (script) 88
rccourier-pop-ssl (script) 88
read messages *see* \Seen (flag)
   number of 31
read permission *see* ACLs
read throughput 56, 57, 60, 61

   for RAID 62
receiving email *see* retrieving email
\Recent (flag) 35
   searching for 306, 307
recipient *see* To header
reconstruct
   Cyrus tool 255, 257
   tool 267, 277
redirect (Sieve command) 248
redundancy 19
regular expressions, in Sieve 247
rehash (tool) 270
ReiserFS
   as email storage medium 54–62
   data loss 54
   journal mode 60–62
   version 4 56
reject (Sieve command) 246, 248
reject8bit (Cyrus option) 204
relay server 17
reliability *see* availability
RENAME (IMAP command) 301
renamemailbox (cyradmin command) 272
renaming
   folders (IMAP) *see* RENAME (IMAP command)
renm *see* renamemailbox
replication (Cyrus) 291
repquota 169
resource consumption 32
retrieving email 18
   via IMAP 111
reverse lookup, on client IP (Courier) 98
RFC
   ACL extension 34
   CHILDREN extension 34
   email format 115, 306
   IDLE extension 34
   IMAP 33
   IMAP4rev1 295
   NAMESPACE extension 34
   POP3 25
      extensions 319
   QUOTA extension 227
   SASL 20, 85
   Sieve 250
   STARTTLS 319

Index

UIDPLUS extension 34
UNSELECT 39
URLAUTH extension 296
rimap (saslauthd plugin) 212
round robin
    via DNS 46
    via iptables 46–47
RSET (POP3 command) 26, 318

S

s (permission) 36
safeguards (Cyrus) 207–224
sam *see* setaclmailbox
SAN, as email repository 20, 45, 55
SASL
    authentication methods (Cyrus) 205
    and Courier 20
    downloading 325
    RFC 20, 85
sasl_mech_list (Cyrus option) 214
sasl_pwcheck_method 212
    Cyrus option 205, 215, 219
    option 189
sasl_sql_hostnames (Cyrus option) 216
sasl_sql_select (Cyrus option) 217
sasl_sql_usessl (Cyrus option) 217
sasl_sql_verbose (Cyrus option) 217
saslauthd (Cyrus SASL module) 189, 212, 215
    using LDAP with 221, 223
saslauthd.conf (file) 222
sasldb (saslauthd plugin) 213, 216
sasldb2
    as authentication for Cyrus 194, 216
    lack of group management 216, 231
saslpasswd2 (command) 194
scaling *see* performance
SEARCH (IMAP command) 40, 296, 304, 308
    returning the Unique ID 314
searching
    conjunction 304
    for deleted email 40
    in email 29, 40, 304, 308
    negation *see* NOT (search link)
    OR link 307
    specifying a character set 305
    for text containing special characters 305
\Seen (flag) 31, 35

Cyrus database 259, 279
    in the filename (maildir) 113
    permit change 36
    preventing when retrieving emails via FETCH 309
    searching for 307
    searching for email without 40
seenstate_db (Cyrus parameter) 259
SELECT (IMAP command) 32, 35, 75, 298
    and CLOSE 303
Selected (IMAP status) 32
    available commands 303, 314
sending email 17
    via IMAP 178
sendmail 18, 178
    path to the program (Courier) 102
SENDMAIL (Courier parameter) 102
sequence number
    changing when emails are deleted 304
    of an email 29
    of the first unread email 299
server reply (IMAP) 31
servername (Cyrus option) 283, 288, 290
session-based flags 29
setaclmailbox (cyradm command) 230
setaclmailbox (cyradmin command) 272
setinfo (cyradm command) 273, 278
setquota
    cyradm command 228
    cyradmin command 273
SHA, as password hash algorithm 147
shadow (file)
    authentication via (Courier) 119, 120, 143
    authentication via (Cyrus) 212, 214, 215, 219
    restrictions on usernames 151
shadow (saslauthd plugin) 212
share groups 158
share name 156
shareable maildir 163
#shared (directory) 110, 156
shared directory 157, 164
    Courier 96
shared folder 34, 164
    Courier 153, 166
        activating 101
        filesystem-based 163
        group mapping 145

Index

  grouping 158
  index file *see* index (file)
  name space 156
  share name 156
  storage location 110
  virtual 154–163
 Cyrus 188, 230
   authentication sources 231
   setting permissions 230
shared groups
 Courier 159, 162
 index file 161
sharedgroup (user option) 145, 155
 Courier 159–161
sharedindexinstall (tool) 88, 162
sharedindexsplit (tool) 88, 161
shell account
 authentication via (Courier) 94, 119
 authentication via (Cyrus) 215
 creating 215
 email address as username 127
shutdown (file, Cyrus) 279
Sieve 21, 240, 252
 administration *see* sieveshell
 changing a script 244
 configuring 241
 evaluating the envelope 246
 evaluating the header 247
 and KMail 244
 loading additional modules 246
 in the murder cluster 285
 notification (SMS, IM) 254
 packages 240
 regular expressions 247
 reject spam 248
 required Perl modules 190
 RFC 250
 script language 246, 250
 setting up scripts automatically for new accounts 251, 252
 and Squirrelmail 244
 testing the configuration 241
 translating into byte code 268, 269
 with virtual domains 252
 and Webmin 244
 working directory 240
   Cyrus 205

sieve (option) 241
sieve_allowreferrals (Cyrus option) 285
sievec (tool) 269
sievedir (Cyrus option) 205, 241, 285
sievenotifier (Cyrus option) 253
sieveshell (tool) 242, 245
 authentication 242
 commands 242, 244
sieveuserhomedir (Cyrus option) 285
Simple Authentication and Security Layer *see* SASL
Simple Mail Transport Protocol *see* SMTP
sivtesti (tool) 241
size
 determining for an email 311
 of an email as search criterion 306, 307
 of an email file 114
 limiting a data segment's (Courier) 102
 limiting the virtual memory's (Courier) 102
 maximum for email (Cyrus) 204
 restricting for an email for LMTP (Cyrus) 258
skiplist (Cyrus database format) 259
SmartSieve 184, 244
smmapd (daemon) 263
SMTP 17
 after POP, using with Cyrus 206
 separate password for (Courier) 126
 server *see* MTA
sniffing 149
 passwords 81
SNMP support (Cyrus) 329
sockets
 Cyrus 279
 defining for LMTP (Cyrus) 191
 specifying for MySQL (Courier) 136
 specifying for PostgreSQL (Courier) 139
SORT (IMAP command) 34, 100, 315
sorting, on the server 34, 100
spaces, in folder names 110
spam
 fighting via Sieve script 248, 251
 fighting with custom IMAP flags 289
special characters
 in folder names 110, 158
 searching for 305
specifying the default domain (Cyrus) 203
sq *see* setquota

349

Index

sql (auxprop plugin) 213
squat index 267, 274
squatter (tool) 267
Squirrelmail 68–70
    and Sieve 244
    migration problems 80
    problems with filter settings 80
    user profiles 80
SqWebMail 85, 138
    disabling login (Courier) *see* disableweb
SSL
    activating (Courier) 103
    caching connection information 260
    configuring (Courier) 102–105
    encryption
        of the database connection (Cyrus) 217
        starting *see* STARTTLS (IMAP command)
    forcing (Courier) 103
    generating keys (Courier) 88
    password-transfer methods
        Courier IMAP server 100
        Courier POP server 97
    start scripts for Courier (OpenSuSE) 87
    version, selecting (Courier) 104
    wrapper 208
SSL certificates
    checking the client's (Courier) 104
    commercial vs. free 208
    creating 209
        with Courier 96, 104
    paths to (Cyrus) 205
    specifying the path
        Courier 104
        Cyrus 205, 210
        LDAP server 222
    warning for custom 208
SSL/TLS (Courier) 102
SSLADDRESS (Courier parameter) 103
SSLLOGGEROPTS (Courier parameter) 103
SSLPIDFILE (Courier parameter) 103
SSLPORT (Courier parameter) 103
start/stop script *see* initscript
STARTTLS
    capability 296
    IMAP command 103, 208, 296, 297
    activating (Courier) 103
    for POP3 *see* STLS (POP3 command)
    POP3 command
        selecting SSL version (Courier) 104
    RFC 319
STAT (POP3 command) 318
STATUS (IMAP command) 32, 302
status information
    for a mailbox 31, 296
    for an email *see* flags
    for an IMAP folder 35, 39, 296, 298, 302
STLS (POP3 command) 103, 208, 319
    activating (Courier) 103
    selecting SSL version (Courier) 104
storage *see* email, repository, central
    restrictions *see* quotas
STORE (IMAP command) 35, 113, 116, 312
    using the Unique ID 313
subfolders (Courier)
    format 109
    names 108
subject header
    as search criterion 307
SUBSCRIBE (IMAP command) 41, 302
subscribed folders
    list (Courier) 109
    list (Cyrus) 280
    listing *see* LSUB (IMAP command)
    migrating 78
    on different backend servers 287
subscribing to (folders) *see* SUBSCRIBE (IMAP command)
    shared folders 166
    and visibility in the mail client 162
subscription_db (Cyrus parameter) 260
symlinks 164
    shared folder 154
system flags 35, 113

T
t (permission) 37
tagged server replies 31
tags 31
tcpd 73
TCPDOPTS (Courier parameter) 98
tcpdump 149
telnet

Index

setting IMAP flags 116
testing the POP/IMAP function 89, 289
test email, sending 93–94, 288
testsaslauthd (tool) 222
text message, when email is received 254
TheBat 209
THREAD
    IMAP command 315
    IMAP extension 34, 100
threading, on the server 34
Thunderbird 17, 279
timeout
    Cyrus option 205
    specifying for POP3 (Cyrus) 259
timsieved 240
    daemon 263
    SuSE package 186
TLS see SSL
    cache (Cyrus) 260
    Courier 102
tls_ca_file (Cyrus option) 206, 210
tls_ca_path (Cyrus option) 206, 210
TLS_CACHEFILE (Courier parameter) 104
TLS_CACHESIZE (Courier parameter) 104
tls_cert_file (Cyrus option) 205, 210
TLS_CERTFILE (Courier parameter) 104
tls_key_file (Cyrus option) 205, 210
TLS_PROTOCOL (Courier parameter) 104
tls_prune (tool) 202, 269
tls_session.db (file) 269, 279
TLS_STARTTLS_PROTOCOL (Courier parameter) 104
TLS_VERIFYPEER (Courier parameter) 104
tlscache_db (Cyrus parameter) 260
tmp
    creating directories (maildir) 88
    directories (maildir) 108, 115
To header, as search criterion 308
TOP (POP3 command) 26, 319
transaction state (POP3) 317
transactions
    simultaneous per Cyrus database 258
translatesieve (tool) 252, 271
trash folder (Courier) 101
    emptying after a specified period 101
\Trashed (flag) 113
trust network 208

TRYCREATE (server reply) 313
Tso, Theodore "Ted" 58, 61
tune2fs 59

U

UID see Unique ID
    IMAP command 313, 314
UIDL (POP3 command) 320
UIDPLUS (IMAP extension) 34, 315
ulimit 102
umask, of the Courier server process 102
UMASK (Courier parameter) 102
uname -n 175
unanswered email, searching for 308
undelete (POP3) 26, 318
undo, when deleting email (Courier) 101
undohash (tool) 271
unique email ID (POP3) 320
Unique ID 29, 299
    determining 312, 315
    as search criterion 308
    using in IMAP commands 313–314
    Value 29, 36, 299
universe 159
Unix account see shell account
Unix separators see /, as mailbox separator
unixhierarchysep (Cyrus option) 205, 235
\Unmarked (folder flag) 34
unqualified users (Cyrus) 233, 276
unread email
    finding 308
    number of the first 299
    querying for 40
UNSELECT (IMAP command) 39
UNSUBSCRIBE (IMAP command) 41, 302
unsubscribing (folders) see SUBSCRIBE (IMAP command)
untagged server replies 31
Update state (POP3) 318
upgradesieve (tool) 271
URLAUTH (IMAP command) 296
URLs, for IMAP messages see URLAUTH
USER (POP3 command) 24, 317–319
user ID
    field in a MySQL table (Courier) 135
    field in a PostgreSQL table (Courier) 139
user options (Courier) 144–147

maintaining in LDAP) 143, 146
saving in the userdb 146
specifying in MySQL) 137, 147
specifying in PostgreSQL) 147
user profiles *see* profile files (Squirrelmail)
user/ (directory, Cyrus) 280
userdb
   creating file from passwd *see* pw2userdb
   directory 125, 129
   file 125
      converting into a database 128
      displaying an entry 127
      maintaining separately by domain 129
      manipulating an entry 127
      saving user options in 146
      separating 129
   file structure 125–127
   tool 127–129
userdb.dat (file) 128
userdbbpw (tool) 128
userdbpw (tool) 129, 130
userdbshadow.dat (file) 128
userid.seen (file) 280
userid.sub (file) 280
username
   converting to lowercase 205
   entry (IMAP) *see* LOGIN (IMAP command)
   entry (POP3) *see* USER (POP3 command)
   field in a MySQL table (Courier) 136
   field in a PostgreSQL table (Courier) 139
   logging (Courier) 99
   selecting 150–151
username_tolower (Cyrus option) 205
users, virtual *see* virtual accounts
usrquota (mount option) 168
UW-IMAP 186

V

vacation (Sieve command) 246, 249, 250
variables *see* configuration parameters
/var/lib/imap 188, 203, 277
/var/lib/sieve 205
Varshavchik, Sam 59, 139, 149
/var/spool/imap 188, 204, 275
/var/spool/imap/user 195
vchkpw library *see* QMail
VDA patch 173

Venema, Wietse 73
version (cyradm command) 274
virtdomains (Cyrus option) 205, 233
virtual (MDA) 172
   quota patch 173
virtual accounts 120
   per authuserdb *see* authuserdb
virtual domains (Cyrus) 232
   activating 205
   adapting Sieve scripts 252, 271
   and assigning permissions 236
virtual memory, limiting size of (Courier) 102
virtual users *see* virtual accounts, 94, 120,
   with Postfix 94
vpopmail library *see* vchkpw library

W

w (permission) 36
WAFL, as email storage medium 55
Web-cyradm 184
webmailer 67–73
   accelerating the *see* IMAP, Proxy (project)
   for cell phones 70
   for the Courier project 85, 132, 138
   migration problems 80
   problems with filter settings 80
Webmin
   Cyrus plugin 184
   and Sieve 244
websieve (web interface) 244
WHERE (SQL command) 137
write permission *see* ACLs
write throughput 56, 57, 60, 61
   for RAID 62
writeback (journal mode) 60–62

X

x (permission) 37
X-commands (IMAP) 316
X-IMAP-Sender (header) 99, 178
xfermailbox (cyradm command) 274, 287
XFS, as email storage medium 54–56
XMPP notification (Sieve) 254

Z

Zephyr 254
ZFS, as email storage medium 54